Ferret!

USAAF Airborne Signals Intelligence Development and Operations, 1942–1945

Ferret!

USAAF Airborne Signals Intelligence Development and Operations, 1942–1945

William M Cahill

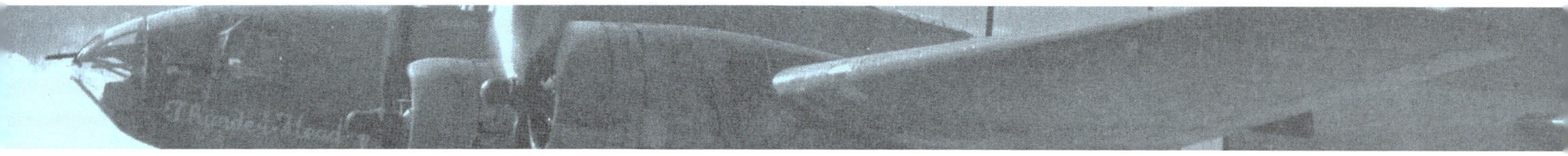

First published in 2024 by Crécy Publishing

ISBN 9781800352971

Printed in Malta by Melita

Crécy Publishing Limited
1a Ringway Trading Estate, Shadowmoss Rd, Manchester M22 5LH
www.crecy.co.uk

Front cover top: Left forward fuselage of B-24M s/n 44-41996 Ferret XVIII Ramp Champ on 7 June 1945. Of note is the black camouflage on the underside of the aircraft and the small radome under the nose housing the spinning AN/APA-17 direction-finding antenna.
Air Force Historical Research Agency via George Cully

Front cover bottom: 16th RS B-17F Ferret 42-3055/Ferret V The Pointer parked in the squadron area at Foch Field. Ferrets III and V had this interesting mottled camouflage scheme, which appears to be black spray painted on the factory paint scheme. B-17F s/n 42-30437 had a different scheme with larger black patches applied while undergoing modification in the UK.
Air Force Historical Research Agency via George Cully

Front flap: A 28th Composite Group B-24D taxiing along the runway after returning from a bombing raid in September 1943. Early ferret missions in Alaska were hosted by the group's 404th BS and utilised crew members from the group to augment the RCM Observers deployed from the US.
National Museum of the United States Air Force

Back cover top: A US Navy 'Black Cat' PBY-5A with radar installed for night reconnaissance and bombing. In April 1944 two PBY Catalinas were fitted out as dedicated ferret aircraft with AN/ARC-1 radar receivers and assigned to the operational control of Section 22.
Air Force Historical Research Agency via George Cully

Back cover middle left: Ramp Rooster, B-24J-1-FO s/n 42-50671, was initially equipped with a SX-28 receiver on 17 August 1944 and Mandrel jammers a week later. The aircraft maintained its jammer and receiver combination through early 1945. *Stephen Hutton*

Back cover middle centre: 42nd Bomb Group (M) B-25J s/n 43-27983 Beautiful Ohio was converted to a radar-hunting ferret by Field Unit 13 personnel in October 1944. This photo was likely taken in September 1945 at Palawan's Puerto Princessa airfield.
Air Force Historical Research Agency via George Cully

Back cover middle right: Lt Holt, one of three RCM Observers associated with the 36th BS P-38 effort, poses beside a P-38J converted to ferret configuration. One of three transferred to the squadron from the 100 (SD) Group in mid-March 1945, the aircraft only flew nine operational sorties before the end of the war. The 'droop snoot' Perspex appears to have been removed and the flat panel bomb-aiming panel has an antenna mounted in its place.
Air Force Historical Research Agency via George Cully

Back cover bottom: At first, flight operations at Boca Raton were constrained by a lack of aircraft. Initially reliant on aging Lockheed A-29 and B-34 aircraft and used and weary B-17s transferred from operational units, it was not until mid-1944 that things started to improve. A 'used' B-17F is seen undergoing flight line maintenance with a newer B-17G in the background.
Air Force Historical Research Agency via George Cully

Page 3 top: Ferret B-17F s/n 42-3358 Thunder Head in flight circa September 1944. By the end of squadron operations at the end of September, Thunder Head had flown forty-five operational missions with the squadron. It was ferried back to US after thesquadron shut down and was turned in to the depot at Hunter Field, Georgia, on 14 November 1944.
Air Force Historical Research Agency via George Cully

Page 3 bottom: B-17F 42-3358 was modified to ferret configuration in theatre by the 16th RS. The aircraft, named Thunder Head, had standard olive drab over grey camouflage and was the first ferret fitted with Yagi DF antennas on the fuselage spine. The SCR-717 navigation radar was fitted in place of the ball turret by squadron technicians at the time of modification.
Air Force Historical Research Agency via George Cully

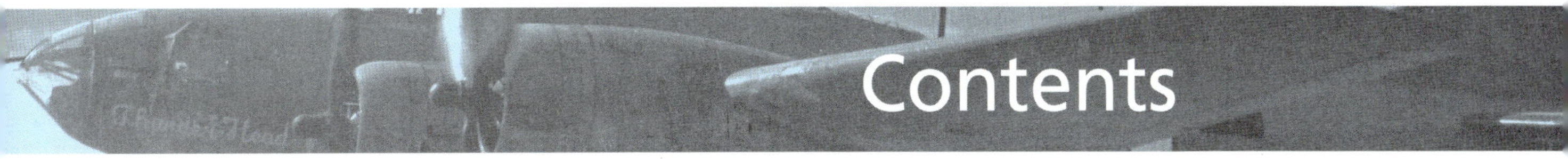

Contents

Foreword

The concept of airborne signals intelligence aircraft – ferrets – has always intrigued me. Inspired by my first US Air Force assignment with EF-111s, my curiosity grew and as I sought out published works on the topic. What little existed was contradictory in nature and pushed me to start writing articles on the topic. A decade or so later, this book is the result of that journey. My aim with this volume is to present an in-depth study of the technical and operational development of USAAF airborne signals intelligence aircraft. Possibly the biggest surprise during my research was that more aircraft were modified for the ferret role than previously thought – with a virtual production line starting at the end of the war.

One of the greatest challenges in preparing this book was to source relevant photographs of good quality. Due to the rarity of ferret images, I decided to include many photographs that under 'normal' circumstances would not meet the threshold for publication due to image quality. Locating primary source material was also difficult – I was unable to provide a complete accounting of all SWPA missions due to gaps in records. Similarly, there is no readily available production list of purpose built and field modified ferrets. I pulled together what was available into a database to analyse and make sense of the fragments and to try and fill in the gaps.

I have been fortunate to draw upon a global band of dedicated "ferret geeks" who, like me, want to tell the story of technical advancement and human ingenuity that the history of ferrets encapsulates. This book would not have been possible without the steadfast support of George Cully. George was more than a researcher – his rolodex of historians and authors is incredible and his dedication and love of aviation history shine through in every interaction. Robert Hopkins, a phenomenal researcher and author of all things Strategic Air Command, encouraged me to move from magazine articles to books and provided introductions and recommendations along the way. One of Robert's introductions, Chris Gibson, created the beautiful maps included in this volume.

Craig Bellamy provided his research into early SWPA ferret operations and was most helpful in locating photos on the topic. The University of Otago in New Zealand provided 'virtual' access to the Hocken Collections and Chuck Varney helped track down photos of late war Pacific ferrets and their crews. Trent Telenko was gracious enough to bring me into his 'Section 22' email group which aided in contacts in the Southern Hemisphere for all things SWPA. Stephen Hutton, Alan Griffith, Robert Livingstone, Jim and Alderman Jr. were all kind in lending photos that help flesh out the textual story of ferrets and their crews. Megan Hallinan took pity upon this poor engineer turned author and worked to slowly hone my writing skills through kind editing of articles – a brave soul she is. Finally, my parents tolerated my love of anything aviation while growing up and encouraged my inquisitive nature – without them this book would never have been started.

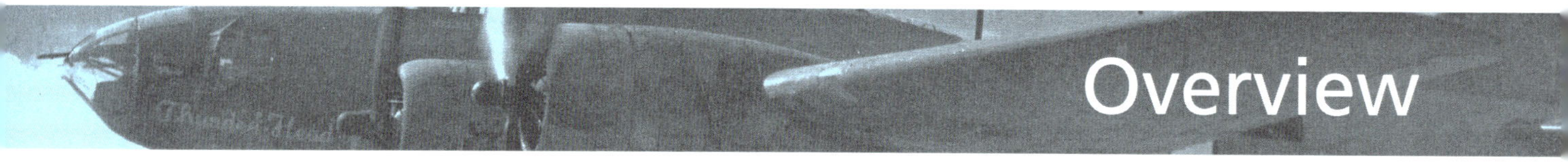

Overview

During the Second World War, the training manual used by USAAF Radar Observer officers defined Radar Countermeasures (RCM) as 'any method or means whereby the enemy is hindered or circumvented in his use of radar. Radar Countermeasures includes the location, signal analysis, and jamming of enemy radar equipment, as well as deception and confusion of enemy radar personnel.' Another broader definition from a different manual stated that RCM referred to the 'activities undertaken to restrict or confuse the use of radio and radar units by the enemy' and included search equipment as well as jamming transmitters. Rather confusingly, this definition encompases another term used durng the period, Radio Countermeasures, which dealt with radio communications interception as well as jamming![1]

These relatively broad definitions encompass what today is termed electronic warfare and includes contemporary SIGINT (Signals Intelligence, composed of radar-seeking Electronics Intelligence or ELINT as as well as communications-focused Communications Intelligence or COMINT) as well as Electronic Attack (jamming of radars and communications links). Electronic Support Measures – the monitoring of enemy electronic activity for purposes of self-defence – is also rolled into the RCM term. I will use the contemporary term RCM throughout the text, although my focus will be on the passive side – mainly ELINT with COMINT where appropriate.

Just as terminology on the topic can be contradictory, so can the aircraft themselves. While the book focuses on 'purpose-built' ferret aircraft that were assembled in the United States, forces in theatre built their own ferret aircraft using whatever components and facilities they had available to them. I will cover these aircraft as well since their primary function was airborne SIGINT. There were also 'ad hoc ferrets', a contemporary term used by aviation historians of the Southwest Pacific Area (SWPA) to describe bomber aircraft that were fitted with RCM gear as an adjunct mission and had a Radar Observer or trained radio operator as a crew member but flew 'regular' bombing missions. I will make mention of these aircraft, whose numbers far exceed ferrets, but they will not be the focus of this text.

Finally, a note on documentation. RCM was treated at a higher classification than regular bombing operations and its discussion in unit histories and reporting was spotty. Some units made separate reports, others included mission data with their regular reports, and sometimes the only references are at the theatre level. This, coupled with the different standards associated with the writing of unit histories and the vagaries of what records were saved for posterity, have made the research of ferrets a unique and challenging endeavour akin to a treasure hunt.

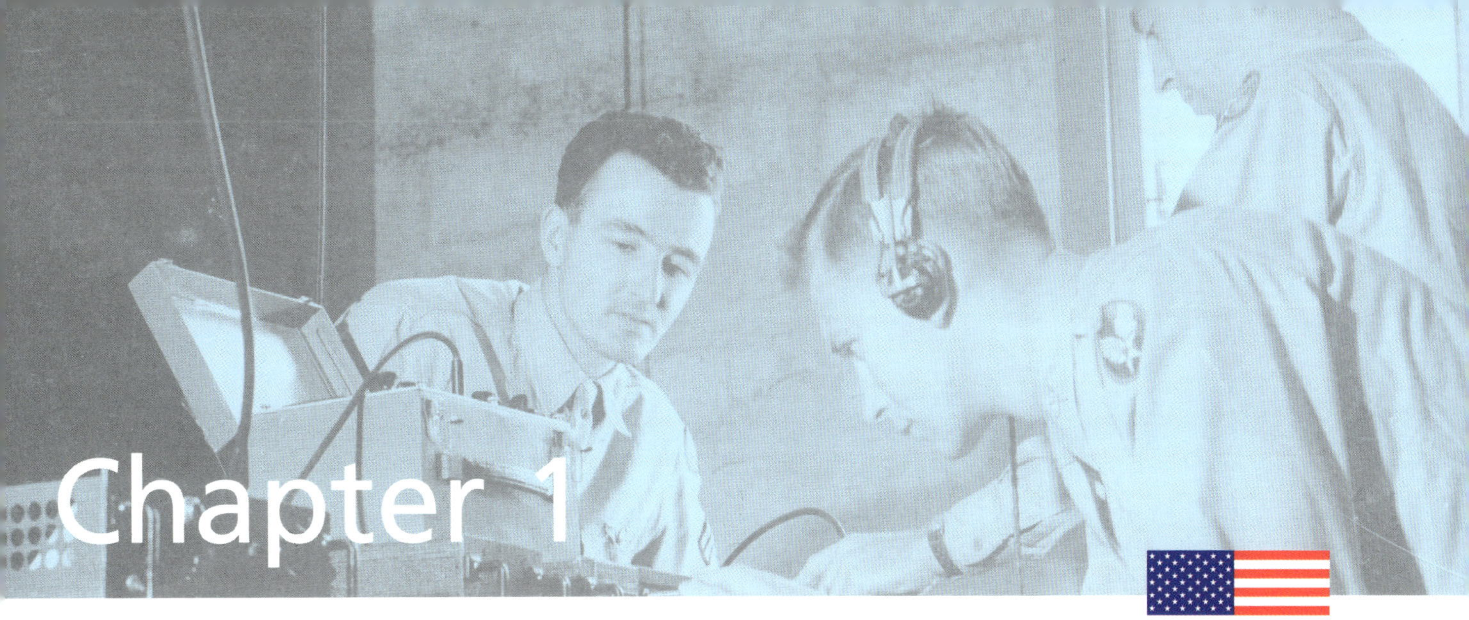

Chapter 1

The development of ferret aircraft by the US Army Air Forces in the Second World War is an interesting story of the management of research and development and the rapid adjustment of technology to keep up with an adversary. Ferret aircraft as a group owe their name to the code name of the project to build the first of their type in late 1942. Radars and ferret aircraft had a symbiotic relationship – without the former, the latter would have little reason to exist. A brief review of radar development will aid in understanding the context of the development of ferret aircraft.

Many technologies come to fruition in multiple locations at the same time with little or no interaction between research staffs; the timing is based on perceived need and the availability of critical components used as the building blocks of the new invention. Automobiles and aircraft shared this type of birth as did radar, although radar development was shrouded in secrecy by nations concerned about national security and inventors concerned about market share. A radar can be broken into five simple components: a transmitter, a receiver, antennas for both the transmitter and receiver, and a display. Often the transmitter and receiver share an antenna, but Japan's Type A radar and the UK's AMES Type 1 Chain Home are examples of 'bi-static' radars that had two antennas.

To detect the presence of an object – an aircraft or a ship – the transmitter generates radio waves that are radiated out by an antenna. The receiver listens for the echoes of these transmitted waves hitting the object and bouncing back towards the radar. If a target is detected, an indication appears on the display. The radio wave is usually generated in pulses, the elapsed time from the beginning of one pulse to the beginning of the next pulse being known as the Pulse Repetition Interval or PRI. The reciprocal of the PRI, PRF or Pulse Repetition Frequency, is the number of pulses of a repeating signal in a specific time unit, normally measured in pulses per second. The radio waves generated by the transmitter have a specific radio frequency (RF), a measurement of the oscillation rate of an alternating electric current. Frequencies for radars are commonly measured in Mega Hertz (MHz) or million cycles per second. Land-based radars in the Second World War usually operated from 60 to 600 Mega Hertz (MHz), which encompasses the High Frequency (HF), Very High Frequency (VHF), and Ultra High Frequency (UHF) bands. The last major characteristic of a radio wave is the pulse width, the duration of the pulse measured in microseconds. These three measurements – PRI, RF and pulse width – were used by Allied forces to characterise the radar signals they were seeing on their reconnaissance missions and helped identify the specific radars they were detecting. The radars themselves followed a development path dependent on the needs of the nation doing the production.

Germany

The German firm GEMA was incorporated on 16 January 1934 to investigate underwater sound and develop radio telephone sets. Soon they were experimenting with radar and by summer 1935 had delivered a prototype radar set to the German navy,

A typical Luftwaffe ground-controlled intercept (GCI) site was composed of two Würzburg-Riese radars and one Freya radar. A German GCI site in Romania, possibly near Bucharest, depicts this layout with two Würzburg radars visible with a Freya Egon to the left of the upturned Würzburg at left centre. *Author*

the Kriegsmarine. In late 1936 the Kriegsmarine contracted with GEMA for the development of a surface search radar designated Seetakt. Further radar testing in 1936 inadvertently revealed the ability of the set to track aircraft, and the Luftwaffe continued this development with a system designed for air surveillance and soon fielded the first Freya radars in 1938.[2]

A second German radar firm, Telefunken, developed the Würzburg fire control radar for directing anti-aircraft artillery and searchlights. First fielded in 1939, it also spawned the larger though electronically similar Würzburg-Riese ground-controlled intercept radar used to direct night fighters. By early 1942, the Luftwaffe had developed an integrated air defence system centred on a number of night fighter control stations known as Flugmeldemess Stellung. Each Stellung was equipped with a Freya early-warning radar and two Würzburg-Riese radars – one to track the targeted bomber and one to follow the friendly night fighter. A fighter controller watched the local picture and guided the fighter to intercept the bomber.

The Kriegsmarine fielded its Seetakt radars along the coastline of occupied Europe to provide warning of an invasion and to aid in the employment of coast artillery. Though operated separately from the Luftwaffe radars, they soon started to operate in a cooperative manner. The Luftwaffe continued to evolve its radar sets, fielding longer-range surveillance radars such as the Mammut and Wassermann and improved fire control radars as well as upgrading Freya and Würzburg radars to compensate for Allied RCM efforts.

Germany first fielded the Würzburg fire control radar in 1939. This Würzburg is in an earthen revetment outside of Bucharest, Romania. The Würzburg was operated by six personnel, with one operator seated in the position at right, two in seats at left, and three standing. *Author*

The German Kriegsmarine fielded its Seetakt radars along the coastline of occupied Europe to provide warning of an invasion and to aid in the employment of coastal artillery. Though operated separately from the Luftwaffe radars, they soon started to operate in a cooperative manner. A tactical reconnaissance photo shows a FuMO 2 Seetakt coastal surveillance radar located atop a concrete hexagonal tower at Hoek van Holland, Netherlands. *Air Force Historical Research Agency via George Cully*

As the war continued the Luftwaffe evolved its radar sets, fielding longer-range surveillance radars such as the Mammut and Wassermann. These radars were emplaced along the coast of occupied Europe to provide maximum warning time of Allied raids on Germany. This Wassermann L early-warning radar is deployed near a small coastal town. *Air Force Historical Research Agency via George Cully*

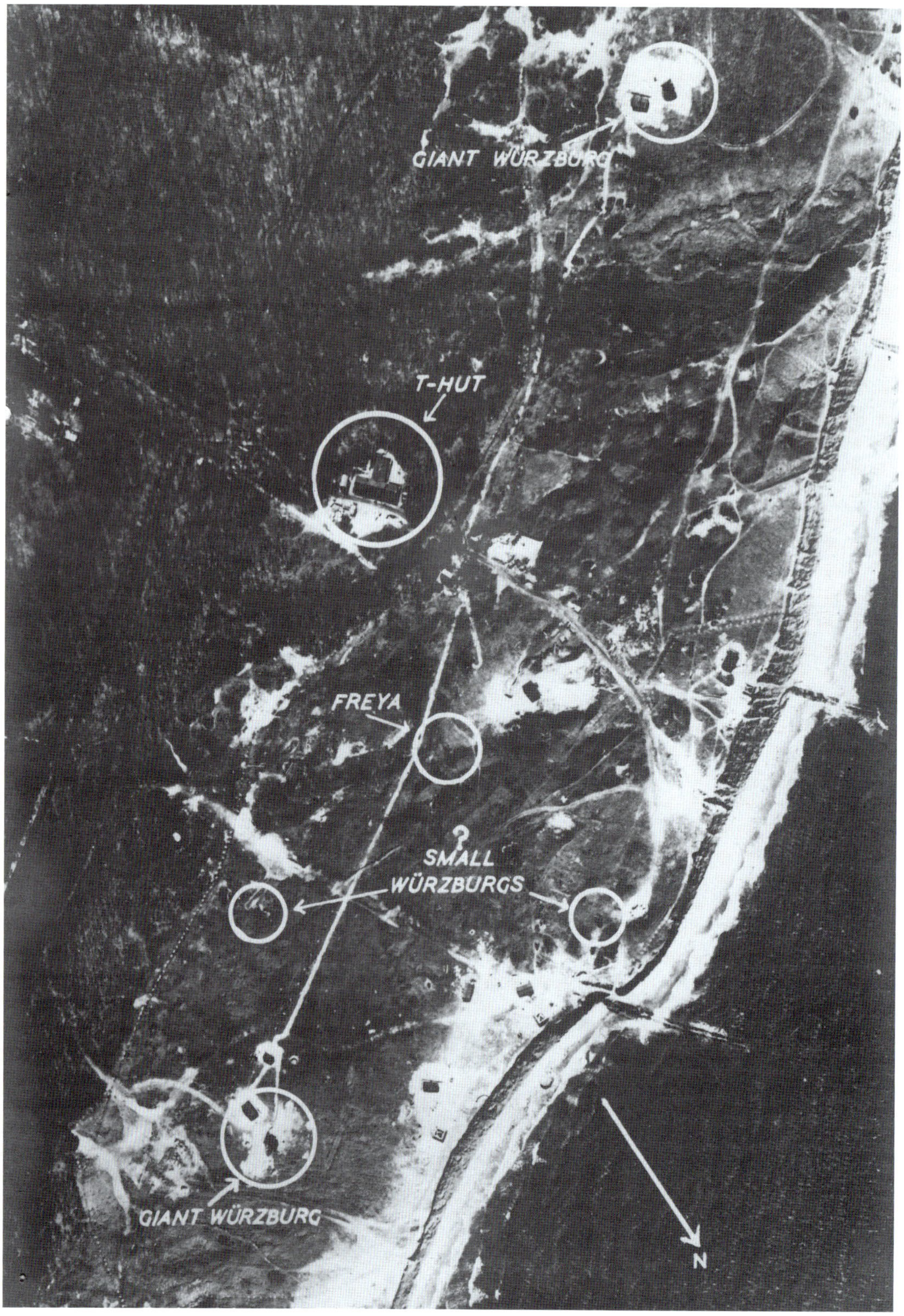

Vertical reconnaissance photo of a German radar site at Domburg, Walcheren, Holland, taken on 12 February 1943 clearly depicts all the elements of a typical GCI site. The site has two Würzburg-Riese radars and one Freya radar providing radar control to night fighters, while the two Würzburg radars provide fire control to protecting anti-aircraft artillery batteries. *Air Force Historical Research Agency*

The Wassermann radar was a development of the Freya used for long-range detection. Developed beginning in 1942, it was based on Freya electronics with additional antenna arrays. The Wassermann S depicted here had eight Freya antenna arrays mounted on a 60m-high (200ft) pipe mast in two columns and is seen at Normandy on 22 June 1944. *US National Archives*

GEMA's Freya LZ radar provided early-warning coverage for the Germans at the start of the war and was integral at GCI sites to provide cueing to the Würzburg-Riese. This example was captured at the end of the war at Lysgaard, Denmark. *US National Archives*

Telefunken developed the Würzburg-Riese GCI radar by scaling up the smaller Würzburg fire control radar. This example is seen at a German GCI site in Skørping, Denmark, after the Second World War. *US National Archives*

Imperial Japanese Navy Type 2 Mark I Model 1 early-warning radar captured on Makin Island, Gilbert Island Group, in November 1943. When emplaced on low-lying coral islands such as Makin, the Japanese would normally elevate the radar to improve performance – in this case, mounting it atop a concrete pillar. The Type 2 Mark I Model 1 was encountered across the Pacific by US ferrets. *US National Archives*

Japan

Like many nations in the 1930s, Japanese technical research was split between Army and Navy factions. The Imperial Japanese Navy's (IJN) Naval Technical Research Department started their initial work into what became radar in 1935. Neither the Naval General Staff nor the Bureau of Naval Construction displayed much interest in the effort, so development was slow.[3] A visit in March 1941 to Germany that included inspection of German and captured British radars revealed the state of radar development to Japan, spurring interest and development. Tests in September 1941 led to the production of the first IJN land-based radar, the Type 2 Mark I Model 1, in early 1942.[4] A more mobile radar, the Type 2 Mark I Model 2, appeared at the end of 1942, with the smaller Type 2 Mark I Model 3 following in 1943.[5]

The Imperial Japanese Army (IJA) was also sponsoring radar development in the 1930s. The IJA was charged with the protection of the Japanese Home Islands; this not only included coastal defences and land forces but also applied to air defence. The air defences of the Home Islands centred on a protective ring of early-warning radars that detected incoming bomber strikes and provided the command and control structure advance notice and time to scramble fighters. The Type A continuous wave radar system was initially deployed on the Japanese Home Islands in 1941, providing longer range but poorer resolution compared to a pulsed radar system. An IJA technical commission spent many months in Germany in 1940, and their summary reports coupled with Japanese research resulted in the production of the Tachi-6 search radar in 1942; the more mobile Tachi-7

The smaller Type 2 Mark I Model 3 radar was fielded by the Imperial Japanese Navy in 1943. An example is seen here on Saipan after liberation by US forces, with the radar and its wooden operations building well camouflaged in a tree line. The Japanese were masters at concealing their radar sites, making their destruction in the war a difficult task. *US National Archives*

Like the Tachi 6, the Imperial Japanese Army Tachi 3 fire control radar was also bi-static. The transmit array depicted here could adjust the elevation of the radar beam by altering the phase of the signal. Electronics for the radar were located underground beneath the base of the radar and electric motors rotated the structure in azimuth. *US National Archives*

followed in 1943. The Tachi 6 was the most common early-warning radar operated by the Japanese Army in the Second World War. Operating between 68 and 80 Mega Hertz (MHz), the Tachi 6 was different from American radars of the time by having separate transmit and receive stations. The transmitter blasted out energy in 90, 180 or 360 degree sectors, while separate receivers (three to six per site) were manually scanned in a sector looking for a return out to a nominal range of 300km. By 1944 the Tachi 18 was finally being fielded, providing a more advanced capability for Japan's air defenders. Operating between 94 and 106 MHz, the Tachi 18 was similar to the US SCR-270 early-warning radar in being truck-transportable and having both transmit and receive elements combined in the same antenna structure.[6] Searchlight and fire control radars based on captured US and British radars appeared with the Tachi-1, -2 and -3 sets in 1943.[7]

Except for half a dozen army sets in such rear areas as the Philippines and the former Netherlands East Indies, the majority of the radar sets used in the outer reaches of Japan's expanded 1942-era territory were built and operated by the IJN. Even in the Home Islands where there was overlap between army and navy radar sets, little to no coordination existed between the services, leading to a duplicative navy air defence net that was used almost exclusively to protect navy bases.[8] By the time the bomber campaign against the Japanese islands started in earnest in late 1944 the IJA and IJN had fielded over 850 ground-based radar sets.

The Tachi 3 receiving antenna shown post-war outside Tokyo. Like the transmitter, all electronics were located underground. Signals from the four receiver dipoles determined direction and elevation by lobe switching. A fifth array at centre determined the range of the target. *US National Archives*

The Imperial Japanese Army Tachi 6 early-warning radar was bi-static with separate transmit and receive elements. The transmitter radiated energy in 90, 180 or 360 degree sectors, while separate receivers (three to six per site) were scanned manually in a sector looking for a return out to a nominal range of 300km. Shown here is a Tachi 6 receiving antenna captured on Noemfoor Island, Dutch New Guinea, in early July 1944. *US National Archives*

UK

Radar development in the UK can be traced back to a fateful test on 26 February 1935 involving a Heyford bomber flying near a BBC radio transmitter at Daventry with a rudimentary receiver noting the disruption of the radio waves caused by the bomber. Radar underwent a painful and at times political development over the next three years until the UK started to field its first developmental systems in late 1938. In early 1939 the initial production AMES Type 1 Chain Home search radars started to be emplaced. A supplementary Type 2 Chain Home Low radar set provided low-altitude coverage, with both sets only being able to be emplaced along coastlines and search over water. The network was still being deployed in July 1940 when the Battle of Britain commenced, with twenty-one Chain Home and twenty-nine Chain Home Low stations in operation. The RAF radar stations passed their radar track data to filter rooms, where the information was combined with visual observers and other radar data into a fused air picture.[9]

US

US Navy radar research dated back to Naval Research Laboratory (NRL) work on HF radios in 1930. Engineer Lawrence Hyland noted a disturbance caused by an aircraft flying between an HF beacon and a test antenna, similar to what occurred in the UK five years later. Over the next four years, the NRL continued its work with a test in 1934 confirming the presence of an aircraft flying along the Potomac River. Work continued over the next two years, raising the frequency from 10 MHz to 80 MHz and then 200 MHz. A prototype search radar set designated the XAF was mounted aboard the battleship USS *New York* in December 1938.

The US Army's relationship with radar technology dates back to early the 1930s, with development activities at the Signal Corps Laboratories, located at Fort Monmouth, New Jersey. Despite concurrent experimental activity occurring in Europe, American radar research was independent of outside influences. Though hampered by a lack of funds and personnel, within a few years a practical demonstration was possible. On 14–15 December 1936, a successful test of the technology was conducted. This test resulted in the construction of a hand-built prototype, which was presented to the Chief of the Signal Corps on 18–19 May 1937, with an exhibition to the Secretary of War a week later.[10] The technology was well received and gave birth to a development programme that led to the SCR-268 searchlight controlling radar.[11] Chief of the Air Corps Maj. Gen. Oscar Westover, who also attended the May demonstration and one on 3 June 1937, proposed an operational specification for a long-range early-warning radar to meet Air Corps needs.[12] Emphasis was placed on the Air Corps requirement and Fort Monmouth went back to the drawing board. By early 1939, both a mobile (soon designated SCR-270) and fixed (SCR-271) version of an early-warning radar had been developed. An engineering model of the SCR-270 was tested in June 1939, and a November demonstration to the Secretary of War — involving two radars located at Twin Lights, N.J. and Meriden, Connecticut, was deemed a success.[13] The Army established the 1st Aircraft Warning Company at Fort Monmouth, on 1 March 1940, and soon thereafter took delivery of the initial production SCR-270A radar sets for operational testing.[14]

USAAF

The ferret aircraft described in this volume were all operated by the United States Army Air Forces (USAAF). The USAAF was created on 20 June 1941 as successor to the United States Army Air Corps. The USAAF was one of three components of the United States Army, which also included the Army Ground Forces and the Services of Supply (which in 1943 became the Army Service Forces). Each component had a commanding general who reported directly to the Army Chief of Staff. The USAAF administered all parts of military aviation formerly distributed among the Air Corps, General Headquarters Air Force, and the ground forces' corps area commanders.

Numbered air forces (NAFs) began as named organisations in the Air Corps before the Second World War. The first four NAFs were established on 19 October 1940 as Air Districts to provide air defence for the United States. These Air Districts were redesignated as the 1st, 2nd, 3rd, and 4th Air Forces on 26 March 1941, changing from Arabic numerals on 18 September 1942 to the First, Second, Third, and Fourth Air Forces. Other organisations established during this period that became NAFs include the Philippine Department Air Force (became Fifth Air Force), the Panama Canal Air Force (became Sixth Air Force), the Hawaiian Air Force (became Seventh Air Force), and the Alaskan Air Force (became Eleventh Air Force). By the end of the war, the USAAF had created sixteen numbered air forces (First to Fifteenth and Twentieth) distributed worldwide to prosecute the war, plus a general air force within the continental United States to support training and provide air defence. By late 1942 the management of RCM overseas was done by a special staff within a NAF.[15] The development and procurement of the RCM equipment to equip a ferret aircraft crossed organisational boundaries, taking in existing units as well as new institutions birthed during the Second World War.

Aircraft Radio Laboratory

The Signal Corps Laboratories established a liaison staff at McCook Field in 1922 in order to supervise the testing of air communication and air navigation sets. McCook Field and adjacent Fairfield Air Depot were incorporated into Wright Field in 1927, becoming the headquarters of the Air Corps' Material Division. The liaison group there became the Signal Corps Aircraft Radio Laboratory; from 1927 on, it proposed as well as tested the equipment that the Signal Corps developed for the Air Corps. The Office of the Chief Signal Officer in Washington coordinated with the Air Staff to ensure that these airborne receivers were developed to meet the USAAF's specific requirements.[16]

The War Department divided RCM responsibility between the Army Air Forces and the Signal Corps rather awkwardly. For years, radio and radar progress had been hampered because airborne equipment fell to the Aircraft Radio Laboratory (ARL), while ground equipment, even Air Forces ground radios that functioned intimately with airborne counterparts, was developed in the Signal Corps' Fort Monmouth laboratories in New Jersey. RCM activities conducted in aircraft were charged to the AAF, along with the responsibility for recommending the type, number, and assignment of AAF units engaged in RCM. Countermeasures other than those conducted in aircraft fell to the Signal Corps. Soon this arbitrary division would prove troublesome.[17] While Washington wrestled over organisational lines of responsibility, the engineers at ARL continued to respond to requests from the field. In 1942 ARL initiated development of a panoramic search receiver, the SCR-587, equipped with a radar-like oscilloscope in which an operator could see the received radar pulse and read out its radio frequency.[18]

In 1943 project and personnel cuts in Signal Corps laboratories hurt the Corps' ability to provide research and development services to the Army as well as the AAF. Because aviation electronic development was set back by the personnel reductions, airmen could cite an obvious reason in support of their argument that Signal Corps research and development of aviation equipment was unsatisfactory. This argument no doubt had a bearing on the 26 August 1944 transfer of aircraft electronics activity along with the Signal Corps installations and personnel from Signal Corps to the Air Forces.[19]

Air Proving Ground

In the early 1930s the Air Corps Tactical School at Maxwell Field, Alabama, began surveys for a bombing and gunnery range to support their activities. Officers from the school centred on Valparaiso, Florida, and in 1935 leased the small municipal airport there along with land for a range. In August 1937 the range became Eglin Field. At the same time, the Air Corps was looking for a suitable proving ground for the testing of aircraft and armament and in April 1939 a board of officers recommended Eglin for this function. On 19 May 1941 the Air Corps Proving Ground was established at Eglin and subordinate units were organised to conduct test activities. Personnel assigned to manage activities at the base were originally assigned to the Air Corps Proving Ground Detachment, redesignated the 1st Proving Ground Group on 16 April 1943.[20]

As the SCR-587 airborne receiver was being developed in late 1942, the USAAF designated Eglin Field as the location of its electronics proving ground. The rapid growth in this field in this time period soon led to the proving ground not only working with radar but also RCM. On 16 February 1943 the USAAF asked the Signal Corps to provide permanent facilities at Eglin for both ARL and for the Radio Research Lab, a Harvard University research organisation (see below). The next day, the USAAF established the 1st Proving Ground Electronics Unit to support these activities to include the testing of RCM capabilities and training personnel in RCM techniques. Later that month, the Air Forces asked ARL to equip ferret aircraft.[21]

Harvard RRL

On 27 June 1940 the President established the National Defence Research Committee to correlate and support scientific research on the mechanisms of warfare and to contract with individuals, educational or scientific institutions, and industrial organisations for studies, experimental investigations, and reports. NDRC was the forerunner of the Office of Scientific Research and Development (OSRD) and the chief civilian governmental agency to which the Signal Corps looked for technical research during the war.[22]

In March 1942 the NDRC sent Dr David B. Langmuir to Cambridge, Massachusetts, to organise RCM research. Assigned to NDRC's Division 15, a shadowy organisation that dealt with RCM matters behind triple-barred secrecy, Langmuir worked with Harvard University's Dr Frederick E. Terman to establish the Radio Research Laboratory (RRL) under an OSRD contract to act as Division 15's research laboratory.[23] RRL at Harvard was a spin-off of the Radiation Laboratory (RL) at Massachusetts Institute of Technology (MIT), OSRD's research centre for radar. RRL's focus was electronic countermeasures to enemy radars and communications, as well as electronic counter-countermeasures (ECCM) to circumvent enemy ECM. By the end of the war, virtually every American heavy bomber and naval vessel carried anti-radar equipment designed by the RRL.

Operating in a converted wing of the huge Biological Laboratory, the RRL, which employed some 800 technicians and spent more than 15 million dollars on research, developed more than 150 anti-radar devices for the Allied armed forces. RL and RRL set up a model shop, the Research Construction Company, specifically to turn out crash items. By 1944 the Signal Corps established a Research Division in the Aircraft Radio Laboratory (ARL) somewhat similarly, to specialise in airborne RCM devices, including crash production of them.[24] All through the war, the Harvard and MIT laboratories, just a mile apart, carried on a friendly but deadly serious rivalry: RL developed better and better radars, and the RRL produced better and better jammers. From the roof of the Bio Lab, the Harvard technicians took delight in jamming RL radars across the rooftops of Cambridge.[25]

Boca Raton Course

In the spring of 1942 the USAAF established an airborne radar school at Boca Raton in Florida. The War Department acquired 5,860 acres nearby to develop an airfield and supporting ranges. To house students in the interim, the Army leased the palatial Boca Raton Club to act as a training facility with nearby Morrison Field at West Palm Beach providing an airstrip for training aircraft. As Harvard's RRL prepared its first production run of airborne RCM equipment for the autumn of 1942, the USAAF looked for a location to establish a training course for the operators of the new equipment. Major Mel Jackson journeyed from Headquarters Army Air Forces in Washington down to Boca Raton to investigate integrating RCM instruction with the existing airborne radar course. Pleased with what he saw, Jackson returned to Washington and soon one of the staff instructors at Boca Raton, Lt Hugh Winter, developed a four-week RCM course. The first class, with four students, started on 2 November 1942. Students were drawn from the existing airborne radar courses at MIT and Boca Raton and received theoretical instruction as well as practise in operating the SCR-587 receiver.[26]

In December 1942 the training moved to Boca Raton Army Air Field. The course Technical Order Directives and all other regulations originated in Washington, with the local school having no control over the course.

Now designated Course 73, instruction for RCM Observers included training missions flown in a single B-24, later augmented with two B-18s, with some training still carried out up at Harvard with RRL. Graduates received an MOS classification of 'Radio Officer "C"'.[27] The Boca Raton schoolhouse also started Course 35, instruction for Radar Mechanic (RCM), in 1943 with fifty students attending each eight-week course. Like the RCM Observers, the initial academic situation was lacking with only one actual piece of equipment, an SCR-587, available for instruction at the school. In August 1943 Academic Headquarters started setting up directives and additional equipment started arriving for training.[28]

Two airmen in the RCM Mechanics Course 35 tuning up AN/APT-3 jamming transmitter for proper output in February 1945. Boca Raton Army Air Field provided instruction for USAAF personnel to maintain the increasingly complex gear that was being fielded with ferrets late in the war. *Air Force Historical Research Agency via George Cully*

Course 73 RCM Observer training at Boca Raton was initially more theoretical in nature, creating versatile students with a broad understanding of abstract electronic theory but without ever having touched actual equipment before arriving in a combat theatre. Instruction was dramatically revised in late 1943 based on a training memo issued on 25 October 1943 that called for training to be predominantly of a practical nature focused on hands-on instruction using actual equipment. It took the school over seven months to develop the new curriculum, acquire equipment and train instructors. In the interim, the instructors at Course 73 did what they could to refine and formalise the existing coursework. A comprehensive Course 73 'RCM Instruction Manual' was issued in March 1944 to provide an book of instruction as well as a reference for use in the field. Documentation was also put in place, formalising the class with an objective to train Radar Officers (SSN 0141) to 'supervise installation, operation, adjustment, and maintenance of all airborne RCM equipment and to operate RCM equipment in the air'. The class ran for twenty-four academic days to include four days on the SCR-587, twelve days on circuit analysis and maintenance of RCM equipment to include receivers, pulse analysers, and jammers, and six days on anti-jamming devices and general RCM tactics.[29]

By June 1944 Boca Raton kicked off the new Course 73 directed by the October 1943 memo. Training was expanded to fifteen weeks consisting of ninety academic days, with pipeline students changed from Radar Officers (SSN 0141) to Communication Officers (SSN 0200). The student flow started with twelve-week Aviation Cadet Pre-Tech School training, followed by eighteen weeks at Yale for Communications Officer Training where those qualified for flight combat duty were selected to continue their studies in Florida. Class size was set at sixteen students, with new classes starting every week. Curriculum expanded to include principles of radar, principles of countermeasures, and 'the operation and airborne maintenance of countermeasures sets in general use'. Graduates of the class were designated Radar Observer (RCM), SSN 7888. The Radar Mechanic (RCM) Course 35 expanded from eight to nine weeks and covered first- and second-echelon maintenance of receivers such as APR-2/4, analysers like APA-11, and jammers like ARQ-5 and APT-1/3. Mechanic classes had forty-two students and started every week.[30]

Course 73 RCM Observer training at Boca Raton was initially more theoretical in nature, but by 1944 included hands-on training of ferret equipment on the ground and operations in the air. Officer cadets in the RCM Observer course are adjusting the frequency of an AN/APQ-9 jamming transmitter in February 1945. *Air Force Historical Research Agency via George Cully*

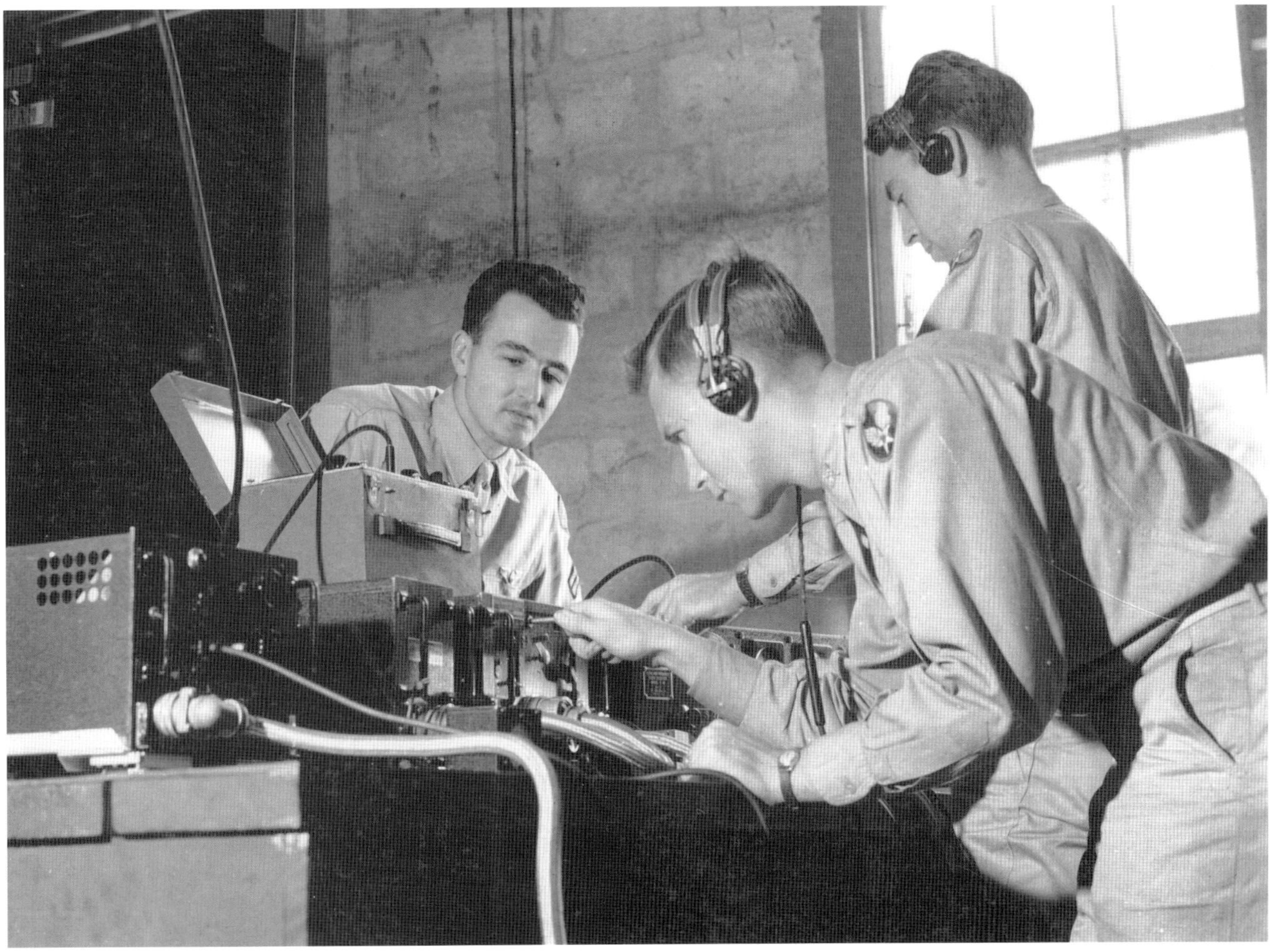

B-17 aircraft were used in the flying training phase of many of the courses taught at Boca Raton, with two B-17Gs supporting Course 73 RCM Observer flight operations in early 1945.This B-17 is on the ramp at Boca Raton Airfield with other bombers in early 1945. *Air Force Historical Research Agency via George Cully*

Even though B-24s were available for training flights at Boca Raton, Course 73 RCM Observers were confined to B-17s and would not fly on the type of aircraft they would employ in combat until later. This B-24 at Boca Raton was utilised primarily by Course 76, Radar Observer, Bombardment. *Air Force Historical Research Agency via George Cully*

Operations at Boca Raton Airfield generated two flights per day per aircraft in support of bombardment radar officer and RCM officer training. Although forty-eight planes were assigned for flight training, many were tired B-17s transferred from operational units and only about one third were available at any given time. Six of the B-17s that arrived in May 1944 were B-17Fs with a backlog of Tech Order changes and had to route through Miami Air Service Depot. When these aircraft arrived, they were able to replace the aging Lockheed A-29 and B-34 aircraft still in use at Boca Raton until August 1944. The additional B-17s allowed aircraft to be aligned against specific courses, with four B-17s being dedicated to Course 73. In the fifteen-week programme, eight weeks involved flight training, with seventy-two hours of flying time per student keeping each assigned aircraft in the air ten hours per day. Boca Raton school staff requested an additional eight B-17s to better support RCM Observer training. The schoolhouse was not only dealing with older aircraft, it was also facing a shortage of RCM equipment for training students due to a lag in equipment production. The shortage of equipment delayed Course 73 classes, as did insufficient numbers of students sent to Florida from prior training.[31]

At first, flight operations at Boca Raton were constrained by a lack of aircraft. Initially reliant on aging Lockheed A-29 and B-34 aircraft and used and weary B-17s transferred from operational units, it was not until mid-1944 that things started to improve. A 'used' B-17F is seen undergoing flight line maintenance with a newer B-17G in the background.
Air Force Historical Research Agency via George Cully

In mid-September 1944 Course 73 was reduced from sixteen students per week to six per month, starting with Class 45-14, which entered training on 2 October 1944. By the end of 1944 the radar school at Boca Raton had sufficient radar-equipped aircraft and radar equipment to meet instructional needs, yet was still low on instructors and unable to achieve the optimum ratio of one instructor per eight students. Ground equipment included SCR-587A and AN/APR-4 receivers and AN/APA-6X pulse analysers as well as SCR-717B search radar. Flying training for Course 73 was broken into three phases: RCM reconnaissance covered eighteen days, RCM planning twelve days, and jamming lasted six days. Two B-17Gs supported Course 73 flight operations in early 1945. Starting with class 45-18 commencing on 5 February 1945 the class duration dropped from fifteen weeks to six weeks.[32] This action was likely linked to the commencement of the formal ferret training course at March Field. This two-month course incorporated flight training, negating the need for this activity at Boca Raton. The March Field training was centred on recently graduated crews from the AAFPOA B-24 training course, to which were added two SSN 7888s (Radar Observer RCM) and one SSN 0142 (Radar Observer).

On 7 May 1945 the RCM Mechanics Course 35 was combined with the Gun Laying AN/APG-15B course and expanded to twelve weeks. Course 73 also changed, eliminating coverage of older RCM equipment and dropping academics on German radars, instead concentrating on Japanese electronic systems.[33] Later that month Course 73 was ordered to discontinue with the class graduating on 9 June 1945, but subsequently it was reinstated in mid-August. This one class, starting on 13 August, was the last as the student pipeline flow into Boca Raton stopped after VJ Day on 21 September. Students started flowing again in late October into an uncertain future.[34]

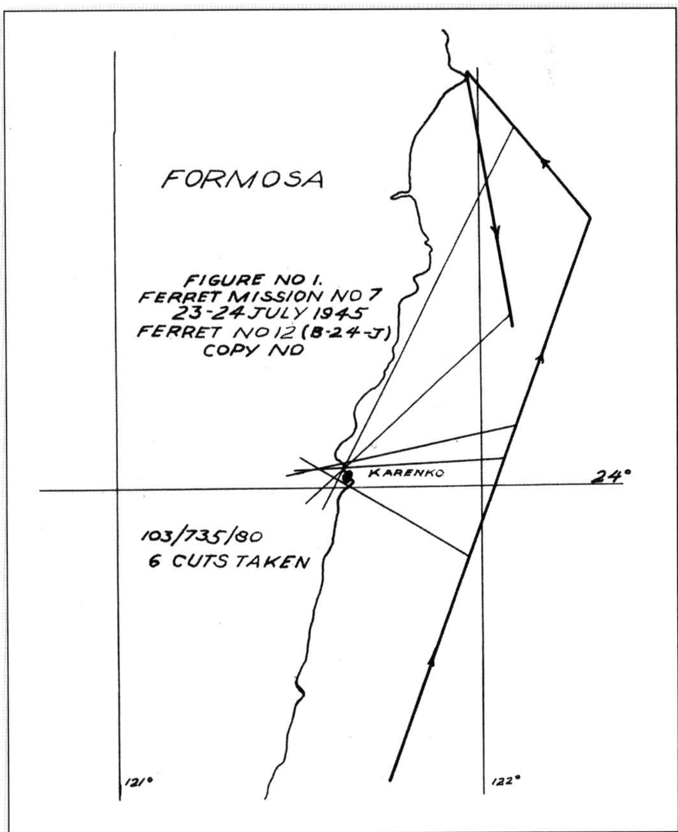

A graphical depiction of direction-finding 'cuts' used to locate a radar. This figure is from a report associated with Ferret Flight No. 7, 26 July 1945 and depicts six bearings taken to locate a Japanese radar on Formosa. *Air Force Historical Research Agency via George Cully*

Ferret Basics

The newly minted 7888s were assigned to an aircraft type and mission that was only a couple of years old and still evolving. The primary function of a ferret aircraft was to monitor enemy radars for changes and improvements and gather technical information to be able to develop countermeasures that could protect friendly forces. Ferrets also located enemy radar stations to determine their coverage and look for blind spots caused by terrain as well as precisely place them for follow-on attacks.

To accomplish the ferret mission an aircraft was required that had endurance to be able to fly long-distance missions or loiter near enemy defences for extended periods of time. This need generally resulted in the conversion of heavy bombers – B-17s and B-24s – to the ferret role. The mission itself was undertaken with a series of electronic boxes and antennas added to the former bomber aircraft. These boxes enabled the ferret crew to answer the questions associated with its base mission – where is the radar and what are the characteristics of its signal?

Determining the location of the target radar is relatively straightforward. The aircraft location needed to be known precisely – normally accomplished with a navigation radar. A direction-finding antenna was used to determine the correct azimuth of the target signal. Multiple azimuth shots – bearings – were then taken. The movement of the aircraft enabled each bearing to be slightly different in azimuth, and the location of the radar was revealed by the intersection of these bearings. This process was normally calculated post-mission by the ferret crews. Search receivers were used to scan across the radio frequency (RF) spectrum for enemy radar transmissions for the purpose of discovering the frequency and PRI of the signals. These receivers would be coupled to Tuning Units that work in a specific RF range and would have their own antenna units, usually dipole/rod antennas. Pulse analysers were used to determine the characteristics of an enemy radar signal such as pulse width and pulse shape that could provide details into the circuitry of the target radar. Finally, if it was desired to document the signal for post-mission playback a wire recorder was used to capture the data for post-mission analysis.[35]

Chapter 2

The Beginnings

The radar development of the 1930s came to the fore when war broke out on 1 September 1939. After the conclusion of the Polish campaign, Britain and Germany stared down each other in the 'Phoney War' as the adversaries strengthened their armed forces and sought to understand their opponents through reconnaissance. At the outbreak of war Britain had twenty-one operational Chain Home radar stations. After the Battle of France in 1940 the network was expanded to cover the west coast of Great Britain and Northern Ireland, in time for the radars to play a key role in the Dowding system's defence of the UK during the Battle of Britain.

After the fall of France, Germany slowly built up its radar-centred air defences. Starting in 1941, the Luftwaffe started to field its own radar-based air defence built on Stellung equipped with Freya and Würzburg-Riese radars. Operating in front of the Stellung was a screen of early-warning radars acting as a tripwire to alert defenders of an impending attack. Also introduced at this time was the FuG 25 identification friend or foe (IFF) transponder that sent back a coded response to enable German radar operators to distinguish their aircraft from those of the Allies.

The Allies' first dip into the world of airborne SIGINT was the RAF's Wireless Intelligence Development Unit, formed in June 1940 under Wing Commander Robert Blucke. Equipped with three Avro Anson maritime reconnaissance/trainer aircraft, the first target of the unit was Luftwaffe navigation beacons that guided German bombers over the UK. On 10 December 1940 the unit was redesignated 109 Squadron. Soon Vickers Wellington bombers joined the organisation, along with the added mission of development of navigation systems. On 6 August 1942 109 Squadron's B Flight split off to continue the airborne SIGINT role and became 1474 Flight, flying Wellington IC aircraft. This unit was redesignated 192 (Special Duties) Squadron on 4 January 1943 and soon gained Handley Page Halifax bombers in addition to the Wellingtons.[36] In the summer of 1941 148 Squadron, a bomber unit assigned to the Middle East, started to experiment with a SIGINT receiver on one of its Wellington aircraft. Soon a detachment of 109 Squadron arrived to help in the effort, conducting both SIGINT and jamming missions. On 4 January 1942 this detachment became 162 Squadron, flying Wellington bombers dedicated to the airborne SIGINT mission.[37]

By mid-1942 the tide of the Second World War was slowly turning in favour of the Allies. Nazi Germany was stalled outside of Stalingrad and turned back from Egypt at El Alamein, while the US Navy inflicted a stunning defeat on the Imperial Japanese Navy at Midway. The Southwest Pacific Area (SWPA) was the Allied supreme military command that oversaw operations in the Philippines, Borneo, Dutch East Indies, Australia, New Guinea, and the western part of the Solomon Islands. Commanded by General Douglas MacArthur, the SWPA came into being on 18 April 1942, replacing the failed American-British-Dutch-Australian Command (ABDA) and, after the fall of the Philippines in May 1942, became the sole US force in the region. Airpower under MacArthur was organised under a combined command – Allied Air Forces – with Australian and US air components. The fight for New Guinea was the defining action of the first part of the war for the Southwest Pacific Theatre. First occupied by the Japanese in January 1942, the battle for the island would be waged for the remainder of the war. The Allied campaign to retake the island started with the defence of Port Moresby and the landing at Milne Bay on the eastern end of the island.

Records are scarce, but it appears that Japan started to deploy radars to its overseas conquests in mid-1942. The first Tachi 6 overseas deployment was to an airfield in Sumatra, Netherlands East-Indies, in late 1942, followed up with an additional twenty sets to Palambang, Sumatra, between December 1942 and spring 1944. At least four sets were deployed to Java, Netherlands East Indies, as well. The Tachi 7 started to deploy in 1943, with twenty sets being shipped to the Philippines in October 1944 – the first IJA radars deployed to this former US territory.[38] Although close to fifty IJA radars were shipped to the Southwest Pacific Area, on average fewer than twenty were deployed at any given time, the majority likely in depot for future use or to act as reserves for those in the field. The majority of the Japanese radars deployed overseas were the Imperial Japanese Navy (IJN) Type 2 Mark I Models 1, 2 and 3. The IJN initiated deployment of radars shortly after the Type 2 Mark I Model 1 went into production, with one set being on Guadalcanal prior to the US invasion in August 1942.[39] The Japanese air surveillance network in the SWPA consisted of thinly scattered belts of radars to provide early warning of approaching raids.[40] As the tactical situation changed, the IJA or IJN would shift their radar sites around to increase the coverage of critical avenues of approach.

Shocked by the discovery of IJN Type 2 Mark I Model 1 radar sets by forces liberating Guadalcanal in August, the US scrambled to field a capability to investigate the extent of Japanese radar deployment and identify any Japanese radars still operating in the Solomon Islands. The Americans, though, were late to the game. The initial radar search started as a unilateral Royal Australian Navy (RAN) effort that pre-dated the Guadalcanal radar discovery and that started with a meeting in Melbourne on 29 May 1942. Held before the US victory at the Battle of Midway, with the Japanese air raid on Darwin and victory at the Battle of Java Sea on their mind, the meeting brought together all Australian service radar experts. The consensus leaving the meeting was for the RAN to lead the investigations, with efforts centred at HMAS Rushcutter, a RAN base in Sydney. By August personnel and equipment were starting to arrive from overseas and the group started to look at operations, with the first focus being to ascertain Japanese air warning radar capability in the New Guinea and Timor regions.[41] This organisation was loosely and unimaginatively termed the 'Radio Counter-Measures Organisation' or the 'RCM Organisation'.

Australia started the search for Japanese radars through the use of a few receivers and a select group of personnel. Carefully orchestrating a group of British, Australian and New Zealand Radio-Countermeasure (RCM) observers who rotated through available airborne assets, the RAN started its investigations into Japanese radar activity north of Australia. This intrepid group of personnel first fitted a US Navy ARC-1 receiver (designated SCR-587 in USAAF service) to a 435th Bomb Squadron B-17 flying out of Townsville, Australia, in September 1942. The 435th, an orphan bomb squadron not attached to a bomb group, had been performing long-range reconnaissance missions in northern Australia since its arrival in February 1942.

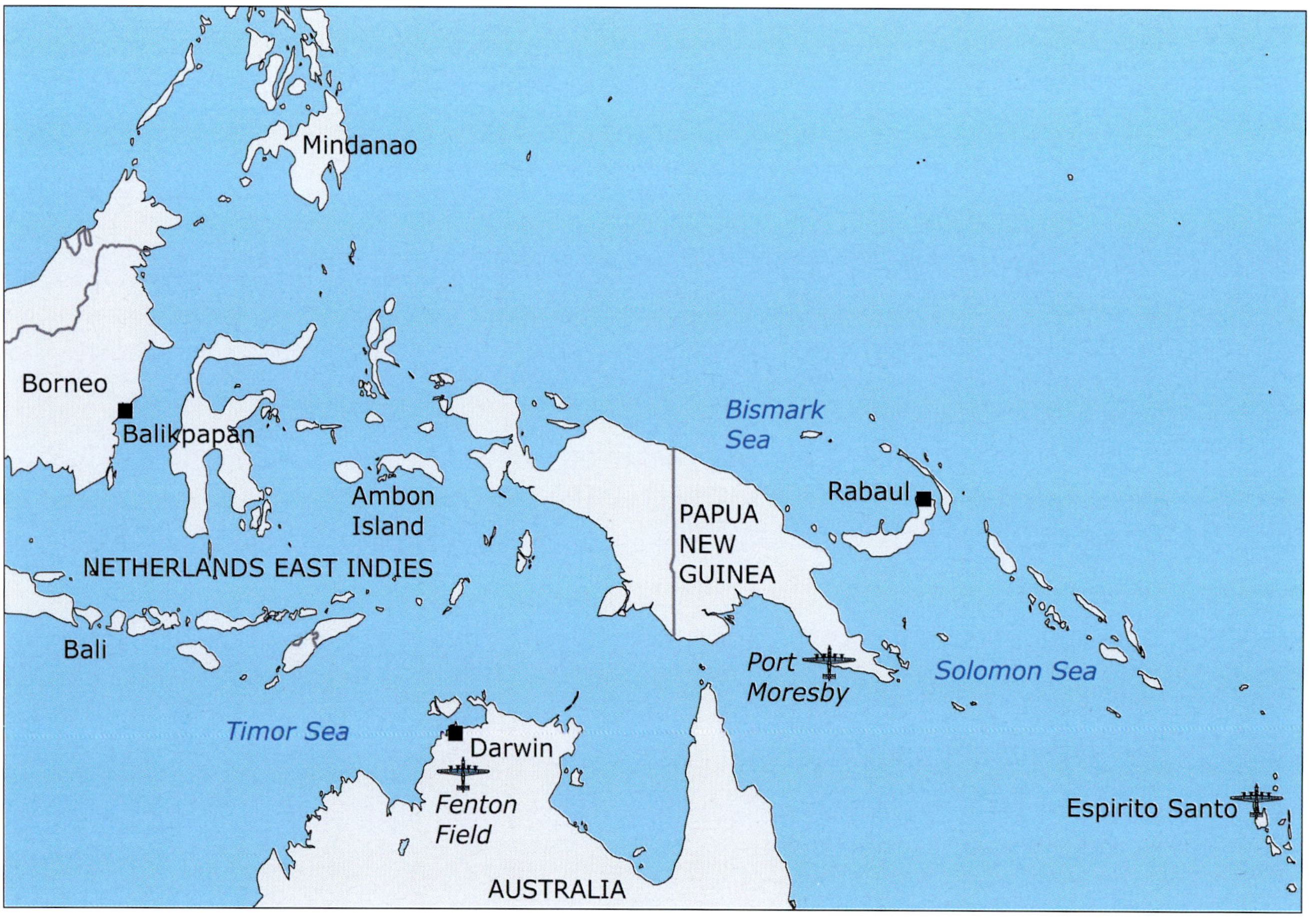

The only US long-range reconnaissance capability in theatre save a handful of US Navy PBY Catalinas in Darwin, the 435th BS (redesignated from the 40th Reconnaissance Squadron in April 1942) flew bombing and long-range reconnaissance sorties for SWPA, including missions over the northern Solomon Islands, New Guinea, and New Britain. Pairing an ARC-1 with one of the B-17s on a photographic reconnaissance mission would have been easy, the Boeing bombers having the payload and space to easily accommodate an additional crew member and his equipment. Besides having the aircraft and mission, the 435th BS had an existing relationship with the Australian military as the RAAF was loaning co-pilots to the undermanned US unit. The squadron flew six RCM missions between 8 and 23 September, concentrating on New Britain and New Guinea. Unfortunately, these missions could not provide conclusive evidence of Japanese radar operations. The RCM observers took their equipment back to Rushcutter and the squadron, run down from multiple months of hard operations, departed the theatre in November 1942.[42]

The second response came from the US Naval Research Laboratory (NRL). The recipient of a captured IJN Type 2 Mark I Model 1 set from Guadalcanal, NRL looked to develop both a receiver and a jammer that could target the set as well as personnel to operate the equipment. The receiver, the XARD, and the personnel, the Cast Mike Project #1, departed for the Pacific in September. Stopping off in Hawaii, Cast Mike #1 installed an ARC-1 set in the submarine USS *Drum* before departing for New Hebrides in the South Pacific. Upon arrival at Espiritu Santo, New Hebrides, the naval personnel installed their XARD receiver in a Boeing B-17E bomber assigned to the 11th Bombardment Group. The bomber with naval operators flew its first airborne SIGINT mission on 31 October 1942, the flight lasting eleven hours and routing to Guadalcanal and Bougainville and return. In November, an additional seven missions were flown to the Solomons and New Britain with American and New Zealand operators but all flights failed to receive any Japanese signals. Undeterred, the Cast Mike #1 team continued their investigations in December using PBY Catalinas of VP-54 and VP-72 flying from Guadalcanal. It would not be until June 1943 before the Cast Mike #1 team found a Japanese radar signal.[43]

Cast Mike #1's lack of results notwithstanding, the search for Japanese radars continued. Trials continued in Australia with RAAF aircraft in December 1942. The RAAF's 20 Squadron flew six missions in December and one each in January and February 1943 with PBY Catalinas fitted with ARC-1 receivers. Similar to the 435th BS missions, the Catalinas were flying surface search reconnaissance missions and the RCM operator and receiver were seen as an adjunct to existing tasking. Missions were flown off the northern coast of New Guinea and against New Britain as well as the Solomons, and again no definitive evidence of Japanese radars was found. Ten missions flown on Lockheed Hudson aircraft between 30 January 1943 and 25 February with 2 Squadron and 13 Squadron aircraft over the Timor Sea and west of Darwin produced similar results. Seven additional RAAF PBY Catalina missions over the next three months produced a few weak signals – a different approach was needed.[44]

Accommodation in ferret aircraft was never luxurious, but the first 'ad hoc' ferrets in the Southwest Pacific Area were decidedly lacking in comfort. RAAF Cpl Ray Hawkins is demonstrating the use of an RCM receiver while seated on the floor among oxygen cylinders above the aft bomb bay of a 380th BG B-24 'ad hoc' ferret. Hawkins was one of a detachment of personnel that became Field Unit 6 assigned to the 380th BG shortly after the bomb group arrived at Fenton Field, Australia, in May 1943. *Frank Cooper Collection via Craig Bellamy*

380th BG's early 'ad hoc' ferrets had simple dipole antennas along the slab side of the B-24 fuselage near the waist gun position. RAAF P/O Frank Cooper in a peaked cap at left is admiring the handiwork performed by his fellow Australians. *Frank Cooper Collection via Craig Bellamy*

Initially, a handful of B-24D bombers of the 380th BG were fitted with racks, cabling and antennas to support radar receivers, with the installation being carried out by Leading Radar Mechanic T.L. Page of the Royal New Zealand Navy and AC 1 Hawkins of the RAAF. This rack of radio equipment was installed above the aft bomb bay of the B-24, with scarce radio receivers only installed when the aircraft was tasked to perform a SIGINT mission. *Official Photo in Frank Cooper Collection via Craig Bellamy*

On 12 February 1943 two RAAF RCM operators reported in to the 43rd Bombardment Group at Port Moresby, New Guinea, lugging two ARC-1 receivers and appropriate antennas and cabling. Within a week, the first RCM mission was flown to Buna, New Guinea and the Solomon Islands. Two or three 43rd Bomb Group B-17Fs were fitted out for the tasking, carrying an RCM observer and an ARC-1 receiver whenever the aircraft were assigned on a bombing mission. Four missions were flown in March and one in April, covering New Ireland, New Britain, and New Guinea with mixed results.[45] At the same time, a similar effort was carried out with the B-24-equipped 90th Bomb Group. Two ARC-1 receivers and six RAAF personnel were assigned to the group and subordinate squadrons in January 1943, although little documentation exists on any operations for the first few months of the year.

The ad hoc nature of the early RCM effort was representative of the SWPA in this era. The 435th BS, short of pilots and aircrew, routinely flew missions with RAAF personnel augmenting their flight crews. The Pacific theatre, and SWPA in particular, was low in priority for the USAAF and personnel in this region learned to make do with what was available. Australian RCM operators lugging aboard their heavy Hallicrafters S-27 or Australian SN-2 radar intercept receivers and riding along for the mission while sitting on the floor was par for the course.

By February 1943 the RCM Organisation had evolved from a RAN to an Allied naval responsibility administered by the Naval Board. On 14 June 1943 MacArthur gave his support to the formation of a 'Radio and Radar Countermeasures Division, GHQ SWPA' under his operational control. By late June there were indications that the RCM Organisation was to be expanded, and on 15 July the Naval Board advised that the RCM Organisation had been transferred from Commander, Allied Naval Forces SWPA to CinC SWPA (MacArthur). The new organisation, known as Section 22, had a writ to oversee the collection, evaluation, and distribution of information and data with regard to enemy radio and radar activities.[46] Section 22 reported to the Chief Signal Officer of General MacArthur's General Headquarters of the Southwest Pacific Area (GHQ SWPA). Geographically separated subordinate elements called 'Field Units' provided information to the headquarters through a myriad of reports. Some of the intelligence was actual 'hands-on' exploitation of captured Japanese equipment, while some was electronic intelligence – intercepts of Japanese radar signals from air, land or sea-based platforms.[47]

A detachment of personnel that became Field Unit 6 was assigned to the 380th BG shortly after the bomb group arrived at Fenton Field, Australia, in May 1943. Many of the RAAF airmen appear to have been assigned to the 44 RDF Wing and did the RCM installation in the aircraft as well as crew the first ferret missions. Initially, a handful of B-24D were fitted with racks, cabling and antennas to support radar receivers, with the installation being done by Leading Radar Mechanic T.L. Page of the Royal New Zealand Navy and Corporal Hawkins of the RAAF. The initial tranche of operators supplied by the RAAF were Flt Sgt Dakeyne and Able Seamen Batstone and Money, although Batstone and Money returned to Brisbane within a few months. By September 1943 the unit had become Field Unit 6, led by Plt Off McCann with a multinational complement of an officer in charge, two RCM officers, one radar material officer, two radar mechanics, and twelve RCM operators. By October McCann and Dakeyne were joined by three RAAF enlisted RCM operators and six USAAF enlisted RCM operators.[48]

As the operational activity of the 380th BG increased, more aircraft were required for the RCM mission. On 4 November 1943 RAAF Plt Off Bevan was appointed as Plt Off McCann's assistant with responsibility for installation, maintenance, and operation of RCM equipment. Additional receivers trickled in and under the oversight of Plt Off Bevan the 380th BG was operating eight 'ad hoc' ferrets by the end of the year.[49]

'Ad hoc' ferrets (a contemporary term used by aviation historians) are standard bomber aircraft field-modified with racks, cabling, and antennas that enable them to carry radar receivers and other SIGINT equipment on a periodic basis, usually as a secondary mission to a primary function of bombing.

Flt Sgt Dick Dakeyne was assigned to 'ad hoc' ferret B-24D s/n 42-40496 *Juarez Whistle* as the RCM Operator and right waist gunner. Dakeyne served with Field Unit 6 from May 1943 until August 1944 and flew his first mission on *Juarez Whistle* the night of 30–31 May, a solo night mission to East Java and Bali. Dick Dakeyne, wearing shorts and second from right in the back row, is seen posed with the crew of pilot Lt John Dennis in about September 1943 at Fenton Field, Northern Territory. *Dick Dakeyne Collection via Craig Bellamy*

With the eight 'ad hoc' ferrets assigned to the group it was possible to fly at least two of the RCM-equipped aircraft per strike, maximising the potential of detecting any Japanese signals. Between May and November 1943 Field Unit 6 flew over thirty 'ad hoc' ferret missions with the 380th BG. Flt Sgt Dick Dakeyne, who was assigned to 'ad hoc' ferret B-24D 42-40496 *Juarez Whistle* as the RCM operator and right waist gunner, served with Field Unit 6 from May 1943 until August 1944 and his flights provide insight into the type of missions flown by the unit. Dakeyne flew his first mission on *Juarez Whistle* the night of 30–31 May, a solo night mission to East Java and Bali. On 11 June 'ad hoc' ferret B-24D 42-40500 *Care Less*, flown by 531st BS CO Capt. Dienelt, accompanied a 380 BG strike on Penfoei airfield near Koepang. *Care Less* was hit by flak and eventually shot down by fighters, the entire crew perishing including RCM operator RAAF Sgt Joe Holohan. Dakeyne was also on the mission in B-24D 42-40492 *Miss Mary*, logging eight and a half hours as a gunner on this non-RCM bomber. Dakeyne flew four RCM missions in *Juarez Whistle* in August, including bomb missions to Balikpapan, Ambon Island, Celebes and western New Guinea. He flew seven missions in September, two in October, and three in November including one mission on B-24D 42-40512 *She Asta*. Targets for Dakeyne's missions included Surabaya, Macassar, Moluccas, Kendari, and Ambon. On 21 November Field Unit 6 suffered its second loss, B-24D 42-40967 *Black Widow* taking a direct hit from AAA while bombing Manokwari, New Guinea, and crashing in a ball of flame, the crew, including RAAF Plt Off Keith Bevan operating an SCR-587 receiver, being killed on impact.[50]

MacArthur's planned offensive against Rabaul, a key Japanese base on New Britain, was given approval by the Joint Chiefs of Staff in spring 1943. Executed as Operation CARTWHEEL, the plan required detailed knowledge of Japanese defences in the region. This action likely galvanised the creation of Section 22 and provided the impetus and priority to move from an ad hoc approach of radar reconnaissance to a more formal structure with proper equipment. In early July Section 22 staff started discussing future requirements for RCM in the SWPA, including the need for two ferret aircraft. Backed by a Joint Chiefs directive, the staff at GHQ SWPA soon went calling to Washington and at a meeting on 22 July attended by Maj. Gen. Akin, GHQ SWPA's Chief Signal Officer, and Maj. Gen. McClelland, the Air Communications Officer at Headquarters, Army Air Forces in Washington the Army Air Forces agreed to build two ferret aircraft to aid GHQ SWPA in gathering SIGINT for current and proposed operations.[51]

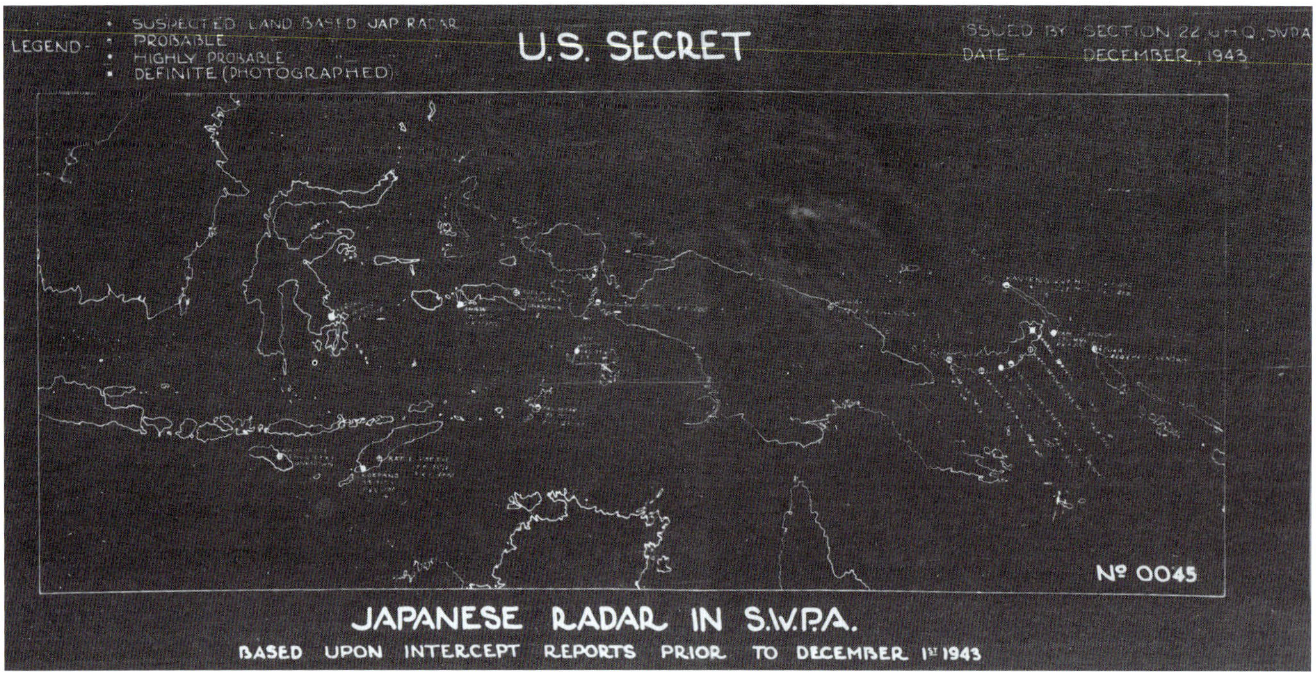

The Section 22 knowledge of Japanese radar capabilities and locations increased dramatically with the fielding of ferrets. This map depicts Japanese radars in western New Guinea, Borneo and Dutch East Indies *circa* December 1943.
Air Force Historical Research Agency via George Cully

The two ferrets were a rush job, with SWPA desiring the receipt of the aircraft little more than a month after the USAAF's Material Command was notified. With no time to build a prototype, the Air Staff recommended Material Command use the ongoing work on a modification named Ferret I and developed for use in Alaska as a starting point for installing the necessary RCM equipment.[52] In January 1944 the two modified B-24Ds, now identified as Ferrets VII and VIII, arrived in theatre. Although administratively assigned to the 63rd Bomb Squadron, 43rd Bomb Group (H) for maintenance, the mission tasking of the ferrets was controlled by Section 22 through Field Unit 1.

Chapter 3

The US purchased Alaska from Russia in 1867. Although in the late 1800s and early 1900s there was a military presence due to the gold rush, by the 1920s the US Army presence was minimal and reached a low of two infantry companies by 1939. Part of this was due to the 1922 Washington Conference Treaty limiting US overseas forces in the Pacific and part due to the finite budget available to the military after the Great War. As the war in Europe kicked off and the US started to expand its forces, Alaska witnessed a slight increase in deployment. In 1940 a cold weather testing facility for aircraft and equipment was approved for Fairbanks and the Civil Aeronautics Administration initiated a programme to build emergency landing fields north from Puget Sound and out to the Aleutians. The build-up was slow until mid-1941, geography and the frenetic pace of growth of the War Department impairing rapid progress in Alaska. In May 1940 General Marshall approved an expansion of Alaska defences, with the Air Corps creating the 28th Composite Group as a cornerstone for air power defences in the north-west. Forces started to flow in theatre in February 1941 as construction started on additional air bases and a plan was put in place to augment air defences with a chain of early-warning radars. By May 1941, one pursuit and two bomber squadrons were in Alaska. Additional squadrons slowly trickled into Alaska after the start of the war, the deploying squadrons following a route pioneered seven years earlier by then Lt Col H.H. Arnold, who led a flight of ten B-10s up to Alaska. After a carrier attack on Dutch Harbor, Alaska, on 25 May 1942 Japanese forces landed on two Aleutian Islands, Attu and Kiska, in early June.

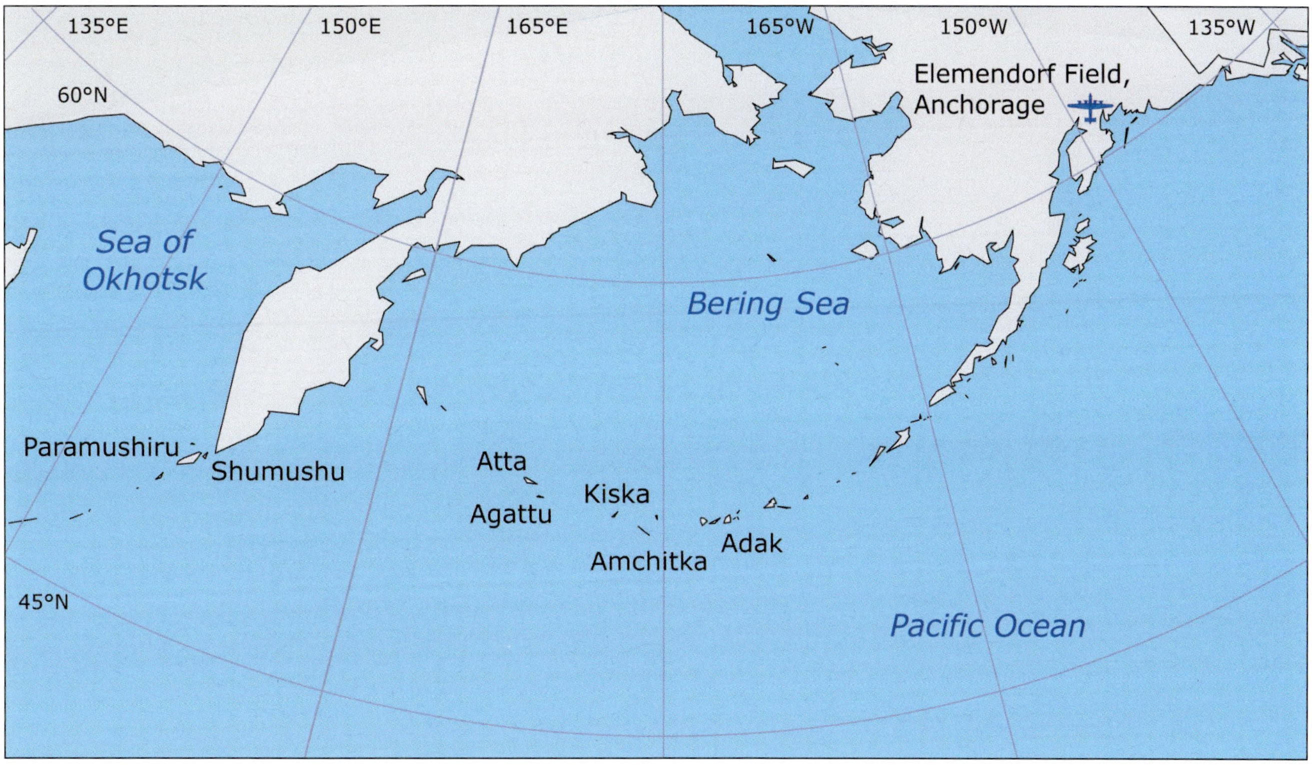

The Army responded by sending an additional three bomber squadrons and a fighter group of four squadrons up north to further bolster defences. As the units acclimated and bases expanded, attacks against the Japanese on Attu and Kiska expanded slowly.[53]

The enemy occupying forces were mainly infantry, but Japan did send equipment to aid in the aerial defence of the islands. Anti-aircraft guns and eight Nakajima A6M2-N floatplane fighters were sent to Attu; to aid in warning these assets that American aircraft were approaching, Kiska and Attu both had two IJN Type 2 Mark I Model 1 radar sets emplaced, a standard deployment where one set could search while the other tracked a specific target. The Imperial Japanese Navy also had radio intercept posts, with two Type 94, No. 1, medium-frequency direction-finder sets deployed to Attu. The radar on Kiska was operational first, in September 1942, followed by the Attu sets starting in March 1943.[54]

In September 1942 a fighter pilot flying over Kiska observed what he thought was a radar, a fact confirmed in early October when imagery from a photo reconnaissance mission revealed what was determined to be an installation similar to that on Guadalcanal. In late January 1943 Eleventh Air Force radio operators started to report Japanese jamming of 'portions of the radio wave bands', a possible sign that the Kiska radar was operational.[55]

Lt Ed Tietz poses in front of B-24D Ferret '23941 shortly after arrival in Alaska at Ladd Field. Prior to WWII, Ladd Field provided cold weather testing to the Air Corps, but by 1943 aircraft testing had become a second priority as Ladd became the hub for fighters and bombers destined for the Aleutians. *AOC via David Stern*

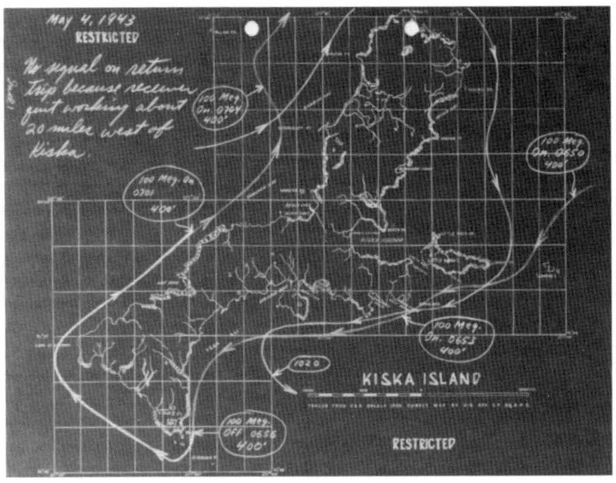

Plot from the mission log for the 4 May 1943 'ad hoc' ferret mission flown in a 21st BS B-24 by Cpl Charles Waid. After departing Amchitka the aircraft flew out to Kiska and circled the island, where Waid noted a 100 MHz signal, the frequency associated with the IJN Type 2 Mark I Model 1. *US National Archives*

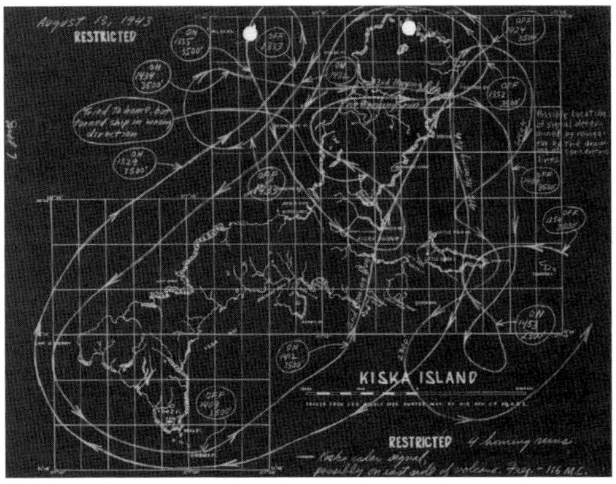

The second deployment of ferret B-24D s/n 41-23941 was not as successful as the first due to the fact that the Japanese had evacuated Kiska within a week of the bomber arriving in Alaska. On 13 August Sgt Waid and Lt Neely thought they found a possible radar on Kiska with a new 116 MHz signal, but the Japanese radar had been out of commission for over two weeks. Electronic anomalies were a routine part of the ferret mission. *US National Archives*

In early November 1942 Lt Col James McRae from the Air Staff in Washington met with Maj. George Haller of the Aircraft Radio Laboratory (ARL) at Wright Field in Ohio to discuss the Alaskan developments. Haller offered his group to modify an aircraft to carry existing receivers and other necessary equipment for the task of airborne SIGINT collection. After returning to DC, McRae drafted a requirement document for the signature of USAAF Chief of Staff General Henry 'Hap' Arnold, directing Wright Field to perform the work. This project, code-named 'Ferret', called for ARL to team with the Naval Research Laboratory in outfitting a new Consolidated B-24D Liberator bomber with a suite of military and commercial radio receivers for the radar reconnaissance. A Consolidated B-24D Liberator, s/n 41-23941, was allocated to the project and flew to Wright Field on 12 November to be fitted with an SCR-587 receiver, a commercial Hallicrafters S-27 receiver, a direction-finding antenna, and a hand-built pulse analyser. The electronic gear was likely fitted in the radio compartment or waist gunner's area of the aircraft, as '23941 maintained the ability to carry and drop bombs. While the aircraft was undergoing modification at Wright Field, Lts Edward Tietz and William Praun, graduates of Lt Hugh Winter's first four-week RCM course at Boca Raton, were assigned to the aircraft and travelled to Ohio to familiarise themselves with the equipment being installed in the aircraft.[56]

After receiving its electronic fit, the B-24 flew to Fort Worth, Texas, in early January 1943 to modify the engines for cold weather operations. After flights against US Army radars along the West Coast the aircraft and crew deployed to Adak, Alaska, in February 1943. As '23941 was being designed and built, the US had slowly been marching out the Aleutian chain. Adak Island was secured in a howling gale on 30 August 1942 followed by Amchitka Island on 11 January 1943. The impending invasion of Kiska scheduled for later that summer required suppression of Japanese air and defensive efforts in the Aleutians, and the new ferret was just the aircraft to do so. After weeks of weather delays, the ferret flew its first operational mission over the Aleutians on 6 March, piloted by Captain Wernick. RCM Observers Tietz and Praun soon started receiving signals from two Japanese radar sets located on enemy-held Kiska Island. Two additional missions were flown on 7 and 15 March to map out radar coverage and investigate Attu and Agattu. After summarising their discoveries to Eleventh Air Force staff, the crew flew the aircraft back to Wright Field. Before departing Alaska, the RCM Observers provided input to an Eleventh Air Force attack on the Japanese radar with B-24 and B-25 bombers scheduled for 16 March.[57] Lts Tietz and Praun returned to Boca Raton as instructors, passing on their real-world experience to the crews of Ferrets III to V heading to the Mediterranean.

After the ferret had departed, interference on radio channels near known Japanese radar operating frequencies was noted by radio operators on bombers attacking Kiska and soon Eleventh Air Force staff suspected the radar had survived the bombing attack on 16 March and was operational again. This anomaly was noted again on 3 May 1943 and resulted in an investigation the following day. Corporal Charles Waid, a 404th Bomb Squadron (BS) radar operator, brought a receiver aboard a scheduled 28th Composite Group weather reconnaissance mission, likely flown in a 21st BS B-24, on 4 May to try and characterise the radio interference. After departing Amchitka, the aircraft flew out to Kiska and circled

Pacific Huts made of laminated wood proved to be ideal for use in Alaska. While flying out of Adak, Lieutenants Praud and Tietz made one their home. Here Ed Tietz stands by his quarters at Adak in February 1943 waiting for the weather to clear to fly his first ferret mission. *AOC via David Stern*

Adak Alaska was a forbidding location for operations. This February 1943 photo of the airfield captures the gloom of an Alaska winter as B-24s, including Ferret '23941, wait for weather conducive to flight operations. *AOC via David Stern*

the island and Waid noted a 100 MHz signal, the frequency associated with the IJN Type 2 Mark I Model 1. The aircraft then circled Attu, where he picked up another signal at 100 MHz when off Chirikof Point south-east of the radar position. A spurious 65 MHz signal was also picked up, one of many that would occur in the Aleutians over the next few months.[58]

The island of Attu was assaulted by US and Canadian forces on 11 May 1943 and liberated by 30 May. Two IJN Type 2 Mark I Model 1 radar sets were captured on the promontory west of Chichagof Harbor, confirming what Waid and photo reconnaissance had assessed.[59] Planning continued for the assault on Kiska, scheduled for later that summer. On 18 July, six B-24s flown by volunteers from the 21 BS, 36 BS and 404 BS made the first US attack on the Japanese island of Paramushiru, part of the Kuril Islands that ran north from the Japanese home islands. This attack was a prelude for more operations over the Kurils in the future months.

B-24 '23941 returned to Alaska, apparently unannounced and without prior coordination. The ferret arrived without any trained RCM Observers, so Corporal Waid was roped into flying in this position.[60] The aircraft forward deployed to Amchitka. Corporal Waid flew as RCM operator on '23941's first mission on 22 July, circling Kiska twice and picking up two distinct signals at 101.5 and 108 MHz. A mission four days later was flown with Corporal Waid being accompanied by Lt Col Mitchell, Lt Huffman, Mr Wolf and Dr Jeffers of the Operational Analysis Section. Two signals, at 101 MHz and 107 MHz, were observed and it was noted that there was an unusual amount of radar activity that evening. The next mission was flown from Adak on 4 August by 21st BS pilots with newly promoted Sgt Waid as RCM operator. After circling Kiska for over an hour with no radar activity '23941 made a bomb run on the Kiska main camp, dropping six 500lb general-purpose bombs.[61] Waid's equipment was correct – the Japanese had evacuated the island on 29 July.

A 28th Composite Group B-24D taxiing along the runway after returning from a bombing raid in September 1943. Early ferret missions in Alaska were hosted by the group's 404th BS and utilised crew members from the group to augment the RCM Observers deployed from the US. *National Museum of the United States Air Force*

On 11 August Waid searched in vain from 40 to 450 MHz without finding any enemy signals as the ferret B-24, flown by 21st BS pilot Lt O'Donnell, circled Kiska and stayed within radar range for two and a half hours. The following day, 12 August, another mission was flown around Kiska with Waid accompanied by Major John Wiegraffe. No signals at 101 MHz were heard, although a spurious 160 MHz signal was heard for short intervals. Three photo runs were made over the island by 21st BS pilot Lt Lock at the end of the mission.[62] On 13 August the unconquerable Sgt Waid, accompanied by Lt Neely, took off from Adak in '23941 flown by Lt Meigs of the 404th BS. Using their SX-27 receiver, the RCM observers thought they found a possible radar on Kiska with a new 116 MHz signal, with the pair confirming the same signal as 'definitely a radar' on a flight the following day. After its seventh mission on 14 August '23941 was no longer needed for radar reconnaissance as Kiska was invaded on 15 August by US forces.[63] Liberating forces confirmed that two Type 2 Mark I Model 1 radar sets were still emplaced on the ridgeline overlooking Kiska Harbor. The radars had been damaged by the Japanese before they departed, so it is unknown what signals Waid had been receiving on the August missions.[64] To support the assault on Kiska, the 1st Special Services Platoon established a jamming station on the western tip of Amchitka Island in order to degrade Japanese radar coverage during the initial landings. Findings from '23941's initial missions were used to determine the type of jamming equipment required and although the equipment was in place it was not needed.[65]

After Kiska was cleared, Western Defence Command and Fourth Army commander Lt Gen. John DeWitt recommended to Gen. Marshall that the US follow up with an invasion of Shumshu and Paramushiru, the northernmost of the Kuril Islands. There was no support in Washington nor Hawaii for such a venture and its early 1944 timeline, although additional contingency planning was undertaken for such an operation in spring 1945. Within two weeks of the securing of Kiska, four bomber squadrons in the Eleventh Air Force were designated for withdrawal in September 1943.[66] Before the majority of the bombers departed, one last strike was planned. Already, a second strike to the Kurils had been flown by nine B-24s on 11 August. On 11 September twelve B-25s and eight B-24s attacked Paramushiru for the third time in 1943. Heavy fighter and AAA defences caused the loss of two B-24s and seven B-25s, with Sgt Waid flying as the radar operator on one of the B-24s lost on the raid. Waid's B-24A crash-landed in the Soviet Union and after enduring internment with his erstwhile Allies he eventually returned to the US. Also flying on the ill-fated 11 September mission was '23941, its intercept gear removed and the B-24D drafted to fly as a standard bomber. Though credited with three kills against attacking Japanese fighters, '23941 was considered beyond repair due to extensive damage caused by the attacking aircraft and once it returned to base it was pushed out of the way and used for parts.[67] Bombing was considered the highest priority for the Eleventh Air Force, so the RCM equipment was transferred to a 'barely flyable' B-24D, s/n 41-23886, which was sent to the continental United States (CONUS) for the installation of more modern equipment. The B-24D, a veteran 404th BS aircraft that had arrived in Alaska in December 1942 and participant in the ill-fated 11 September raid (with one Zeke kill), departed Alaska in September 1943.[68] Eventually '23941 was made flyable and eventually returned to the US in January 1944, conducting no further RCM work.[69]

Ferret '23941 shortly after arrival at Ladd Field, Alaska, in late January 1943. Fitted with SCR-587 and Hallicrafters S-27 receivers, a direction finding antenna, and a hand-built pulse analyzer, there was little to see on the exterior of the B-24D to denote the function of this unique aircraft. *AOC via David Stern*

The withdrawal of the four USAAF bomber squadrons did not mean the demise of airpower in Alaska. Starting in March 1943, the US Navy initiated rotations of squadrons equipped with Lockheed PV-1 Ventura twin-engine patrol aircraft under the control of Fleet Air Wing Four (FAW 4). On average two squadrons were based out of Attu, flying patrols and, starting in mid-1944, photo reconnaissance and light attack missions against the northern Kurils.[70] The primary target of FAW 4 was Japanese shipping in the Kurils. As US and Japanese forces shadow-boxed in the Kurils, '23886 was sent to the 1st Proving Ground Electronics Unit at Eglin Field to be outfitted as a ferret aircraft. According to the 1945 Proving Ground Command official history, the electronics unit, although assigned to the Proving Ground Command, was responsible to the Commanding General, Army Air Forces, for special projects such as 'limited scale installations of special countermeasures equipment in aircraft proceeding overseas'.[71]

Florida's next iteration in the ferret design, likely built shortly after '23941 departed in late 1942, was named Ferret II and was built based on experience from the construction of the original ferret. Unfortunately, its performance was dubbed 'inadequate' and the aircraft was never operationally used, instead staying in Florida for test and training purposes.[72] After arrival in Florida for fitting out, '23886 was dubbed Ferret I. The ferret production line was still nascent, with each aircraft being hand built. The bomb bay was converted to an RCM compartment with two seats and the electronics updated and laid out logically based on experience from the Alaska missions. The aircraft was sent to Oklahoma City Air Depot for nose turret installation at the end of 1943. Unfortunately for Alaska, SWPA submitted a requirement in September 1943 for two ferret aircraft. With Alaska moving to the back-burner after the liberation of Kiska, SWPA had priority and Ferret I moved aside to allow Ferrets VII and VIII to be built.[73]

Serial Number	Aircraft	First Mission	Last Mission	Total # Ops Missions	Notes	Fate
41-23941	B-24D-10-CO	6 March 43	14 August 43	10	Original CONUS production	Returned to US after flying routine bomber missions

A 404th BS B-24D taxiing past two parked B-24Ds at Shemya AAFB, Alaska. All aircraft are fitted with SCR-521 ASV radars, a necessity for operations in the Aleutian weather. Take-off, navigation, and landing in the Alaskan theatre were all made more difficult by reduced visibility and high winds. *National Museum of the United States Air Force*

Chapter 4

While most of the USAAF ferret programme was focused on the Pacific theatre and used B-24s as a host aircraft, what would become the 16th Reconnaissance Squadron broke the mould in many ways. The primary strategic air war was Europe, with few assets devoted to the Mediterranean theatre, which was more of a close air support and interdiction fight. Although the Allies knew Germany had operationally deployed radars, little was known about the ranges of these radars nor the frequencies on which they operated – or even where they were located in the Mediterranean. The Royal Air Force (RAF) started examining this problem with 148 Squadron. A bomber unit flying Vickers Wellington medium bombers against German targets in North Africa, 148 Squadron had started to experiment in summer 1941. A few of their aircraft were modified to carry receivers and an operator and operated as 'ad hoc' ferrets, flying bomber missions while monitoring the radio waves. A detachment from the dedicated RCM unit, 109 Squadron, joined in the effort in November 1941, being formally designated 162 (Special Duties) Squadron on 4 January 1942. This action continued through 1944, with the main focus being on North Africa and the desert fight.[74]

With combat operations against the Germans in North Africa winding down, the Casablanca Conference in January 1943 provided the strategic direction for the next move by the Allied forces in Europe. The decision was made to invade Sicily later that year as a stepping stone to the invasion of mainland Italy. The USAAF had a requirement to map German surface search and early-warning radars in preparation for the assault on Sicily and in February 1943 asked ARL to equip three ferret aircraft to support this operation.[75]

Three B-17F aircraft were allocated for conversion to the electronic reconnaissance role, with their sensor suite based on the original ferret, B-24D s/n 41-23941. The first aircraft, Boeing B-17F-50-DL s/n 42-29644, was designated Ferret III and sent to Wright Field and Radio Research Laboratories (RRL) in Boston for its transformation. Additional fuel tanks were installed in the bomb bay and a RCM Observer's position built in the radio room with racks for receivers and seats for two observers. The RCM Observers, meanwhile, were undergoing training at Boca Raton, Florida. Simultaneous to the ferret training and construction was another endeavour involving targeting German radars. It was not enough to locate enemy radars, something had to be done to counter their threat to Allied operations.[76]

The RRL at Cambridge, Massachusetts, developed two airborne barrage jamming transmitters designed to counter the two biggest German threats – the RC-183 'Mandrel' to jam the Freya early warning and surface search radar and the RC-156 'Carpet' to suppress the Würzburg gun-laying and fighter control radar. In May 1943 thirty-five Boeing B-17 bombers were sent to Eglin Field for modification to accommodate one of each type of jammer, with operators and maintenance personnel undergoing training at Boca Raton for a deployment to the Mediterranean in support of Operation HUSKY, the Allied invasion of Sicily.[77]

The crew of Ferret III met up with their aircraft and after processing at Salina, Kansas, flew to Eglin Field in Florida and conducted a practise flight over the Gulf of Mexico. With everything looking good, the crew of Ferret III left Morrison Field at West Palm Beach, Florida for Algeria on 22 April 1943. Pilot 1Lt Harold Millen took '644 via the southern ferry route of South America to West Africa via Ascension Island and on to Algiers. The B-17F arrived at Blida, an RAF base about 30 miles outside Algiers. Assigned to the 64th Troop Carrier Group for rations and administration but essentially on their own, Ferret III's crew quickly found common cause with 162 (SD) Squadron.[78] Ferret III's RCM Observers, 2Lts Matthew Slavin and Roger Ihle, chatted with their equivalents in 162 (SD) Sqn and with the help of technical adviser Dr D.B. Sinclair of RRL did the first of many modifications to their aircraft, rearranging their equipment for ease of operation and modifying

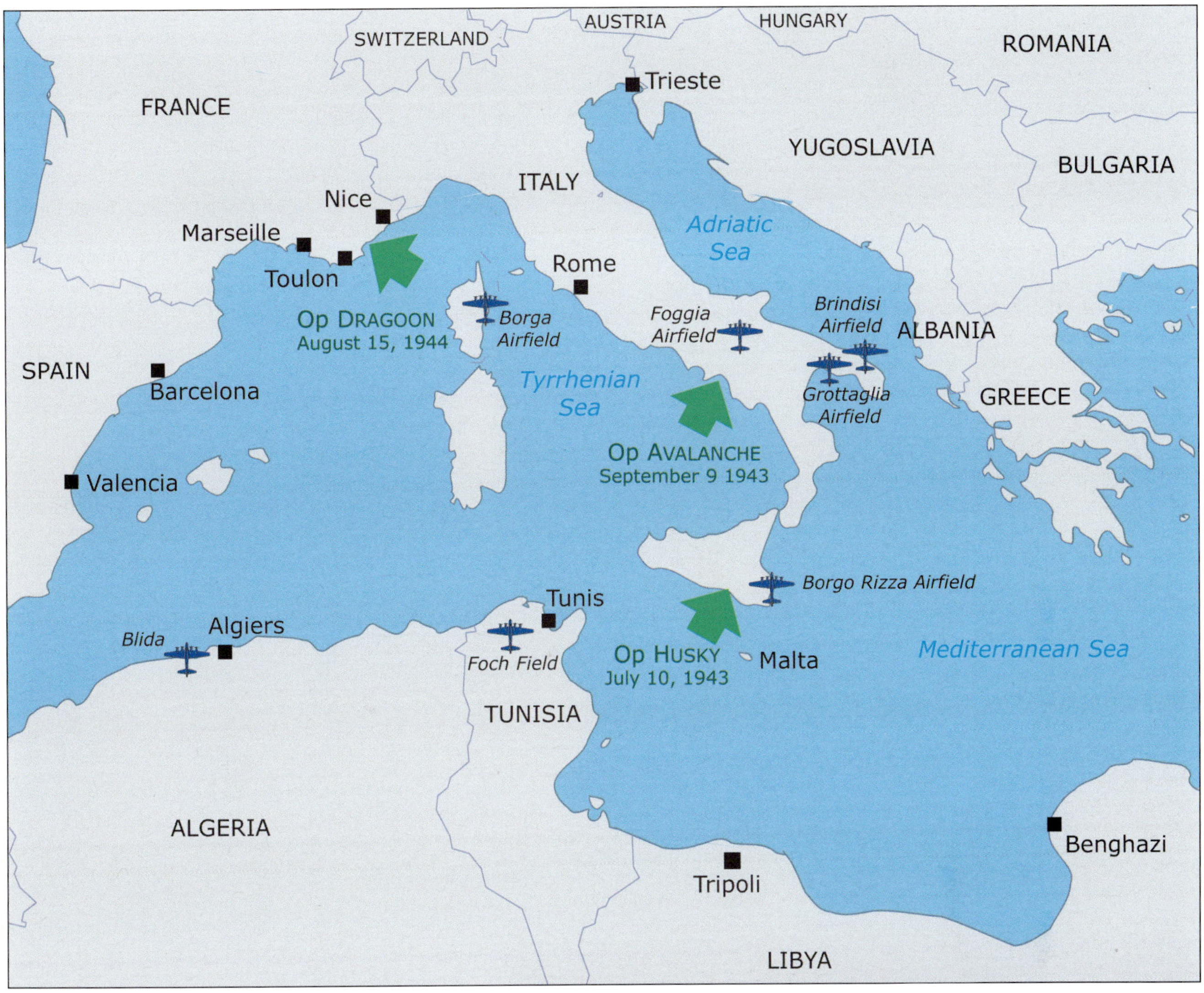

their direction-finding antennas for increased accuracy.[79] Initial test missions were flown in May 1943, with operational sorties starting on 17 May. In line with their RAF brethren, the ferret crews operated at night, alone, and over the Mediterranean 10–15 miles off the enemy coast. Missions were flown at low level, 500–1,000ft in altitude, with the pilots flying visually without the benefit of a navigation radar. By 9 July, when Operation HUSKY kicked off, Ferret III had flown nine missions along the coasts of Sardinia and Sicily and contributed valuable intelligence to invasion planning. The missions were flown from various bases, ranging from Blida, Algeria to Enfidaville, Tunisia. Back in the States, the second leg of the electronic war against Germany was preparing to join the fight. On 6 July, the jammer B-17s departed the US for Algeria. Coming late to the dance, four of the B-17 jammers had arrived before the start of Operation HUSKY. Even though their maintenance personnel were still en route via ship, the flight crews with support from Ferret III's personnel maintained and flew their aircraft for jamming missions supporting the invasion.[80]

Allied focus in the Mediterranean starting in mid-1940 resulted in the Luftwaffe shifting a portion of its Integrated Air Defence System south to protect strategic locations including Italian bases and Romanian oilfields. Key to providing warning of Allied raids were coastal early-warning radars such as this Freya LZ radar sited inside a circular concrete blast wall on the island of Sicily. *US National Archives*

The nucleus of what was to become the 16th Reconnaissance Squadron pose in front of B-17 Ferret V, s/n 42-3055 *circa* September 1943. Initially christened the 'GR' (General Reconnaissance) Squadron, the unit contained the pilots and crews of Ferrets III, IV and V as well as administrative personnel from Northwest African Air Forces. *Air Force Historical Research Agency via George Cully*

Ferrets IV and V left the US together on 20 June, following a route similar to Ferret III's journey to North Africa. Arriving at Blida in mid-July after delays in routing through Africa, the two new aircraft and their crews joined Ferret III in mapping German radars. Ferret IV, crewed by RCM Observers 2Lts Harrison Lehman and James Magnuson, and Ferret V, with 2Lts Norman Weed and John Pheley, had brought with them Dr Richard Raymond of RRL, who was to replace Dr Sinclair as the Technical Observer for the group. With the invasion of Sicily done, the Northwest African Air Forces (NAAF) needed a mid-term solution for what to do with the ferrets. Blida was distant from future action, so the ferret detachment was ordered to move east to Foch Field outside of Tunis, Tunisia, on 26 July. The ferret detachment was also formally made into an organisation – before departing for Foch, the detachment was christened the 'GR' (General Reconnaissance) Squadron and aligned under the Communications Section of Twelfth Air Force.[81] The unit absorbed the radar jammer personnel, airborne jammers, and the four 'orphan' jammer aircraft sent over to support the Sicily invasion and took on a broader mission for the remainder of its existence.

Foch Field's 5,000ft sod and clay runways were not ideal but would serve the squadron for the moment. When it rained, aircraft were mired in mud and when a dry spell set in, aircraft movement caused a dust cloud the height of a Fortress. Despite these challenges, with Sicily secured by 17 August, radar reconnaissance of the west coast of Italy began in earnest to support the Allied landing at Salerno planned for September. Ten missions were flown in the last two weeks of August, providing thorough coverage of German radars on the islands of Sardinia, Corsica and Elba as well as the west coast of Italy around Genoa and Naples areas. After the Operation AVALANCHE amphibious landing at Salerno in early September, another ten missions were flown off the

The 16th RS operated from Foch Field outside of Tunis, Tunisia, from July 1943 to March 1944. An aerial view from October 1943 depicts the following: 1. North–south runway, Foch Field. 2. 16th RS squadron area. 3. Sub-depot, 17th Air Depot Group. 4. Bay of Tunis. 5. Tunis. 6. City of Machrin. *Air Force Historical Research Agency via George Cully*

Maintenance at Foch Field was primitive. 16th RS maintenance personnel work on a ferret B-17F out in the open, performing routine engine work. Squadron personnel relied on tools and equipment borrowed from the local 17th Air Depot Group. *Air Force Historical Research Agency via George Cully*

east coast of Italy as the Fifth Army fought to gain a foothold on the Italian peninsula. After two weeks of hard fighting, the Allies were able to break out of the coastal area and the GR Squadron started to spread its wings to mapping radars further afield. The first mission off southern France was flown on 16 September, followed by missions in the Adriatic on 24 and 26 September that investigated Greece, the east coast of Italy and west coast of Yugoslavia and Albania. Prior to 16 September, Allied knowledge of German radar locations in the Mediterranean was mainly confined to Sicily, Sardinia and the southern part of Italy. With the capitulation of the fascist government in Rome, Allied intelligence needed additional information to plan follow-on amphibious landings. The mission flown the night of 16–17 September also revealed that the German radar operators appeared to comprehend the function of a lone aircraft flying at low altitude at night, the RCM Observers noting that the Germans seemed to turn their radar away and not track their aircraft, making the job of the ferret crew that much harder.

Many of the missions continued to be flown at night and at low level, usually 500ft over the water. For the first fifteen missions, this was accomplished by dead reckoning and celestial navigation but by late August squadron technicians had fitted their aircraft with the SCR-521 navigation radar to aid in their nocturnal flights. The early recording equipment turned out to not work well, Lt Weed noting 'the accurate data for the location of the enemy radar was logged by the observers, then plotted on the navigator's charts'.[82] The autumn time period was busy for the squadron, first up being another reorganisation.[83] The GR Squadron was redesignated the 16th Reconnaissance Squadron (Bomber) on 26 September 1943, an action designed to ease supply and personnel challenges by providing a standard organisational structure that could be referenced for requisitions. Besides flying ferret radar reconnaissance missions, the 16th pursued a new mission area, radar jamming.

On 1 September, one of the four 'inherited' jammer B-17s, B-17F-100-BO s/n 42-30379, was flown with Ferret V s/n 42-3055 on a mission to determine the effectiveness of 'Mandrel' jamming against a Wassermann early-warning radar at Pula and a Freya early-warning radar at San Antioco Island in the Cagliari area of southern Sardinia. Ferret V, flown by Captain Balaban with Dr Raymond and Lts Ihle and Hovee as RCM Observers, was outfitted with Hallicrafter S27 and SCR 587 search receivers and an oscilloscope and audio oscillator for measuring pulse repetition frequency. The action appeared to excite the Luftwaffe as '379 soon drew the attention of German night fighters and flak. On the second leg of the orbit in the target area, the jammer was jumped by Luftwaffe fighters. Cautious about flying down to 500ft in the dark, the Germans resorted to dropping flares to highlight the B-17 to the flak batteries. The pilot of '379 turned hard left and dropped to 200ft, losing the inquisitive German flare droppers. A follow-up mission on 5 September was tame by comparison and allowed the RCM Observers to watch the German efforts to work around the 'Mandrel' jamming.[84]

With a growing interest in attacking the radio waves, the jammer section of the GR Squadron had already started to look for the remaining thirty-one 'lost' jammer aircraft and their accompanying 100 jammers. After arriving in theatre, the bombers had been assigned to four bomb groups within the Fifth Wing. Bomb group maintenance personnel, unaware of the 'top secret' jammers and wiring, removed the non-standard equipment and put the bombers into regular service without the 'excess' weight, damaging some of the gear in the process. Eventually all the aircraft were accounted for, one having crashed by the time the search was completed. The remaining thirty bombers were routed through Foch Field in late August to have their wiring restored and jammers reconditioned in order to support the AVALANCHE landing at Salerno. The aircraft, though, were apparently needed more in their primary role of bombardment and their jammers were not fitted prior to AVALANCHE. However, the squadron did not give up that easy.[85]

Post-AVALANCHE, there was a hesitancy to use the jammers in support of daily bombing strikes lest they fall into German hands. After discussions with the NAAF staff, it was decided to equip one Twelfth Air Force bomb group with 'Carpet' jammers as an experiment to screen bomber formations from radar-directed flak.[86] The 97th Bomb Group located at Deppien, Tunisia, not far from Foch Field, was selected for the task. After the cable-equipped bombers were collected and forwarded to the 97th BG, by late September 1943 the GR Squadron was in the jamming business, installing and maintaining equipment through a pool of maintenance personnel that 'commuted' to work each day. Before focusing solely on 97th BG 'Carpet' operations, the 16th RS (B) tried one experimental mission. Four jammer-wired B-17s of the 99th and 301st BGs were fitted with 'Mandrel' transmitters to jam early-warning radars and, accompanied by Ferret IV s/n 42-29881, conducted a raid into Italy the night of 3–4 October. B-17 '881 flew behind the formation with receivers tuned to watch the German activity. Analysis by the squadron showed that 'Mandrel' jamming appeared to alert the enemy of an incoming raid. Based on this evidence, 'Mandrel' jammers were put into a warehouse and not used again by the 16th RS (B).[87]

Once settled in stone stables and farm houses at Foch Field, the squadron engineering section started to improve their electronic gear based on feedback from missions. This technique was more responsive than acquiring equipment from the US and helped the squadron stay abreast of evolving threat radar technology. Besides tinkering with SCR-587 receivers and other components, the engineering section also modified entire aircraft. The three original ferrets continued to soldier on, though they were starting to show their age due to heavy usage. Three months of long missions flown at low altitude was hard on the airframes, so the 16th RS solved the problem just like they addressed other equipment shortages – they modified what was on hand. Three B-17s – B-17E s/n 41-9016 and B-17Fs s/n 42-30379 and s/n 42-3358 – were acquired in theatre through unknown methods and converted to ferret aircraft in October 1943. Ferrets III and IV, crewed by men who had completed their fifty combat missions, departed for the US in late November for repair work and were stricken from squadron records.[88] Also departing for the US was Dr Raymond, who had completed his temporary duty as Technical Observer and was replaced by Wallace Caufield. On 5 November, the squadron received back from the UK B-17F s/n 42-30437, which had been dispatched there on 25 September; it was an ex-97th BG aircraft that had flown jamming tests with the squadron in September. Accompanied by Tech Rep Dr Raymond, '437 was fitted out with British Gee radio navigation equipment, British ELINT equipment, and painted in a new black paint scheme. While the ferret was being modified, Raymond visited various British organisations engaged in RCM work to stay abreast of the latest developments. Aircraft, though, was not the limiter for 16 RS operations – it was equipment, one of the reasons why '437 went to the UK for modification. Although all squadron aircraft were likely equipped with Group A equipment – racks, cabling and antennas – to operate as a ferret, the unit only had enough receivers and pulse analysers for two or three aircraft at most.[89]

By late October the 97th BG had commenced jamming operations and the 16th RS (B) dispatched ferrets to fly with their formations to observe the impact of the 'Carpet' jamming on the Würzburg radars – as well as contribute some bombs to the target area. Missions flown on 24 October and 2 November against Wiener Neustadt, Austria, and on 1 November against Spezia, Italy, let ferrets monitor the effectiveness of jamming and scan for new German radars in the target area. The mission flown by B-17E ferret '016 on 24 October was the first time a ferret had accompanied a bomb group on a daylight strike. The ferret flew on the wing of the lead ship in order to observe German radar tracking of the lead formation, monitor radar activity, and witness the impacts of the radar jamming. After the 2 November mission the squadron was satisfied that the jamming was having the right effect and the 16th RS stopped flying its ferrets with the daylight bomber formations.[90]

Right: Lt Harold Millen, 16th RS Operations Officer, and Captain Harold Dollinger, 16th RS Executive Officer, bid farewell to Ferret III. Ferrets III and IV, crewed by men who had completed their fifty combat missions, departed for the US in late November 1943 for repair work and were stricken from squadron records.
Air Force Historical Research Agency via George Cully

Below: B-17F 42-3358 was modified to ferret configuration in theatre by the 16th RS. The aircraft, named *Thunder Head*, had standard olive drab over grey camouflage and was the first ferret fitted with Yagi DF antennas on the fuselage spine. The SCR-717 navigation radar was fitted in place of the ball turret by squadron technicians at the time of modification. *Air Force Historical Research Agency via George Cully*

16th RS B-17F Ferret 42-3055/Ferret V *The Pointer* parked in the squadron area at Foch Field. Ferrets III and V had this interesting mottled camouflage scheme, which appears to be black spray painted on the factory paint scheme. B-17F s/n 42-30437 had a different scheme with larger black patches applied while undergoing modification in the UK. *Air Force Historical Research Agency via George Cully*

To continue to monitor jammer performance, RCM Observers were placed on detached service to the 97th BG to oversee RCM operations and ensure the 16th RS was getting feedback on the performance of the jammers as well as German tactics. The 16th RS maintenance personnel also took burned out SCR-587 receivers and turned them into frequency monitors to aid with in-flight adjust of 'Carpet' jammers carried by 97th BG. Two B-17Fs assigned to the 97th BG's 340th Bomb Squadron were fitted with these modified SCR-587s in October 1943 for use by the assigned RCM Observers to monitor jamming impacts and German tactics to work around the intrusion. Lt Roger Ihle, one of the original RCM Observers assigned to Ferret III, flew on one of the 340th BS-modified B-17Fs for an attack on an airfield at Istres-Le Tubé in southern France on 16 November. The next day Lt Slavin, Ihle's crewmate from Ferret III, flew on a strike against an airfield at Eleusis, Greece. Both RCM Observers noted the effectiveness of the 'Carpet' jammers, witnessing the Würzburg radars sweeping the bomber formation but unable to lock onto a target. In late December the 97th BG moved to Italy, although the relationship did not end. The 16th RS transferred one officer, Lt Weed from Ferret V's crew, and three enlisted personnel to the group. Weed and his crew would install receiving and analysing equipment in the group commander's bomber and fly missions, sitting in the radio room to monitor the German radars and the effectiveness of their jamming. Success of the 97th BG jammers in reducing flak losses saw the expansion of jammers to other bomb groups. Jammer maintenance was soon transferred from the 16th RS to the Twelfth AF Service Command. The 16th RS trained Twelfth AF personnel as their last contribution to the successful programme they had birthed.[91]

Although the daytime missions provided value to Twelfth Air Force, the 16th RS was more comfortable flying its missions at night. Partners in nocturnal Mediterranean flight operations were the RAF Wellington bomber squadrons. Starting on 22 October, the 16th RS flew five missions in conjunction with the RAF over a one-month time period. The intent was to let the British raid 'stimulate' the defences while the ferret collected the resulting radar activity. The ferrets would arrive over the target area prior to the bombers, set up in an orbit at 12,000ft, and remain until the last bomber had passed. Although there were few German radar signals on the first flight, the ferret did attract the attention of several RAF Beaufighter night fighters. On the night of 1–2 November, though, ferret '016 had a narrow escape from both combat and weather hazards. Flown by Lt George Jordan with Lts Lester Manbeck and John Pheley accompanied by S/Sgt John Howard as observers, the target was Viareggio in northern Italy. On take-off the weather appeared threatening and worsened en route, resulting in delays for the flight to the target area. As '016 approached the island of Elba, the Germans started to jam the ferret's SCR-521 navigation radar. With weather and jamming impacts, '016 did not arrive near the target until after the Wellingtons had started to bomb. The now alert flak batteries started to engage the ferret and despite manoeuvring by Jordan '016 was bracketed by AAA fire. Passing from AAA into weather again, '016 hit an intense thunderhead, with Jordan almost losing control of the aircraft. Finally in the clear, the ferret flew westbound and spent a further ninety minutes logging eight Freya early-warning radars on the coast of southern France. The missions were mutually beneficial, the RAF gaining updated target defence data and the 16th RS acquiring new and unique signals or radar tactics.[92]

The crew of 1Lt William W. Redman with Radar Observers 2Lts M. Slavin III and J.E. Magnuson flew Ferret IV s/n 42-29881 on the night of 22–23 October 1943 on a mission to accompany RAF bombers to Ancona, Italy. The crew is seen here after recovery from the night mission, blinking in the morning sunlight at Foch Field, Tunisia. *Air Force Historical Research Agency via George Cully*

Besides RCM equipment, another limiter of squadron operations was trained personnel. Graduates of the RCM Observer course at Boca Raton were in short supply, so the 16th RS started to train enlisted men to fly as RCM Operators on ferret reconnaissance flights. The squadron established a training school with the graduates being worked into the flight schedule in October 1943. Training for the enlisted operators was a combination of classroom instruction, training flights against a simulated Würzburg radar built by the squadron and American

The 16th RS flew ten sorties in support of or accompanying RAF bombers, usually Vickers Wellington twin-engine aircraft. Here a Wellington is being refuelled at Foch Field after a mission with Ferret IV the night of 22–23 October 1943 against a railway bridge at Ancona. *Air Force Historical Research Agency via George Cully)*

SCR-270 and SCR-268 radars, and operational missions. With this extra manning for flights, the Boca Raton graduates were able to devote more time to equipment modification, jammer work, and detached service to aid in theatre-level RCM activities. Soon Lt Ihle was transferred to the Fifteenth Air Force as an RCM advisor and Lt Slavin to the Twelfth Air Force Service Command to oversee RCM supplies.[93]

Reconnaissance flights were flown from dusk till dawn, lasting up to twelve hours at altitudes from 200 to 500ft in the mission area. These long and gruelling missions were often flown in zero visibility and were taking a toll on men and machines – something needed to change to reduce the time spent flying from Tunisia to the target area. One alternative was forward-basing aircraft in Italy, a practice that started in late October with Ferret III flying two night missions over the Adriatic from Grottaglie airfield, Taranto, Italy, before returning to Foch Field. A week later Ferret V arrived at Grottaglie to fly two additional Adriatic missions, while at the end of November ferret B-17E '016 deployed to Brindisi for four Adriatic missions; overall, 30 per cent of the missions in October and 10 per cent in November utilised forward basing.[94] These missions highlighted the flight savings of such basing and set the stage for future 16th RS operations and eventual basing changes. Tasking for this time period, beyond the Adriatic missions, was split between the Italian west coast and the French Mediterranean coast.[95]

The 16th RS was not above trying new tactics to elicit a response from the German radar operators, who were starting to not pay attention to single aircraft trawling off the coast. On the night of 16 November the 16th RS launched three ferrets to parade up the west coast of Italy from Rome up to Nice, France, at fifteen-minute intervals; the tactic was tried again, with two ferrets flying off France from Nice to the Spanish border. The Germans, undoubtedly amused, did nothing out of the ordinary and the squadron decided it wasn't worth the effort to repeat. Another experiment was dubbed a 'J-Mission', which entailed two ferrets on a single mission, one at 500ft, the other at 1,000ft. Each ferret carried a RC-183 'Mandrel' jammer tuned to known operating frequencies of Freya radars, with the two jammers covering the known frequency range of the radar. The purpose of the 'J-Mission' was to see how the Germans worked around jamming of the Freya radar and what additional radars might be activated to work around the electronic interference. 'J-Missions' were flown on 27 December and 8 January 1944 but little additional intelligence was discovered that warranted the flying of two aircraft and the concept was dropped.[96]

Thirteen missions were flown during December 1943, a decrease from the twenty-one flown in November – a high water mark for squadron operations. The end of the year brought winter weather that, coupled with older equipment, had a negative effect on flight operations. On 6 December B-17E '016 flew into a hillside in northern Spain with a complete loss of the mission crew. Piloted by Lt Earl Clement (originally co-pilot of Ferret V) with Lt John Pheley (originally crewed on Ferret V) and Cpl Christian Becht as RCM Observers, the aircraft had been on a mission to investigate German radars in southern France from Toulon to the French–Spanish border. A cold front was forecast and the ferret was likely flying at low altitude in instrument conditions when it flew into rising terrain. The SCR-521 radar carried on board should have negated this from occurring, but the squadron write-up characterised this equipment as 'war weary' and needing replacement. Not only did the squadron lose a well-trained crew, it also lost the RCM equipment aboard '016. The unit history noted 'most of our good equipment was on 016' and after the loss, there was only enough gear to equip one ferret.[97] The arrival of spares mid-month still only included another ferret's worth of equipment. The hits kept coming, as the following month B-17F '379 was lost returning from Italy, likely crashing into the Mediterranean on 25 January after searching for evidence of German jamming of American radars at the Anzio beachhead. The 16th RS was back to only enough equipment to outfit one aircraft. Even worse, '379 had the primary instructor for the enlisted RCM Operator course on board along with three students, further straining the unit. Beyond '379's fateful mission, ten additional flights were flown in January 1944 including three missions flown from Brindisi against Adriatic targets and a co-operative mission with the RAF on a night bombing raid to Klagenfurt, Austria. To support this mission, flown on 21 January, B-17F '379 forward deployed to Foggia, Italy, returning to Foch on 23 January. The mission saw much in the way of radar activity, with twenty-one intercepts being logged. At Ljubljana, Yugoslavia, approximately 50 miles south of the target area, two Luftwaffe night fighter radars were noted searching for targets under the direction of a Würzburg-Riese GCI radar.

Weather coupled with loss of equipment ground flights to a halt. Four missions were flown in February as the unit struggled to get back into an operational tempo. The primarily dirt runway at Foch Field turned to mud, closing the airfield for operations for half of February. B-17 '437 somehow took off from Foch Field's atrocious runway and made it to Grottaglie to fly three missions against littoral Yugoslavia, but all were cut short due to weather. One benefit to the downtime was the ability to carry out deeper maintenance on the aircraft, with '437 and '055 flying to El Aouina Airport in Tunis for repair work.[98]

On 17 February replacement personnel, radar receivers, C-2100 direction-finding antennas and AN/ARN-1 radio altimeters arrived at Foch Field – it was a delayed Christmas for the squadron that had been enduring a tough winter. The next day the 16th RS was officially assigned to the Fifteenth Air Force. In March, the gifts kept on coming in – the squadron's 'scrounger' supply system located two slightly used aircraft, B-17F #412 and B-25D #463,

Luftwaffe fighters posed a minimal threat to the nocturnal missions of the 16th RS. Squadron Lts Redman, Lehman and Jenks pose with a Bf 109 in a scrapyard of destroyed German aircraft at El Aouina airfield outside of Tunis. The destroyed aircraft was likely assigned to II./JG 77. *Air Force Historical Research Agency via George Cully*

and two new SCR-717C radar sets still in their packing crates at a depot in Italy. The loot was quickly returned to Foch Field; the radars were installed in '358 and '055 and #412 was stripped of armament and converted to an 'admin ship' for future scrounging flights and other non-operational missions. The B-25D was modified for use as another liaison aircraft as well as for radar calibration. The additional aircraft helped the squadron supply mission as well, with flights throughout the region turning up 'excess' supplies such as tools and flying equipment located at Fifteenth Air Force Depot No. 5 in Bari, Italy.[99]

Scrounger flights notwithstanding, the weather in March was still having an impact on ferret flight activity. Only eight operational missions were flown that month, including three against southern Adriatic radars by '358 from Brindisi and Amendola. Aircraft '358 was testing out the new C-2100 direction-finding antenna on these missions and the results were impressive – the location derived from six direction-finding cuts against a Freya radar located north of Pola was shown by subsequent photo reconnaissance to be accurate within a mile. On 18 March, '437 flew a mission up the west coast of Italy starting at La Rocca Fort and continuing to Marseille before returning directly to Foch Field across the Mediterranean. Mandrel jammers were carried on the mission and tuned to the lower-frequency band of the Freya. The jamming of the known radar operating frequencies resulted in the Germans tuning their radar to 194 MHz, the first time Freyas were seen operating this high; other interesting signals including an air intercept radar operating at 485 MHz were also noted. A mission was flown the next day along the same route to follow up on the signals of interest. This mission did not reveal any high-frequency Freyas but an unusually large number of Seetakt coastal surveillance radars operated by the Kriegsmarine were active, likely assisting the Luftwaffe in tracking the troublesome ferret.

Capt. George W. Jordan, standing second from left, poses with his crew in front 16th RS ferret B-17F s/n 42-3358 *Thunder Head* at Foch Field in early 1944. *Air Force Historical Research Agency via George Cully*

Ferret B-17F s/n 42-3358 *Thunder Head* posed with a B-25D and what appears to be P-40F s/n 41-14559 at Foch Field, Tunisia. The B-25D is #463, the Mitchell 'acquired' by the 16th RS for use as a liaison aircraft as well as for radar calibration work. *Air Force Historical Research Agency via George Cully*

Overview of the 16th RS squadron area at Foch Field, Tunisia, with B-17F Ferret V in the background. The flight surgeon's tent is in the foreground, while the radar laboratory was housed in the white stone structure at right. *Air Force Historical Research Agency via George Cully*

S/Sgt Thriffley and T/Sgt Gray, Radar technicians with the 16th RS, pause from their task of electronics maintenance. Ferret B-17F s/n 42-30437 exhibits its unique camouflage picked up while undergoing modification in the UK. *Air Force Historical Research Agency via George Cully*

Radar and electronics personnel of the 16th RS pose in between maintenance work. Squadron personnel, at the end of the supply line, worked miracles in scrounging spare parts and creating modified equipment to enable continued improvement of the squadron mission.
Air Force Historical Research Agency via George Cully

Two ferret B-17Fs preparing for the 16th RS move from Tunisia to Italy. B-17F s/n 42-3358 *Thunder Head* appears to be the aircraft at right. By this time period, most of the squadron tasking was in the Adriatic and a survey of airfields in Italy revealed room at Foggia. *Air Force Historical Research Agency via George Cully*

Through flight tests, the 16th RS determined the best way to combat the *Freya* early-warning radars was with ground-based jammers. Starting the prior December, the unit surveyed Corsica for a location to emplace a system to fill the air waves with constant barrage jamming and spent the next few months tinkering with five British 'ground Mandrels'. By April 1944 the system was in place and turned over to the 1st Signals Service Platoon (SP) for operations. The 16th was also on the hunt for German radars to bring back to Tunisia for testing with their jamming equipment. After a few bad leads, the unit finally located a Würzburg radar at Taranto, Italy. The radar was delivered to Foch Field on 1 March and by mid-month it was operating again with a crew of 16th RS personnel. By 25 March six missions were flown against the radar to train its operators and establish a baseline performance for future tests. Once these flights were complete Lt James Magnuson and Dr Raymond, back in theatre to replace Mr Caufield as Technical Observer, planned and executed tests against the radar to determine optimum settings for 'Carpet' jammers and preferred methods to deploy 'chaff' as well as ran missions to train jammer operators from the bomb groups. The squadron also played host to visitors, including the commanding officer of 162 (SD) Squadron and US Navy personnel interested in conducting tests against surface vessels.[100]

Although Foch Field had become home, the war had long since passed by Algeria and something needed to be done to shorten the all-night missions. A survey of airfields in Italy revealed room at Foggia, and by mid-March the squadron started to pack their material. B-17 '437 flew the last mission from Foch Field, launching on 25 March for a survey of southern France and recovering at Foggia, with all subsequent missions flown from Italy. This change of venue saved four to five hours' transit time off each mission and was much appreciated by the aircrews.

The 16th RS took their job as RCM experts seriously and after a few bad leads finally located an intact Würzburg radar at Taranto, Italy. The radar was delivered to Foch Field on 1 March and by mid-month it was operating again with a crew of 16th RS personnel. By 25 March six missions were flown against the radar to train its operators and establish a baseline performance for future tests.
Air Force Historical Research Agency via George Cully

The 16th RS dragged their prize Würzburg radar with them to Italy and conducted a series of tests in April and June. Lt Blumenschein, facing the camera, ran the June tests and worked to prove the effectiveness of chaff against this version of the radar. *Air Force Historical Research Agency via George Cully*

The 16th RS used its aircraft to haul much of the unit's cargo, with a ground echelon moving by land and sea at the end of April. As a result of the move, only five missions were flown in April, two of which accompanied RAF night raids. The first, flown by B-17F '437 on the night of 4–5 April 1944, accompanied an RAF strike against Budapest. Aircraft '437 orbited near the target area for thirty minutes collecting German signals, including many night fighter air intercept radars. If the night fighter crews turned their attention on the B-17, the crew of '437, forewarned of German intentions by the SCR-587 receiver, would take evasive action until the signal was lost. The Luftwaffe fighters focused on the Wellingtons and the ferret's crew witnessed two of their number being shot down. Flak had been intense but inaccurate, but as the last of the RAF bombers retreated the German gunners turned their attention to '437. Captain Millen, piloting the B-17F, shoved the throttles past full throttle and into War Emergency Power position and got the Fortress up to 230mph indicated in level flight, quite a feat for the Boeing. After a few minutes, he throttled back and continued on the way to Foggia. As '437 passed Kapsovar on the Hungarian border it was once again engulfed in accurate flak and Millen responded by shoving the throttles back to War Emergency Power. After a short time the engines started to misfire and the ferret, throttled back to a low speed, limped across the Adriatic. The 'red-line' performance by Millen to leave the danger zones resulted in three engines requiring replacement post-mission. Two of the remaining April missions were flown by '358 from Pomigliano near Naples in search of a reported U-boat radar in the Tyrrhenian Sea, while the last was a routine flight by '437 from Foggia to survey the northern Adriatic. No U-boat radars were picked up on the maritime surveillance sorties.[101]

With their bags packed for Italy, the crew of one of the ferrets prepares to depart Foch Field for Foggia. This change of venue saved transit time for each mission and was much appreciated by the aircrews, though the initial crew quarters left little to be desired.

Ferret B-17F s/n 42-3358 running up its engines, ready to depart Tunisia for Italy. The ferret's Yagi antennas and navigation radar are clearly visible. Foggia was closer to operational areas where the ferrets flew, saving four to five hours of transit time on each mission.
Air Force Historical Research Agency via George Cully

Although Foggia offered easy access to the Adriatic, the German radars in north-west Italy and southern France still required surveying. In May B-17F '358 forward deployed to Borga, Corsica, to fly cooperative missions with the 1st Signals Service Platoon (SP), the operators of the ground-based radar jammers the squadron had installed earlier in the year. The 1st Signals Service Platoon also operated ground-based direction-finding equipment and '358 flew seven cooperative missions collecting signals to allow a comparison between the airborne and ground-based collect. Sorties were flown up the west coast of Italy and along the southern French coast. The remaining six missions flown in May were focused on the Adriatic and collecting signals along the Yugoslav coast line. Nothing terribly unique was found on any of the missions, the logged signals including Freya early warning and Seetakt coastal surveillance radars as well as Würzburg gun-laying and GCI radars. As new APR-1, APR-4 and APR-5 receivers arrived and were fitted to the ferret aircraft, the now redundant SCR-587s were repurposed as frequency monitors to help Fifteenth Air Force bomb groups tune their 'Carpet' jammers in flight against new radar signals. The Army rotation policy began to be felt as many of the squadron 'old guard' were transferred out en route to the US. Among those leaving the unit was Lt Magnuson, whose job as the captured Würzburg radar project officer was filled by Lt Carl Blumenschein. At the end of May the squadron was reassigned from Fifteenth Air Force to Army Air Forces, Mediterranean Theatre of Operations, aligning administrative and operational channels for the first time in the squadron's existence.[102]

June saw fifteen missions flown by the squadron: seven in the Adriatic, three along the southern French coast, four along the Italian west coast, and one with an RAF night raid. The raid, flown the night of 13–14 June by Ferret V '055 against Munich, provided a little excitement for the crew. The route to the target area passed close to Venice, where '055 first picked up flak. Just as the crew was passing over Linz, Austria, at 18,000ft the superchargers on engines three and four died and moments later flak from the city started firing on the aircraft. Pilot Capt. William Redman quickly wheeled '055 into a turn as the aircraft started losing altitude. Redman was able to maintain enough altitude to clear the 8,000ft Alps and return to Foggia, flak chasing the aircraft for most of the way. RCM Observers Lts Manbeck, Hovee and Hauck were still able to intercept twenty-three signals and make use of the newly installed APR-5 receiver to search for higher-frequency radars. After safely landing in Italy, the crew cycled through the Flight Surgeon's tent to receive their well-earned double shot of mission whiskey.[103]

By mid-1944 the 16th RS had become the Mediterranean theatre's centre of knowledge on German radars through mapping of locations, evaluating captured equipment and managing the Fifteenth Air Force RCM programme. This background knowledge contributed to three unique missions in June. That month, the 16th RS was called on to assist an RAF raid against the heavily defended port city of Trieste with the use of chaff. Chaff, not available in quantity in theatre until January 1944, was just starting to be fully integrated into operations in the Mediterranean. On the evening of 22 June, ferret '437 dropped chaff near known Würzburg locations in the southern Adriatic and monitored the effect it had on the German air defences. The next

Though far from palatial, the squadron had made Foch Field comfortable through their scrounging efforts and reconditioning local stone structures; Italy was a step backward. Although the squadron headquarters was housed in a Nissen hut seen at right in July 1944, the airmen were housed under canvas in a large tent city.
Air Force Historical Research Agency via George Cully

evening '437 and its crew were at it again, this time in the central Adriatic, but still there was no apparent reaction. Finally, on 26 June, the Germans flinched. For almost two hours, ferret '437 flew around the northern Adriatic dropping chaff corridors to give the impression of bomber streams attacking different targets in the region. During this time period, RAF Wellingtons were able to slip into Trieste and drop their bombs with minimal resistance from the Germans. Luftwaffe Ju 88 night fighters had been scrambled and vectored by their controllers across the Adriatic, chasing aluminium strips and unable to concentrate in the target area. The 16th continued to refine its knowledge on the impacts of chaff on the Würzburg radar. On 24 June Lt Blumenschein conducted a test involving six runs against the radar by eighteen B-17s from the 99th BG and another seventeen from the 463rd BG. The flights proved the effectiveness of chaff against this version of the Würzburg radar and helped refine tactics for bomb groups of the Fifteenth Air Force.[104]

The aircrew were not the only ones being kept busy with work – engineers and technicians of the 16th RS stayed occupied though the spring with many new projects. The logjam finally broke with the supply system and airborne jammers and receivers started to flow into theatre. Command of the strategic air war had switched over to the Fifteenth Air Force and direction came down to equip all bomb groups with jammers. The 16th RS set up an RCM Operators school in June, running a two-week course for 'Carpet' operators as well as training B-17 and B-24 radio operators in the use of APR-1 and APR-5 receivers to note details on radar signals. A B-25 of the 57th Bomb Wing (Medium) and a 320th Bomb Group B-26 were fitted with SCR-587 receivers and an operator, Sgt Clarence Payne, was sent to the 320th BG to train personnel how to operate the equipment. The new RCM gear finally allowed all three ferrets ('055, '437, '358) to be fitted with equipment at the same time.[105]

Lt McKeever, squadron Engineering Officer, stands at left with engineering personnel in front of one of the squadron ferrets at Foggia. *Air Force Historical Research Agency via George Cully*

A 16th RS family portrait, taken in July or August 1944 at Foggia, depicting the operational aircraft of the squadron. Numbered are 1. Ferret B-17F s/n 42-30437; 2. B-17F Ferret V; 3. Ferret B-17F s/n 42-3358; 4. Admin B-17F #412; 5. Radar calibration/admin B-25D #463. Unnumbered but visible between 1. and 2. is a P-38, likely the squadron's P-38G that was modified for ferret work but never used operationally. *Air Force Historical Research Agency via George Cully*

B-17F Ferret V undergoing maintenance at Foggia, Italy, circa September 1944. She now appears to be fitted with Yagi antennas on her fuselage spine similar to those used by Ferret B-17F s/n 42-3358. *Air Force Historical Research Agency via George Cully*

Be it the dust of Foch Field or the mud of Foggia, the 16th RS maintenance troops kept their aircraft ready to fly a relatively high operational tempo; in summer 1944 the individual ferret aircraft could fly up to ten times per month. Ten maintenance airmen pose in front of what appears to be B-17F Ferret V with B-25D admin bird #463 in the background.
Air Force Historical Research Agency via George Cully

The squadron 'laboratory' also converted radar calibration B-25D #463 into ferret configuration in July along with a P-38G the squadron had picked up along the way. The B-25 was equipped similarly to the B-17 ferrets while the P-38 carried a SCR-587, SCR-522 and an automatic recorder. Although flight tests were flown, no operational missions were scheduled and the equipment was uninstalled from both aircraft after a couple of months. The laboratory continued with SCR-587 installation in bombers and also installed APR-5 receivers in aircraft of the 99th and 2nd Bomb Groups to aid in the hunt for higher-frequency German radars. A second RCM Observer course graduated in mid-July, with radio operators trained in the use of APR-1 and oscilloscopes to be able to monitor Würzburg frequencies. Squadron testing of their captured Würzburg ended due to the failure of the radar's transmitter tube.[106]

The squadron flew thirteen missions in July – four in the southern Adriatic, three in the northern Adriatic and six in southern France. The French missions were flown from Borgo Rizza, Sicily; two by '437 and the remainder by '358. The northern Adriatic mission flown on the night of 24–25 July went over northern Italy as far west as Monte Venda, 10 miles west of Padua. Flown by Operations Officer Lt Norman Garland, ferret '358 drew intense flak fire with several shell fragments striking the aircraft and coming close to the crew.[107] As the summer wore on, the 16 RS – renamed from 16th RS (Bomb) to 16th RS (Heavy) Special on 9 July – prepared to support Operation DRAGOON, the Allied invasion of southern France. Seven missions were flown in August in the lead up to the 15 August assault, with ferret '358 forward deploying to Borgo Rizza in early August. The ferret flew two missions on the nights of 4–5 and 5–6 August to confirm the location of German radars, concentrating on the Seetakt surface search radars that would reveal the incoming invasion fleet. On 7 August a special mission was flown at the request of Troop Carrier Command. This organisation requested

After the move to Italy, the 16th RS laboratory continued providing RCM support to Fifteenth Air Force bombers. After the squadron was fully supplied with the new APR-5, the receivers were then fitted to aircraft of the 99th and 2nd Bomb Groups to aid in the hunt for higher-frequency German radars. 16th RS RCM Observer Lt Hovee, in charge of the APR-5 installation team, is seen examining equipment in a 99th BG bomber prior to mission take-off, *circa* June 1944. *Air Force Historical Research Agency via George Cully*

Once US RCM production hit its stride in spring 1944, for the first time in its existence the 16th RS had an excess of equipment. As new APR-1, APR-4 and APR-5 receivers arrived and were fitted to the ferret aircraft, the now redundant SCR-587s were repurposed as frequency monitors to help Fifteenth Air Force bomb groups tune their 'Carpet' jammers in flight. Two 16th RS airmen are seen next to 99th BG B-17G s/n 42-102855 during the installation of receiver equipment. *Air Force Historical Research Agency via George Cully*

23358

By mid-1944, the 16th RS ferret electronics had moved from improvisation to standard production. This view looking forward from the waist gun position in a B-17F ferret shows the SCR 717 operator's position at right and the racks of RCM equipment on the other side of the bulkhead in the radio operator's room. *Air Force Historical Research Agency via George Cully*

a strip of continuous radar scope photos from the French coast to the paratrooper drop zones. B-17F '437 was selected for the mission as its SCR-717B radar was the same type as the ones fitted to the Troop Carrier Command pathfinder aircraft. Squadron Radar Intelligence Officer Captain Lester Manbeck designed a mount for a K-24 camera that was able to record the scope of the SCR-717 radar. For the mission, pilot Major James McElhone, the squadron CO, kept the ferret at 300–400ft while over the water, pulling up to 2,000ft when nearing the coastline. Manbeck started the camera, having to manually trigger the shutter when the automatic control failed. As the aircraft crossed the coast, Würzburg radars came alive and started to track the aircraft. The ferret crew responded with a flurry of chaff, the dispensing rate confirmed by earlier squadron tests. The aircraft was unable to manoeuvre due to the scope photographic requirements, relying on the chaff to divert the Würzburg radars and stay alive for the fifteen-minute target run.[108]

Opposite top: Ferret B-17F s/n 42-3358 *Thunder Head* in flight *circa* September 1944. By the end of squadron operations at the end of September, *Thunder Head* had flown forty-five operational missions with the squadron. It was ferried back to US after the squadron shut down and was turned in to the depot at Hunter Field, Georgia, on 14 November 1944.
ir Force Historical Research Agency via George Cully

Bottom: Lt Dale E. Shaffer returns to Foggia in B-25D #463 after a ferret test flight. The squadron 'laboratory' converted the radar calibration B-25 into ferret configuration similar to the B-17 ferrets in July 1944. Although flight tests were flown, no operational missions were scheduled and the equipment was uninstalled after a couple of months. When the squadron deployed back to the US in November the aircraft was disposed of in theatre. *Air Force Historical Research Agency via George Cully*

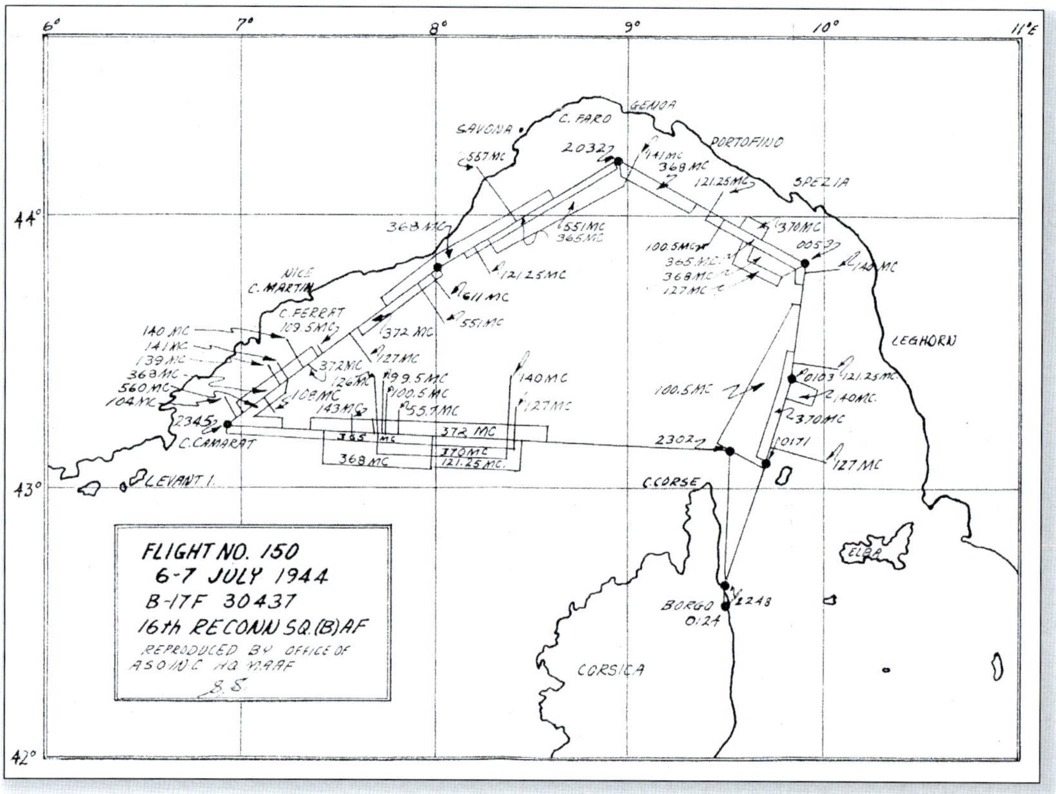

16th RS Investigative Flight 150 was flown the night of 6–7 July 1944. Ferrets '437 and '358 forward deployed to Borgo Rizzo, Sicily, to fly four missions over the Ligurian Sea. Signals received by the RCM Observer are annotated on the mission plot. *Air Force Historical Research Agency via George Cully*

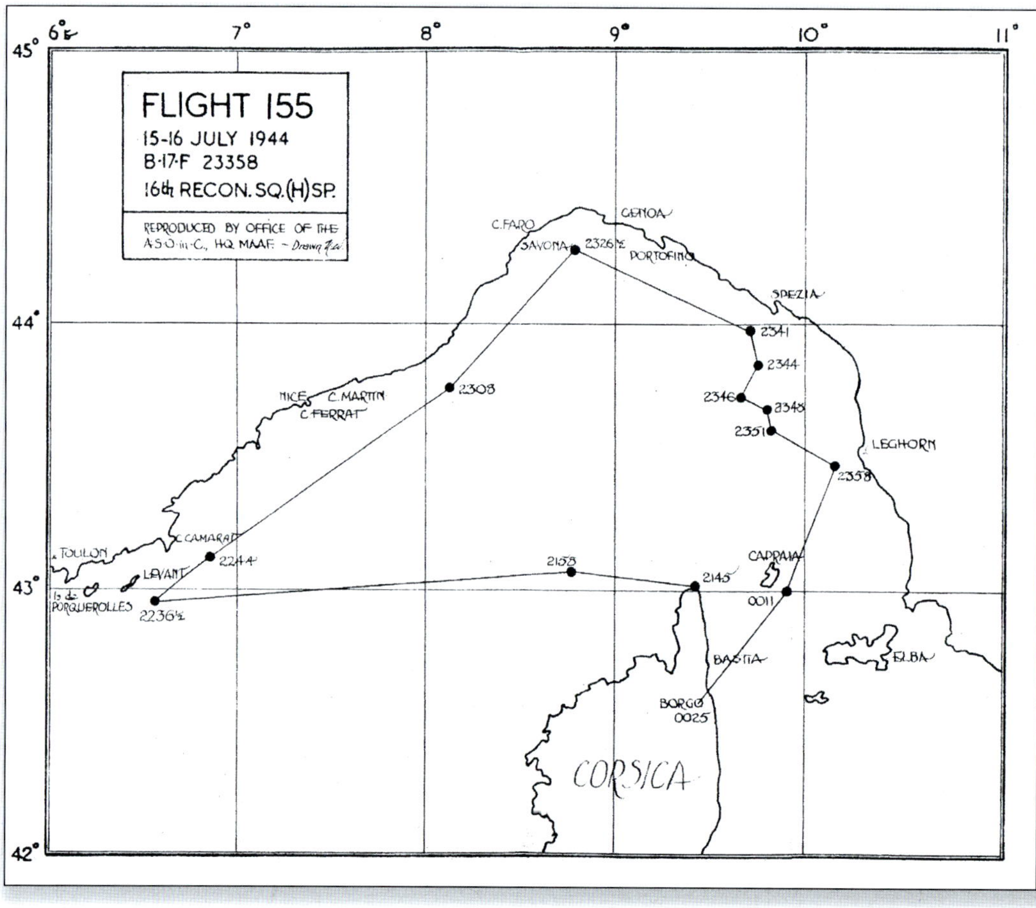

On the night of July 15-16 1944 16th RS ferret B-17F s/n 42-3358 flew a short night mission from the forward deployed airfield at Borga around the Ligurian Sea. Routine missions such as this flight kept track of German radar locations and also searched for new radar types. '358 was one of three B-17s that the squadron acquired in-theater and converted to ferret aircraft in October 1943. *Air force Historical Research Agency via George Cully*

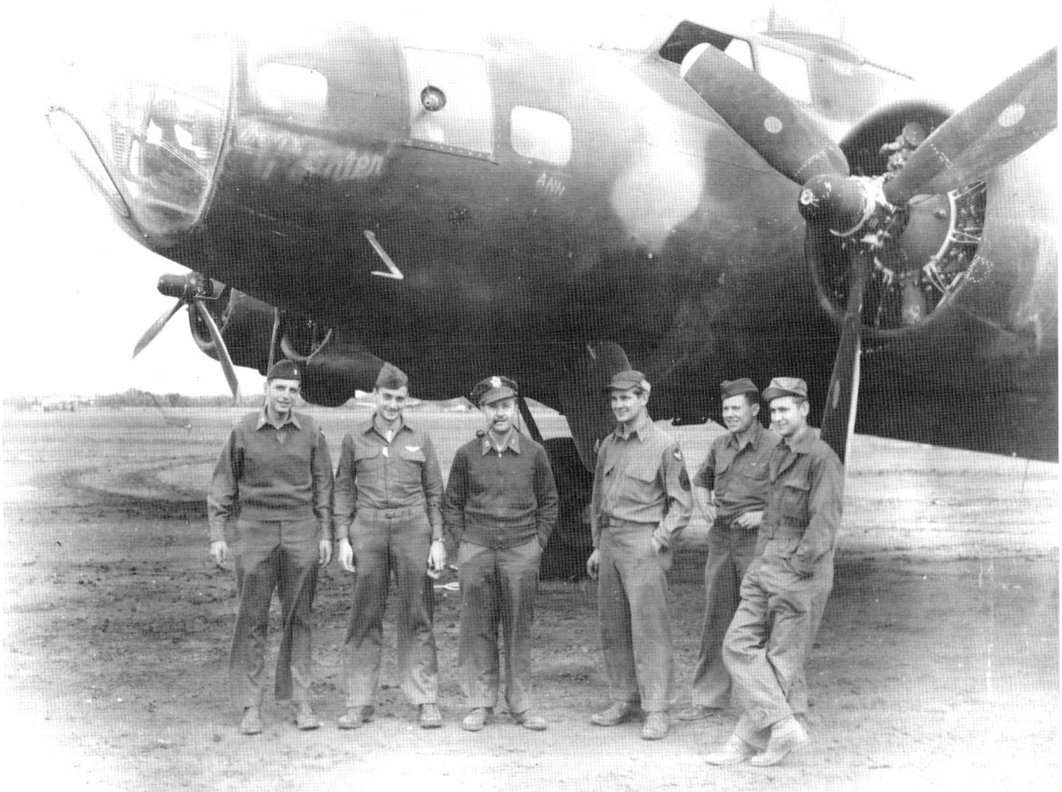

Lt Blumenschein, S/Sgt Grossman, Capt. Eaton, T/Sgt Kruta, T/Sgt Walker, and S/Sgt Webb pose in front of Ferret V *The Pointer* at Bari Airport en route to Bucharest, Romania, for exploitation of German radar technology. Eventually mechanical problems with Ferret V resulted in the substitution of B-17F '358 for the mission on 8 October. *Air Force Historical Research Agency via George Cully*

As 16th RS personnel started to hit fifty operational missions they were rotated back to the US. Even though the squadron was starting to close down, an adequate number of crews was needed for the remainder of flight operations. Four new bomber crews were assigned to the 16th RS from local bomb groups in August 1944. Lt Wright and his crew, recently assigned to the squadron, are posed near the nose of Ferret B-17F s/n 42-3358 *Thunder Head* with admin B-25D #463 in the background. *Air Force Historical Research Agency via George Cully*

Airmen and Romanian soldiers posed near the nose of *Thunder Head* after arrival at Popesti Airport outside Bucharest, Romania, on 8 October 1944. The photo was taken by Lt Hovee, one of the RCM Observers who came up with the plan to fly to Romania to get spare parts for the squadron's Würzburg radar as well as examine other German radars.
Air Force Historical Research Agency via George Cully

Prior to DRAGOON, the Mediterranean Allied Tactical Air Force under Maj. Gen. John Cannon committed a large number of sorties to knock out the German radars along the French southern coast. The 16th RS flew three missions on succeeding nights to evaluate the effectiveness of their work, all flown by ferret '437. Pilot Major James McElhone lifted off in '055 Ferret V at 2245 from Algerho, Sardinia, the night before the invasion tasked with observing the German electronic reaction to the Allied onslaught. Allied jamming commenced at 2300 and McElhone kept '055 at 4,000–5,000ft for the eight-hour mission. Ferret V flew a large triangular route in the Gulf of Lyon, steering clear of the invasion beaches. Nothing significant was noted about the German radar activity, although it appeared that a few German radars did start operating on the coast of Spain.[109]

After DRAGOON there was little left for the 16th RS to do. Allied advances in France and Italy and partisan activity in the Balkans negated much of the need for coastal missions and with five heavy bomb groups monitoring the Germans with APR-1 receivers the war was essentially over for the ferrets. The squadron flew three missions after the initial DRAGOON landings to surveil the target area. The remaining six missions flown in August were in the Adriatic. Nine missions were flown in September against northern Adriatic and north-west Italian targets – the last flown by the unit. Later that month, plans came down for the 16th RS to deploy to another theatre – either the Pacific or China. Due to an unavailability of equipment in theatre, the squadron would need to route back to the US to re-form and re-equip. There was one last mission to do, though.[110]

A conference with the Fifteenth Air Force on 17 September gave birth to a plan to fly to Ploesti, Romania – newly liberated after signing an armistice the week prior – to get spare parts for the squadron's Würzburg radar, which was broken and needed transmitter tubes among other things. The plan, hatched by Lts Blumenschein and Hovee, would have squadron RCM Observers and intelligence personnel also inspect other radars to look for any new variants as well as interview Romanian radar operators. The idea worked its way through staff channels and up to the AAF/MTO A-3 for approval.[111]

The original objective of the 16th RS trip was to scavenge spare parts for their Würzburg radar. This was not necessarily an easy task, as the Romanians had been belligerents in the not too distant past and were not excited to see the Americans. This Würzburg radar has its electronics cabinets open and is missing major components. The concrete revetment for the radar denotes its permanence as part of the protection of the Ploesti oil fields, with a searchlight position in the field in the background. *Air Force Historical Research Agency via George Cully*

After a false start with Ferret V '055, which had to turn back to Italy with engine issues, the Ploesti radar investigation mission finally departed Bari, Italy, in B-17F '358 on 8 October. Flown by Lt Norman Garland, RCM Observers Hovee and Blumenschein were joined by Lt Col Vanda from the OSS, Squadron Leader Jennings from the Air Ministry, and Capts Haley and Ihle from Fifteenth Air Force. Other than moderate flak south of Budapest the night flight was uneventful. Upon landing, the ferret was greeted by Romanian spectators and armed guards. The airfield, lately occupied by the Luftwaffe, was still packed with German aircraft including a Bf 110 night fighter that attracted the attention of the RCM Observers. Later in the morning the 16th RS personnel met with the American mission. The airmen were billeted in hotels in downtown Bucharest and that afternoon the 16th RS RCM Observers and their Fifteenth Air Force companions headed to Ploesti for the afternoon. Over the next five days, the four RCM Observers – Blumenschein, Haley, Hovee and Ihle – studied the radar defences of Ploesti, interrogated Romanian radar operators, and investigated the Bf 110 night fighter. At the end of their fact-finding expedition spare transmitting tubes and other parts for their Würzburg radar were loaded into '358's bomb bay and on 16 October the weary but happy 16th RS crew winged westwards to Italy.[112]

Looking like tourists, 16th RS airmen tour a Romanian GCI site outside of Bucharest. At centre is a Würzburg-Riese GCI radar with a Freya Egon surveillance radar off to the left. Spread over five days, the Romanian trip let the four RCM Observers – Blumenschein, Haley, Hovee and Ihle – study the radar defences of Ploesti, interrogate Romanian radar operators, and investigate a Bf 110 night fighter. *Air Force Historical Research Agency via George Cully*

Above: Posing for a 'hero' shot in front of a Würzburg-Riese GCI radar, one of the 16th RS 'tourist' airmen pauses from exploring a GCI site. Top on the list of activities was to inspect radars to look for any new variants that they had not previously encountered. *Air Force Historical Research Agency via George Cully*

Right: The Freya Egon radar was fielded mid-war by the Germans and technically was a 'secondary' radar, tracking FuG 25 IFF responses from German fighter aircraft. Like many of the radars seen during the Romanian trip, this one appears to have been vandalised or cannibalised for parts. *Air Force Historical Research Agency via George Cully*

The squadron ground echelon departed Italy aboard the SS *Santa Paula* on 3 November. The air echelon included admin ship #412 and ferrets '437 and '358; '055, an original ferret, was considered too tired for the trip across the Atlantic and was unceremoniously disposed of in theatre along with the squadron B-25D. The air echelon returned via the south Atlantic ferry route and up to Florida. After arriving at Palm Beach, Florida, on 14 November the aircrew proceeded to the air depot at Hunter Field, Georgia, and turned in the aircraft. After generous amounts of leave, the squadron re-formed at Buckley Field, Colorado, but was deactivated in April 1945. The Pacific War already had existing reconnaissance units and needed ferret crews, so the combat-experienced RCM Observers, officer and enlisted, were transferred to March Field to set up a school to train new ferret crews en route to the Pacific. Fitting of their hard duty the prior year, 16th RS personnel spent the last days of the war in Riverside, California.[113]

Serial Number	Aircraft	First Mission	Last Mission	Total # Ops Missions	Notes	Fate
42-29644	B-17F-50-DL	17 May 43	30 Oct 43	At least 19	Original CONUS production – Ferret III; 'The Archangel'	Returned to US
42-29881	B-17F-75-BO	Unk – Aug 43	22 Oct 43	At least 14	Original CONUS production – Ferret IV	Returned to US
42-3055	B-17F-20-DL	Unk – Aug 43	26 Aug 44	At least 22; only used once between 4 Dec 43 and 12 Aug 44	Original CONUS production – Ferret V; 'The Pointer'; mottled camouflage	Disposed of in theatre
42-3358	B-17F-65-BO	1 Nov 43	26 Sep 44	45; all but two flown Mar–Sep 44	Ex-jammer? Field modification; 'Thunder Head'	Turned in to depot, Hunter Field, GA, 14 Nov 1944
42-30379	B-17F-100-BO	2 Nov 43	25 Jan 44	17	Ex-jammer? Field modification	Lost on mission, 25 Jan 1944
41-9016	B-17E	24 Oct 43	6 Dec 43	15	Ex-jammer? Field modification	Lost on mission, 6 Dec 1943
42-30437	B-17F-105-BO	13 Nov 43	19 Aug 44	46	Ex-97 BG; Field modification; British equipment; black paint scheme?	Turned in to depot, Hunter Field, GA, 14 Nov 1944
#412	B-17F	N/A	N/A	None	Squadron admin hack	Turned in to depot, Hunter Field, GA, 14 Nov 1944
#463	B-25D	N/A	N/A	None	Originally used for radar calibration; modified to ferret configuration but no operational missions flown	Disposed of in theatre
	P-38G	N/A	/A	None	Modified to ferret configuration but no operational missions flown	Disposed of in theatre

Chapter 5

Within a few months of establishment, Section 22 defined a requirement for dedicated USAAF ferret aircraft to support their activities. This was a rush job, with SWPA desiring the receipt of the aircraft little more than a month after the USAAF's Material Command was notified. With no time to build a prototype, the Air Staff recommended Material Command use original ferret B-24D '23941 as a starting point for installing the necessary RCM equipment.[114]

Material Command was established on 9 March 1942 when the pre-war Air Corps Material Division was expanded to command status. Material Command oversaw research and development activities as well as procurement of aircraft and other items for the USAAF. Led by Brigadier General O.P. Echols, Material Command was based at Wright Field, where the command conducted the majority of its work. Initial ferret design work was done by the Engineering Division, an organisation that enabled the service to modify existing aircraft for new purposes or to fit theatre-specific requirements. The Production Division, also at Wright Field, coordinated with aircraft manufacturers for the actual production of wartime aircraft.[115]

Plans for Project 96288R – the production of two ferrets for SWPA – were quickly drawn up by the Engineering Division and sent to the 1st Proving Ground Electronics Unit of the Air Service Command at Eglin Field, Florida. Two new production Consolidated B-24D aircraft left the Tucson Modification Centre after having post-production work performed on them and arrived at Eglin in late September for their transformation into ferrets. A plywood compartment was built in the aft section of the bomb bay to house two RCM Observers, with seats on the right side and equipment racks on the left. SCR 587 and RC 160 search receivers were installed along with a C-2100 direction-finding antenna and an SCR-521 navigation radar – SWPA would have preferred an SCR-717 but this was all that was available at the time.[116] Personnel from Wright Field and the Radio Research Laboratory assisted in the modifications.[117]

RCM compartment of an early ferret, possibly Ferret VII while still at Eglin Field. Visible equipment includes Hallicrafters S-27 and SX-28 receivers, a rudimentary pulse analysis capability formed through the use of a 1930s Dumont 'oscillograph' and an HP audio oscillator. Above the operator's head is a magnetic compass repeater indicator on the left, driven by the flux gate compass in the wing of the aircraft. To its right is a slave indicator that provided directional information from the AN/APA-24 rotatable Yagi antenna that was mounted outside the fuselage. *Michael Hanz*

While Material Command was building two new ferret aircraft for SWPA, Section 22 looked at what it could do in theatre. In late July 1943 it asked Headquarters Army Air Forces staff for any information they could provide on design and performance data on radar search receiver antennas for B-24 aircraft.[118] As the organisation grew, Section 22 asked the War Department for additional RCM-trained personnel to perform non-ferret work, likely planning and tactics development.[119] Section

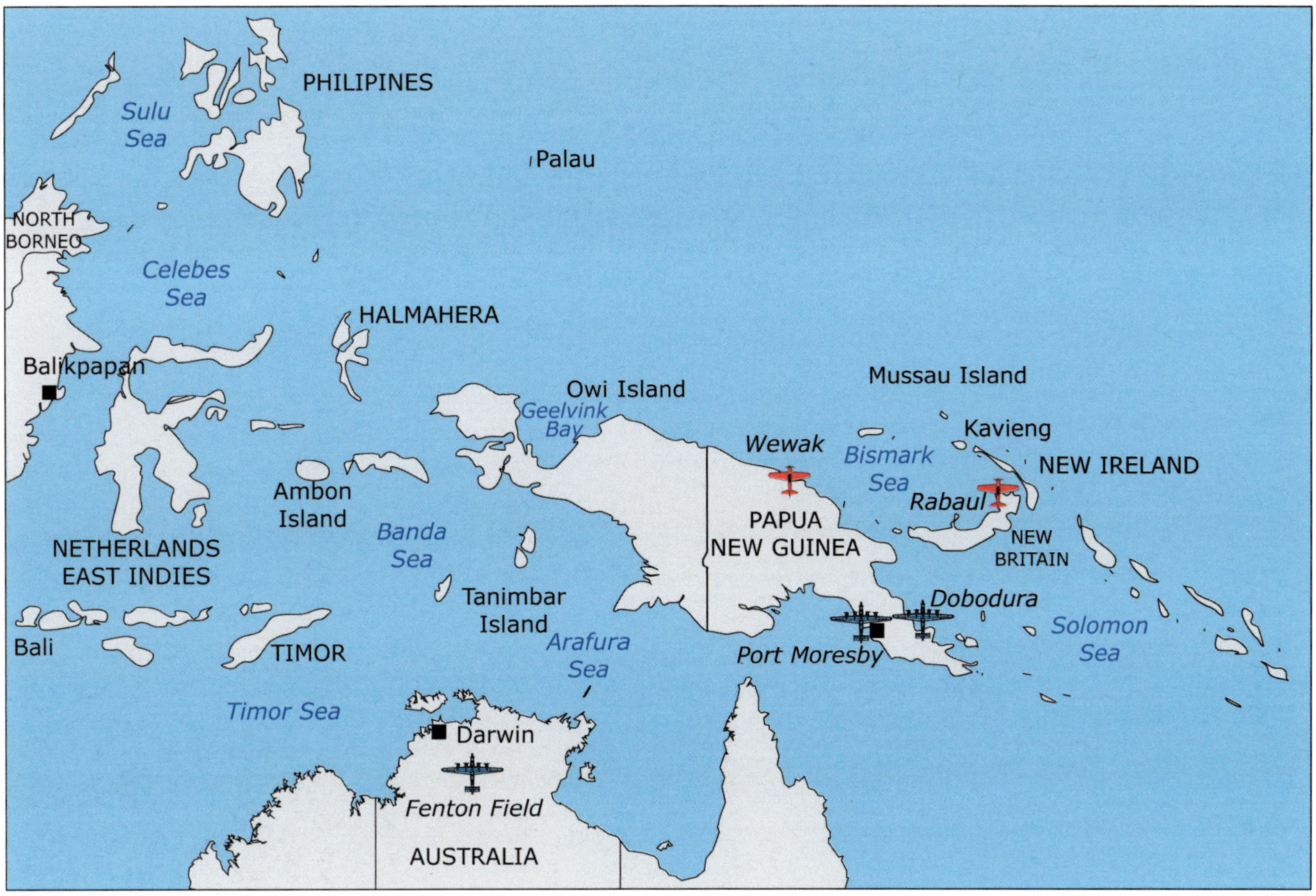

22 endeavoured to stay abreast with developments in electronics that were occurring on an increasingly faster pace, requesting the shipment of prototype RCM equipment to Australia so the theatre would be ready to fully utilise the new receivers when they came into production.[120] Section 22 was also building its inventory of operational equipment as well. Likely driven by the memory of having to borrow equipment from the US Navy for outfitting 'ad hoc' ferrets in 1943, Section 22 requested a long list of equipment from War Department ranging from AN/APR-4 and Hallicrafter S-36 receivers to test equipment.[121]

In January 1944 the two modified B-24Ds, now identified as Ferrets VII and VIII, arrived in theatre. The Ferret number VI was skipped for unknown reasons, with Ferret XI #1 being redesignated as such at a later date. Flight personnel for ferret aircraft were not available in theatre, so four RCM Observers and four enlisted RCM mechanics joined the ferrets in the US and were assigned to V Bomber Command.[122] In addition, a Radio Research Laboratory Technical Observer, Clark Cahill, accompanied the ferrets to the theatre at the request of SWPA to observe and report on the performance of the aircraft.[123] Although administratively assigned to the 63rd Bomb Squadron, 43rd Bomb Group (H) for maintenance, the mission tasking of the ferrets was controlled by Field Unit 1 of Section 22.

The 63rd BS was not new to the RCM business. 'Ad hoc' ferret flights had been flown in squadron B-17s starting in March 1943 with RAAF RCM operators, lasting until at least June. Starting in May 1943, the 43rd BG converted from B-17s to B-24s, the 63rd BS being the last squadron to do so. On 20 October, new crews arrived at the squadron with B-24s and the old crews departed with their B-17s. The squadron then moved to Dobodura, New Guinea, on 25 October 1943. Dobodura Airfield was actually a complex of airfields located in Australian Papua in western New Guinea built by US Army Air Forces between December 1942 and early 1943. Based on 63rd BS records, it is estimated that the ferrets arrived with the unit in early February 1944 and departed before the end of March, with the first combat mission flown by 10 February.[124] The first twenty-one operational ferret missions in SWPA were flown from Dobodura around New Britain, New Ireland, and the north coast of New Guinea. In March the ferrets were ranging far north, with one mission flown by Ferret VII on 10 March crossing New Ireland to investigate radars at Kavieng harbour and further west at Mussau Island. This nine-hour daylight mission was flown alone, steering clear of Rabaul but still at risk of interception from Japanese fighters. The next day Ferret VIII ranged up the north coast of New Guinea to Wewak. USAAF attacks against Wewak on 17–

18 August 1943, had reduced IJAAF Fourth Air Army strength at the airfield from about 200 aircraft down to thirty and had gained air superiority for Allied forces along the north central coast of New Guinea. Ferret VIII detected the Tachi 6 still at the airfield, even though most of the fighter force had departed the prior month. That evening, the night of 11–12 March, Ferret VII flew up to Wewak but spent the entire mission scanning from 75 MHz to 1000 MHz with no success. On 13 March, Ferret VIII again ventured alone into enemy territory with a daylight survey of St George's Channel; Kavieng, New Ireland; and Wewak, New Guinea. A large number of signals were recorded and many plotted, including multiple IJN Type 3 Mark 1 Model 3 and Type 2 Mark I Model 2 radars and a lone signal at 96 MHz that may have been either an IJA Tachi 6 or a ship. On 16 March Ferret VII was sent off to confirm a signal at 70.3 MHz near Wewak. The signal was intermittent and turned off because of an Allied air raid. A frustrating ten hours were spent by RCM Observers Lts Armour and Meehan tooling along the north coast of New Guinea to capture minimal signal activity. The same day four RCM Observers squeezed into Ferret VIII for a mission on the other side of the Bismarck Sea to surveil the southern coast of New Ireland. There was significant radar activity and additional radars were plotted and confirmed along the St George Channel and in the Rabaul area.[125] Five additional missions were flown before the ferrets departed Dobodura.

These missions, combined with earlier efforts, greatly contributed to the understanding of the eleven Type 2 Mark I Model 1 and Type 2 Mark I Model 2 radars protecting Rabaul and aided Fifth Air Force and US Navy air strikes on the base. Once the ferrets were able to precisely locate the sites they were targeted for attack. Destruction of Japanese radar sets started in April or May of 1944, with half the sites out of action by August.[126] In late March the Ferrets moved from Dobodura, New Guinea, to Fenton Field, Australia, and were temporarily assigned to the 530th Bomb Squadron of the 380th Bomb Group (H). On the same date, Ferret VII was flown to Brisbane for modification. The upgrade to the ferrets – Ferret VIII would follow Ferret VII once it had returned to flight operations – was something that had been planned for a while. Section 22 had noted that the direction-finding antennas on the aircraft required improvement and apparently wanted to upgrade the SCR-521 navigation radar as soon as a replacement SCR-717B was available.[127]

The assignment of the ferrets to the 380th BG made sense, as the unit had been operating 'ad hoc' ferrets since June 1943. Although controlled by two different Section 22 Field Units, the co-location of these assets from a supply and maintenance standpoint had many benefits. While on its own Ferret VIII flew eight missions at approximately three-day intervals, covering the Timor Sea and Banda Sea and encompassing the islands of Sumba,

Although the mission tasking of the ferrets was controlled by Field Unit 1 of Section 22, the aircraft were administratively assigned to the 63rd Bomb Squadron, 43rd Bomb Group (H), for maintenance and housing. The 43rd BG Headquarters at Buna at this time period was housed in this wooden structure with a thatched roof. *National Museum of the USAF*

Timor and Ceram and western New Guinea. The first two flights involved flying circuits around the Tanimbar, Kai and Aroe Islands, but no radar activity was picked up. The next mission, up to Geelvink Bay in western New Guinea, plotted out a Type 2 Mark I Model 1 radar at Utarom in western New Guinea. Additional activity was also found on the next five missions flown by Ferret VIII, with the last two missions flown against Timor Island on 25 and 28 April. Evaluated data from the eight flights revealed four Type 2 Mark I Model 1 radars on Timor, Ambon Island and western New Guinea and one probable Tachi 6 radar sites on Timor.[128]

The ferret modification was carried out in Brisbane, Australia, by a group in Section 22 responsible for development work and adaption of existing equipment. The equipment location within the RCM observer compartment was altered to ease operation, with the SCR-587, AN/APA-6 pulse analyser and HP audio oscillator moved in front of the operator's position. A second operator's chair and a small heater were added to the RCM compartment. The navigation radar was also upgraded from the SCR-521 to the SCR-717B and the navigator's station was rearranged for optimum employment with the navigator moved to the rear of the flight deck. Enlisted radar mechanics were recruited and trained to become radar operators for the ferret flight crews, the radar operator's position being moved to the nose of the ferret where the navigator used to be located. Section 22 would continue to modify SWPA ferrets through the end of the war, tweaking antennas and equipment to optimise performance and passing results back to the US for incorporation into future ferret development.[129]

Above left: Part of the Ferret VII/VIII upgrade in Brisbane, Australia, in April–July 1944 saw the navigation radar upgraded from the SCR-521 to the SCR-717B and the navigator's station rearranged for optimum employment and moved to the rear of the flight deck. The hooded instrument above the window of the relocated navigation position is the indicator for SCR-717-B. *Air Force Historical Research Agency via George Cully*

Above right: The Brisbane upgrade of Ferrets VII and VIII altered the equipment location within the RCM Observer compartment for ease of operation, with the SCR-587, AN/APA-6 pulse analyser and HP audio oscillator moved in front of the operator's position. A second operator's chair and a small heater were also added to the RCM compartment. *Air Force Historical Research Agency via George Cully*

Right: Ferrets VII and VIII had their navigation radars upgraded when rotated through Archerfield, near Brisbane, Australia, in April–July 1944. The ferrets were delivered with the SCR-521, all that was available at the time. SWPA preferred the SCR-717 and acquired the units to enable the ferrets to be upgraded when they went to Australia for rework. Shown are the mounts for the antenna, the transmitter and the modulator units of the SCR-717B installation in Ferret VII. *US National Archives*

The new navigator's position post-Brisbane upgrade in Ferrets VII/VIII pulled the navigator out of the nose and closer to the pilot to allow precise plotting and interaction between the pilot and navigator. Repeater instruments (altitude, airspeed, heading) helped the navigator plot the aircraft location in real time, a necessity for the ferret mission. *US National Archives via Peter Dunn*

B-24D s/n 42-64045, Ferret VIII, named *Atom Smasher*, arrived in theatre in January 1944. *Atom Smasher* had different nose art on each side of the forward fuselage; depicted is the art on the right side. *Author*

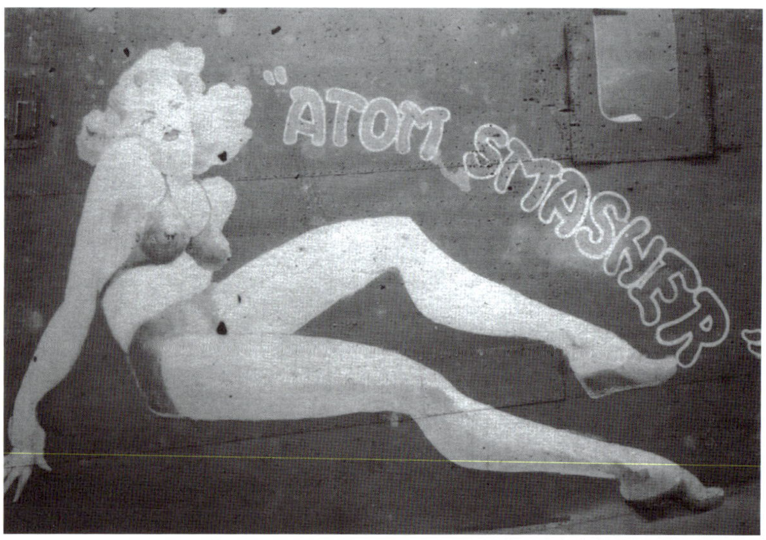

On 1 May, Ferret VIII was sent to Brisbane for modification work, replaced by Ferret VII in the operational search role. Ferret VIII did not return to operations until early August. Ferret VII flew twenty-eight missions between 19 May and 16 August. Little documentation exists on specific missions, although one mission was flown to Balikpapan via Makassar Strait. On 6 August, Ferret VII departed Fenton Field and surveilled the Tanimbar, Aroe, and Kai Groups before recovering on Owi Island. At least two missions were flown from Owi Island against the Palau Group on the nights of 7–8 and 9–10 August; possibly two or three additional missions were flown in this vicinity, likely in preparation for the planned landing by US Marines on Peleliu in the Palau Group on 15 September 1944. Ferret VII only flew two missions between 7 and 31 August, while Ferret VIII, back from refitting, flew five. Again, details are lacking on specific mission locations.[130]

By the end of August the Fenton Field-based ferrets had mapped the Banda Sea and Borneo region and were ready to join the fight for the Philippines. The Allied liberation of Owi Island enabled the ferrets to move northward and rejoin the 63rd Bomb Squadron in early September, arriving in time to survey Morotai and the Palaus again before the allied landings.[131] With their assignment to the 43rd Bomb Group (H), the ferrets would be linked to Fifth Air Force operations for the rest of the war, leaving the Netherlands East Indies without a dedicated USAAF ferret platform. Thankfully the Navy patrol community was able to cover some of this gap.

In late 1943 the replacement for the USN Cast Mike #1 team, teams of officer aircrews dedicated to the radar search missions, started to arrive in the South Pacific. A VP-104 Consolidated PB4Y-1 was modified for the ferret mission and flew about twenty missions in February 1944 against radars at Truk, the Caroline Islands, and New Britain. The missions proved successful and VPB 116, a PB4Y-1 squadron flying out of Eniwetok, was tasked with performing electronic reconnaissance of the region with three aircraft fitted out with receivers.[132] The Navy saw success in this endeavour and expanded the deployment of RCM equipment. By August 1944 thirteen of the eighteen land-based patrol squadrons had aircraft fitted out with AN/APR-1 receivers, AN/APA-6 pulse analysers, direction-finding (DF) antennas, and AN/APT-1 jammers. Most USN land-based patrol aircraft RCM tasking was controlled by Field Units 3 and 11 of Section 22.[133] In April 1944 two PBY Catalinas were fitted out as dedicated ferret aircraft with AN/ARC-1 radar receivers at Palm Island near Townsville in Australia and assigned to the operational control of Section 22. Operations began in May 1944 with missions based out of Port Moresby searching for Japanese radars in New Guinea, Halmahera, and the Philippines.[134] Like B-24 Ferrets VII and VIII, they were administratively attached to various units for support, including VP-33, VP-34 and VP-71. Times were changing and soon the USN aircraft would be joined by a group of 'ad hoc' ferrets from the Thirteenth Air Force

Maj. Jarek and his crew pose beside Ferret VIII *Atom Smasher*, around April–August 1944. Maj. Jarek and his crew primarily flew Ferret VIII while the aircraft was assigned to the 380th BG at Fenton Field, Australia. *Robert Livingstone*

B-24D s/n 42-64045, Ferret VIII *Atom Smasher* shortly after arrival in theatre is pictured at Dobodura, New Guinea, in February 1944. The Hawaii Air Depot modified a number of early B-24Ds by fitting the Consair A-6 tail turret to new framework in the nose. Both Ferret VII and Ferret VIII were so modified when passing through Hawaii en route to SWPA. *Robert Livingstone*

B-24D-20-CF s/n 42-63991, Ferret VII *The Duchess of Paducah* followed Ferret VIII through assignments in SWPA. Lt Bailey and his crew flew Ferret VII on a number of missions during the aircraft's time at Fenton Field, Australia, in mid-1944.
Robert Livingstone

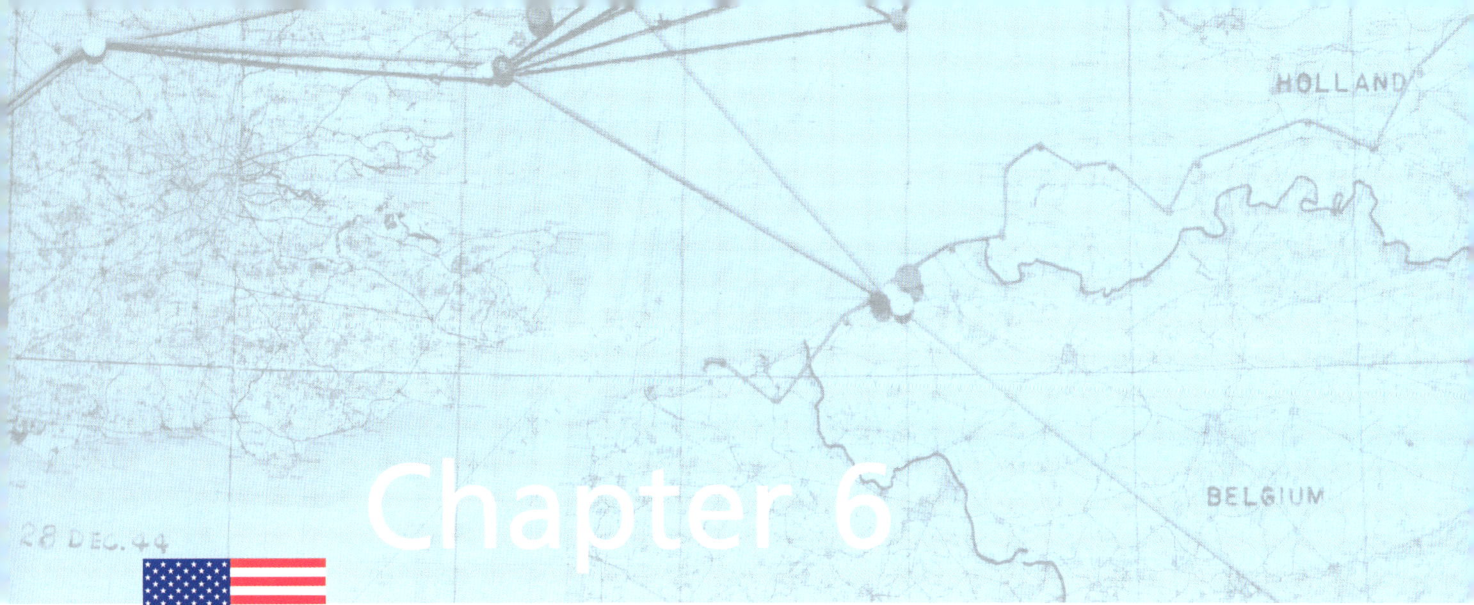

Chapter 6

At the Argentia Conference in August 1941 the US and the UK agreed to cooperate in an aerial campaign to wear down Germany in preparation for a cross-Channel invasion of occupied Europe. The US proposed a daylight strategic bombing campaign against Germany in accordance with their inter-war doctrine. The focus of this aerial effort on the US side was the Eighth Air Force. Eighth Air Force was established as the VIII Bomber Command on 19 January 1942 and activated at Langley Field, Virginia, on 1 February. An advanced echelon of VIII Bomber Command was established at RAF Bomber Command Headquarters at RAF Daws Hill (near High Wycombe, Buckinghamshire) on 23 February in preparation for the arrival of subordinate units in the United Kingdom.

The 15th Bomb Squadron was the first USAAF bomber unit sent to the UK. Flying personnel arrived without aircraft on 13 May 1942. On 4 July 1942, six of its crews accompanied six British crews of the RAF's 226 Squadron on a low-level attack against enemy airfields in Holland. The first combat group of VIII Bomber Command to arrive in the United Kingdom was the ground echelon of the 97th Bombardment Group, which arrived at RAF Polebrook on 9 June 1942. VIII Bomber Command started the USAAF's strategic bombing campaign against Germany on 17 August 1942 with a small raid against occupied France. The invasion of North Africa and Italy over the next year was a resource draw and it was not until the summer of 1943, and the initiation of the Combined Bomber Offensive, that the Eighth Air Force started to have an impact on the German war effort. As USAAF bombers started to fly deeper and deeper into Germany, the Luftwaffe recognised the growing threat for what it was and rapidly committed more resources. On 17 August 1943 VIII Bomber Command launched a two-pronged raid against ball bearing plants at Schweinfurt and the Bf 109 factory at Regensburg. High casualties for this raid forced the USAAF to back off its cherished concept of self-defending bombers and accelerate efforts in fielding an escort fighter. This only addressed one aspect of the German defences – fighters. Anti-aircraft artillery and the overall coordination of Luftwaffe air defences would need to be addressed through electronic means.

The RAF had confronted similar challenges and responded with the creation of 100 (Special Duties) Group, established on 23 November 1943 to employ RCM equipment to 'deceive or jam enemy radio navigation aids, enemy radar systems, and certain wireless signals'. The first operational squadron joined the group on 3 December and by the end of the war the group had twenty-four squadrons. Pioneers in the art of electronic attack, 100 (SD) Group jammed radars, radio communications, and navigation aids as well as flying SIGINT search missions to support these activities.[135] The RAF squadrons within 100 (SD) Group operated a myriad of platforms to perform these missions, with many of the 'special duty' jamming squadrons flying former bomber aircraft. The first squadron to operate 'heavy' four-engine bombers, 214 Squadron, joined 100 (SD) Group on 17 January 1944 and was slated to re-equip from Short Stirlings to Boeing B-17s. In an effort to rapidly convert the unit, Eighth Air Force 'loaned' fourteen B-17F aircraft already in the UK, which were flown to British bases and fitted out with electronics for their new mission.[136]

Birth of the 803 BS

Personnel from a myriad of VIII Bomber Command units were placed on detached service and sent to RAF Sculthorpe to train 214 Squadron in operating and maintaining the Flying Fortress. Personnel started arriving on 17 January 1944 and training continued for the next two months. Once the British crews were checked off on the B-17 in mid-March the original mission of the Americans was expanded to encompass a detachment flying RCM missions with 214 Squadron in support of Bomber Command raids.[137] Using the airmen who were training 214 Squadron as a nucleus, six crews and aircraft from 96th Bomb Group (BG) were ordered from their home at Station 138, RAF Snetterton Heath, to

Be it radar jamming operations in support of the RAF Bomber Command or VHF screening operations in support of the Eighth Air Force, the intended victim of the 36th BS was the Luftwaffe command and control structure within the German integrated air defence system. This photo was taken at the end of hostilities in Europe and shows the filter plotting boards and controller positions in the operations room of the 'Gyges' headquarters for Luftwaffe operations in Denmark located at Grove airfield. *US National Archives*

Sculthorpe on 21 March 1944. The six crews all had twenty-five missions under their belt and had been part of the 96th BG radar countermeasures programme. The new RCM unit would report directly to the Eighth Air Force with tactical control going through RAF 100 Group. The unit would fly operations with 214 Squadron, assisting Bomber Command operations and providing the USAAF with insight into British RCM operations. The unit's charter was to investigate and analyse 'enemy radio and radar activity of particular interest' to the USAAF and make recommendations on equipment and tactics.

The idea of a USAAF RCM unit dated back to at least December 1943. A study on a countermeasures programme for the Strategic Air Force in the European Theatre produced by the Eglin Field-based 1st Proving Ground Electronics Unit on 7 December 1943 recommended a layered approach to confronting German radar and radio communications. Among the proposals was the activation of an RCM squadron of twelve heavy bombardment aircraft that would carry jammers as well as 'radio and radar reconnaissance equipment' in each aircraft. Reconnaissance would be carried out by individual aircraft outside enemy territory as well as escorted formations inside enemy territory or accompanying bomber formations.[138] Designated the 803rd (Provisional) Bomb Squadron (Heavy) on 28 March 1944, the organisation would eventually have a strength of twelve aircraft, with the original six from the 96th BG providing a solid start. Five of these aircraft, all B-17Fs, were already equipped with Carpet and Mandrel jammers while the sixth, a B-17G, had jammers as well as search equipment in the form of SCR-587 and Hallicrafters S-27 VHF receivers for monitoring Luftwaffe early-warning radars and radio traffic. Once at Sculthorpe the aircraft had additional equipment installed and were modified for night flying. Soon the six 96th BG crews and three additional crews composed of training personnel and new arrivals were training for night flying and navigation, foreign to VIII Bomber Command but critical for nocturnal Bomber Command operations.[139]

The squadron transferred to RAF Oulton with 214 Squadron on 16 May and was directed to undertake experimental work in support of Operation OVERLORD. In the first two weeks of May seven additional B-17Fs were added to the squadron. There was a rush to train personnel on RCM equipment and have aircraft ready for supporting the invasion. On the evening of 5 June Captain Robert Stutzman, squadron operations officer, led three other B-17s on the unit's first operational mission. Between 2235 and 0450 local time the B-17s were orbiting off the Normandy beachhead, jamming the German early-warning radars and screening the approaching Allied invasion force. After the invasion, it was finally decided to have the squadron focus on supporting RAF operations. The original crews from the 96th BG rotated back to the US and were replaced by crews who had not completed an operational tour. Extensive training continued within the squadron for night flying and navigation as well as preparing more aircraft for upcoming operations.[140]

Into Operations

The second operational mission flown by 803rd BS was on the night of 16–17 June 1944. Six B-17s joined sixteen Stirling B.III aircraft of 199 (SD) Squadron to form a jamming screen over the North Sea in support of a Bomber Command attack on Sterkrade, Germany. Four similar missions followed by the end of the month, flown in a semicircle over the North Sea at 15,000–19,000ft and in concert with ten to fourteen 199 (SD) Sqn Stirlings.[141] The APT-3 Mandrel noise jammer carried by the B-17s was used to blind German early-warning radars such as FuMG 80 Freya, FuMo 51 Mammut and FuMG 402 Wassermann. These radars were positioned along the coast of occupied Europe, passing radar tracking for consolidation at a Jagd Division to enable tracking of Bomber Command operations and orchestration of defences. Operations continued in July but at a higher pace with fourteen missions flown, averaging five B-17s. Critical to the success of the jamming operations was updated intelligence on German radars – both locations, operating frequencies, and any new radar types. For this, the 803rd BS relied not only on 100 Group SIGINT collection but also their own ferrets.

The sole B-17G transferred from the 96th BG in March, B-17G-10-DL s/n 42-37743, had its search equipment removed on 15 June and transferred to B-17F-75-DL s/n 42-3518. The 803rd BS commenced four- to six-hour ELINT missions on 6 July with this B-17F, flying five in July and four in August to include one flown on 1 August with two aircraft – it is uncertain what the identity of the second aircraft was.[142] Little detail exists on the actual target of these missions or their locations, though it can be presumed it was off the North Sea coast of occupied Europe. Tasking for these search missions came from the Anglo-American Laboratory of Division 15, Office of Scientific Research and Development (ABL-15), a joint US–British organisation established in fall 1943 at Telecommunications Research Establishment, Malvern, to work with the Eighth Air Force to develop engineering solutions for RCM activities.[143]

In May, the Eighth Air Force had started to field the 'Carpet-Blinker' system composed of one to three tunable Carpet jammers and the Blinker search receiver optimised against the Würzburg gun-laying radar. The Carpet-Blinker system allowed USAAF bomber crews to monitor Würzburg signals and tune their Carpet jammers accordingly, a tactical improvement as the majority of Carpet jammers flew with pre-set frequencies. An 803rd BS B-24 was fitted with the Carpet-Blinker system and in July the unit started running training classes with flights on this aircraft for personnel from the 2nd Bombardment Division. This 'training' B-24 was one of many that started to arrive as the 803rd BS transitioned from the B-17 to the B-24.

On 14 August the 803rd (Prov) BS (H) merged with the 856th BS (H) to become the 36th BS (H) (RCM) and moved to Station 113, Cheddington. Sixteen missions were flown in August, each consisting of four to six B-24s flying Mandrel

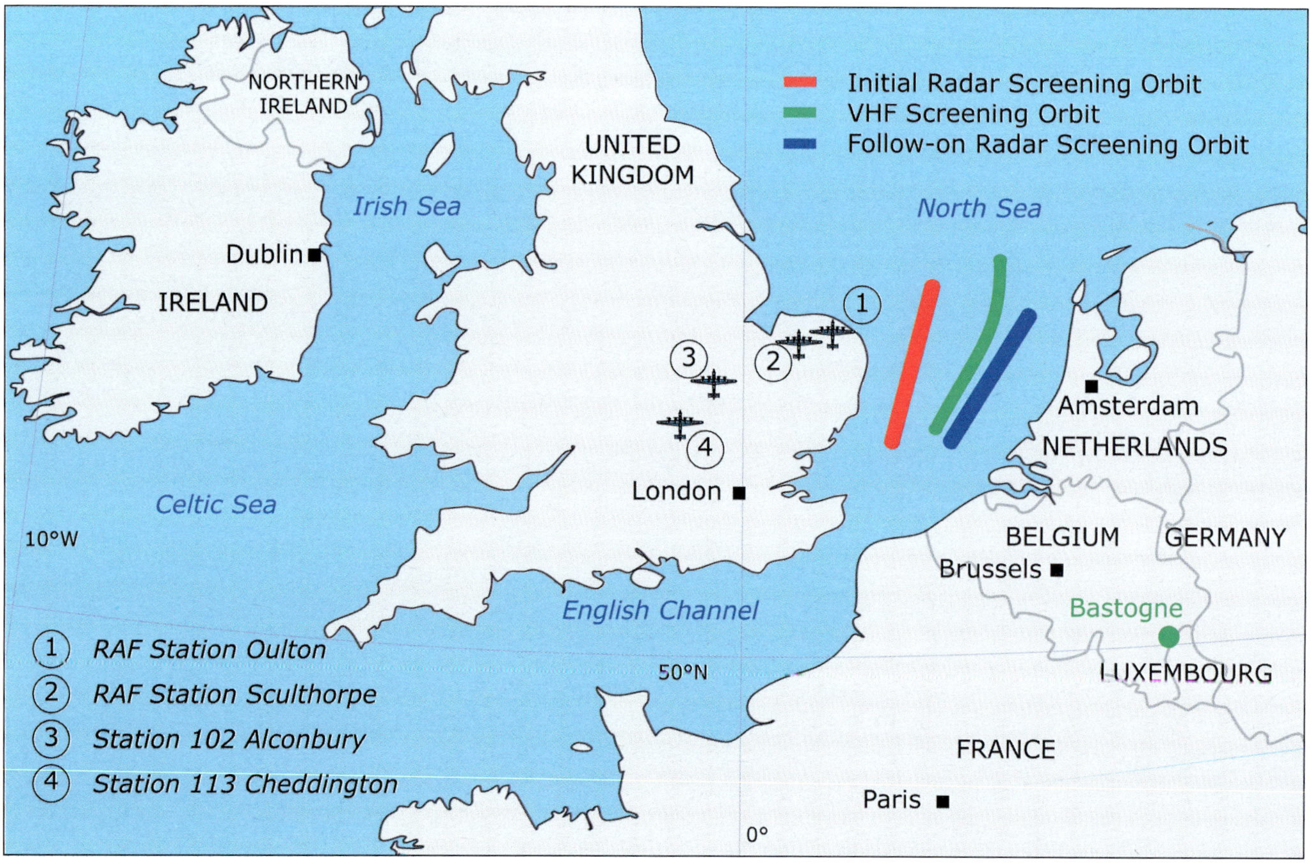

Ramp Rooster, B-24J-1-FO s/n 42-50671, was initially equipped with a SX-28 receiver on 17 August 1944 and Mandrel jammers a week later. The aircraft maintained its jammer and receiver combination through early 1945. *Stephen Hutton*

B-24J-40-CF 'R4-J' s/n 42-50476 was a 'standard' jamming aircraft assigned to the 36th BS in December 1944, while *Ramp Rooster* s/n 42-50671, 'R4-F' carried search receivers as well as jamming gear. The three antennas under the outer port wing of R4-J are associated with the jamming equipment. *Stephen Hutton*

screening operations. Operations increased in September with the 36th BS supporting eighteen missions of six to seven aircraft each. Starting on 22 June, B-24H and J models arrived at the squadron to replace the existing B-17Fs. Five Liberators arrived in June, followed by five in July and two in August. Starting on 1 July, RCM equipment was removed from B-17s and installed in the newly arrived B-24s. The search equipment was removed from B-17F-75-DL s/n 42-3518 on 26 August 1944, the aircraft leaving the squadron a week later. An interim ferret appears to have existed with B-24J-1-FO s/n 42-50671, which had a SX-28 receiver installed on 17 August, with Mandrel jammers added on 28 August.[144]

Construction started on a new 'ferret' search aircraft in September, with B-24J-5-DT s/n 42-51308 undergoing a conversion with an enclosure in the entire rear section of bomb bay for installation of search equipment along with oxygen and heated suit fittings for two operators and additional oxygen bottles. The aircraft was probably fitted out with SCR-587 and S-27 VHF SIGINT receivers, the AN/APR-1 search receiver for radar and radio signals, and equipment to measure pulse repetition frequency. Carpet Blinker training equipment was installed in the cockpit aft of the pilot and in November additional VHF sets were installed for spoofing missions. Many of the B-24s in the squadron that carried jammers had a similar 'room' constructed in the aft bay for their jamming equipment. No search missions were flown in September, but they resumed in October.[145]

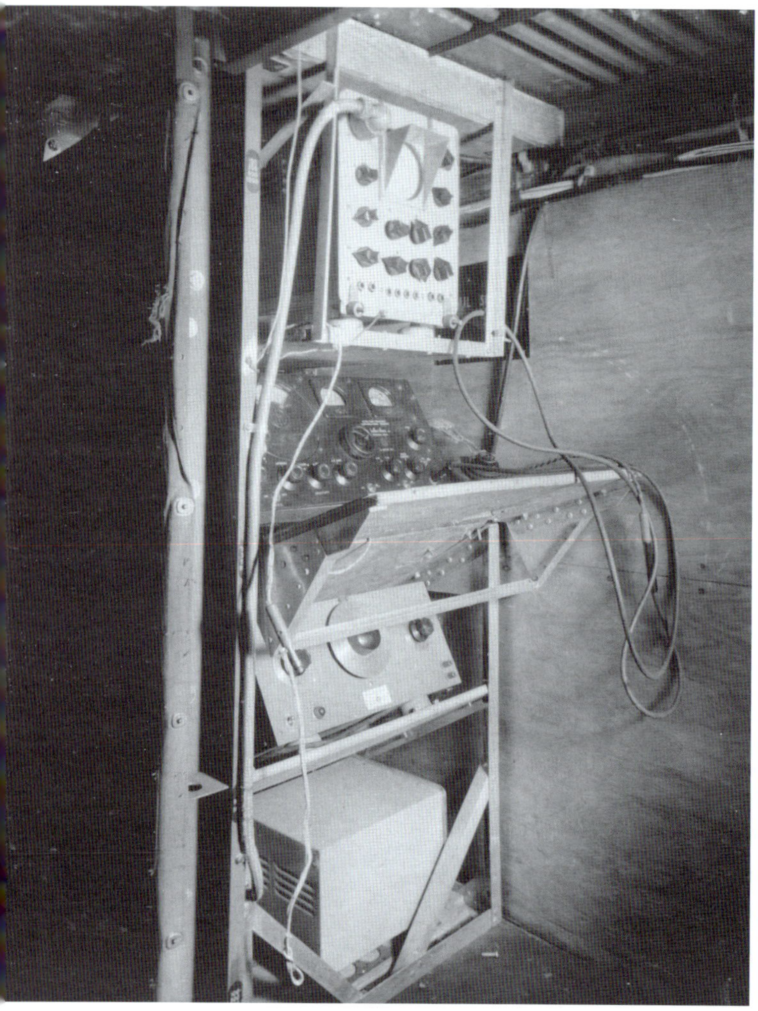

A rack of search equipment mounted in the rear bomb bay compartment of an unknown 36th BS B-24. At the top is British Type 32 Monitor for determining PRF and pulse analysis. Below that is a Hallicrafter S-27 receiver, while under the S-27 is a Hewlett-Packard audio oscillator for accurate PRF determination. At the bottom is a power supply for the Type 32 Monitor. *Air Force Historical Research Agency via George Cully*

What appears to be an RCM Operator's search position in the rear bomb bay compartment of an unknown 36th BS B-24. Rack-mounted receivers are seen here, with a SCR-587 (with Tuning Unit TU-58-A) at the top and AN/APR-1 below. The 36th BS ferrets carried SCR-587 and S-27 VHF SIGINT receivers to enable the tuning of jammers, AN/APR-1 search receivers for radar and radio signals, and equipment such as the H-P audio oscillator to measure pulse repetition frequency. *Air Force Historical Research Agency via George Cully*

B-24J-1-FO s/n 42-50622 received ferret equipment from B-24J s/n 42-51308 in December 1944 and had the racks installed into an enclosure in the entire rear section of bomb bay built for two RCM Observers and their equipment. The aircraft sports an enlarged nose compartment usually associated with Carpetbagger B-24s assigned to the 801st BG (P)/492nd BG. *Stephen Hutton*

B-24J-5-DT s/n 42-51308 *Modest Maid* had an enclosure built in September 1944 in the entire rear section of bomb bay for installation of search equipment and space for two operators. Search equipment possibly came from B-17F s/n 42-3518. Search equipment was uninstalled and transferred to B-24J-1-FO s/n 42-50622 in December 1944. *Stephen Hutton*

The 36th BS flew thirteen search sorties in October 1944, five flown as missions with two aircraft. Again, it is unknown what configuration the second aircraft was as the squadron only had one permanently configured search aircraft at this time. There are no records for search missions flown in November, with the next search mission not being logged until the last week in December. During the early part of December, ferret B-24J '51308 had all receiver equipment pulled and jammers put in its place. The receiver equipment was then installed in B-24J-1-FO s/n 42-50622, which also had the 'complete room' modification for the rear bomb bay.[146] The search mission flown by '50622 at the end of December was not ELINT but in support of communications jamming. The AN/ART-3 Jackal was a high-power VHF barrage jammer built to target German Army tank radios. The original request for this capability dated back to just after Operation OVERLORD in June but the jammers were not used.[147] In the wake of the German Ardennes counteroffensive in December 1944, the 36th BS was called upon to fly Jackal missions in the region of Bastogne, Belgium. The first mission was flown on 28 December and involved three Jackal-equipped B-24s orbiting west of Bastogne at 15,000–20,000ft with ferret '50622 orbiting 10–20nm away with its S-27 search receiver manned by a German linguist. A similar mission was flown on 31 December, this time east of Bastogne and with two jammer aircraft and ferret '50622. Three additional Jackal missions were flown between 2 and 7 January 1945 with similar compositions of jammer and search aircraft, with fighter cover being provided to the orbiting B-24s for protection from marauding Luftwaffe fighters. These five Jackal missions were all that were flown by the squadron for the duration of the war, although the 36th BS remained ready to execute additional missions.[148]

The lack of interest in ELINT missions for the 36th BS ferret may be attributed to other assets being capable of performing this mission. During this time period, one bomb group each in the 1st Bombardment Division (457th Bomb Group) and the 3rd Bombardment Division (94th Bomb Group) fielded twenty-two aircraft fitted with 'Group A' for AN/APR-4 search receivers, enough to enable a search aircraft to fly on every group mission. In addition, two aircraft assigned to the 94th Bomb Group were fitted with the AN/APA-17 airborne direction finder to allow direction finding of signals.[149]

Lt Col Robert F. Hambaugh, Squadron Commander of the 36th BS, stands beside his aircraft, B-24J-2-FO s/n 42-50622. The aircraft has gained nose art, possibly added at the end of the war as the aircraft was being prepared to return to the US. The aircraft name is a reference to Hambaugh's hometown of Birmingham, Alabama. *Air Force Historical Research Agency via George Cully*

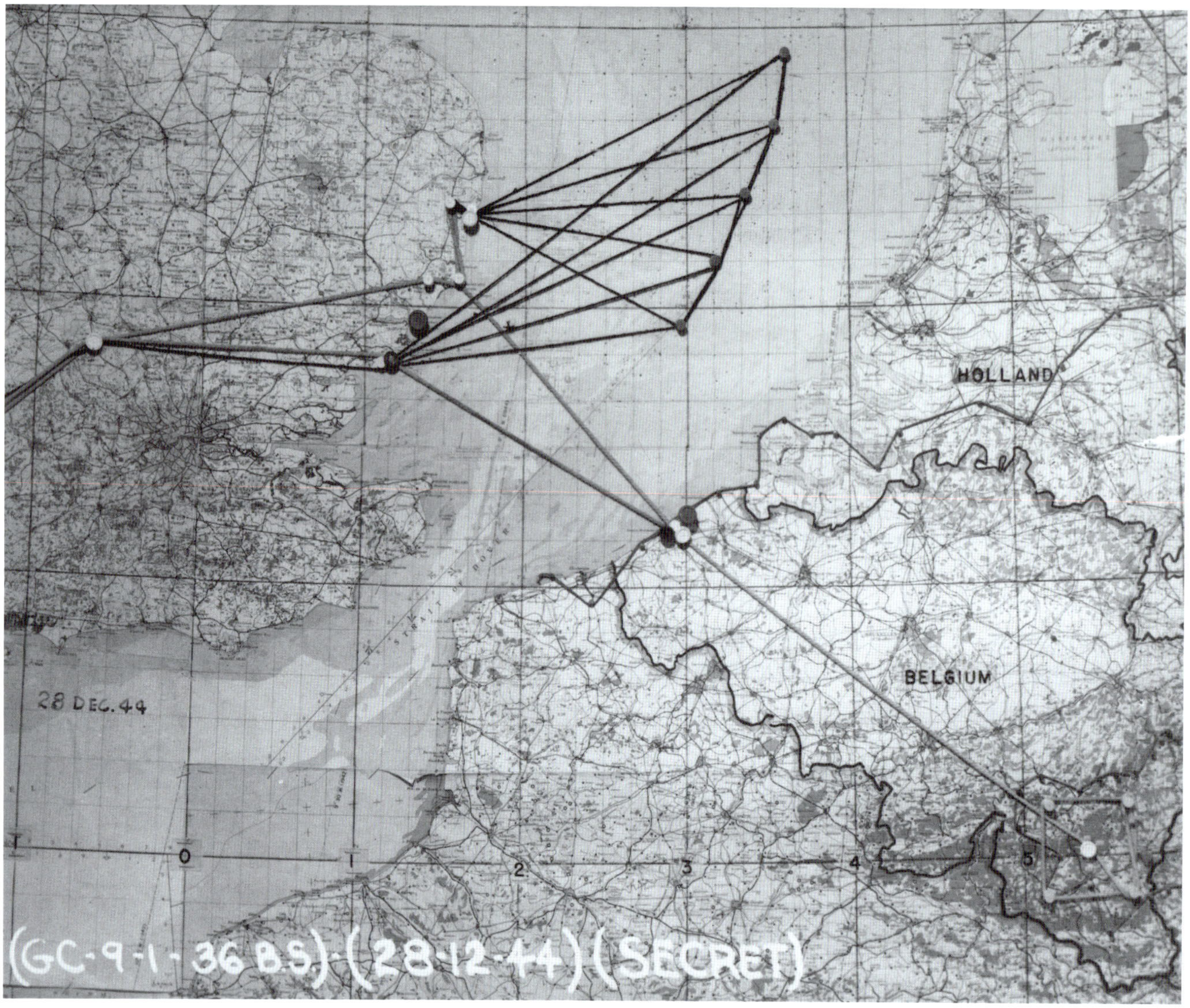

28 December 1944 was a busy one for the 36th BS. Missions are depicted in a string on a map; the northern routes depict nine B-24s performing VHF screening off the coast of Holland for 2nd Bomb Division efforts. The route to the Ardennes battle area in southern Belgium used for Jackal operations is also shown, supported with three jamming B-24s and one B-24 performing search operations. *Air Force Historical Research Agency via George Cully*

This increased search capacity for analysts at United States Strategic Air Forces (USSTAF) headquarters probably helped lessen the demand for 36th BS search missions. The VIII Bomber Command was not only monitoring radar activity, select bombers were also listening in on German communications.

Like other aspects of SIGINT in the European theatre, the Eighth Air Force looked to the Royal Air Force for the lead in monitoring German voice communications. While the RAF had been doing ground-based voice intercept since the early part of the Second World War, the British use of airborne linguists did not begin until the summer of 1942 in the Mediterranean. In the UK, a 192 Squadron Handley Page Halifax was fitted with two S-27 receivers and on 19 June 1943 two RAF German language linguists flew a forty-minute test flight followed by an operational mission over the North Sea the next day. This flight proved the viability of the concept and a follow-on test was ordered to listen in on the Luftwaffe reaction during an VIII Bomber Command daylight bombing mission. On 25 June a 192 Squadron Halifax accompanied B-17s of the 306th Bomb Group on a mission to Hamburg, Germany. As the attacking force approached the German shoreline, the Halifax established an orbit about 75 miles north of the coast and listened in on the Luftwaffe fighters as they attacked the B-17s.[150]

Eager to obtain similar intelligence, the Americans followed the British lead and began programmes of their own. The Air Ministry and VIII Bomber Command met to devise a plan based on voice recorders vice flying linguists. Beginning in the fall of 1943, VIII Bomber Command planned for a series of operational tests to prove the feasibility of their idea. Delays in equipment resulted in a series of tests flown at the end of the year using borrowed British equipment. On 20 February 1944 a COMINT-configured B-17 flew an operational mission over Germany to test unmanned recorder-only versus manned voice intercept; the manned option provided better results. On 15 March 1944 Major General Doolittle, commander of the Eighth Air Force, ordered his three bombardment divisions to implement airborne voice intercept operations. Within three weeks of the order, Doolittle's bombardment divisions began flying with linguists on board their B-17s and B-24s. After the initial training build-up and implementation, the Eighth Air Force used as many as twelve linguists per mission spread across its three bombardment divisions.[151]

A New Year and New Tasking

Support to the RAF took a back seat in the month of December, with missions flown with 100 (SD) Group ending in early January 1945. This reduction reflected not only the growing size of 100 (SD) Group, which was increasingly able to handle all of Bomber Command's needs, but also the growth in demands being placed on the 36th BS. The 36th BS was being directed to screen the VHF radio communications of VIII Bomber Command aircraft forming up over the UK. Twenty-two VHF screening missions supporting the Eighth Air Force were flown in January with four to eight jamming platforms, while twenty-four were flown the following month with six to eight B-24s.[152] In January 1945 the 36th BS also graduated its last RCM training class for 210 men of the 1st Air Division and shut down its Carpet-Blinker training section. Enough experience had been built within Eighth Air Force's air divisions for this activity to continue at the group level. All told, the squadron had trained about 600 men since August 1944 while operating under the direct supervision of the RCM Section, Headquarters Eighth Air Force.[153]

In February 1945, the Eighth Air Force directed the 1st Air Division to organise the 36th BS to be able to carry out four distinct functions: 1) Prevent German interception of VHF radio traffic during assembly; 2) Jam early-warning radars to screen assembly; 3) Jam enemy tank communications; 4) Investigate German radar frequencies. According to the Eighth Air Force, the squadron would require nineteen B-24s and three Lockheed P-38 Lightnings to accomplish these mission areas. Eighteen B-24s would be configured as jamming aircraft, fourteen equipped with ten Dina jammers and four carrying twelve SCR-522 'Orvils' jammers. The squadron already had twenty B-24s on hand, so it was only a matter of procuring an adequate number of 'Group B' jammers – still a problem in early 1945. For the investigation function, the Eighth Air Force recommended a dedicated ferret B-24 and three P-38s. Although the 36th BS had built its own ferrets in the past, the 1st Strategic Air Depot at Station 375, Honington, was fitting out a B-24 specifically for the ferret mission. The P-38s were already built and serving with 100 (SD) Group and had an interesting background.[154]

In August 1944 the Eighth Air Force provided four P-38s to 100 (SD) Group to aid in searching for signals associated with the V-2 ballistic missile. The aircraft were P-38Js with the pathfinder 'Droop Snoot' modification, but with SIGINT receivers operated by an RCM Observer in the nose replacing bombing equipment. The Lightnings were assigned to 192 Squadron at RAF Foulsham and flew daytime missions with USAAF crews on detached service from the 7th Photographic Reconnaissance Group. One P-38 was lost on 26 October 1944 and the remaining three were transferred to the 36th BS in mid-March 1945.[155] The renewed interest in SIGINT at this late stage in the war was based on intelligence's latest assessment of the Luftwaffe. Although the war was almost over, new threats were seen as on the horizon: more effective AAA controlled by centimetre-wavelength radar; proximity fuses for AAA; and a day fighter force composed principally of jet fighters with 'extensive and detailed control by radio and radar'.[156]

As the 36th BS prepared to institute its new direction, at the end of February it moved to Station 102, Alconbury, and was placed under the 482nd Bombardment Group (P) for local administrative support.[157] In March 1945, the 36th BS flew twenty-seven VHF screening missions and ten radar screening missions. Similar to earlier missions flown with 100 (SD) Group, the radar screening missions were directed by the Eighth Air Force and may have been based not only on proven 100 (SD) Group success, but also intelligence coming from British analysts at Bletchley Park, who noted Germans complaining that the VHF screening operation was also jamming some of their German early-warning radars. The objective of these missions was to screen the assembly operations from prying German eyes using seven to nine Dina jammer-equipped B-24s. The radar screening missions were first flown 20 miles off the coast of East Anglia, paralleling the UK coast, but later moved to 50 miles from the Dutch coast.[158] The target of the Dina jammers were the remnants of the Luftwaffe early warning system still active in the western Netherlands. Although Allied ground forces had advanced up the coast of France and Belgium, the Netherlands was still occupied by German forces and was in contact with the remainder of the German air defences through existing cable networks or the use of powerful, long-range HF radios. One way to confirm what was operational was through the use of ferret aircraft.

In early March the 36th BS took delivery of its new ferret, B-24J-60-CF s/n 44-10507, from the 1st SAD. The aircraft was rapidly worked into the flight schedule and flew its first search mission on 7 March. Thirteen additional search missions would be flown during the month, both monitoring the effectiveness of the VHF screen and looking for German early-warning radars, while flying an orbit between the VHF screen and occupied Europe. The aircraft's direction-finding antenna enabled the crew to plot and forward to USSTAF staff for analysis active German radars, while the aircraft's

Lt Holt, one of three RCM Observers associated with the 36th BS P-38 effort, poses beside a P-38J converted to ferret configuration. One of three transferred to the squadron from the 100 (SD) Group in mid-March 1945, the aircraft only flew nine operational sorties before the end of the war. The 'droop snoot' Perspex appears to have been removed and the flat panel bomb-aiming panel has an antenna mounted in its place. *Air Force Historical Research Agency via George Cully*

receivers enabled RCM Observers to note German radar parameters. Based on data received from the ferret, the squadron adjusted its Dina jammers to better cover the German radars still operating.[159] With the new ferret '10507 performing well, existing ferret '50622 had all its search equipment removed in April and was likely placed in storage with the unit as new B-24J and B-24M aircraft arrived at the squadron.

The ferret's data, when combined with information received from 94th and 459th Bomb Group AN/APR-4-equipped bombers, gave USSTAF analysts a good idea of what the Germans were doing towards the end of the war.[160] Another system also fed into this pool of knowledge – the P-38 ferrets assigned to the 36th BS. The three P-38s arrived at Alconbury in mid-March with their first search mission flown on 17 March with a single P-38. Four more solo missions and one with two aircraft were flown in March. The P-38s, their pilots, and maintenance personnel were on detached service from the 7th PRG, as they were with 192 Squadron. Three RCM Observers were assigned the rather uncomfortable role of flying in the aircraft's nose and operating the receiver, made more exciting by the fact that P-38s were reserved for missions 'within enemy territory'. Capt. Howard Kasch, a liaison officer for the Director of Intelligence, HQ USSTAF, coordinated the tasking of the SIGINT Lightnings. Original guidance called out three specific tasks for the aircraft: 1) searching for new radars in the 30–70 MHz range as well as monitoring the existing Freya radar range of 70–220 MHz; 2) general search of the 600–15,000 MHz spectrum; 3) search for navigation buoys with transmitters for use by He 111 aircraft launching V-1s over the North Sea.[161] Missions in March were directed at German radars in Holland and along front lines, with patrols along the coast from Dunkirk to Denmark and along the length of the Ruhr Valley. The coastal tasking provided feedback to the 36th BS radar jammers, while searches in the Ruhr region looked for new electronics such as developmental 2cm radars.[162]

April 1945 was the last month the 36th BS flew operational missions. VHF screening missions were flown for eighteen days, all missions flown over the North Sea with the 36th BS's last operational mission of the war flown on 25 April. Radar screening missions had stopped on 30 March with Allied ground forces overrunning a few additional German radar posts, but the jamming itself did not appear to have been effective. Studies conducted by SIGINT units in Europe note that 'the enemy has been able to "look through and around" the screen sufficiently to secure desired information', negating the primary purpose of the radar screening mission. Search missions also slowed down, with the USSTAF liaison officer returning to London on 1 April. The three ELINT missions flown in April – one B-24 over the North Sea, one P-38 over Baltic seaports and one P-38 over the Munich region – were all conceived and directed by the squadron, with the P-38 mission on 13 April the last search mission flown by the unit.[163]

Hostilities against Germany ceased on 7 May. Since the squadron had already stood down from flight operations almost two weeks earlier, there was little to do other than wait for orders dictating the future of the squadron and its personnel. The 36th BS was maintained in the UK as an administrative unit for 'high-point' personnel en route to being sent back to the States for discharge.[164] No thought was given to rotating the unit back for conversion to B-29s and shipment to the Pacific, as the Twentieth Air Force had a robust RCM capability already in place. As the war in Europe closed down, so did the unique 36th BS.

Serial Number	Aircraft	First Mission	Last Mission	Total # Ops Missions	Notes
42-3518	B-17F-75-DL	Receivers from '7743, 15 Jun 44	Receivers removed 26 Aug 44	At least 8	Departed squadron 4 Sep 44
42-37743	B-17G-10-DL	Unk	Receivers removed o/a 15 Jun 44 and transferred to '3518	Likely none	Ex-96 BG search aircraft
42-50622	B-24J-1-FO	Receivers from '51308, Dec 44	All search equipment removed by Apr 45; possibly only flew Jackal support	5, Dec 44–Jan 45	Enclosure installed in rear bomb bay
42-50671	B-24J-1-FO	SX-28 receiver installed 17 Aug 44	Receiver likely removed Sep 44	Likely none	
42-51308	B-24J-5-DT	Sep 44	Receivers removed Dec 44 and transferred to '50622	At least 9	Enclosure installed in rear bomb bay for SCR-587, S-27, APR-1 receivers and two crew positions
44-10507	B-24J-60-CF	7 Mar 45	3 Apr 45	15	Built by 1st Strategic Air Depot at Station 375, Honington, UK
44-23156	P-38J-20-LO	First P-38 mission 17 Mar 45	Last P-38 mission 13 Apr 45	Total of nine P-38 missions	
44-23501	P-38J-20-LO				
43-28479	P-38J-15-LO				

Members of the 36th Bombardment Squadron (H) pose atop a squadron B-24 two weeks after the end of hostilities in Europe. Aircraft and personnel were preparing to fly back to the US for either discharge or preparation for the Pacific Theatre.
Air Force Historical Research Agency via George Cully

Chapter 7

South West Pacific Strategic Picture – Autumn 1944

In September 1944 the staff in SWPA were tense. The years of slow fighting along New Guinea were about to change as MacArthur was poised to return to the Philippines through an amphibious landing on Leyte Island – an operation accelerated by two months in mid-September to a 20 October assault date. The seizure of western New Guinea also opened up air bases for operations against the Philippines and the Netherlands East Indies. In September 1944, the island of Noemfoor was captured and two 7,000ft runways were completed. This action set in motion air boss Lieutenant General Kenney's next move – a series of five raids by his Far East Air Forces against the major oil refinery complexes at Balikpapan and Lutong, Borneo. The first raid was on 30 September – hence his interest in Japanese radars in the region. That month, Ferrets VII and VIII started flight operations from Owi Island, positioning them to range deep into the Philippines and over Borneo. As the fighting dragged on in the southern Philippines, SWPA planners charted out follow-on actions for the theatre. In February 1945, GHQ SWPA outlined operations for the next six months, with plans centring on clearing the remainder of the Philippines and the Australian invasion of Borneo.[165] Japanese forces in the Netherlands East Indies, although bypassed by MacArthur, were still prevalent and considered dangerous. GHQ SWPA looked to the Thirteenth Air Force to soften up these enemy forces.

Airpower under MacArthur was organised under a combined command – Allied Air Forces – with Australian and US air components. Australian forces were organised under the RAAF Command, which by October 1944 had fielded the Australian First Tactical Air Force. US forces would eventually comprise three numbered air forces. The Fifth Air Force was created from the remnants of Philippine air power and the Far East Air Force in February 1942, while the Thirteenth Air Force was assigned to SWPA under a re-formed Far East Air Forces in June 1944, followed by the Seventh Air Force in July 1945. By early 1945, the Thirteenth Air Force had three bomb groups assigned to XIII Bomber Command – the 5th Bomb Group (H), the 42nd Bomb Group (M), and the 307th Bomb Group (H) – along with the 868th Bomb Squadron. In September 1944, the 307th Bomb Group (H) commenced operations in the Netherlands East Indies, hitting targets in Halmahera, Ceram and at Balikpapan, Borneo. The 307th would continue flying missions in this region until mid-1945, targeting Japanese shipping, oil refineries, and airfields. The 5th Bomb Group (H) followed a similar course of action, alternating between the oil refineries of Borneo, Japanese shipping from Morotai to the Sulu Sea, and airfields throughout the Philippine Islands, Celebes, Halmahera, and Borneo. In between these missions, the 'Bomber Barons' of the 5th Bomb Group (H) supported clearing operations in the Philippine Islands (Luzon and Mindanao) and the Australian invasion of Borneo. The 42nd Bomb Group (M) and the Australian First Tactical Air Force played similar roles, keeping the pressure on Japanese forces and supporting clearing operations throughout the region. Though bypassed by the main war effort, the Japanese forces in the Netherlands East Indies were far from pacific and, supplied with fuel from Borneo, were able to resist Allied incursions aggressively.

The split of SWPA into two lines of effort – north through the Philippines and west into the Netherlands East Indies – divided the airborne RCM effort. Ferrets VII and VIII and the two US Navy Consolidated PBY Catalina ferrets could only cover so much territory and by the end of September 1944 were mainly devoted to missions against the Philippines. This left the Netherlands East Indies – which had received some radar reconnaissance from the ferrets during their stay at Fenton Field – lacking dedicated airborne collection. A requirement for two 'radar investigational search' aircraft for service with the Fifth Air Force in the Southwest Pacific Area was passed on to Material Command in late March 1944.[166] These two aircraft, designated Ferrets X and XI, arrived in Ohio in mid-July 1944

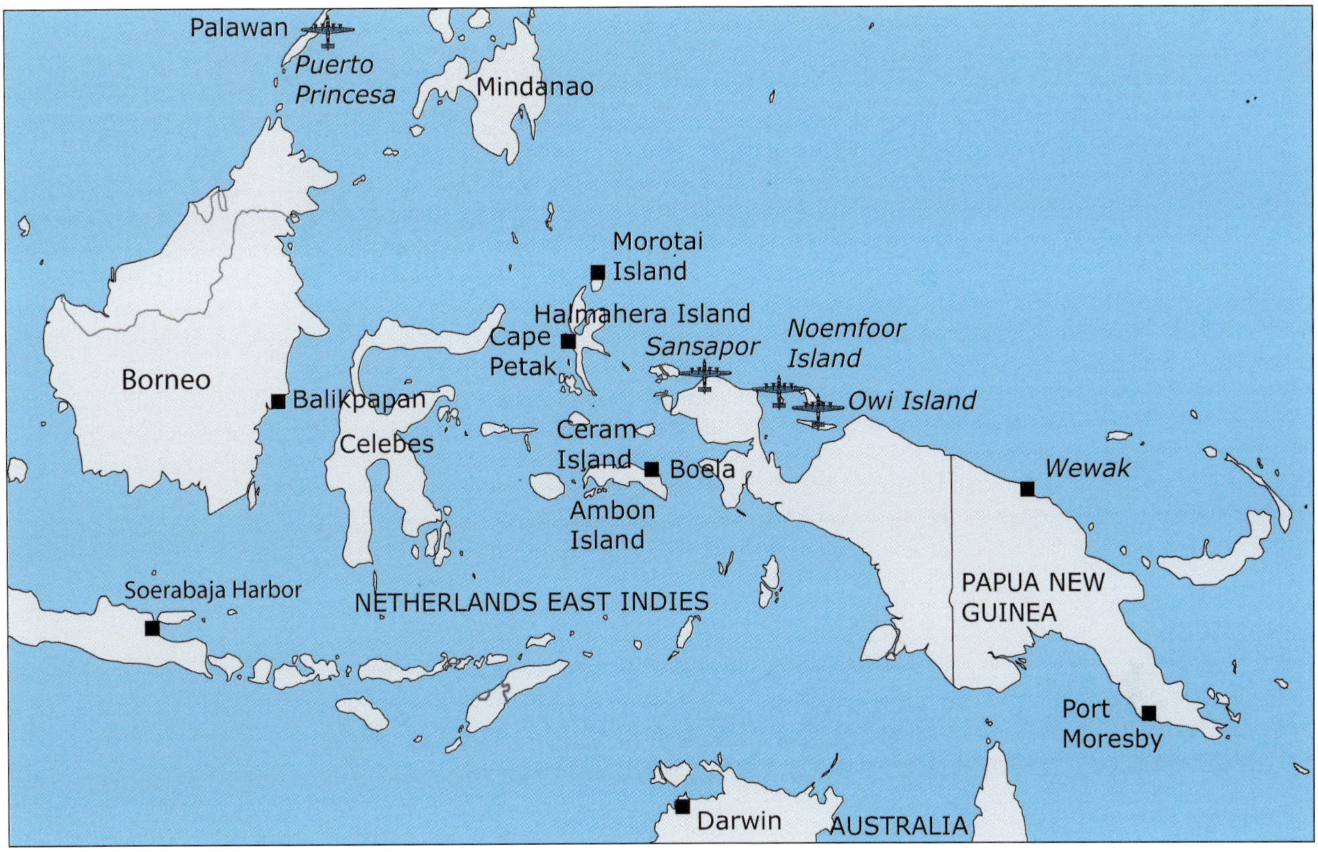

from a pool of B-24J but it would not be until early 1945 that they would be ready to depart the US. With the hard use of Ferrets VII and VIII, the new aircraft were likely just going to replace old airframes rather than add new capacity. Something clearly needed to be done – and the solution lay with the Field Units of Section 22.

Section 22

By mid-1944 Section 22 had the personnel and equipment in hand to start addressing the needs of the theatre. Ferrets VII and VIII, coupled with the other elements of Section 22, were gathering details on Japanese radar deployment and employment to enable staff planners to start developing ways to counter Japanese air surveillance. Radar jammers and window were on hand from shipments earlier in the year, giving SWPA aircraft the ability to mask their actions from Japanese radars.[167] On 10 September 1944 air commander Lieutenant General George Kenney sent an urgent message to General MacArthur requesting assistance in circumventing Japanese radar coverage of Goerango Point on Morotai Island in preparation for upcoming bombing operations. Section 22's exhaustive response noted that any bombers would need to be masked from both the Goerango Point radar and the Cape Petak radar on Halmahera; while jamming or window could be used, it was recommended that the offending radars be located precisely and bombed.[168]

It was realised that only by searching during a strike could it be determined how the Japanese used their radars against enemy aircraft, be it searchlight, gun-laying, or ground-controlled intercept by fighter aircraft. For this reason, before 'ad hoc' ferrets proliferated, Ferrets VII and VIII accompanied several strike missions.[169] The 380th Bomb Group (H) 'ad hoc' ferrets were still operating and had actually received six 'updated' aircraft by mid-1944.[170] By this time Section 22 had accumulated a large number of AN/APR-1s receivers and AN/APA-6 pulse analysers and work started to create 'ad hoc' ferrets for all the bomb groups in Fifth Air Force.[171] The Seventh Air Force had taken a similar approach to the vexing problem of too many SIGINT requirements and not enough ferrets. In November 1944 Headquarters Seventh Air Force set forth a Radio and Radar Reconnaissance Plan that required that provisions be made for rack, power and antenna installations in four aircraft per heavy bomb squadron to carry radar receivers.[172] The Thirteenth Air Force, left to cover the 'backwater' Netherlands East Indies, needed its own 'ad hoc' ferret force – and Field Unit (FU) 13 of Section 22 provided a solution.

Japanese Radar Development Until 1944

The Japanese air surveillance network in the SWPA consisted of thinly scattered belts of radars to provide early warning of approaching raids.[173] As the tactical situation changed, the IJA or IJN would shift their radar sites around to increase coverage of critical avenues of approach. As the US moved into the southern Philippines, the Japanese rapidly reoriented their air surveillance coverage to better screen their southern flank.[174] Many Japanese radar posts had more than one radar set assigned to them. A review of the February 1945 electronic order of battle for the Netherlands East Indies shows this to be the case with approximately 15 per cent of the sites, with a slightly smaller percentage of sites in the Philippines following this rule.[175] Some Japanese radar sets could also receive US Identification, Friend, or Foe (IFF) signals, a factor likely taken into account when equipment was deployed. The IJN Type 2 Mark I Model 3, along with some variants of the Type 2 Mark I Model 2, the Type 2 Mark I Model 1 Modification 3-K, and land-based adaptations of the Air Mark VI Mod 4 radars operated in the same frequency band as the US Type III IFF transponders that came into universal service in the Pacific in late 1943. These radars could and did trigger an IFF response that enabled the Japanese to monitor Allied aircraft not only at medium altitude but also allowed them to track aircraft at altitudes lower than the radars could normally pick up targets at ranges out to 300km.[176]

What became Field Unit 13 had been associated with the Thirteenth Air Force since mid-1943. When still assigned to the South Pacific Area, COMSOPAC RCM Group provided the theatre and Thirteenth Air Force with a consolidated RCM organisation. With little RCM equipment being available, COMSOPAC RCM Group started to acquire the necessary RCM gear – receivers, pulse analysers, and antennas – from other units in theatre, mainly US Navy squadrons. The equipment was gathered at Thirteenth Air Force and sorted out while waiting for a host aircraft. When the 868th Bomb Squadron arrived in theatre in January 1944 one of the squadron aircraft was configured as an 'ad hoc' ferret with an AN/ARC-1 radar receiver, but since the plane was still assigned bombing duties the ferret equipment was removed every time it flew a 'standard' bombing mission to preclude unnecessary loss. In late February and early March 1944 the aircraft flew only three electronic reconnaissance missions.[177] After transfer to SWPA in June 1944, this expertise followed and likely formed the foundation of Field Unit 13. Figuring out how the Japanese used their radars was an international effort that ended up using young men from around the world to solve the problem.

James Alderman grew up on a farm outside of Wartrace, Tennessee, a small town 70 miles south of Nashville. In June 1942 James applied for Aviation Cadet training and enlisted in the reserves but was not called to active duty until May 1943. After completing Communication Cadet training at Boca Raton, Florida, in December 1943 he was commissioned and sent to Radio Technical School at Yale University. Placed on flying status as an RCM Observer in June 1944, he was shipped overseas to SWPA and Section 22 in November. Section 22 was unique in that it also contained technically oriented personnel – engineers, physicists, or civilian technical representatives – that could build and modify equipment in theatre to meet specific tactical needs rapidly. Included on its rosters were two New Zealand physicists who, despite their academic background, fit easily into the unrefined war in the Pacific.

Bob Unwin was born in Timaru, New Zealand, in 1918. After completing his degree at Canterbury University, he stayed on for an additional year studying radar technology before joining the Radio Development Laboratory (RDL) at Wellington. At RDL, Bob was commissioned as a New Zealand Army Lieutenant and met Ted Collins, another physicist who was now an Army major. In addition to radar development, Bob trained army personnel in the operation of radar before joining Lab E, a special RCM section at RDL, along with Ted and another physicist. Soon Ted and Bob were reassigned to New Zealand's Radio and Radar Countermeasures Division in December 1943, being detailed to South Pacific Area Headquarters in New Caledonia as part of COMSOPAC RCM Group. As the effort in the region wound down, Ted and Bob were assigned to SWPA and dispatched to Section 22's Field Unit 13 in September 1944.[178]

One of the first orders of business for the intrepid New Zealand physicists was to assist the Thirteenth Air Force in locating Japanese radars in the region. About the time the Kiwis arrived at Field Unit 13 Ferrets VII and VIII shifted north to assist the Fifth Air Force in operations over the Philippines and littoral China. After looking at the resources available to them, Collins and Unwin determined the 868th Bomb Squadron's (BS) operations – 'snooper' radar-equipped bomber aircraft going in at night that could stir up Japanese radar activity – as the perfect fit.

Commonwealth soldiers assigned to the COMSOPAC RCM Group at to South Pacific Area Headquarters, Camp Barnes, Noumea, New Caledonia. Seen in early 1944 are (L to R) Syd Slatter, Robert S. Unwin, Ted Collins, and Charles W. Munroe. Unwin and Collins were reassigned to Section 22's Field Unit 13 in September 1944. ***Hocken Collections, University of Otago, Dunedin, NZ***

Collins, commanding the Field Unit, worked out a plan to kit out one of the squadron's B-24J aircraft as an 'ad hoc' ferret. Equipment racks, cabling, and antennas were permanently installed, and when an aircraft was scheduled for a ferret mission it was fitted out with the appropriate receivers and analysers. The now-modified bomber would fly its standard night anti-shipping or strike mission but on board a Section 22 RCM Observer would also monitor the gear and record signals of Japanese radars. Eventually six 868th BS B-24 aircraft would be equipped for the 'ad hoc' ferret role, with Field Unit 13 technicians performing the work on site.[179] Field Unit 13 also constructed homing antennas and cockpit displays to enable the pilots of these aircraft to make bombing runs against Japanese radar sites.[180] 'Ad hoc' ferret missions started on 18 September 1944 and continued until at least June 1945. The RCM Observers were largely a mix of trained USAAF RCM Officers like James Alderman and non-commissioned officers trained in theatre by Section 22 personnel.

Just as the equipping of the 'ad hoc' ferret fleet was achieved on a shoestring, so was the manning. The USAAF RCM Observer Course at the Radar School at Boca Raton, Florida, had a limited throughput. Officers who graduated from this course were generally put in leadership positions at the Field Units or on staff with Section 22. The majority of the personnel used to operate the equipment on the SWPA 'ad hoc' ferret aircraft were enlisted airmen and Allied personnel. RAAF airmen continued to fly with the Field Units associated with US Heavy Bomb Groups until May 1945, slowly being augmented by then replaced by USAAF radar mechanics. Section 22 set up an RCM School in theatre to train enlisted radar mechanics to be flying RCM Operators, with classroom academics and flights in a C-47 augmenting the stateside training they had received.[181]

The US Navy was also helping with the reconnaissance mission over the Celebes Sea. By October 1944 each land-based squadron was authorised three aircraft fitted out with a variety of receivers and ordered to maintain a 'continual RCM survey' of the enemy, with tasking from fleet commanders.[182] In the SWPA, Section 22 Field Units 3 and 11 supported Navy patrol units. Field Unit 3 worked with multiple squadrons, but with the exception of two ferret PBY missions flown against Celebes in October the thrust of the unit's work was in the Philippines. Field Unit 11, based out of Morotai, started to support missions in October 1944.

After looking at the resources available to them to fill the gap of departing Ferrets VII and VIII, Section 22 determined the 868th Bomb Squadron's (BS) operations – 'snooper' radar-equipped bomber aircraft going in at night that could stir up Japanese radar activity – as the perfect fit. This is a right side view of B-24J-185-CO s/n 44-40899 *Lady Luck II*, one of the 'ad hoc' ferrets assigned to the 868th BS. *Alan Griffith*

Eventually six 868th BS B-24 aircraft would be equipped for the 'ad hoc' ferret role, with Field Unit 13 technicians performing the work on site. Right side view of B-24J-190-CO s/n 44-41025 *So Round, So Firm, So Fully Stacked*, one of the 868th BS bombers converted to 'ad hoc' ferret status. *Alan Griffith*

Ad hoc ferret B-24J-185-CO s/n 44-40899 *Lady Luck II* in its original version without nose art, just *Lady Luck II* with nine ship symbols and fifty bomb symbols. 'Ad hoc' ferrets had equipment racks, cabling, and antennas installed permanently, and when an aircraft was scheduled for a ferret mission it was fitted out with the appropriate receivers and analysers. *Darryl Ford*

A simple dipole antenna in front of nose gear used for direction finding in 868th BS 'ad hoc' ferrets. Noemfoor, New Guinea, December 1944. *Hocken Collections, University of Otago, Dunedin, NZ*

Initially working with three VPB-146 Lockheed PV-1 Ventura aircraft that flew dedicated SIGINT missions, the unit switched to supporting VPB-101 and VPB-104 Consolidated PB4Y-1 Liberators. The nine Ventura flights fanned out in the north-west quadrant from Morotai, with the majority of the missions covering the Celebes Sea. The ten PB4Y-1 flights in November 1944 covered similar territory, reaching out to Palawan and Makassar Strait. Reporting from both Field Units dies off by the end of 1944, but the Navy VPB squadrons continued to send reports on Japanese radar activity to Section 22. By this time most of the Navy patrol community was no longer flying in the Celebes Sea region; after supporting the invasions of Mindoro and Luzon they were ranging between Formosa and Indochina along the western edge of the China Sea, leaving the 868th BS to cover the Celebes Sea.

While most 'ad hoc' ferret sorties were for tracking deployments of Japanese radars, Ted Collins' first mission on the night of 2–3 November 1944 with Major Newbury, a veteran of six prior 'ad hoc' ferret missions and RCM Officer for the Thirteenth Air Force, was different. Taking off at 1500 from Noemfoor, New Guinea, B-24J 'ad hoc' ferret s/n 44-40902 transited through Morotai for fuel and a quick break before continuing on the mission. Ferret '0902 crossed the Celebes Sea alone en route to the Mindanao Sea for an armed shipping search. Newbury located an IJN Type 2 Mark I Model 3 radar on Sebago Island and the pilot proceeded to make three bombing runs, dropping

Opposite top: The US Navy version of the USAAF B-24 was the PB4Y-1. In early 1944 US Navy patrol squadron VP-104 had one of its PB4Y-1s modified to fly ferret missions. The missions proved successful and VPB-116, a PB4Y-1 squadron flying out of Eniwetok, was tasked with performing electronic reconnaissance of the region with three aircraft fitted out with receivers.
Air Force Historical Research Agency via George Cully

Bottom: A US Navy 'Black Cat' PBY-5A with radar installed for night reconnaissance and bombing. In April 1944 two PBY Catalinas were fitted out as dedicated ferret aircraft with AN/ARC-1 radar receivers and assigned to the operational control of Section 22.
Air Force Historical Research Agency via George Cully

Radar hunting in SWPA was a combined effort using all available assets. This view out the navigator's bubble of a RAAF Beaufighter shows the mountain top clearing housing the Cape Tekoe Radar, Celebes, Philippines, during a November 1944 strike. *Hocken Collections, University of Otago, Dunedin, NZ*

single 500lb general-purpose bombs on the first two attacks and two on the third. The bombs appeared to miss the radar by a few hundred feet each time.[183] In the past, Japanese radar sites in the SWPA had been viewed as targets of opportunity or had been struck when seen as a particular problem. Thirteenth Air Force P-70s and P-38s had targeted the Japanese radar installation protecting Rabaul at Cape Saint George, New Ireland, on at least three occasions between January and March 1944, using data from Ferrets VII and VIII. Starting with the 3 November attack on the Sebago radar site, the 868th Bomb Squadron 'ad hoc' ferrets performed strikes against Japanese radar sites but not on a routine basis. Their primary mission was still anti-shipping or attacks on Japanese facilities, the 'ad hoc' ferrets usually having neither the time nor the ordnance to go after enemy radar posts.

Attacking Japanese radar posts was not an easy endeavour. The Japanese concealed radar towers with palm fronds and sometimes attached antenna elements to live trees, so plotting out a radar site via electronic means was not good enough – photographs were needed to lock down the radar location for follow-on bombers to find and strike. On 1 October 1944 Section 22 requested information on an antenna fit for a B-25 aircraft to enable it to home in on an enemy radar set while making a bombing run.[184] Field Unit 13 personnel started working on modifying 42nd Bomb Group (M), 100th Bomb Squadron B-25J s/n 43-27983 in November 1944 using equipment on hand that was being used with the 868th BS 'ad hoc' ferrets – the AN/APR-1 receiver and AN/APA-6 pulse analyser. The RCM observer sat in the waist section of the aircraft, listening to the radar signal in one of his earphones, with the crew's intercom system on the other. Signals were received by means of a rotating, directional antenna, mounted on the end of a retractable pipe that extended through the bottom of the plane and manually turned by the RCM observer. With all of this kit, the Thirteenth Air Force now had the capability within one aircraft to precisely locate and destroy hard to find Japanese radar sites that were passing warning of inbound Allied bomber raids.

XIII Fighter Command, based at Sansapor, Dutch

Opposite top: An Imperial Japanese Navy Mk I Model 3 radar station radar at Sibago Island, west of Mindanao, Philippines, under attack from 868th BS 'ad hoc' ferret B-24J s/n 44-40902 on 3 November 1944. This photo was taken by a K-20 camera shot out the waist gun window. Starting with this attack, 868th BS 'ad hoc' ferrets performed strikes against Japanese radar sites, but this was not the primary function or mission of these aircraft. *Air Force Historical Research Agency via George Cully*

Bottom: Once radars became a target, the Japanese went to great lengths to camouflage them. This IJN Mk I Model 3 radar station at Cape Mangkalihat, eastern Borneo, was imaged from low altitude by US Navy patrol squadron VPB-130 on 17 January 1945. *Air Force Historical Research Agency via George Cully*

42nd Bomb Group (M) B-25J s/n 43-27983 *Beautiful Ohio* was converted to a radar-hunting ferret by Field Unit 13 personnel in October 1944. This photo was likely taken in September 1945 at Palawan's Puerto Princessa airfield.
Air Force Historical Research Agency via George Cully

New Guinea, tasked the B-25 ferret to assist in the systematic destruction of enemy radar installations.[185] The aircraft's first mission was flown on 28 November, with an additional six flown from Sansapor by 9 December 1944. The missions concentrated on locating strategically important radars on Halmahera Island. XIII Fighter Command was undertaking a major strike against Japanese facilities at Goeroea, Halmahera, with eleven A-20s, twenty four B-25s, and twelve P-38s on 11 December. That day, ferret B-25 '983 was teamed up with another 100th BS B-25 to suppress the Japanese radar at Cape Petak, 30 miles

Detail shot of the direction-finding antenna fitted to B-25J s/n 43-27983 *Beautiful Ohio* of the 42nd BG (M). Once an RCM observer such as Lt Alderman had a fix on a site, the pilot could fly over the radar and either take photographs or attack the installation.
James Alderman via Jim Alderman Jr

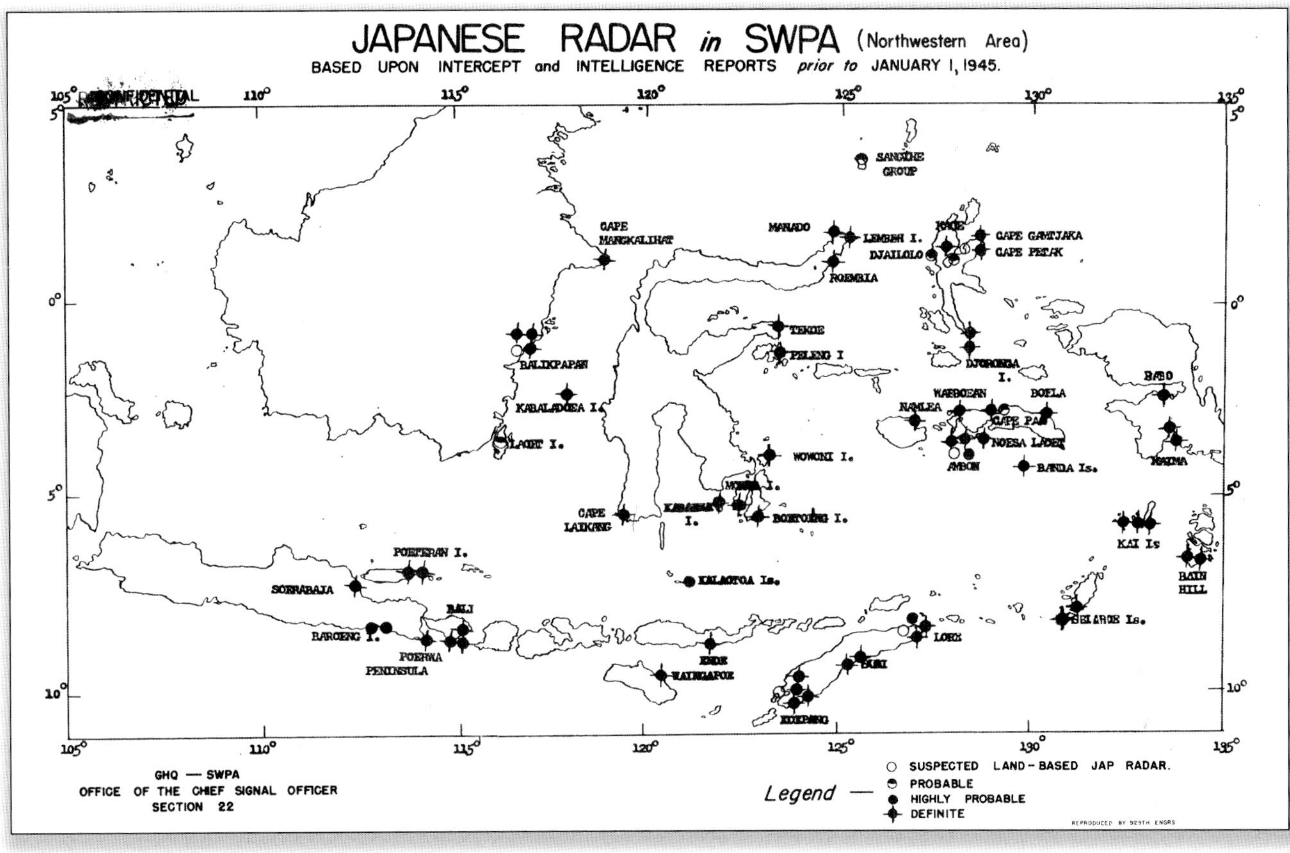

Japanese forces in the Netherlands East Indies, though bypassed by MacArthur, were still prevalent and considered dangerous. This Section 22 map of western New Guinea, Borneo and Dutch East Indies highlights the Japanese radars faced by Field Unit 13 in January 1945. *Air Force Historical Research Agency via George Cully*

away from the target area. Bombing and strafing runs against the hapless radar enabled complete surprise for the strikers at Goeroea, the A-20 bombers receiving no anti-aircraft fire until they were departing the target area. Additional attacks were flown against the Cape Noesanive radar on 14 December with a follow-up attack against Cape Petak on 17 December, both strikes flown at the behest of XIII Fighter Command.[186] With the Halmahera apparently cleared out, B-25 ferret '983 was directed to operate further south against Ceram Island on Banda Sea.[187] Over the next two months, the B-25 ferret flew twenty-eight sorties, including a dozen that resulted in attacks against radar sites. On 28 December, '983 and another B-25 successfully suppressed a Japanese radar on Laoet Island to prevent detection of a XIII Fighter Command strike headed for Ambon and Haroekoe Islands.[188] While '983 had demonstrated its efficacy, the key to these missions was the two dedicated RCM observers who flew with it – 1Lt Dylowski and Sgt Plant. Dylowski (promoted to captain in December) would continue to fly with '983 until mid-January, when he trained up two lieutenants as replacements – 2Lt Wally Fenn and 2Lt James Alderman. James Alderman had bounced around New Guinea and the Philippines between various Section 22 locations for a month or so before being assigned to Field Unit 13 at Thirteenth Air Force Headquarters on Morotai Island. During this time he met another lieutenant also newly assigned to Field Unit 13, Wally Fenn. Within a week of arriving at Morotai, James and Wally were shipped to Sansapor to meet up with the 100th Bomb Squadron of the 42nd Bomb Group.

On 6 February, ferret '983, with Wally Fenn as the RCM Observer, was accompanied by another B-25 to attack the Japanese radar site at Boela, Ceram. This installation had led a charmed life, being attacked six times previously by the ferret. The offending radar was only on for a few minutes before shutting down, forcing both bombers to drop their bombs from medium altitude and depart the area with unknown results.[189] While the strike missions were exciting, the majority of the missions flown by '983 were to 'obtain intercept and photographic information on radar activity' at specific tasked locations for XIII Fighter Command and XIII Bomber Command. The job of finding Japanese radars started to increase in complexity as enemy radar operators were learning to recognise the homing runs flown by '983 and would switch off the radar when the aircraft was miles from the coast. Still, the B-25 ferret was indispensable in building an understanding of radars in the region and was credited with finding radars on eastern Ceram at Boela, Banda Islands south of Ceram, and at Ambelau Island.[190]

On 16 February, ferret '983 accompanied a

strike mission of twenty-four 42nd Bomb Group (M) B-25s against the Kendari supply area and adjacent Mega village on south-east Celebes Island. RCM Observer Lt Alderman was tasked to ascertain the effectiveness of the low-level ingress routes planned to evade Japanese radar detection. No Japanese signals were heard after the formation dropped down to 500ft, thus validating the mission plan and the mapping of Japanese radars in the region by Section 22.[191] With this mission complete, the crew prepared to relocate their ferret operations to Puerto Princesa, Palawan, situated between the Sulu Sea and the South China Sea. As the ferret B-25 crew packed their belongings for the trip to Palawan, recently liberated from the Japanese on 28 February, the remainder of the Field Unit continued to work with the 868th BS.

In between missions over Luzon and the South China Sea, Ferret VII flew a single sortie against Japanese radar sites on Halmahera.[192] The intelligence take from the 15 January 1945 mission confirmed the location of radars plotted by 'ad hoc' ferrets and highlighted the need for a dedicated ferret aircraft for the Thirteenth Air Force. As strikes by XIII Bomber Command against Borneo and the southern Philippines increased, the command became aware of the need to better understand Japanese air defences. Although US Navy patrol aircraft were starting to use Section 22 radar data to attack radar installations around the Celebes Sea, Thirteenth Air Force personnel acknowledged the need for a long -range ferret aircraft that could aid in radar destruction.[193] With this requirement in mind, Section 22 Field Unit 13 commander Major Ted Collins lobbied for a B-24 fitted out as a ferret but capable of dropping bombs for attacking radars. The Commanding General of Thirteenth Air Force concurred and released a B-24 to Field Unit 13 for conversion to a ferret.[194]

Major Collins immediately started fitting out the aircraft as both a radar reconnaissance and a radar attack platform. Working with scrounged equipment and no outside assistance, Field Unit 13 engineers hand built a ferret aircraft in the jungles of New Guinea. Two RCM Observer positions were installed in the aircraft, one in the nose and one in the waist position, leaving the bomb bay clear for weapons. Each location had an AN/APR-4 receiver and an AN/APA-11 pulse analyser to allow reconnaissance against multiple signals. Radar jammers were also fitted in the waist area and waist gunners were tasked to drop radar jamming 'window'. K-17 and K-20 cameras enabled radar installations to be photographed, while homing gear and displays for the pilot similar to those in B-25 ferret '983 were installed in the cockpit. The first operational mission was flown on 1 March 1945, although only one RCM position had a complete equipment installation for the flight.[195]

The Thirteenth Air Force ferret – B-24L-5-CO s/n 44-41464 – flew dedicated RCM reconnaissance missions with the 868th BS. Between 15 March and 13 April it flew six sorties across the SWPA, including two missions to Makassar Strait, two to Mindanao, and two to Halmahera and Ceram Islands. Major Collins flew on the first three missions of '464, joined by fellow Kiwi Bob Unwin on its second flight. The use of the ferret B-24 was similar to the ferret B-25 – confirming radar coverage in target areas and precisely locating radar sites for attack. On 9 April '464 took a run at the immortal radar site at Boela, Ceram, but cloud cover kept it from going in on the final bomb run. Two days later '464 tried its luck against another radar site. Five bombing runs were made against the radar site at Dongala, Celebes, but all the bombs burst short and to the right of the station. Undoubtedly frustrated, the pilot lined the aircraft up and made two strafing runs against the radar post. On 17 April 1945 Ferret '464 took off from Morotai to plot radars accurately on Tarakan Island off north-east Borneo and obtain photo coverage of the Lemo and Donggola areas. When complete, it landed at Puerto Princesa, Palawan where the Field Unit 13 Detachment was working with 42nd Bomb Group (M) B-25 ferret '983. Major Collins, Lt Fenn and Sgt Kunhart accompanied the ferret B-24 for this short deployment. Aircraft '464 remained for three days, flying a mission along the coast of French Indochina before taking off on 21 April for a mission to observe Balikpapan and Tarakan Island en route to Morotai. Ferrey '464's mission to the Indochina coast was likely to augment '983's work from the past month.

Field Unit 13 commander Maj. Collins lobbied hard to get a dedicated ferret aircraft that could also act as a radar hunter/killer. The commanding General of the Thirteenth Air Force concurred and released a new bomber, B-24L-5-CO s/n 44-41464, that had been in theatre a couple months to Field Unit 13 for conversion to a ferret. The aircraft was named *Lady June II* and flew missions from March through June 1945. The original 868th BS *Lady June* was B-24J s/n 42-100271, an 'ad hoc' ferret. *Alan Griffith*

Thirteenth Air Force ferret B-24L-5-CO s/n 44-41464, operated by Field Unit 13 and attached to the 868th BS. It sports the 868 BS 'snooper' 'S' in a diamond insignia on the tail and is shown at Morotai shortly after conversion in March 1945. As opposed to the purpose-built ferret aircraft coming from the States, Field Unit 13 located RCM Observer positions in the nose and waist of the aircraft, leaving the bomb bay available for weapons. *Hocken Collections, University of Otago, Dunedin, NZ*

Once at Palawan, James Alderman became the Officer in Charge of the Field Unit 13 Detachment – which consisted of one officer (him) and one enlisted airman (Corporal Maguire). B-25 ferret '983 flew its first mission from Puerto Princesa on 26 March with the first five missions along the north-east and north-west coast of Borneo picking up no radar signals. On 31 March, '983 ventured into the South China Sea to look for a reported radar installation on Itu Aba Island, but again the receivers picked up no signals. Searches of the Turtle Islands and the China Coast in early April also provided similar results, although range limitations kept '983 150 miles off of China. With a bomb bay full of fuel tanks and an escort of six P-38s, the intrepid '983 took off at 0735 on 14 April and flew due west to Saigon, French Indochina. Alderman noted seven radars active during the mission, including IJN Type 2 Mark I Model 1 Modification 2, Type 2 Mark I Model 2, Type 2 Mark I Model 3, and Imperial Japanese Army Tachi 6 radars. While the 21 April flight to Brunei revealed no radar activity, the flight activity over the next two weeks provided a change of pace for the crew of '983. Between 22 April and 6 May, five missions were flown to Indochina, with '983 acting as a pathfinder for fighter sweeps into the area and taking advantage of the extra air activity acting as a stimulus to note radar signals. A similar mission was flown on 26 April with the target being Kuching on the west coast of Borneo.[196]

On 24 April '464 joined two 868th BS B-24J 'snoopers' in a night attack against Soerabaja harbour, Java, a major naval base for the Japanese and shipping terminal for oil from local refineries. Ferret '464, fitted with three radar jammers and carrying CHH-2 'rope' window, entered the target area at 14,000ft, jamming searchlight and fire control radars and dropping rope at five-second intervals to support the two bombers attacking shipping and warehouses. Three days later a more aggressive mission was planned with '464, crewed by veteran Field Unit 13 operators Lt Everett, Sgt Plant, and Sgt Powers. Though it was planned for B-24 #397 to light up the target area with flares, its H2X radar was inoperative and '464 quickly made two passes, dropping ten flares over the target area. Five 'snooper' Liberators then came in for the attack at one-minute intervals. The searchlights and AAA appeared to be controlled visually, with the bombers only encountering inaccurate ground fire. Although Japanese radars started tracking the bombers at 225 miles out from the target area, American jamming did not commence until they were 75 miles from the target area. Starting at 20 miles out, 'window' was dropped, with one of the three RCM observers on '464 noting the jamming as 'very effective'. 'Ad hoc' ferret B-24J 44-40899 *Lady Luck II*, with Bob Unwin as the RCM Observer, led the bombers over the target area, dropping 'window' when seven minutes out. Fourteen signals were noted on the mission by ferret '464 to include Type 2 Mark I Model 1, Type 2 Mark I Model 2, and Type 2 Mark I Model 3 radar sets. The snoopers then set course for Truscott, Australia, landing just before 6 am.[197]

By 10 May the war in the Southwest Pacific was nearing its climax. The southern Philippine islands were being cleared, with the Sulu Archipelago liberated on 3 April. Australian forces had landed on Tarakan Island a few miles off the coast of Borneo in preparation for their main assault on Balikpapan planned for July. On this day, Bob Unwin climbed into '464 for a low-level visual and photo search mission against the radars at Dongala and Lemo on northern Celebes Island. The skies were still dark as the ferret B-24 departed Morotai at 0450. As the aircraft transited across the northern Gulf of Tomini at 7,000ft, Bob started to receive signals from the radar at Lemo. Pilot Lt Gilman banked the aircraft to fly a few miles inland and upon reaching the Celebes isthmus he turned south and started to lose altitude. By the time the aircraft was opposite Lemo it was flying 700ft above the water and 5 miles offshore. As the aircraft closed to within a few miles the radar suddenly shut down, a standard defensive manoeuvre by Japanese radar technicians when an aircraft was spotted close by at low altitude. Lt Gilman then headed west, crossing the Celebes isthmus to Makassar Strait and the Dongala peninsula. The Dongala radar was not heard on approach and the crew spent two hours performing a thorough low-level search of the peninsula. Binoculars located in the nose turret, nose, waist positions, and tail turret were used by crew members to scan the jungles for the camouflaged radar arrays, but to no avail. With no luck and hitting time to fly back to the east, the crew moved on to search for the Lemo radar site, and this time it was found and several bomb runs were made.

Two days later Field Unit 13 made another run at the Lemo radar site. Ted Collins joined the crew of 'ad hoc' ferret B-24J 44-41025 for a mission against this site as well as tasking to locate the Japanese radar at Boengkoe. These radars, along with the elusive Dongala site, were opposite Balikpapan, which was scheduled for an invasion in six weeks and were likely of high interest to Thirteenth Air Force staff. No signals were heard as the crew flew over the Molucca Sea en route to the target area. The B-24J flew direct to Lemo and spent two hours in the target area trying to find the radar. A broken cloud layer covered the region between 2,000 and 3,000ft, so the pilot took the bomber down under the cloud deck to search for the radar site. With their bomber highlighted against the cloud layer, Japanese gunners easily saw the attacker and light anti-aircraft fire greeted the bomber. Undeterred by the AAA, the crew made ten separate bombing runs from 500 to 1,500ft altitude. Because the bomb damage could not be confirmed, four additional strafing attacks were made on the Lemo radar post. With all weapons expended and nothing heard from any radar, the crew headed for home. On the way home, with the aircraft low on fuel and 120 miles away, the Boengkoe radar came up for a few minutes as a parting shot to '025 and its crew.

Personnel assigned to Field Unit 13 pose in front of their office at Morotai, around March 1945. Identified as (L to R back row) Max Kuniansky, Ericson, Fred Everett, Bob S. Unwin; (L to R middle row) Sgt Foord, Unk., S/Sgt Kunhart, Tony Yakutis, Ted Dylowski, Ted Collins (C.O.), Wally Fenn, Unk., Aldy Stucke. Front row not identified. Lt Alderman was absent with XIII Fighter Command at Palawan. *Hocken Collections, University of Otago, Dunedin, NZ*

James Alderman started to view '983 as his aircraft and, being in charge of his own detachment, decided to modify it to better serve its purpose. Since bombardiers were not carried on low-flying attacks, the RCM equipment could be moved up to that position in the nose. A retractable antenna was located just in front of the nose wheel, placing it in front of the propellers as these could cause distortion on incoming radar signals. On 30 May 1945 '983 was in the vicinity of Balikpapan, Borneo, when its left engine blew a piston. Although the engine did not catch fire, the pilot mistakenly thought it had and smothered the engine with carbon dioxide, which fouled the ignition wiring enough to cause that engine to shut down. To make up for the dead engine, power was increased on the right engine. Before long, the increased demand caused the right side to blow a piston as well. The co-pilot, who had more experience, persuaded the pilot to try to restart the now dried-out left engine. With both running at reduced power '983 limped to a recovery airfield at Sanga Sanga, an island in the Sulu Archipelago north-east of Borneo.

James worked long hours for the next several days, removing the RCM equipment from '983 and reinstalling it into another squadron B-25J, #958 (likely s/n 43-27958). After a mission on 6 June along the north-west coast of Borneo, #958 was preparing for another sortie on 9 June when it too faced misfortune. Going too fast on a wet taxiway, the pilot skidded into a parked plane and effectively totalled #958. Damaged beyond repair, James was now back to where he started. He waited for '983 to return – its engines were being changed at Sanga Sanga – but decided to go ahead and work on another B-25, #126 (likely s/n 43-28126). Starting on 22 June, James flew five more operational missions, mainly against Balikpapan and central Borneo, before standing down after a mission on 4 July. By this time Australian forces were ashore on Borneo and fighting Japanese forces in the central part of the island. With no more missions to fly, James was assigned to XIII Fighter Command in the Philippines. He flew two missions as an observer on US Navy PBMs and PB4Ys but for him the air war was over.

With the invasion of Borneo and the pacification of most of the Philippines the Japanese radar threat was greatly reduced in the SWPA. Most ferret operations ceased in July 1945, with the aircraft retiring or being dispersed for other missions. B-25 ferret '983 was abandoned in place on Palawan, with James Alderman finding it in the weeds off the side of the runway a few weeks after the war ended. B-24 ferret '464 somehow made it back to the US to be turned over for scrap to the Reconstruction Finance Corporation at Kingman,

Thirteenth Air Force ferret B-24L-5-CO s/n 44-41464 performing its intended mission of radar location and destruction. Here '464 is in the process of attacking a Japanese radar station at Koetai (Mahakam) River delta, Borneo, on 20 June 1945. *Air Force Historical Research Agency via George Cully*

Above: A few weeks after the war ended, Lt Alderman went down to the Puerto Princessa flight line and found 42nd Bomb Group (M) B-25 ferret #983 with weeds growing around it. He took a few photos for posterity and as a reminder of the missions he flew on this aircraft. *James Alderman via Jim Alderman Jr*

Arizona, in October 1945. With the over-production of bombers such as the B-24 and B-25, most aircraft such as the 'ad hoc' ferret fleet that had been flown hard were scrapped – there were plenty of new airframes at home and both aircraft types were considered nearing obsolescence. Even before the ferrets had ceased flying, organisational changes had been taking place. On 1 May 1945, operational control of the RCM mission had passed to Far East Air Forces and 7th Fleet. With this transfer, the Field Units were dissolved and their personnel and equipment turned over to their respective commands. Day to day operations had continued as before, with flying squadrons still filing their post-mission reports back to Section 22 for collation and dissemination.

B-25J s/n 43-27983 *Beautiful Ohio* of the 100 BS maintained its full attack capability, with 'cheek guns' and an operational bomb bay available to attack and destroy Japanese radars once they were located. *James Alderman via Jim Alderman Jr*

Even before the transition of the RCM mission to the services, many Navy radar receiver-equipped aircraft were arriving on the island of Palawan. First to arrive were detachments from two Martin PBM-3D Mariner squadrons, VPB-17 and VPB-20, operating from the seaplane tender USS *Pocomoke*. The aircraft arrived on 11 March, with flights mainly covering the China Sea. VPB-17 departed on 22 April, and within one week VPB-20 and the USS Pocomoke moved to Tawi-Tawi, Sulu Archipelago. The squadron provided convoy coverage and reconnaissance flights in support of the invasion of Borneo. Between mid-April and early May the US Navy relocated three land-based patrol squadrons to Puerto Princessa, placing them under the operational control of Fleet Air Wing 10. VPB-109 deployed to the island from Hawaii with its Consolidated PB4Y-2 Privateers, starting to attack land and maritime targets in Borneo and Celebes in late April. VPB-106, also equipped with Privateers, deployed from Iwo Jima and started flying anti-shipping patrols along the Malay coast on 6 May. VPB-111 arrived on 11 April from Tacloban with PB4Y-1s but started conversion to the Privateer on 1 May and joined VPB-109 in hitting Borneo and Malayan targets. VPB-117, flying PB4Y-1s from McGuire Field, Mindoro, starting in February 1945 under the operational control of FAW-17, also contributed sorties over the north-west coast of Borneo, the coastline of Indochina and the waters in between. The RCM A-kit wired into the Privateers during production enabled great flexibility in the missions they were assigned, with many RCM reconnaissance missions flown in support of the upcoming invasion of Borneo. The addition of these long-range aircraft,

Consolidated PB4Y-2 Privateer attributed to VPB-106 parked between missions at Puerto Princessa, Palawan. VPB-106 started flying missions from Palawan in May 1945, joining VPB-109 and VPB-111 in maritime patrols and contributing to radar reconnaissance efforts around Borneo. *Air Force Historical Research Agency via George Cully*

many with radar receivers, literally flooded the region with aircraft able to map the remaining Japanese radars.[198]

On 7 May 1945 HQ RAAF took over operational control of Field Unit 15 from Section 22. Later that day, it directed the Field Unit to fit out two B 24s of 12 Squadron, RAAF, with equipment similar to the 'ad hoc' ferrets of the Thirteenth Air Force. Field Unit 15, bereft of any RCM-equipped aircraft, had already been working on modifying a 24 Squadron B-24. This aircraft flew three missions in May before the 12 Squadron aircraft took over. The two 12 Squadron B-24s flew operational missions from Darwin over the Celebes Sea region, usually shipping searches or strike missions against land targets in the region. Plans were made to equip two aircraft from 99 Squadron with a similar equipment load.[199] The Australians – who had started it all with RCM observers assigned to the 380th BG – were fully transitioned to independent operations.

Most of the Americans in Field Unit 13 transferred to the Thirteenth Air Force and its components, while the Kiwis transitioned to other work. Bob Unwin went ashore with Australian troops at Balikpapan on 1 July as part of an intelligence-gathering mission, exploring Japanese radar sites while attached to a commando unit. In October 1945 James Alderman was ordered to Japan as part of the Air Technical Intelligence Group to study Japanese radars and technology. By January 1946 the demobilisation process caught up to him and he boarded a ship bound for the United States.

Serial Number	Aircraft	First Mission	Last Mission	Total # Ops Missions	Notes	Fate
44-41464	B-24L-5-CO	1 Mar 45	20 Jun 45	25	*Lady June II*	RFC Kingman, AZ, Oct 1945
43-27983	B-25J	28 Nov 44	30 May 45	62	*Beautiful Ohio*	Abandoned at Palawan

Chapter 8

The China Burma India Theatre (CBI) was the United States military designation during the Second World War for the China and Southeast Asian or India–Burma (IBT) theatres. Operational command of Allied forces (including US forces) in the CBI was murky in the early part of the war, not formally aligning under an allied theatre command, South East Asia Command, until 4 October 1943. Two numbered air forces provided the command structure for USAAF assets in theatre. The Tenth Air Force was established at New Delhi, India, on 12 February 1942 for operations in India, Burma and Indochina. The China Air Task Force was a component of the Tenth Air Force with the mission to defend the aerial supply operation over the Himalayan mountains between India and China and to provide air support for Chinese ground forces. It formed the nucleus for the Fourteenth Air Force,

established on 10 March 1943 to command air operations in China. RAF forces in the theatre originally were under Headquarters Air Force Far East Command but became Air Command, South East Asia (ACSEA) on 30 December 1943. Basing for most US and RAF forces was in eastern India, although the Fourteenth Air Force operated from China.

The basing of B-29s in the CBI was always seen as an interim step before the acquisition of bases in the Marianas. Logistically difficult, the endeavour allowed experience to be gained on the new weapon system and politically showed backing to the Chinese government. The first USAAF staff for the very heavy bomber effort arrived in December 1943 to oversee base construction, a task mainly complete by April 1944. To avoid the risk that B-29s might be wasted by theatre commanders on the battlefields when they would be much more useful against the Japanese home islands, the Joint Chiefs Staff (JCS) agreed in April 1944 to establish the Twentieth Air Force as a non-theatre command controlled directly by the JCS. As the USAAF prepared to assault the Japanese islands with XX Bomber Command (BC) B-29s, staff officers were concerned with the gap in knowledge on Japan's Chinese and Home Island radar nets. Up until this time, what little was known about radars deployed around Japan was based on initial ELINT taken by US Navy submarines off the coast of Japan's islands. Fortuitously, Radio Research Laboratory's (RRL's) AN/APR-4 radar receiver was starting production in early 1944 and offered a capability that could be integrated into the bomber force. Air Staff in the Pentagon directed these receivers be allocated to the building B-29 bomber force that was destined to deploy to the Far East.

When the 58th Bomb Wing deployed with its B-29 bombers to airfields in eastern India near Calcutta in April 1944, the original intent was to have one aircraft in four equipped with countermeasures. These RCM aircraft would be fitted with an AN/APR-4 receiver and an AN/APA-6 pulse analyser operated by a trained RCM Observer, with AN/APA-17 and AN/APA-24 direction finders as well as AN/ARR-5 receivers also available to the wing. Sixteen receiver-equipped B-29s flew on the first mission, a strike against rail yards at Bangkok, Thailand, on 5 June 1944. Each XX BC strike mission usually contained between six and eight radar receiver-equipped aircraft and although the AN/APR-4 provided insight into Japanese radar activity it was not capable of divining the radar's location. To address this problem, a few planes were equipped with AN/APA-24 direction-finding (DF) antennas during the last half of 1944 to start the process of locating the Japanese early-warning net in northern China. The plotting was a laborious process, not helped by the fact that India-based B-29s could only manage three to five strike missions per month due to being on the end of a long logistics chain. The receivers continued in use throughout the 58th Bomb Wing's existence, seeing action over Japan with the initial B-29 strikes later in June.[200]

Two RRL Technical Observers, Dr Joseph Pettit and Donald MacQuivey, had accompanied the wing overseas to work with the RCM equipment. Pettit had recently graduated with a doctorate in electrical engineering from Stanford University and had joined his professor, Dr Terman, at MIT RRL after receiving his diploma in May 1942. He started in the receiver group, working on the SCR-587, AN/APR-1 and AN/APR-4. In January 1944 RRL received a request from Brig. Gen. McClelland for assistance in sending the first B-29 wing into combat. MacQuivey and Pettit joined the 58th Bomb Wing overseas in India as Technical Observers in late April, with Pettit returning to RRL in September 1944.[201]

Due to logistical challenges and low priority in the global war, the China-based Fourteenth Air Force did not field heavy bombers until March 1943, when the 308th Bomb Group was assigned and started flying out of Chengkung, China, with its three subordinate bomb squadrons.[202] As the tempo of the 308th Bomb Group increased, Fourteenth Air Force staff recognised that their knowledge of the IJA air defences in China was lacking and by April 1944, a ferret aircraft was requested from Air Staff. SWPA had priority and was receiving the next two aircraft, Ferrets X and XI, leaving the follow-on pair, XII and XIII, for CBI. When a ferret wasn't immediately forthcoming, the Fourteenth Air Force decided to construct one locally. Lt R.E. Friedman, the RCM officer of the India Burma Sector, cabled back to Washington for drawings and installation data for a B-24 ferret. Dr Pettit and Donald MacQuivey were joined by Captain Robert Perry, the 58th Bomb Wing RCM Officer, in designing the aircraft.[203]

The aircraft chosen to modify into a ferret was SCR-521 radar-equipped B-24D s/n 42-40635. This had arrived in theatre on 19 June 1943, a little over two months after the USAAF had taken delivery from Consolidated. The aircraft was flown up to Bengal Air Depot at Dum Dum Airport, Calcutta, British India, from its base at Ondal on 29 May after minor repairs from high wind damage. MacQuivey and Capt. Perry loaded RCM equipment aboard and flew to other bases to collect additional gear before settling down at Agra Airfield, British India, in June to start conversion work in earnest. Agra Airfield housed the Central India Air Depot, a major Air Technical Service Command Depot, and it had the tooling and equipment necessary for the conversion process. Lt Swanberg of the India Burma Sector was detailed to assist in the work with MacQuivey providing technical direction. Pettit remained at Dum Dum working with the 58th Bomb Wing.[204]

Plywood was used to construct an RCM compartment in the rear bomb bay and RCM equipment on hand with the 58th Bomb Wing was fitted to the aircraft. Flight testing at Agra started in early July but aircraft maintenance issues slowed completion. Rework delayed completion until mid-August. The resulting aircraft was referred to as the 'Interim Ferret' by the Fourteenth Air Force, although its crew dubbed it *Tail Heavy* with appropriate nose

B-24D-80-CO s/n 42-40635 *Tail Heavy* was also referred to as 'Interim Ferret' in official correspondence. The small radome under nose housed the spinning AN/APA-17 direction-finding antenna. The aircraft carried SCR-587, AN/APR-2, AN/APR-4 and AN/AAR-5 receivers and the AN/APA-6 pulse analyser. *B-24 Best Web via Dan Stockton*

art. The aircraft carried SCR-587, AN/APR-2, AN/APR-4 and AN/AAR-5 receivers, AN/APA-6 pulse analysers, and an AN/APA-17 direction-finding antenna with seats for two RCM Observers. After a final test flight in India, '0635 was flown to Kunming, China, on 13 August and formally transferred from the 374th BS to the 375th BS for 'radar intelligence work' on 21 August 1944.[205]

Ferret Production Picks Up

Before the Fourteenth Air Force had even requested a SIGINT aircraft, Air Staff had started refining requirements for the next group of ferrets. Project 90754-S called for the building of two B-24J ferret aircraft for service in the China–Burma–India theatre and also the transition of ferret aircraft from B-24D to B-24J aircraft. The 'J' model, like the earlier 'H' model, was the result of a design effort to improve the defensive firepower of the B-24D aircraft. Consolidated's San Diego plant started producing the 'J' on 31 August 1943, with the Fort Worth plant starting a month later. The two aircraft of Project 90754-S would become Ferrets XII and XIII when their conversion was complete. The designers were able to consolidate the equipment in the RCM compartment, increasing efficiency from the scattered placement in previous aircraft. The forward bomb bay was outfitted with two 450-gallon fuel tanks to extend the range and a manually turned AN/APA-24 was fitted for direction finding.

In late 1943, after completing training at Boca Raton and earning his 7888 MOS, 1Lt Charles Beard was assigned as Project Manager for Ferret XII. He was sent to Wright Field to oversee the conversion of B-24J s/n 44-40815 into a ferret aircraft. Upon completion, Charles and the crew of Ferret XII departed the US on 30 September 1944 for assignment to the Tenth Air Force's 7th Bomb Group at Pandaveswar Airfield, India.[206] The ferret, dubbed *Alec Tronix* by its crew, arrived in theatre in October 1944 and was administratively assigned to the 436th Bomb Squadron as Plane No. 72. Ferret XIII, B-24J s/n 44-40817, also left the US on 30 September but did not arrive at its Fourteenth Air Force Chinese base until 9 November. Ferret '0817 was administratively assigned to the 375th Bombardment Squadron of the 308th BG base at Chengkung, China.[207] Like the XX Bomber Command, the 308th BG was at the end of a long supply line, stretching back to Indian ports via the aerial supply line over the Himalayas, 'the Hump'. By mid-1944 the 308th BG was mainly flying anti-shipping, mining, and unarmed maritime reconnaissance sorties over the South China Sea as well as along major Chinese rivers to attack the Japanese logistics line. Interspersed into this mix were attacks against Japanese airfields to help with the air superiority effort of the Fourteenth Air Force. These wide-ranging missions required knowledge of Japanese radar sites.

The Fourteenth Air Force, though, got a jump on their SIGINT missions. After a test flight at Chengkung on 2 September, Captain Perry was joined by another RCM Operator, Lt Claud Pinson, and with a 375th BS crew of Lt George Uthe as pilot, Lt Stephan Koss, co-pilot, and Lt Theodore Pulich, navigator the Interim Ferret was ready to fight. On 4 September Uthe piloted '0635 on its first mission, a survey of the Luichow Peninsula and Canton. No radar signals were picked up and in frustration Uthe dropped *Tail Heavy* down to low

B-24J-180-CO s/n 44-40815 Ferret XII *Alec Tronix* with RCM Operator Lt Charles Beard and his crew. Beard was assigned as Project Manager for Ferret XII and sent to Wright Field to oversee the conversion of B-24J s/n 44-40815 into a ferret aircraft. Upon completion, Charles and the crew of Ferret XII ferried the aircraft to Pandaveswar Air Field, India. *Charles Beard via Roger Cook*

Claud Pinson, one of the RCM Observers assigned to the 308 BG, stands beside the 'Interim Ferret', B-24D-80-CO s/n 42-40635. Captain Robert Perry, the 58th Bomb Wing RCM Officer, was the second RCM Observer that normally crewed *Tail Heavy*. *B-24 Best Web via Dan Stockton*

altitude and buzzed Canton. The action had the desired effect, the Japanese turning on their radars and Perry and Pinson logging enemy signals.[208] Although '0635 launched from Chengkung, Uthe recovered the B-24D at Liuchow. Mission tasking for the ferret was directed by the local RCM staff but the aircraft were directly responsible to Headquarters Fourteenth Air Force. The data from each mission was originally retained locally, but by mid-October mission reports were being distributed to HQ USAAF in Washington, XX Bomber Command, Air Command SEA, SWPA Section 22, Pacific Ocean Area, and RRL at Cambridge.

The Interim Ferret operated from Liuchow from 4 to 9 September, likely flying three operational missions. After returning to the 375th BS home base at Chengkung, *Tail Heavy* departed for Chabua, returning three days later. The Assam Air Depot at Chabua was technically a depot supply facility, as it did not have a depot-level maintenance or repair capability associated with most air depots. Located in the north-east Indian state of Assam along the Brahmaputra River, the depot supplied aircraft parts and supplies to USAAF units in China, Burma, and the Upper Assam Valley of India and '0635's trip was probably to retrieve parts. *Tail Heavy* returned to Chengkung on 15 September and flew its next mission on the morning of 23 September. Unfortunately, '0623 had been airborne for less than an hour when engine issues caused the crew to abort the mission and return to base. The next day the Interim Ferret flew to Chengtu, flew a night mission, then recovered back at Chengkung. The night mission was to investigate the Yochow and Hankow areas and was flown by the same crew as the first mission. The RCM Observers logged two signals, minimal return on a night mission in poor weather. The next mission for *Tail Heavy* was the night of 30 September–1 October. Uthe piloted the B-24D on a mission to accompany a bombing mission to the Canton area. The RCM Observers also investigated Hong Kong and Liuchow Peninsula, plotting four radars, three of which were new to them, and noting what had been observed by others – the impact of timing a ferret mission with a bombing mission. Two weeks later the Interim Ferret was back out again, targeting the Liuchow Peninsula and Hainan Island and two nights later Liuchow Peninsula, Kiungsha, and Hanoi. Both missions only logged a few radars on the Liuchow Peninsula and nothing at the other locales.[209]

Ten days elapsed before the Interim Ferret flew again. On the night of 27–28 October '0635 was in the air again, headed to the Changteh–Shasi–Hankow area. RCM Observer Captain Perry noted the lack of radars intercepted on the prior missions and speculated that the Japanese only kept one radar active in the Canton area and one in the Hankow region until an apparent bomber raid was in progress when several more radars would come on the air for a few hours before returning to silence. In a change of pace, the Interim Ferret flew a night mission on 30–31 October, accompanying mine-laying aircraft to the Canton–Hong Kong area. Even with all this activity, only three radars were active. The night of 5–6 November was even more boring. *Tail Heavy* flew down along the coast of French Indochina from Haiphong to Tourane (Da Nang) and back with no recorded radar activity. Three nights later the Interim Ferret flew out to the East China Sea, crossing over the Liuchow Peninsula and returning to base by crossing over Hainan Island. Weather caused the mission to be cut short due to lack of a navigation radar but there was not much of a loss as only one signal was logged, already seen on two prior missions. Although stated as carrying an SCR-521 radar when modified, the Interim Ferret's radar was either functioning poorly or it had been removed. As '0635 landed from its mission on the night of 8–9 November, Ferret XIII was winging into Chengkung. With two ferret aircraft and crews on hand, the Fourteenth Air Force had greater flexibility in tasking RCM missions.[210]

Before Ferret XIII arrived, the original plan was to uninstall the RCM equipment from the Interim Ferret and hold it in storage, but there appears to have been a change in plans and the Fourteenth Air Force decided to keep two ferrets in inventory.[211] Ferret XIII flew its first mission the night of 16–17 November. Lt Uthe joined the new crew, as did RCM Observers Pinson and Perry, accompanying Lt Charles Gordon for his first operational mission. A search of the Yochow–Hankow–Changsha area revealed three radars active but also issues with the RCM fit of the ferret. After it flew its first mission, it was decided to rearrange the RCM equipment for greater ease of operation. The AN/APA-24 DF antenna was rebuilt to address vibration causing intermittent shorting, the Adcock antenna removed and a high-frequency (165-275 MHz) horizontal dipole antenna installed in its place. On the night of 22–23 November *Tail Heavy* patrolled the same location as Ferret XIII, although this time a 308th BG bombing attack was occurring. Five radars were

The CBI theatre offered varied terrain, including wide open expanses not encountered in other ferret areas of operation. A B-24 flies over the Yalu River, with the 'Old Yellow River bridge', connecting Chenghsien and Sinsiang for the Phin Han railway, in the distance. The bridge, China's longest river structure, was a vital lifeline link for Japanese lines of communications northward to Manchuria and Korea and typical of infrastructure targets supported by ferrets.
National Museum of the United States Air Force

active during the four hours and thirty minutes the ferret was in the target area. The next mission, flown by the Interim Ferret two nights later during a 308th BG raid, also had more radar activity. Patrolling in the Changsha–Tuagting-lae Shahi area, Perry and Pinson noted that only early-warning radars had been noted in the region with no evidence of gun-laying or searchlight control radars. With modifications complete, Ferret XIII was back out on patrol the night of 26–27 November, investigating Hainan Island. Five signals were recorded and the equipment checked out fine. Ferret activity appeared to taper off, with Ferret XIII undergoing additional maintenance work and Interim Ferret spending close to two weeks at Chabua, Calcutta and other locations in India.[212]

Although the 58th Bomb Wing B-29s continued to fly with their AN/APR-4 receivers, the Japanese air defences did not warrant any radar jammers and the equipment was removed soon after arrival in India. The Fourteenth Air Force saw things differently and in December 1944 started to set up an RCM organisation to oversee electronic warfare in theatre, stockpiling jammers and window for use if required. The ferrets continued to get their tasking from Headquarters, Fourteenth Air Force.[213] The same month, the Joint Chiefs of Staff made the decision that the 58th Bomb Wing's B-29s would be moved to newly captured bases in the Marianas in the central Pacific. The 58th Bomb Wing flew its last operations from India and China on 8 February 1945, leaving the strategic bombing campaign in the CBI theatre to the 308th and 7th Bomb Group B-24s.

The assignment of Ferret XII to the 436th Bomb Squadron, 7th BG, in October 1944 started the aircraft on its ten-month war against Japan that spanned two operational theatres. Ferret XII flew its first patrol mission in late October 1944, but the exact date escapes documentation. For its second mission, *Alec Tronix* flew south along the west coast of Burma on the night of 10–11 November, turning back when it came near Rangoon. Piloted by 2Lts Sheppard and Short, the RCM Observers for the mission were Capt. Jose Nin, Lt Ralph Shinn and Lt Beard. Captain Nin was the RCM Project Officer from Tenth Air Force staff likely accompanying the mission to better understand the capabilities of the new ferret. One radar was detected on a mountain east of Gwa Bay, but the site appeared to shut down when only one aircraft was detected. Another mission was flown on the night of 14–15 November to the same region, followed by a third on 19 November. This daylight sortie saw Ferret XII join eleven B-24s of the 436th BS and RAF Liberators of 356 Squadron for a strike against Burma Railways locomotive repair shops at Mokpalin. Light and heavy flak was experienced but it was inaccurate and Japanese fighters kept their distance from the sixteen escorting P-38s. The nine-and-a-half-hour mission was profitable, logging many intercepts and plotting three radar sites, including the one located north-east of Gwa Bay. RCM Observers Beard and Shinn also searched for Japanese air-ground communications; although not Japanese linguists, they logged frequencies that had activity on them.[214]

Ferret XII's fifth mission was flown on the night of 27–28 November with the task of searching the west coast of Burma up to and including St Matthew's Island. Only one radar was plotted, causing consternation with the RCM Observers and leading Capt. Nin to speculate how the Japanese knew that only one aircraft was airborne. On 1 December Ferret XII accompanied a daytime 7th BG strike to Morgui, Burma. The ferret crew again logged many intercepts due to the aircraft activity and plotted two radar sites including one probable gun-laying radar in the target area. RCM Observers Beard and Shinn once again searched for Japanese air-ground communications, although no activity was noted. On the return leg Ferret XII had to make an emergency landing at Cox's Bazaar due to low fuel. On 21 December Ferret XII accompanied five 436th BS B-24s to attack a supply depot at Taungup, Burma. Two days later a repeat strike on the supply depot was undertaken with six B-24s and *Alec Tronix*. The last mission of the month was flown the night of 29–30 December down the coast of Burma to Rangoon and back. The ferret trailed a night strike of B-24s and was rewarded with activity from two early-warning radars in the Rangoon area. Four additional missions were flown in December,

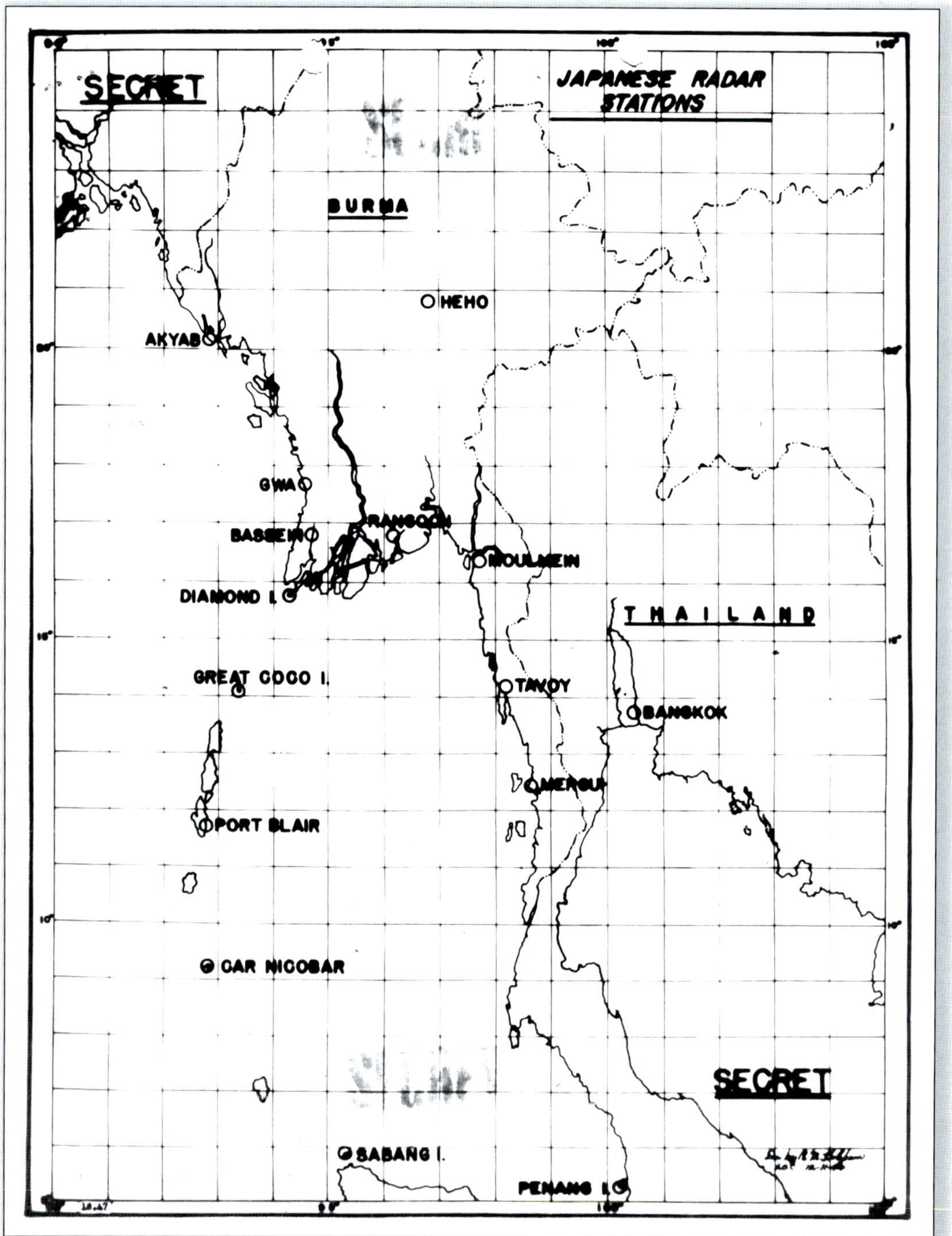

Japanese radar stations of Southeast Asia, *circa* December 1944. Many of Ferret XII's missions were against these radars in support of raids against Japanese transportation infrastructure in the region. *Air Force Historical Research Agency via George Cully*

but no documentation can be found on their targets and dates.[215] Ferret XII's reconnaissance efforts not only aided the Tenth Air Force, they were also of use to the XX Bomber Command when they struck targets in Thailand.

The Fourteenth Air Force ferrets were busy in January 1945, flying eight missions mainly in the Kunming region of China. A curious entry in the unit journal lists Mission 21 as a short two-and-a-half-hour sortie flown on 5 January with the stated purpose of checking on 'Jap comm. channels during the bombing raid on our field'. Mission 26 flown by Ferret XIII on the night of 16–17 January also references tasking to 'obtain information on enemy broadcast and beacon stations' in the Kunming area. This mission, flown with Lt Pinson as an RCM Observer, also carried two enlisted RCM Operators – indications that CBI engaged in training enlisted personnel for this role similar to SWPA. Four additional missions, flown on 8, 11, 12 and 14 January, were also to the Kunming area but documentation as to which aircraft flew or other details is lacking. Ferret XIII flew again on the night of 28–29 January, conducting radar searches in the Shasi, Yochow, Hangkow, and Changsha Areas. A 308th BG B-24 was laying mines in the area at the same time, causing an increase in Japanese radar activity. The last mission of the month was flown on 30 January as a combination sea search and RCM reconnaissance mission near Hainan Island. Three radars were plotted by Lt Gordon and Cpl Swineford.[216]

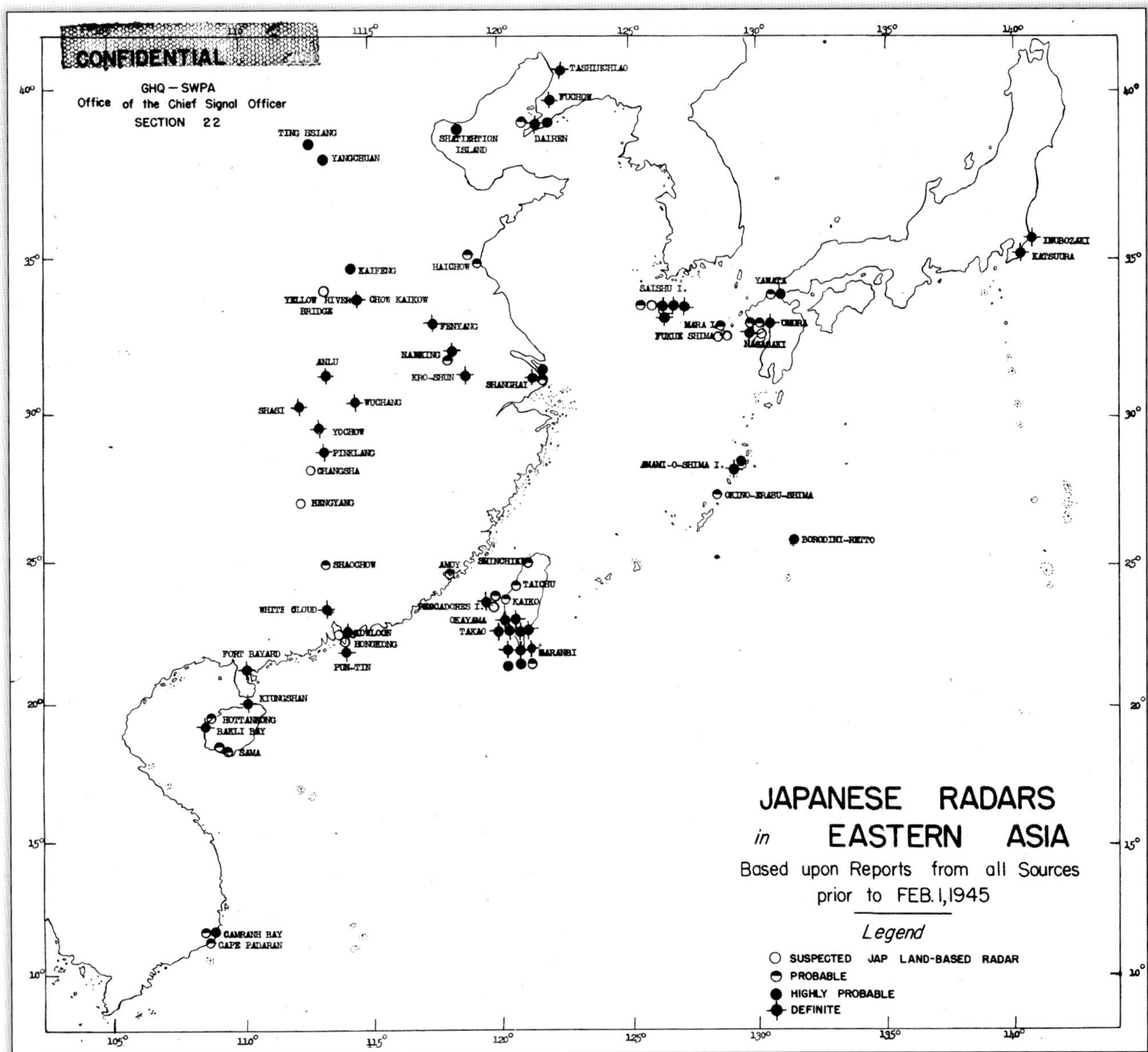

Section 22 map depicting Japanese radars in China *circa* 1 February 1945. Ferret XIII and Interim Ferret flew long-range reconnaissance missions across China and along the South China Sea coast to support Fourteenth Air Force requirements and likely provided much of the intelligence used to construct this map. *Air Force Historical Research Agency via George Cully*

The mission by the Interim Ferret on the night of 2–3 February increased COMINT focus with tasking to 'obtain information on enemy air to ground communication' along the Chinese coast from St John Island to Amoy. Four hours in the target area proved to be lucrative, with four radars plotted and 'several enemy broadcast stations were logged'. Two enlisted RCM Operators joined Lt Gordon along with Lt Wong S. Ching, listed on the mission report as an 'Interpreter'. The Interim Ferret again flew on 6 February, joining three B-24s in a routine radar reconnaissance of the South China Sea around Hainan Island and the Tonkin Gulf. On 12 February 1945 the Interim Ferret and Ferret XIII were transferred from the 375th BS to the 373rd BS and flew to their new base at Luliang, China. The aircraft were accompanied by the aircrew, ground crew and personnel associated with the 'China Ferret Project'.[217] Five missions were flown from Luliang. Evidence is sparse, but it appears that Ferret XIII accompanied at least two anti-shipping patrols along the coast of French Indochina and likely flew two additional missions in February. On the night of 8–9 March, Ferret XIII winged to Hengyang in Hunan province of central China to look for two specific radar signals as well as search the Poyang Lake area. Interim Ferret RCM Observer Lt Claud Pinson joined Lt Stepka and S/Sgt Sauer for a short nine-and-a-half-hour mission that recovered at Kunming. Both target signals were logged along with many others in a relatively active evening for Japanese radars.[218] This one mission was apparently the only one flown in the month of March. Similarly, only one mission was flown in April – and with 375th BS. The Interim Ferret arrived at Hsinching on 1 April for detached service to the 375th BS. On the night of 2–3 April *Tail Heavy* flew a search mission of Hungtze Lake, Shanghai and the Yangtze River, logging seven radars. Weather was not good but the B-24D spent nine hours in the target area. The Interim Ferret departed to fly back to Luliang and the 373rd BS on 7 April.[219] Both ferrets then disappear from documentation for two months. In mid-April, the 374th and 375th Bomb Squadrons were retasked from bombing to fuel transport over the Hump, although the 373rd BS kept up bombing and mining the Yangtze.

Ferret XII flew eight missions in January 1945, all but one accompanying 7th Bomb Group daytime strikes. The solo mission, flown the night of 7–8 January, detected an already plotted radar at Rangoon. The remaining seven were daylight missions spread throughout the month. Targets were up and down the coast of Burma, reaching as far south as Rangoon. These missions ranged from a high of three plotted radars to two missions where no radar activity was noted – a rarity for missions accompanying bombers. Only three missions were flown in February, all accompanying bomber strikes and plotting two to three radars. Of the four missions flown in March, three were flown singly, a change of pace for the crew, all in the Bassein, Gwa, Pagoda Point region of Burma. The one mission flown with a strike package on 29 March was to the same region as well. Seven missions were flown in April, although little documentation exists to provide details on location and activity. On 3 May Commonwealth forces liberated Rangoon, securing Burma and bringing most fighting to a close in Southeast Asia. In mid-May the 7th BG was tasked to start hauling supplies, joining the 308th BG in a rather unglamorous but still dangerous mission.[220] The 436th BS squadron operations orders list no flight activity associated with Ferret XII for the months of May and June.

With no real work for ferrets to do it was determined to transfer the two production ferret aircraft to the Fifth Air Force, which had a growing need for additional ferrets. On 21 June 1945, Ferrets XII and XIII flew from Luliang direct to Clark Field, Philippines, to join the 20th Reconnaissance Squadron.[221] Although the ferrets had departed the CBI theatre, RCM was not over in Southeast Asia. The RAF's Special Flight, 160 Squadron, had been flying ELINT missions from India and Ceylon since January 1944. The flight was equipped with two Liberator Vc aircraft modified for the ferret role and in August 1944 the unit transferred to 159 Squadron, becoming its Special Flight. One Liberator Vc was lost on 10 November, with a replacement Liberator VI arriving in December. By December 1944 RAF's South East Asia Command had five squadrons flying Liberator VI bombers and two squadrons flying Mosquito VI fighter-bombers, supporting British land forces advancing in Burma, attacking airfields and transportation links. During the time with 159 Squadron Special Flight also started to undertake work with COMINT. The second Liberator Vc was lost on 30 January 1945. The flight detached from 159 Squadron in June 1945 and became 1341 Flight. About the same time, six Halifax BIII bombers fitted out for ELINT arrived to augment the unit and flight operations continued until the end of the war.[222]

RAF Ferret Fit

RAF Ferret Fit
S-27 receiver
A.B.R 3 receiver
A.B. 2 receiver
Audio B.F.O.
Cathode ray oscilloscope
No DF system, but used a series of four antennas to derive a crude bearing

The Interim Ferret appears to have been pushed off to the side as the war swept past it. A B-24D with many flight hours had little value to the CBI in June 1945, when new B-24s were available for the taking. Records show it surviving in theatre until October 1945, when it was finally salvaged and stricken from the records on 28 November.

B-24D s/n 42-40635 *Tail Heavy* was a 308th BG bomber modified to ferret configuration at Agra, India, in August 1944. Plywood was used to construct an RCM compartment in the rear bomb bay and RCM equipment on hand with the 58th Bomb Wing was fitted to the aircraft. *Author*

Serial Number	Aircraft	First Mission	Last Mission	Total # Ops Missions	Notes	Fate
42-40635	B-24D-80-CO	Early Sep 44	3 Apr 45	At least 21	Interim Ferret; *Tail Heavy*	Salvaged in theatre
44-40815	B-24J-180-CO	Early Nov 44	24 Apr 45	Likely 35	Ferret XII; *Alec Tronix*	To 20 RS, 21 Jun 45
44-40817	B-24J-180-CO	9 Nov 44	9 Mar 45	At least 10	Ferret XIII; *Rovin' Lady*	To 20 RS, 21 Jun 45

Chapter 9

Overview

Far East Air Forces – created in June 1944 with the Fifth and Thirteenth Air Forces – were focused on supporting the Army drive through New Guinea to the Philippines. This support came in the form of attacks against Japanese supply and transportation forces as well as counter-air attacks against Japanese air assets. By the end of August the Fenton Field-based ferrets had mapped the Banda Sea and Borneo region and were ready to join the fight for the Philippines. The Allied liberation of Owi Island enabled SWPA Ferrets VII and VIII to move northward and rejoin the 63rd Bomb Squadron after being assigned to the 380th BG at Fenton Field, Australia, since April. The ferret B-24s departed Australia in early September 1944, arriving in time to survey Morotai and the Palaus before the Allied landings.[223] As airfields were seized in the southern Philippines in late 1944, the Heavy Bomb Groups assigned to the Fifth Air Force were able to start ranging Japanese transportation and industrial targets in littoral China as well as French Indochina and Formosa. Supporting these efforts were the SWPA ferrets.

63rd BS encampment at Owi island in the Schouten Islands. The Allied liberation of Owi Island enabled SWPA Ferrets VII and VIII to move northward and rejoin the 63rd in September 1944. The tents in the photo include from left to right: radar repair shop, communication repair shop, post office and post exchange.
Air force Historical Research Agency via George Cully

Ferret Operations

As per established practice, the 63rd BS furnished the regular flying crew for the ferret and Section 22 provided the two RCM Observers (or RCM Operators in the case of enlisted crew members) and an additional navigator per ferret. The ferrets first mission flown from Owi surveyed Morotai, Talaud, Davao Gulf, and Palau on 6 September 1944. No Japanese signals were detected, a good sign for planned landings on Peleliu and Morotai on 15 September. A mission scheduled for 10 September only got as far as Noemfoor Island before engine #3 started leaking oil and the crew returned to base. A mission flown the next day headed out west, again observing Morotai Island and northern Celebes before looping back via the Ceram Sea. Again, no signals were detected nor any shipping activity observed.[224]

On the night of 13–14 September Ferret VII, under the command of Lt Hackler, carried out a western sweep past Halmahera but winged across the Celebes Sea up to Moro Gulf off the island of Mindanao – the first time the ferrets had surveyed the Philippines. Only two signals were observed, a rather disappointing return for RCM Observers Lts Witry and Stern and SSgt Duke on this fifteen-and-a-half-hour long mission. The following day, Lt Wilson took Ferret VII out to accompany a 64th Bomb Squadron strike on the Japanese airfield at Kaoe. Kaoe had been struck five times previously over the past month in a Far East Air Forces (FEAF)

effort to gain air supremacy in the region. Six Japanese radars and numerous Allied radars were detected on a short seven-and-a-half-hour mission in excellent weather.[225] On 24 September a flight flew out west to Borneo via Halmahera; that evening, a flight scheduled to survey the Philippines had to return after two hours due to mechanical problems. Two nights later Ferret VII was launched in the late afternoon for a mission to encircle the island of Mindanao. Only three signals were heard on the entire mission, little accomplishment for a gruelling fourteen-and-a-half-hour flight. The following evening, Ferret VII took off at 1800 in the evening on 27 September for another search mission around Mindanao, only detecting one signal on the southern tip of the island. Both the fluxgate compass as well as the SCR-717 failed, as they had the prior evening. Taking off about the same time as Ferret VII was Ferret VIII under the control of Lt Griffiths. Scheduled to verify blind spots in the radar coverage of Balikpapan's defences of Borneo for a bombing mission scheduled in three days, it had to turn back two and a half hours into the flight due to the failure of the liaison transmitter (HF radio). Ferrets VII and VIII were starting to tire, with VHF radios failing twice on mission over the prior two weeks, along with an engine failure and automatic pilot; replacement aircraft were needed desperately. The final ferret mission for September was flown the evening of 28–29 September. Ferret VIII conducted a radar search through the central Philippines via Talaud Island, Zamboanga, Negros, Panay, Leyte and return. RCM Observers Lts Witry and Zwoianek and SSgt Duke detected six signals while their ferret dodged weather fronts, helping start the mapping of the Philippines for future air operations.[226]

Activity in October continued the trend, with missions into the Philippines flown the first three days of the month, although the sortie on 2 October had to return early due to the search radar malfunctioning. A further ten missions were flown

Right side view of B-24D-20-CF s/n 42-63991 Ferret VII, *The Duchess of Paducah*, which carried nose art on both the starboard and port side of the nose. The aircraft was a survivor, enduring at least forty-nine and possibly over seventy combat missions before being replaced in February 1945. *Robert Livingstone*

to the Philippines during the remainder of the month, surveilling Mindanao, Leyte Gulf and the central Philippines, with another mission returning early due to a radar failure. On 20 October the Sixth US Army landed on assigned beaches on Leyte to start the liberation of the Philippines. Section 22 used the ferret sorties from October to update their Japanese Radar Coverage Map for the Philippines, issuing a new version on 5 November. November saw the ferrets fly another ten missions to the Philippines, ranging up through Luzon to cover the Manila region as well as the rest of the island. For northern missions, the ferrets would sometimes make a fuel stop at Morotai to extend the range of their B-24s. The Allies had landed on Morotai Island on 15 September and two major airfields were ready for use in October, all part of the island hopping and amphibious envelopment scheme in use in SWPA and the Central Pacific. The tired ferrets held up well for the month, only returning early once due to weather but no major mechanical discrepancies noted. Each had over a thousand hours and several engine changes to its credit. Long missions through the SWPA weather (the average mission was about fifteen hours, with several over eighteen) aged the planes noticeably.[227]

At the beginning of December 1944, the 63rd Bomb Squadron began to operate from Angaur Island in Palau, staging through the recently opened Tacloban airstrip on Leyte to attack Japanese airfields and shipping. The 63rd BS was scattered throughout the region with operations still continuing from Owi Island and Morotai. Living under canvas on the edge of swamps in the rainy season was a challenge for the crews as well as the assigned maintenance personnel. This dispersal suited the ferret detachment as they flew missions throughout the Philippine archipelago, with four missions flown in December

Two 43rd BG B-24 bombers attack Boram airstrip at Wewak, New Guinea. Fifth Air Force carried out numerous strikes against airfields and installations in New Guinea, the Bismarck Archipelago, Celebes, Halmahera, Yap, Palau, and the southern Philippines – all requiring ferret support to map out Japanese radar coverage. *National Museum of the United States Air Force*

targeting Luzon as well as Cebu and Negros in the central Philippines.[228] On a strike against Clark Field outside Manila at the end of December 1944 a Japanese gun-laying radar was detected by an 'ad hoc' ferret. Section 22-controlled ferret aircraft were sent on subsequent raids to the area, confirming fire control radars at this location as well as on the island of Formosa.[229] Ferret VIII was involved in a landing accident at Angaur Island, Palau, and subsequently scrapped on 29 December 1944.[230]

The 'ad hoc' ferret that detected the gun-laying radar at Clark Field was part of a growing fleet of these aircraft in the Fifth Air Force. By mid-1944 Section 22 had accumulated a large number of AN/APR-1 receivers and AN/APA-6 pulse analysers and started to create a force of 'ad hoc' ferrets for the V Bomber Command. Six 'updated' aircraft were delivered to the 380th Bomb Group (H) to augment and replace their earlier 'ad hoc' ferret force and an initial delivery of aircraft was made to the 90th Bomb Group (H), enabling both groups to fly at least one 'ad hoc' ferret equipped with a receiver and pulse analyser on each strike. By January 1945 all four Heavy Bomb Groups in the Fifth Air Force were operating 'ad hoc' ferrets.[231]

Two missions were flown from Angaur, a mission on the night of 30–31 December and one on the night of 4–5 January. The second mission routed through Tacloban on the outbound leg to fuel up. Tacloban was also used for a fuel stop on an Owi-based mission on the evening of 7 January before Ferret VII recovered there after a mission on the night of 15–16 January and remained on Leyte for the next two months. There were few signals active during this time period, the mission flown the night of 30–31 December only detecting one radar. Possibly due to this light activity, Ferret VII was modified to provide passive and active RCM; a mission flown by it on the evening of 4–5 January carried an AN/APT-1, which happened to be inoperative that night, and also dispensed rope in the Legaspi area of south-east Luzon as per a plan developed by Section 22 to jam a radar in this location. The mission flown the night of 7–8 January focused on Lingayen Gulf, gathering data on Japanese radars in front of the 9 January landing of US forces. Bombers of the 63rd BS were also in the vicinity, bombing Fort Stotsenburg and Clark Field. The ferret was looking to confirm a Japanese gun-laying radar in the vicinity of Manila.[232] During this time period, the Fifth Air Force's priority for RCM ranked neutralising fire control radars first, jamming GCI radars second, and evading early-warning radars to achieve surprise as third. With no GCI radars in theatre, the ferrets chased gun-laying radars and mapped out radar coverage to help medium and light bombers achieve surprise on raids and diminish the possibility of intercept by Japanese fighters.[233]

43rd Bomb Group B-24J-160-CO s/n 44-40395 *Bob's Hope*, one of the 'Raven' RCM aircraft assigned to the 43rd BG. V Bomber Command transitioned from supporting soldiers in the Philippines to hitting Japanese targets in Formosa and littoral China in March 1945 and, with an influx of additional jammers, the 380th and 43rd Heavy Bomb Groups started to field 'Raven' aircraft to escort their attacks. *National Museum of the United States Air Force*

90th BG B-24J-205-CO s/n 44-41332 *Lovely Louise* was one of the group's 'Raven' RCM aircraft. On 19 January 1945, Headquarters Fifth Air Force published a comprehensive RCM programme to equip all heavy bomber formations with jamming capability against fire control radars. The plan was to start with the 90th and 22nd Heavy Bomb Groups, scheduled to strike targets in Formosa and China while the 43rd and 380th Heavy Bomb Groups were busy supporting US troops in the Philippines. *Peter Johnston*

As airfields were seized in the southern Philippines in late 1944, the Heavy Bomb Groups assigned to the Fifth Air Force were able to start ranging Japanese transportation and industrial targets in littoral China as well as French Indochina and Formosa. After the US Army secured the beachhead on Luzon, the Fifth Air Force directed the 90th and 22nd Bomb Groups to strike targets in Formosa and China, while the 43rd and 380th Bomb Groups were assigned to support US troops in the Philippines. On the night of 15–16 January,

Ferrets first started investigating the Philippines in mid-September 1944. By the time the Sixth US Army landed on Leyte on 20 October Section 22 had a decent understanding of Japanese radars in the area, with comprehensive coverage available by the end of 1944. Section 22 analysts sifted through ferret reports to produce radar coverage charts to aid in planning by bomber crews. *Air Force Historical Research Agency via George Cully*

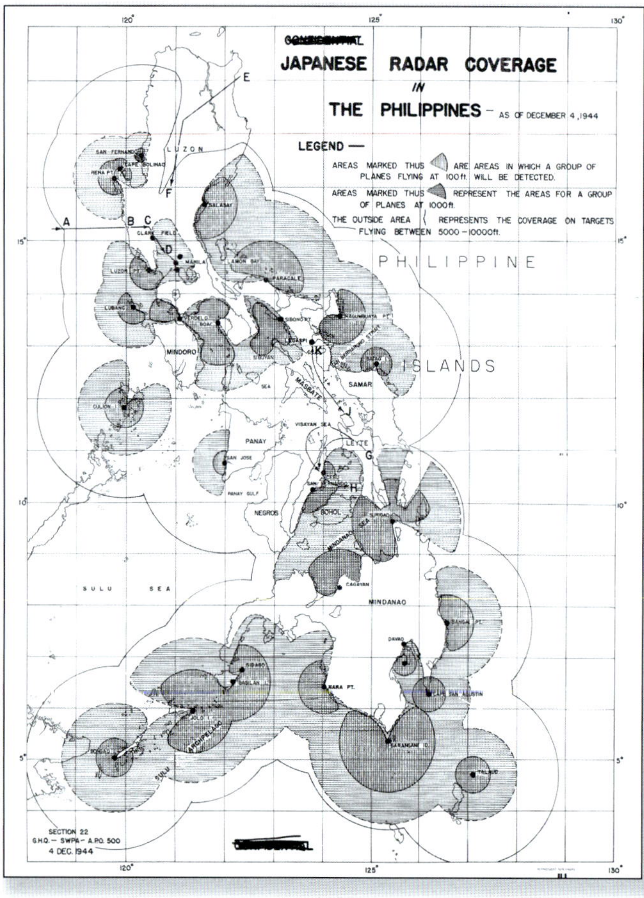

As the ferrets started to fly out of Owi Island in September 1944, many of their missions focused on surveying Japanese radars in the Philippines. This Section 22 map of radars of this region dates to December 1944, showing the result of many months of ferret work. *Air Force Historical Research Agency via George Cully*

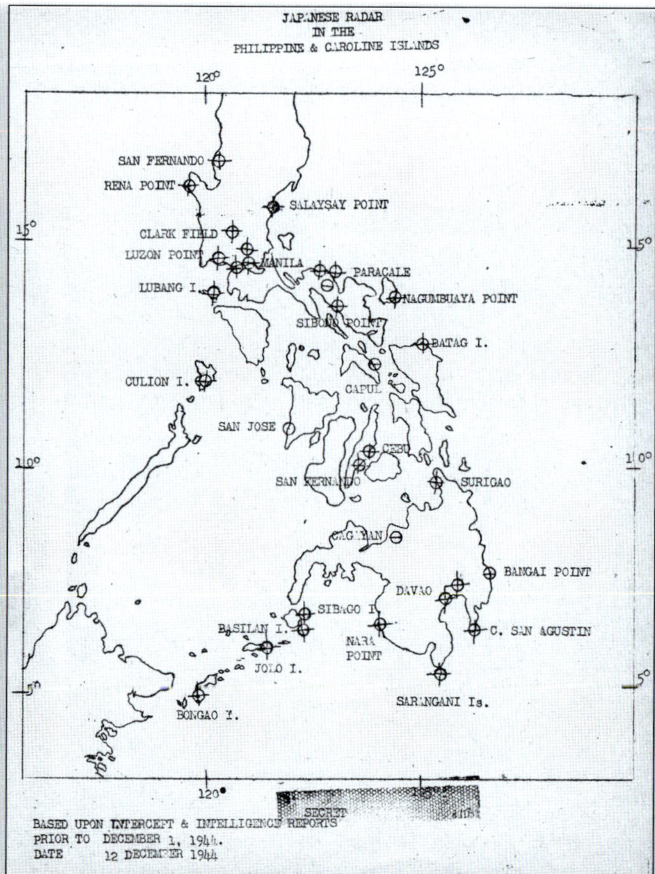

Ferret VII accompanied two 63rd BS bombers to spend the evening harassing Heito and Okayama airfields on Formosa. En route from Owi Island, the ferret confirmed the location of radars plotted by the 'ad hoc' ferrets and cemented the need for a dedicated ferret for the Thirteenth Air Force. After taking on fuel at Tacloban, Ferret VII flew north to Formosa. What appeared to be radar-directed searchlights had been noted by 63rd BS crews on prior nights, so Lts Godwin and Stern, the RCM Observers aboard the ferret, worked to find the Japanese radars. Working with a poorly functioning direction-finding system, the airmen noted two radars active on Formosa but both were early-warning types. On the evening of 18–19 January Ferret VII flew another mission against the northern Philippines and Formosa, the last of the month for the detachment.[234] Shortly after the first of the year, Lts Witry, Morris and Godwin completed their tours and returned to the US. Lt Stern elected to stay in theatre and was assigned to work on the Fifth Air Force B-25 'radar buster' aircraft programme.[235]

A requirement for two 'radar investigational search' aircraft for service with the Fifth Air Force in the Southwest Pacific Area was passed on to Material Command from Lt Col George Hale on Air Staff in late March 1944. Hale, the Communications Equipment Officer who worked for the Assistant Chief of Air Staff, Materiel, Maintenance and Distribution, oversaw requirements for Ferrets VII through XI, deftly overseeing DC bureaucracy from mid-1943 until mid-1944. In spring 1944 the 1st Proving Ground Electronics Unit at Eglin was just completing work on Ferret IX, an aircraft built against requirements for the South Pacific Theatre, but there is no evidence that this aircraft ever made it overseas and it disappeared from the scene by mid-1944. The aircraft did, however, act as a bridge between the earlier ferrets and the next group of aircraft as it carried updated avionics purpose-built for the SIGINT mission as opposed to the modified commercial receivers found in earlier ferret construction.[236] For the new SWPA ferrets, Air Staff recommended Material Command incorporate ideas from a report from Clark Cahill, a civilian RRL technical representative who had worked with Ferrets VII and VIII in theatre. Air Staff also recommended Material Command consult with Air Service Command in Eglin on lessons learned from the construction of prior ferrets such as Ferret IX.[237] These two new aircraft, designated Ferrets X and XI, arrived in Ohio in mid-July 1944 from a pool of B-24J aircraft that had already passed through a modification centre to receive changes for the Pacific theatre.

These aircraft, designated Project 96508R, used some of the existing engineering work from the prior two ferret aircraft. The engineers in Ohio were able to consolidate the ELINT equipment into the rear bomb bay, increasing the efficiency from the scattered placement in previous aircraft. The forward bomb bay was outfitted with two 450-gallon fuel tanks to extend the range.[238] As Ferrets XII and XIII were tested at Eglin Field, results from their trials were fed back into the Project 96508R production line. Following production, Ferrets X and XI departed for Florida, arriving at Eglin Field in late October 1944. While in Florida, Ferret XI was redesignated Ferret VI and its assignment changed from Section 22 to the newly forming XXI Bomber Command, then just arriving at Guam. A new Ferret XI was put into the mix but would be delayed by higher-priority work at Fairfield. Based on evolving requirements from Air Staff based on theatre feedback, its original equipment fit changed considerably in the six months that it bounced between Eglin and Patterson Fields.[239]

Like the two ferrets before them, Ferrets VI and X were not well received by the test engineers at Eglin Field. Wiring was 'mashed', antenna motor shafts sheared, antenna leads mismarked, and 'numerous small items' requiring attention pointed to the inexperience of the Ohio production line with building ferret aircraft. These discrepancies precipitated a letter from Colonel Doubleday on Air Staff that requested Wright Field investigate the matter and report back to Washington with the results.[240] In late January 1945, Ferret X finally left Eglin Field for overseas and checked in with Section 22 in mid-February 1945. Ferret X arrived almost a year after the requirement was identified, a victim of design work, delayed testing and rework performed at Eglin. The new Ferret XI followed two months later. As Ferret XI started production, another aircraft arrived in Ohio for conversion to the ferret mission. Dubbed 'Ferret 0', the aircraft was to be assigned to Eglin Field for testing. A test bed aircraft would allow engineers to wring out new equipment before it was fitted to a ferret aircraft on the production line and hopefully catch errors before the aircraft were deployed overseas.

Ferret VII's penultimate operational flight was a daylight search mission flown on 8 February. The B-24 flew east from Tacloban and circumscribed a rhomboid around the Sulu Sea, flying down to Borneo, then north-east along Palawan. Ten weak signals were detected, most if not all US radars. Its last mission was on the night of 25–26 February 1945. The navigators plotted a course north-west from Tacloban and out over the South China Sea to the coast of China. Ferret VII reconnoitred littoral China until close to Formosa, then flew south-east until off Luzon, which it paralleled until cutting past Manila Bay and back home. Six signals were received on the fifteen-hour sortie, most early-warning radars sweeping the waters off Formosa. After recovering there was likely no ceremony and the aircraft, a veteran of over fifty reconnaissance sorties, was likely rolled into the weeds at the edge of the airfield. It was listed as salvaged on 31 May and stricken from the records on 1 August 1945. The retirement of this veteran B-24 was due to the arrival of its replacements. Ferret X arrived at Tacloban in early February and flew its first mission against Formosa via northern Luzon on 15 February,

B-24D-20-CF s/n 42-63991 Ferret VII *The Duchess of Paducah* apparently getting new nose art painted on in between missions. Its last mission was on the night of 25–26 February 1945, during which it reconnoitred littoral China. After recovering at Tacloban, Leyte, it was likely rolled into the weeds at the edge of the airfield and abandoned. *Robert Livingstone*

looping the Japanese-occupied island to completely catalogue their radars. The next evening it was out again, flying a similar mission profile to confirm radars received from the prior sortie. Seventeen radars were noted, the majority on Formosa, along with eight on the west coast of Luzon assessed to be American. Ferret X's third mission was a general search mission against China.[241]

Since mid-March the 63rd BS and the attached ferrets had been flying from Clark Field in the Philippines. Ferret X flew six missions in March, concentrating on Formosa and the Chinese coast from Indochina north to Hong Kong. An average of four to five signals were intercepted, little return for missions that could last up to eighteen hours. It was more of the same in April, with Ferret X flying five missions and the newly arrived Ferret XI taking over starting on 20 April and flying another four missions that month. On Ferret XI's first operational mission, flown the night of 20–21 April, the 100 MHz stub antenna on the right side of the aircraft was open-circuited; the next mission, flown the night of 22–23 April, the DF antenna was not functioning properly.

Field Unit 1, Section 22, operated the ferret aircraft attached to the 63rd BS, 43rd BG. Eight of the unit are posed in front of a wrecked Japanese aircraft. Front, left to right: Glenn Deakins, Technical Observer; Maj. Carson, Officer in Charge; Lt Brown, RCM Observer, Cpl Krutz, RCM Operator. Standing, left to right: Lt Blatz, RCM Observer; Lt Cowan, Navigator; Cpl Anderson, RCM Operator; Sgt De Weese, Office Supervisor. *Air Force Historical Research Agency via George Cully*

Lt Brown, Field Unit 1 RCM Observer assigned to Ferret X, posing in his 'office' in between missions, around March–April 1945. The equipment identified is as follows: Top row: AN/APA-6, AN/APA-11 signal analysers; Bottom row: AN/APR-5, AN/ARR-5, AN/APR-4 receivers. *Air Force Historical Research Agency via George Cully*

Left to right: Capt. Lefoldt, Navigator; Glenn Deakins, Technical Observer; Lt Miller, Navigator; of Field Unit 1 pose next to a 63rd BS sign. The 63rd BS furnished the regular flying crew for the ferret and Section 22 provided two RCM Observers (or RCM Operators in the case of enlisted crew members) and an additional navigator per ferret. *Air Force Historical Research Agency via George Cully*

Lieutenant Blatz, Field Unit 1 RCM Observer assigned to Ferret X, poses for the 43rd BG Photo Section. Some of the equipment is missing cables for this obviously staged shot.
Air Force Historical Research Agency via George Cully

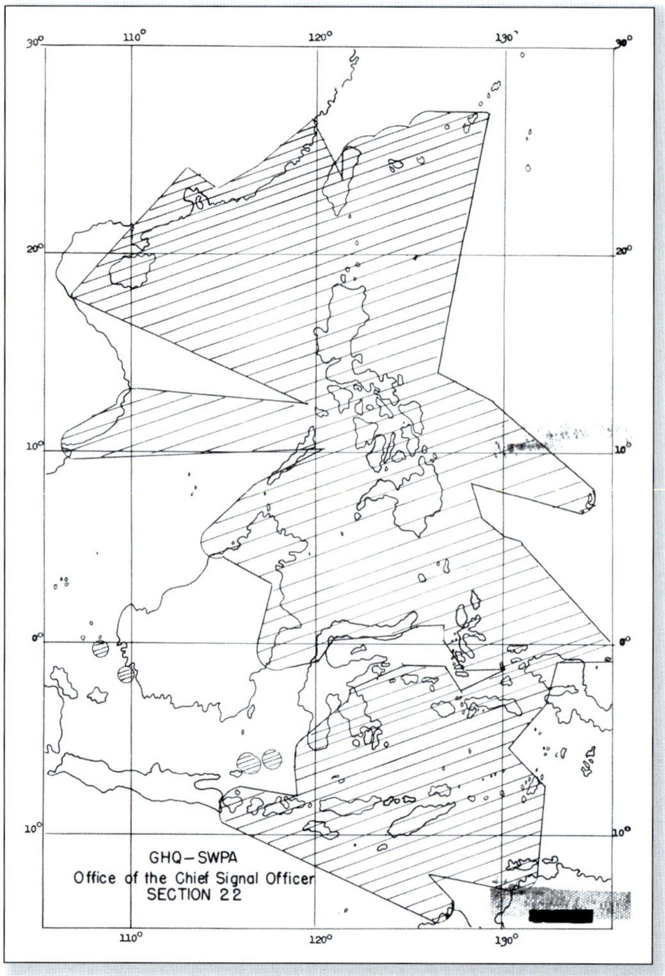

By 1945, ferrets were part of a greater network of platforms collecting intelligence on Japanese radars. Ferrets, ad hoc ferrets and submarines were tasked by Section 22 to provide comprehensive collection coverage over the Philippines, littoral China, Formosa, and the East Indies.
Air Force Historical Research Agency via George Cully

The third mission was fine, but both AN/APA-11s failed on the fourth mission. It appears that Ferret XI may have had some issues from Wright Field that were not caught by the Eglin engineers. Some of the new RCM Observers appeared to copy down every beep and squeak they saw as their missions, noting thirty or so signals, while others averaged ten.[242] Either way, the coast of China and Formosa did provide a more lucrative hunting ground than the Philippines. Joining the ferrets in radar reconnaissance of Southeast Asia were the radar receiver-equipped patrol planes of the Navy. After supporting the invasions of Mindoro and Luzon, the Navy VPB squadrons were ranging between Formosa and Indochina along the western edge of the China Sea, chasing shipping and logging radar signals. One of the signals noted by the ferrets in April was a signal operating in the 10cm/3000 MHz range. Although many US Navy radars operated in this frequency range, it was new for the Japanese and caused concern in the theatre.

To China and Beyond

Up through 1944, the SWPA RCM programme concentrated on the 'passive' side of the house – mapping Japanese radar locations and being on the alert for new signal types. This all changed at the end of the year. Save one or two instances in North Borneo, the only Japanese radars encountered had been those associated with early-warning radars that gave rough range and azimuth to the Japanese to provide warning of an impending raid but not accurate enough to direct searchlights or anti-aircraft fire at night or bad weather. The confirmation of the Clark Field gun-laying radar as well as the spotting of similar radars on Formosa

changed all of this.[243] On 19 January 1945, Headquarters Fifth Air Force published a comprehensive RCM programme that directed the equipping of all heavy bomber formations with jamming capability against fire control radars along with fitting out a smaller number with receivers, pulse analysers and DF antennas.[244] This change would flood the theatre with SIGINT capability, assisting the ferrets and helping reduce the uncertainty in their mission. They could now concentrate on confirming specific signals and mapping radar coverage as opposed to flying into an area with no idea of what radars may exist.

A more active approach was also taken to suppress Japanese radars, apparently with little success. In February 1945 two B-25 'radar buster' aircraft were set up by Fifth Air Force A-3 RCM Advisor Capt. Vic Tatelman to neutralise Japanese radars and make gaps in early-warning radar coverage.[245] The aircraft, assigned to the 345th Bomb Group (M), were fitted out with radar receivers to help the crew locate Japanese radars with the intent of bombing and strafing positions after visually identifying their exact location. Apparently not much progress was made, because in late May the Air Communications officer of Fifth Air Force noted that while the Thirteenth Air Force had 'piled up an impressive score' against Japanese radars, their B-25 'radar busters' had done very little.[246]

Organisational Changes

The transition of airborne radar countermeasures activities from Section 22 to FEAF was gradual. Although the Fifth Air Force had been operating an airborne RCM programme since January 1945, RCM activities were still operationally managed by Section 22 at the joint headquarters in the theatre (SWPA). Initial change of command started in March with Section 22 authorising the Fifth Air Force to task subordinate heavy bomb groups with providing operational summaries of RCM activity as well as weekly inventories of RCM equipment. On 6 May GHQ SWPA transferred administrative and operational control of Air Force radar reconnaissance and radar countermeasures activities to FEAF.[247]

The transformation of SWPA RCM efforts involved not only equipment and procedures, but also personnel. Previously, the Field Units had been 'combined' organisations made up of US, Australian and New Zealand personnel; with their incorporation into the FEAF heavy bomb group structure, they became solely American in nature. The ranking American in the Field Unit became the Group RCM

On 6 May 1945 GHQ SWPA transferred administrative and operational control of Air Force radar reconnaissance and radar countermeasures activities to FEAF. The end result was the ranking American in the Field Unit became the Group RCM Officer and Allied troops departed for Section 22's rear echelon for follow-on assignment. Here RAAF personnel previously assigned to Field Unit 6 attached to the 380th BG pose before departing. Providing the backdrop is 380th BG B-24D s/n 42-72953 *Jezebelle*, a bomber with no RCM affiliation. Identified as: Back row, left to right: W/O Ratcliffe, Flt Sgt Ford, F/O Pike, F/O Agnew, Flt Sgt Pattison; Bottom Row, W/O Carrold, Sgt Butler, Flt Sgt Aberdeen, W/O Nosworthy, F/O Carmen. *Air Force Historical Research Agency via George Cully*

Officer and Allied troops departed for Section 22's Rear Echelon for follow-on assignment. The RCM personnel remained a group-level asset, pooled for assignment at the squadron level. The primary function of the Group RCM Officer was to coordinate RCM support with the Group S-3, work with the Group S-2 on Japanese radar deployment and employment, evaluate all RCM reporting, and oversee the supply of RCM equipment.[248]

Ferret Alignment

In April FEAF requested the War Department provide a RCM flight of four operational and two reserve ferret aircraft.[249] With the transfer of Section 22 assets on 1 May, the Fifth Air Force gained operational control of the two in-theatre ferret aircraft, Ferrets X and XI. The ferrets were placed under the operational control of V Bomber Command with guidance to search areas of operational interest to the Fifth Air Force. An additional 'Ferret Flight' of four operational and two reserve aircraft was promised to arrive in June and July, with the force of six aircraft split between V and XIII Bomber Command operational control.[250] This 'Ferret Flight' was part of a reorganisation of theatre long-range reconnaissance assets. On 10 May 1945 the 20th Combat Mapping Squadron was reorganised as the 20th Reconnaissance Squadron, Long Range, Photo-RCM. The only real change this brought was the formal attachment of an 'RCM rcn Flight' to the existing F-7-equipped squadron. All personnel for the squadron were to be sourced from within SWPA with the exception of this flight, personnel for which would be furnished without requisition. Further orders within FEAF stated the RCM flight would arrive in theatre from the United States 'completely manned'.[251]

Alignment notwithstanding, the SWPA ferrets continued to fly missions under the administrative control of the 63rd BS. In May nine missions were flown, the majority by Ferret XI. Night missions continued to be the norm, monitoring the Chinese coast from Shanghai down to Hainan Island and Formosa, with a mission the night of 11–12 May flying in the Gulf of Tonkin to monitor Indochina. On the afternoon of 15 May Lt Williams lifted Ferret X off Clark Field's runway for what would be an almost twenty-hour sortie. Flying north with RCM Observers Lt McKirnan and Sgt Moskowitz, the B-24 droned across the East China Sea, passing to the east of Formosa and making landfall near Shanghai. Following the Yangtze River, the ferret flew west to Nanking, turned south, then flew east to Hangzhou before turning north past the Yangtze, then east to the sea. Passing to the west of Formosa, Lt Williams had to recover at Lingayen as the B-24 was low on fuel. After gassing up, Williams flew the remaining forty minutes to Clark and finally landed in the afternoon of 16 May. Twenty-two signals were recorded on this iron-man mission. The next mission was a complete contrast. Tasked with looking for Japanese air intercept radars on Formosa, the ten-hour mission to Taihoku Prefecture in north-east Formosa logged no signals. Fighting rain, thunderheads, undercast and overcast the night of 18–19 May with malfunctioning radar and RCM gear, Lt Williams and his crew were likely just happy to return Ferret XI to Clark Field in one piece. Lt Dolley took Ferret XI back to Taihoku on the night of 23–24 May to take another swing at the air intercept radars. Logging fourteen hours, Ferret XI had only clear to mild undercast weather to contend with. The RCM Observer crew of Lt McKirnan and Sgt Moskowitz tracked eighteen signals and noted many additional early-warning radars in the 100 MHz range active. Intense but inaccurate AAA fire was noted as the ferret droned for three and a half hours over Taihoku, at times taking evasive action to avoid barrages. Multiple AI signals in the 500 MHz range were captured and one night fighter was spotted lurking near the ferret by one of the flight crew. Two nights later Lt Croft was back over Taihoku in Ferret XI. No AI signals were noted, although early-warning radars were very active, as were searchlights. Once again, the aircraft's SCR-717 radar was inoperative for most of the flight.[252]

Sometime during their assignment to the 63rd BS, likely in early 1945, Ferrets X and XI had their belly turrets removed and the AN/APA-17 spinning DF antenna moved from its forward position to this location, appreciably increasing its sensitivity while reducing cable length. The SCR-717 was also being used as a receiver for 10cm signals, using the AN/APA-17 presentation equipment to display the signal to the RCM Observer. Updates on design modifications such as this was provided to Air Staff in Washington to aid in future ferret development.[253]

June was the last month that the SWPA ferrets were attached to the 63rd BS. Eight missions were flown, half of which focused on Nanking. Lt Booth set out on 2 June with Ferret X to investigate Nanking but had to return early when the navigation radar failed. Two nights later he took off but once again a failing navigation radar forced mission cancellation. On 15 June the unflappable lieutenant sallied forth for a third time and reached Nanking but had to return early due to a low fuel state. A mission flown the night of 19–20 June finally accomplished all objectives. An additional mission to the Shanghai–Nanking region was flown the night of 27–28 June after two coastal survey missions along littoral China. The last ferret missions flown with the 63rd BS proved to be interesting. The 63rd BS crews had been encountering night fighters in the Formosa Straits and Ferret XI had come across one earlier over Formosa, so the Japanese were lurking about during the night missions. Lt Brim flew Ferret XI on a survey mission in the Hong Kong/Canton region. The weather started to close in and when confronted with violent thunderstorms Brim cut the mission short and started to head back to Clark Field. Off the coast of China near the mouth of the Canton River an unidentified aircraft flew parallel to the ferret for ten minutes. Then it closed from three o'clock high and slid 150 yards under the ferret. The fighter did not fire, nor did the ferret's gunners. Both aircraft then went about their business.[254] At the end of the month the ferret crews and assigned maintenance personnel hopped into some trucks and drove down the flight line to join the 20th RS.

New Ownership

In March 1945 Project 98264-S was identified as a 'POA final recipient' with a requirement for six aircraft – which aligns to the 'Ferret Flight' of four operational and two reserve aircraft. Over the next month there was confusion between Washington and Wright Field over whether these would be C-1 COMINT aircraft or standard 'radar ferret' aircraft. This was eventually resolved, but the requirement disappears by late May. A new requirement, Project 97078-R for two aircraft, then appears with no listed recipient. In mid-May, FEAF still believed they were getting six new ferrets. By mid-June FEAF directed the Fifth Air Force to move Ferrets X and XI from the 63rd Bomb Squadron to the 20th RS. In addition, they were to be joined by Ferrets XII and XIII coming from the Tenth and Fourteenth Air Forces in June.[255] Before the China–Burma–India theatre ferrets arrived in the SWPA, a concept was floated to convert them to 'jamming ships' with high-power AN/APT-4 jammers and other jammers with amplifiers. The aircraft would accompany strikes to heavily defended areas to jam gun-laying radars, fly diversionary raids away from the main effort while jamming to aid the bomb groups, or jam early-warning radars to mask ingressing bombers.[256] Nothing ever came of the concept and the aircraft were put into use as standard ferret aircraft after their arrival at Clark. On 21 June 1945, Ferrets XII and XIII flew from Luliang direct to Clark Field, Philippines, to join the 20th RS.[257]

The Fifth Air Force directed that its newly

assigned ferret force provide weekly reports to the heavy bomb groups with emphasis on new radar locations and searching for new fire control, searchlight or air intercept radars. Bi-monthly radar coverage plots were also required to aid in planning of both medium and heavy bomb group strike missions.[258] The Fifth Air Force tasking for the ferrets mainly came from V Bomber Command requests, with the initial requirements at the end of June focusing on reconnaissance north of Luzon and east of Formosa; the Hong Kong area; and the region between Okinawa and Kyushu.[259]

As US forces continued their drive northward, liberating islands from occupying Japanese forces, while a well-oiled intelligence apparatus followed closely behind inspecting captured equipment and documents. This intelligence data was processed quickly and, among many uses, fed back into the RCM programme. As an example, documentation captured in June 1945 revealed a Japanese low-frequency maritime radar operating at 27.5 MHz. This frequency was at the lower limit of the existing AN/ARR-5 receiver and Headquarters V Bomber Command recommended acquiring more AN/ARR-7 lower-frequency receivers as the only one in theatre was flying on Ferret XI.[260]

The War for Japan

The invasion of Japan was planned as two separate operations – Operation OLYMPIC, scheduled for 1 November 1945, centred on southern Kyushu island and Operation CORONET, planned for 1 March 1946, focused on the island of Honshu. Although CORONET would require forces redeployed from Europe, MacArthur planned on undertaking OLYMPIC with assets already in theatre. Air assets assigned to support OLYMPIC were tasked to isolate and attrite the defending Japanese forces. The United States Strategic Air Forces in the Pacific (USASTAF) would continue to pound away at what remained of Japanese industrial resources, disrupting whatever production remained on the islands and continuing to degrade the morale of the populace. Carrier air forces would attack any remaining air and naval forces, interrupt land and maritime communications, and hit strategic targets in concert with USASTAF bomb groups. FEAF assets based in the Ryukyus would neutralise Japanese air power on the Home Islands as well as China,

On 17 May 1945 the RCM Officer assigned to the Seventh Air Force conducted a test during a routine mine-laying mission to southern Korea. Using an 'ad hoc' ferret, the officer validated the radar coverage charts produced using ferret data. *Air Force Historical Research Agency via George Cully*

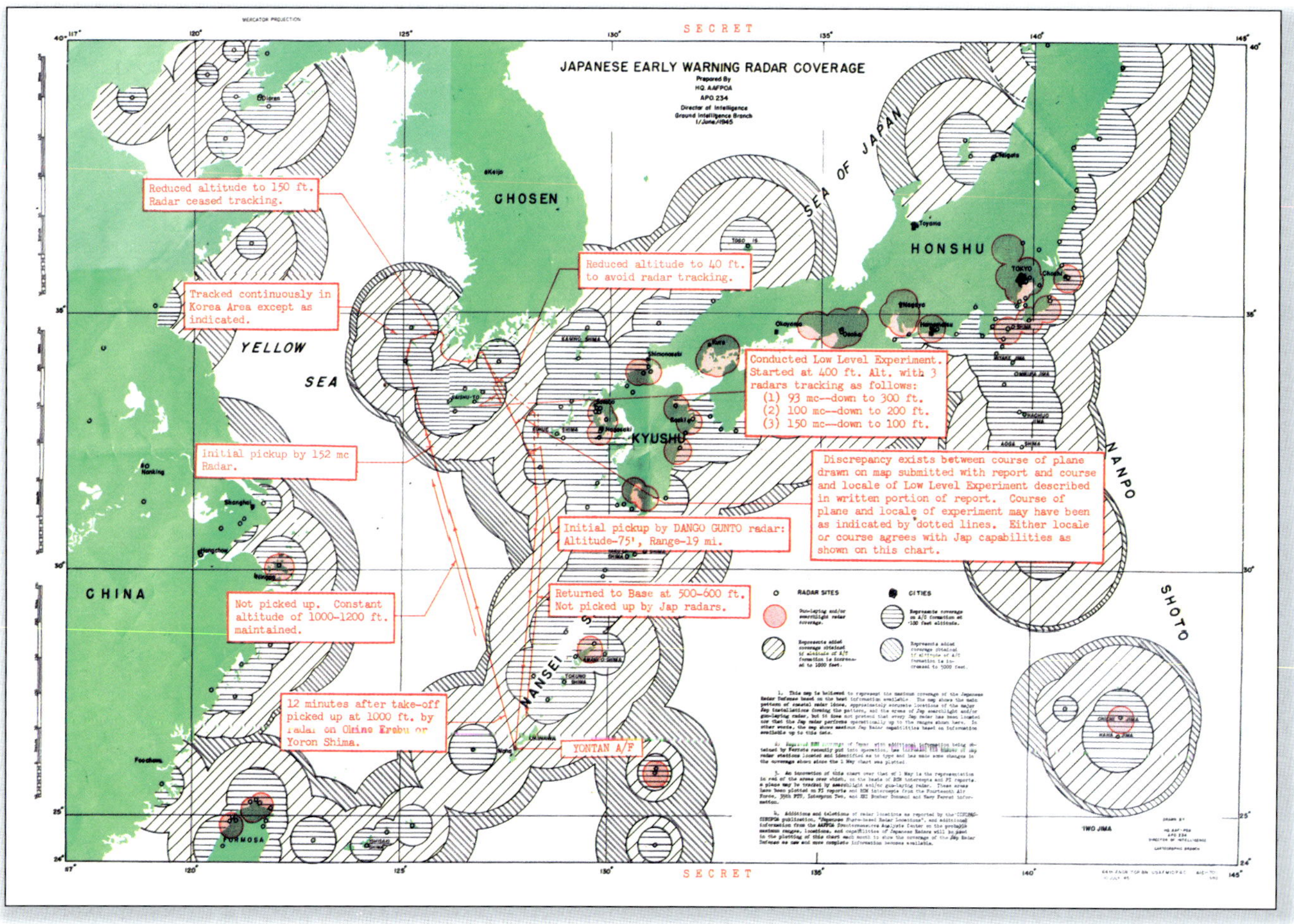

interdict shipping, and prepare Kyushu for invasion by shattering road and rail networks as well as striking defensive installations. To augment the Fifth and Thirteenth Air Forces in this task, the Seventh Air Force transferred to FEAF on 14 July after the majority of its units had reached Okinawa, although most of VII Fighter Command transferred to USASTAF for the strategic air campaign.[261] Seventh Air Force RCM activities were quite limited compared to the Fifth Air Force, both because of a lack of personnel and a lack of equipment. Only three aircraft of the 30th BG were fitted with Group A parts for the AN/APR-4 receiver and the AN/APA-6 pulse analyser. The sole RCM Officer assigned to the Seventh Air Force would fly missions on these aircraft as the RCM Observer. Little appears to have been done to change this before the war ended.[262]

As the FEAF prepared for operations against Japan, it looked to the Twentieth Air Force for lessons learned from flying against that target for over seven months. A study about the Japanese Air Defence System was forwarded to V Bomber Command and the 91st Reconnaissance Wing (parent unit of the 20th Reconnaissance Squadron) for review and use by bombers, ferrets and 'Radar Busters'. Additional reports were also available, including one from the HQ AAF Pacific Ocean Area Countermeasures Air Analysis Center titled 'The Jamming of Gun-Laying Radars by the XXI Bomber Command' that outlined formations and jamming techniques. Many of these reports likely figured into the development of FEAF SOP #31 for RCM operations, issued on 15 July. SOP #30, issued two weeks prior, directed all radar, radar intelligence, and RCM officers to send all RCM, ferret and other radar reports to Fifth Air Force A-2.[263]

The ferrets of the 20th Reconnaissance Squadron flew their first mission on 3 July, with Ferret XI winging north to investigate Japanese radars on Batan Island, Itbayat Island, and Koto-Sho. No signals were logged in the target area, although seven radars were detected likely emanating from Formosa. Ferret XI was out again the following evening to search the Canton–Hong Kong area. Seven radars were plotted, including two stations not previously located. Ferret XI also looked for a radar on Tankan Island that had been attacked by one of Fifth Air Force's 499th BS B-25 'Radar Busters'. The signal was off the air. The SCR 717 was not operating well, making navigation 'difficult and tedious' according to the mission report. Ferret XII flew the next mission, a repeat of the previous one. Nothing significant was found, although it appeared that the Japanese were pulling their radars back from the Hong Kong area as they retreated from this part of China. Ferret X was up the following night, 10–11 July, to reinvestigate Japanese radars on Batan Island, Itbayat Island, and Koto-Sho. No new signals were active and the mission confirmed the location of previously plotted radars. A general search of Formosa Island the night of 13–14 July by Ferret XII had similar results. Ferret X's mission, flown the night of 15–16 July, was different. Concentrating on the east coast of Formosa, RCM Observers Lts Dille and Blatz logged seventeen new radars, plotting out many new sites on Formosa during the nine hours they orbited off the island. The next mission, flown by Ferret XII the night of 23–24 July, had a similar experience and logged twenty-five signals. A night fighter was encountered and two radar contacts and one visual sighting were made. There was no attempt at interception. The last three missions of July focused on the Ryukyu Islands, the chain of islands including Okinawa that run from Formosa to Kyushu in the Home Islands of Japan. Two of these missions were flown from Yontan Airfield on Okinawa to extend the mission time. These missions helped outline the forces that were being bypassed and likely were planned for targeting by FEAF assets. Surprisingly, the ferrets were not surveying Kyushu – the planned primary target for the Fifth Air Force in the upcoming invasion of Japan. The 20th RS felt that ferret tasking exceeded the capabilities of the four assigned aircraft and mission crews, so the Fifth Air Force likely coordinated RCM reconnaissance with other theatre assets. Honshu was covered by the 3rd Photo Reconnaissance Squadron ferrets supporting Twentieth Air Force operations out of Guam, while Fleet Air Wing (FAW) 10 PB4Y-2 Privateers with radar receivers were operating around Kyushu and along the Chinese coast. The Fifth Air Force received all the RCM reports from these units and likely chose to just fill in gaps where other units were not operating.[264]

The Fifth Air Force started bombing Japan in July 1945 and stopped with the end of the war on 15 August. Leading the effort was the 43rd BG, concentrating on shipping as well as airfields and railways.[265] Two ferret missions were flown against Sakishima Gunto in August. The first, scheduled for 2 August, was not accomplished as Ferret XIII, under the command of Lt Hall, turned back before reaching the target area due to weather. Lt French tried again the night of 5 August and while Ferret XIII got further north, the mission once again was scrubbed due to thunderstorms and complete undercast and overcast. This flight proved to be the last RCM mission flown by the 20th RS. Future RCM missions were cancelled once surrender negotiations with Japan commenced.[266]

Closing

On 27 July, the 20th RS advanced echelon departed Subic Bay by LST bound for Okinawa as the squadron prepared to move to this island in preparation for Operation OLYMPIC, arriving on 4 August after encountering a typhoon en route. The air echelon departed Clark on 12 August, but the ferrets were left behind in the Philippines. On 28 August four crews flew back to Clark Field via transport to retrieve the B-24s. No further tasking was required of the ferrets, but they were to be kept in flying condition pending further action as to their disposal. The 20th RS was looking to transfer the now aged B-24s to a service squadron – if no takers could be found, the aircraft would be ferried to Okinawa to join the rest of the squadron. Only three ferrets were listed in the squadron inventory on 31 August, the squadron possibly finding a taker for a heavily used B-24J at Clark Field. The two new ferrets for the 20th RS from Project 97078-R were ferried from Cheyenne to California and were picked up by two newly graduated ferret crews at Salinas, California. The two B-24Ms winged westward and had reached Biak when their progress was halted for unknown reasons. The crews continued to Okinawa via transport aircraft, leaving the new ferrets to gather coral dust at the airport.[267] The Fifth Air Force's association with ferrets had run its course and the mission was no longer needed.

Serial Number	Aircraft	First Mission	Last Mission	Total # Ops Missions	Notes	Fate
42-63991	B-24D-20-CF	Early Feb 44	26 Feb 45	At least 49; possibly 70–80	Ferret VII, *The Duchess of Paducah*	Salvaged 31 May 45, stricken from records 1 Aug 45
42-64045	B-24D-20-CF	Early Feb 44	Dec 44	At least 19; possibly 40–50	Ferret VIII, *Atom Smasher*	Scrapped on 29 Dec 44 after landing accident at Angaur Island, Palau
44-41076	B-24J-195-CO	15 Feb 45	30 Jul 45	23 with 5 AF; 4 with 20 RS	Ferret X	Kingman, AZ, 13 Dec 45; declared excess 14 Jan 46
44-40943	B-24J-185-CO	20 Apr 45	5 Jul 45	12 with 5 AF; 2 with 20 RS	Ferret XI	Declared excess 1 Nov 45
44-40815	B-24J-180-CO	9 Jul 45	25 Jul 45	4 with 20 RS	Ferret XII; ex-10 AF	Declared excess 30 Nov 45
44-40817	B-24J-180-CO	2 Aug 45	6 Aug 45	2 with 20 RS	Ferret XIII; ex-14 AF	Declared excess 27 Nov 45

Chapter 10

The Eleventh Air Force continued the war against the Japanese in the north Pacific even though it was lacking dedicated RCM support. Although the Joint Chiefs in Washington had decided not to use Alaska as an approach to the Japanese Home Islands, the theatre was still useful in tying down Japanese forces with a minimal investment by the US. Few additional assets were allocated to the fight up north, although on 31 January 1944 the 311th Photo Wing was assigned the task to map the Kurils.[268] Slowly, an offensive against the northern islands of Japan was taking shape. The campaign against the Kurils differed from the liberation of the Aleutians in the fact that it was not in support of a land campaign nor was it in Alaska. These differences resulted in a unique chain of command for the USAAF groups and squadrons. While all land forces in Alaska and Canada remained under the control of the US Army's Western Defence Command, forces operating in the north Pacific fell under Admiral Chester W. Nimitz as part of the Pacific Ocean Areas (POA). The Joint Chiefs further divided the Pacific Ocean Areas into the North, Central and South Pacific Areas with Vice Adm. Frank J. Fletcher leading the North Pacific Area after 11 October 1943.

Details on the deployment of Japanese radars to the Kurils are hazy, but it is likely that the first set arrived in mid to late 1942 with additional units being added throughout war. The Kurils, originally seen by the Japanese as a staging area for North Pacific operations to include the Aleutians, became a combat zone starting in mid-1943. A captured document dated 11 October 1943 referenced a radar site at

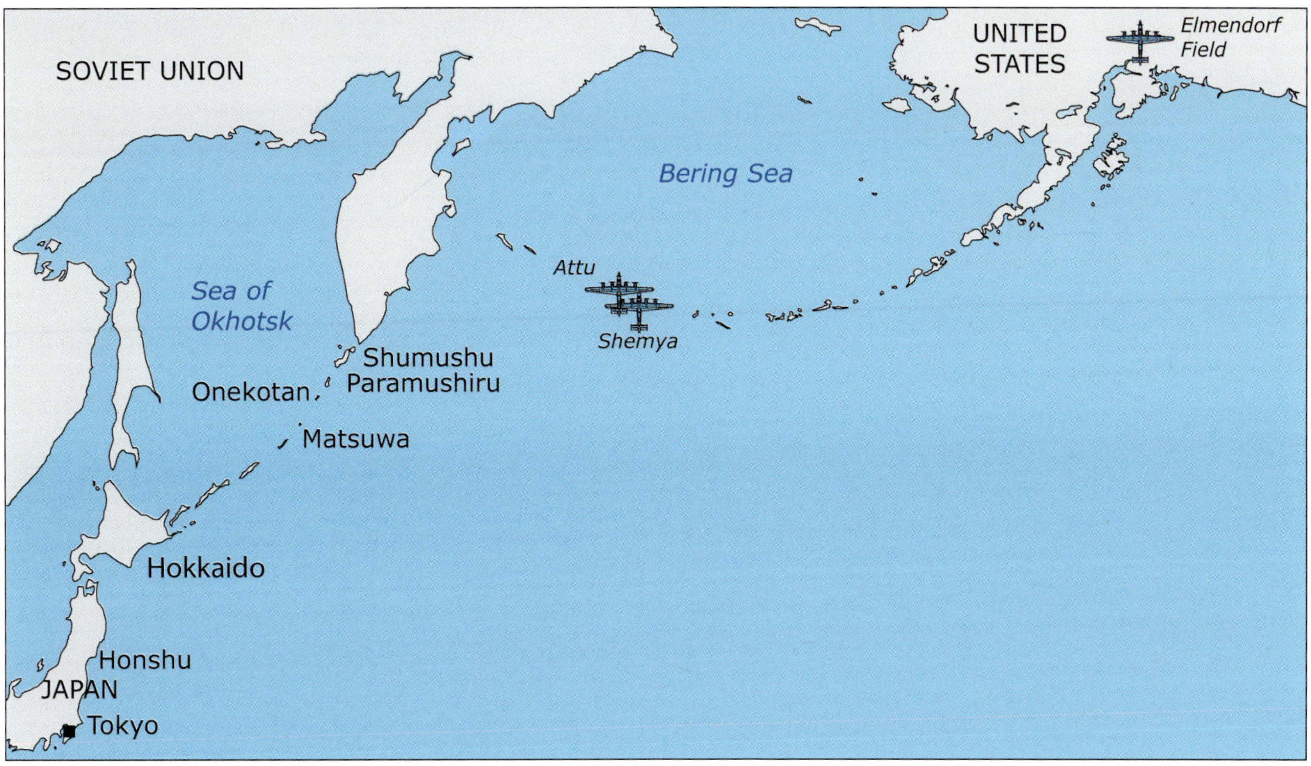

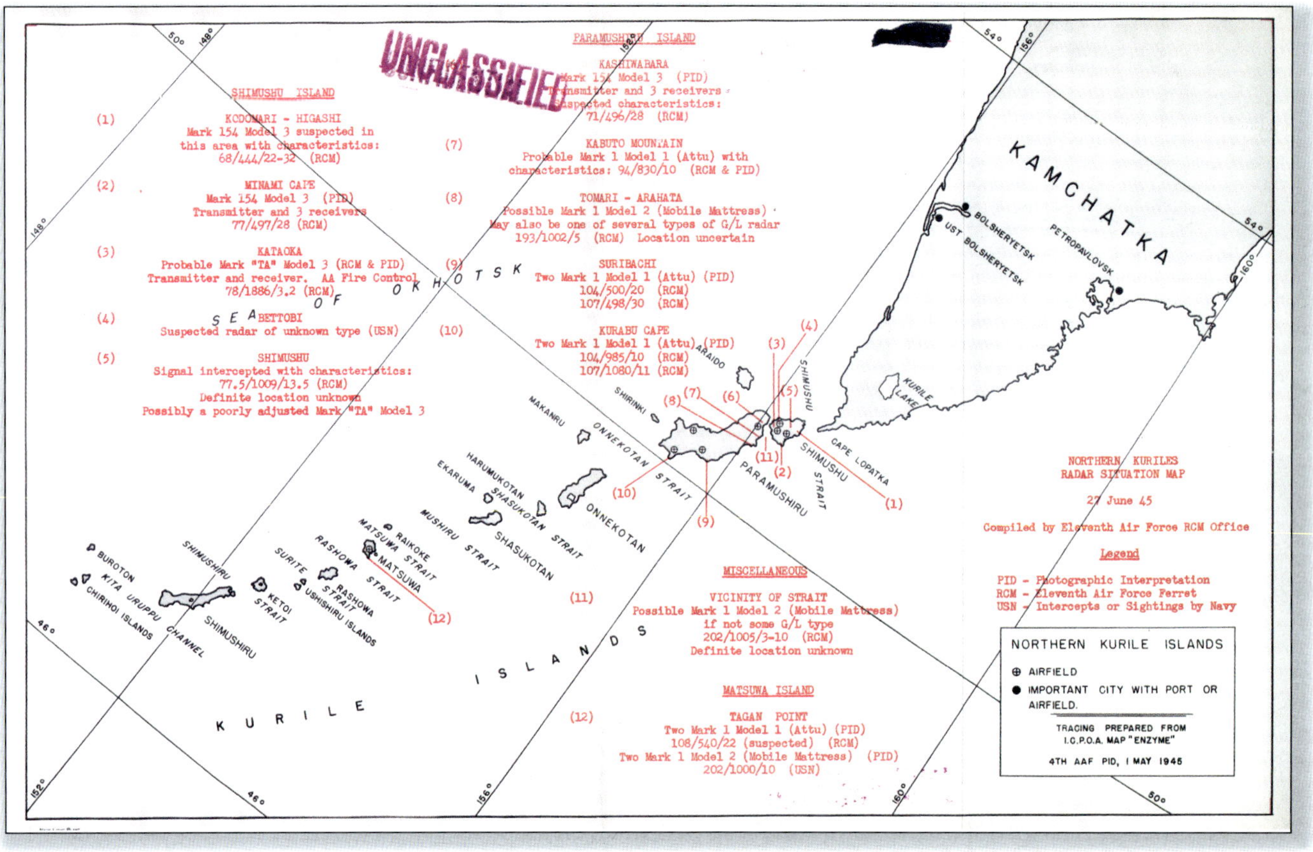

By June 1945 404th BS B-24s, 77th BS B-25s and Fleet Air Wing 4 Lockheed PV-2s were routinely striking targets in the Kurils as well as shipping in the region. Ferret I, working with Navy assets, helped produce this detailed radar situation map from that period that helped aid these strikes. *Ike Skelton Combined Arms Research Library*

Kurabu Cape, Paramushiru.[269] The final deployment of radars provided the Japanese with ample warning of any US raids against the Kurils. Assisting the radars in providing warning of raids were radio direction-finding sites operating in the medium and high frequencies. At least two DF sites existed, at Kurabu Cape and Matsuwa Island, likely able to detect the SCR-717 navigation radar used on Eleventh Air Force B-24s.[270] The Japanese devoted the first half of 1944 to the construction and expansion of air facilities to accommodate an increase in IJA and IJN aviation units. At its peak in June 1944 the Kurils boasted approximately 10 per cent of the entire Japanese operational air strength. The second half of 1944 saw a concentration of Japanese effort towards developing and expanding ground defences for the defence of the islands.[271]

On 24 February 1944 the Eleventh Air Force restarted its campaign against the Kurils with six bombers attempting to fly an armed reconnaissance and shipping search mission, but weather forced the majority to turn back. Though an inauspicious start, over the spring months XI Bomber Command slowly increased its presence over the Japanese-held islands.[272] On 3 March 1944 the 2nd Photographic Charting Squadron was ordered to Alaska to map the Kuril Islands. Although four F-7A aircraft were in place by 7 April, modifications to the aircraft and training for aircrew delayed the first operational photo reconnaissance mission until 14 June. In the interim, weather reconnaissance missions were flown starting in late May 1944. The 404th Bomb Squadron contributed to the effort, flying visual and photographic reconnaissance missions with its B-24D aircraft, while 77th Bomb Squadron B-25 aircraft worked with Fleet Air Wing 4 (FAW 4) Lockheed PV-1s to concentrate on Japanese shipping. By mid-September the reconnaissance mission was deemed complete and the aircraft departed Shemya for Elmendorf Field and their return to the Continental US.[273]

While the 2nd PCS was cataloguing Japanese troops and installations in the Kurils, the Navy started to look into the electronic side of things. Assigned to the Commander North Pacific Force (ComNorPac) was RCM Unit #6. This organisation provided equipment and operators to undertake SIGINT on platforms of opportunity, similar to Section 22 Field Units in the SWPA. In May 1944 RCM Unit #6 started to fly on select FAW 4 PV-1 mission over the Kurils. At least two SIGINT missions were flown in May, one in June, and one in October; likely more were flown. RCM Unit #6 apparently did not have DF equipment, so signal intercepts were broad and precise radar locations were problematic.[274] RCM Unit #6 was not confined to aircraft; on at least two occasions the unit sent resources out aboard US Navy surface combatants that were conducting bombardment missions against Matsuwa and Paramushiru. On both occasions, the unit detected Japanese radars.[275]

B-24D assigned to the 404th Bomb Squadron patiently awaits its next mission at Shemya AAFB, Alaska, April 1944. The 404th BS was detached from the 44th BG and sent to reinforce the 28th Composite Group in Alaska in July 1942.
National Museum of the United States Air Force

A 404th BS B-24D takes off from Shemya AAFB, Alaska, in October 1944. On 28 May 1943, Alaskan Scouts began reconnaissance of Shemya, a small uninhabited island 35 miles to the east of Attu. The following day, Army engineers came ashore to begin construction of a runway suitable for B-29 bombers. Construction started on a 10,000ft runway but due to the challenging weather and remote location the 404th BS did not commence flight operations from the base until February 1944.
National Museum of the United States Air Force

B-24D-12-CO s/n 42-41157 of the 404th BS, over Shemya AFB, Alaska, on 1 November 1944. The aircraft has a nose turret installed at the Oklahoma City Depot at Tinker Field, Oklahoma City. The nose turret modification differed in visual appearance from the Hawaii Air Depot modification by adding additional windows to the nose area, which resulted in a deepening of the fuselage. Ferret B-24D-CO 41-23886 had this style of nose turret. *National Museum of the United States Air Force*

Maintenance personnel working on the engines of a 404th BS B-24D at Shemya AAFB, Alaska, on 17 April 1944. Maintenance of a complex bomber is challenging enough; most maintenance of 404th BS bombers and their attached ferret aircraft was performed outside in the elements, adding an additional layer of difficulty to the task. *National Museum of the United States Air Force*

Two 404th BS B-24 aircraft taxi back after landing in a snow storm after a raid. Both aircraft are fitted with SCR-521 ASV radars for locating Japanese naval activity. Snow storms and fog made flying incredibly challenging; the SCR-717 fitted to Alaskan ferrets was not only needed for the ferret mission, it was also required to navigate in the murky weather. *National Museum of the United States Air Force*

Eleventh Air Force and FAW 4 attack missions continued against the Kurils throughout 1944, mainly striking Paramushiru and shipping. Eleventh Air Force bombers, although limited to one heavy and one medium squadron, had been keeping a light but steady pressure on Japanese forces. Navy patrol squadrons flying out of Attu had performed a similar function, but the level of effort from both services amounted to one or two dozen sorties per week during the good weather months of the shortened summer, with the sortie rate dropping to a handful per month for the rest of the year.[276] A mid-September 1944 intelligence summary lists defences, plots AAA, and mentions radars located at Kurabu Cape on Paramushiru and on Matsuwa Island. The summary also noted, 'It is certain that gun batteries in the Kurile Islands are not equipped with gun-laying radars in order to conduct unseen firing even though it is known that this type of equipment is possessed by the Japanese.'[277]

By late 1944 the US was formulating its strategy for the final push on the Japanese home islands. The plan that emerged saw thrusts up through the Philippines with the Southwest Pacific forces under General MacArthur and an attack from the east by Central Pacific forces under Admiral Chester Nimitz. In order to set the stage for the assault on the home islands, Nimitz first needed to secure Iwo Jima, one of the Volcano Islands located 750 miles south of Tokyo. The operational plan for the advance on Iwo Jima directed the North Pacific Force, subordinate to Nimitz, to 'contain enemy naval and air forces in the North Pacific by conducting reconnaissance and harassing enemy positions in the Kuriles'.[278] With few fleet forces assigned to the region, this was predominantly an air operation.

In preparation for the upcoming air campaign the 28th Bomb Group, re-designated from the 28th Composite Group in December 1943, dispatched its Communications and Radar Officer, Capt. Golistein, to Florida in September 1944 for RCM Observer training.[279] The next month the Eleventh Air Force, frustrated that its B-24D ferret '23886 was still in the US after a year of rework, requested to have a team sent up to Alaska to install RCM gear in one of its existing bombers. The AAF responded by dispatching Lt William Lytle, an RCM Observer, to Alaska. Lytle, one of four children of Judge Nelson and Zelime Lytle, was a fifth-generation Texan born in San Antonio in 1919. Lytle arrived at the Shemya base of the 404th BS in November 1944 to install an AN/APR-4 and an AN/APA-11 into one of the existing squadron aircraft. There were no plans to fit direction-finding capability to the aircraft, which from a capability standpoint was essentially an 'ad hoc' ferret. B-24D-CO s/n 41-11924 had been in Alaska since August 1942 and was already fitted with an SCR-717B radar, standard equipment for operating in the bad weather of the Aleutians and critical for ferret work. Although adequately maintained, the aircraft was the high-time aircraft in the 404th BS and reflected the priority given to bombing over reconnaissance. Apparently few other modifications were made to the aircraft other than fitting the RCM equipment and it appears to have not had its bomb bay modified and could only carry one RCM Observer. Lytle and five enlisted men were assigned to the Eleventh Air Force but on detached service with the bomb squadron to maintain the aircraft. The RCM equipment had been stored at Attu awaiting shipment to Shemya and did not arrive at Shemya until 16 December after a visit by Lt Lytle. Ferret '1924 went into a 100-hour inspection on 29 December and installation of the RCM gear started when the maintenance work was complete. Lytle was lucky in having the new maintenance hangar available; previously, all aircraft work was carried out in the elements on the flight line.[280]

Down south in warmer weather, Ferret I '23886 likely completed its modifications in October 1944 but bounced between Air Transport Command fields for two months before finally starting its journey northward to Alaska at the start of the new year. About this time, the 404th BS started to receive replacement airframes for its tired B-24D bombers. Eight new B-24L/M aircraft arrived at the squadron and the unit transitioned from the night bombing raids of 1944 to daylight raids. With an improved squadron inventory, the 404th BS also doubled in size the average bombing strike, increasing the raid size from three to six aircraft. Lt Glucksman, a second RCM Observer for the detachment, arrived at Shemya on 20 January. A Jamesway hut, a portable and easy-to-assemble shelter designed for Arctic weather, was constructed adjacent to the radar shop for use by the RCM team to include maintenance of their equipment.[281]

The first mission for the Eleventh Air Force's field-built ferret was 20 January 1945. RCM Observer Lt Lytle worked his AN/APR-4 search receiver as the aircraft turned south from the southern end of the Kamchatka Peninsula and flew 20 to 60 miles off the Kuril Islands, from Shumushu to southern Onekotan. Lytle spotted what he assessed as two Type 2 Mark I Model 1 radars, one in the Shumushu–Paramushiru area and one in the Paramushiru–Onekotan area. A Type 2 Mark I Model 2 was also noted in the Paramushiru area, making for a successful collection mission. Due to their location and timing, the ferret missions also pulled double duty performing weather reconnaissance – a critical information need in the Aleutians.[282]

Three days later, '11924 and Lt Lytle were once again surveilling the Kurils. The B-24D flew direct to Onekotan Island and flew along the Kuril chain, maintaining a 35-mile stand-off, until the aircraft was abreast Matsuwa Island. The only signal received was the Type 2 Mark I Model 1 radar at Onekotan.[283] In February, the RCM unit stood down in preparation for the arrival of 'their ferret plane'.[284] A two-month gap occurred between ferret flights, with the next mission being flown on Ferret I s/n 41-23886 in late March. In the intervening nine weeks, the Eleventh Air Force mounted a strike on the IJN Fifth Fleet Headquarters at Kataoka Naval Base, Shumushu Island, with six B-24s and followed up two weeks later with a B-24 attack on Kurabu Zaki, Paramushiru Island and a USN PV-1 attack on south-east Shumushu.[285] Pressure against Japanese forces was kept up in March, with three missions of four to six B-24s attacking the Kataoka naval base on Shumushu. This pressure was needed as US forces had assaulted Iwo Jima on 19 February, drawing an aggressive response from Japan including kamikaze attacks on the US fleet offshore.

It is unknown what Eleventh Air Force did with the ferret data. There is no indication that Alaskan B-24s flew with RCM and mission reports indicate that

B-24D-CO s/n 41-23886 Ferret I *Little Girl* seen in the US in 1944 before departure to Alaska. Its time at Eglin Field was extended due to Alaska's lower priority compared to SWPA, resulting in a stay of over a year. *Historical Electronics Museum, Radar Magazine No. 4*

Liberators stayed at medium altitude, while a portion of B-25 flight profiles appeared to fly towards targets at low level and may have used radar-masking approaches. Naval air assets seemed to have utilised the radar data better as FAW 4 PV-1s approached targets at low level to avoid radar detection, dropping to minimum altitude 100–150 miles from the target.[286] Still, the Eleventh Air Force persisted with its RCM programme. On 22 March, the RCM's lieutenants arrived in the Aleutians with Ferret I '23886, flying up to Shemya from Elmendorf Field. The lieutenants had been in Elmendorf for two weeks, overseeing the installation of RCM equipment in the aircraft. Two local sorties were flown out of Shemya prior to the first operational mission.[287]

The third Eleventh Air Force ferret mission for 1945 was flown on 29 March. Lt Lytle was joined by Lt Glucksman in '23886's first operational RCM mission. A ten-hour sortie was flown from Shemya, focusing on Shumushu and Paramushiru Islands. Two Type 2 Mark I Model 1 radars were located, one at Kurabu Zaki on the south-east corner of Paramushiru and the other at Torishima Retto in north-east Paramushiru. An odd signal at 77 MHz detected on the 20 January mission, possibly an IJA Tachi 6 early-warning radar, was detected again and found to be on the east coast of Shumushu; these three sites correlated to captured Japanese documentation.[288] On the evening of 25 March 1945 five US radars in the Aleutian Chain reported what appeared to be noise jamming for a period of about twenty minutes. During the week that followed, four separate reports were received from individual radars with similar interference. RCM support missions were flown by Ferret I on 2 and 4 April to investigate the jamming of US radars in the vicinity of Attu and Agattu with negative results, although the flight crew did provide useful weather reconnaissance data. The 404th BS history attributed the RF interference to a sun lamp on Attu![289]

The next ferret mission was flown on 7 April, targeting Paramushiru and Kharimkotan. Ferret I picked up six signals that plotted out to locations on northern Shumushu, Kurabu and Onekotan. The other three were received over water and, without any land mass to take a bearing from, were from an unknown location. Three days later, seven B-24s attacked Kataoka on Shumushu in conjunction with Navy PV-1s. At the same time, four B-25s attempted to bomb a radar site on Minami Cape on the south-east corner of Shumushu Island but failed. This may have been the source of Lytle's spurious 77 MHz signal, but why this site was attacked instead of one of the Type 2 Mark I Model 1 radars is unknown. Another ferret mission was flown on 16 April but the SCR 717 radar was unreliable, impairing navigation and precluding accurate direction finding. Five radars were noted when the RCM Observers scanned between 70 and 300 MHz, likely emanating from Paramushiru or Shumushu and including signals similar to those seen previously at Torishima Retto and Kurabu.[290] On 25 April Lts Lytle and Glucksman were once again aboard '23886 for a ten-hour mission off Shumushu and Paramushiru Islands. The April weather at 12,000ft was still unpleasant – ice build-up on the DF antenna made it difficult to rotate and take bearings against target signals. The lieutenants prevailed and noted six signals, including an unlocated Tachi 3 radar, probable Type 2 Mark I Model 1 radars at Suribachi and Kuraba on Paramushiru, two probable Type 2 Mark I Model 1 radars on Shumushu, and a probable IJA Tachi 6 radar near Cape Tomari on Paramushiru.[291] Imagery on 29 April revealed a possible gun-laying radar at Kataoka Naval Base Airfield, the source of the Tachi 3 emanations detected by Lt Lytle. This proved to be the only gun-laying radar in the Kurils.

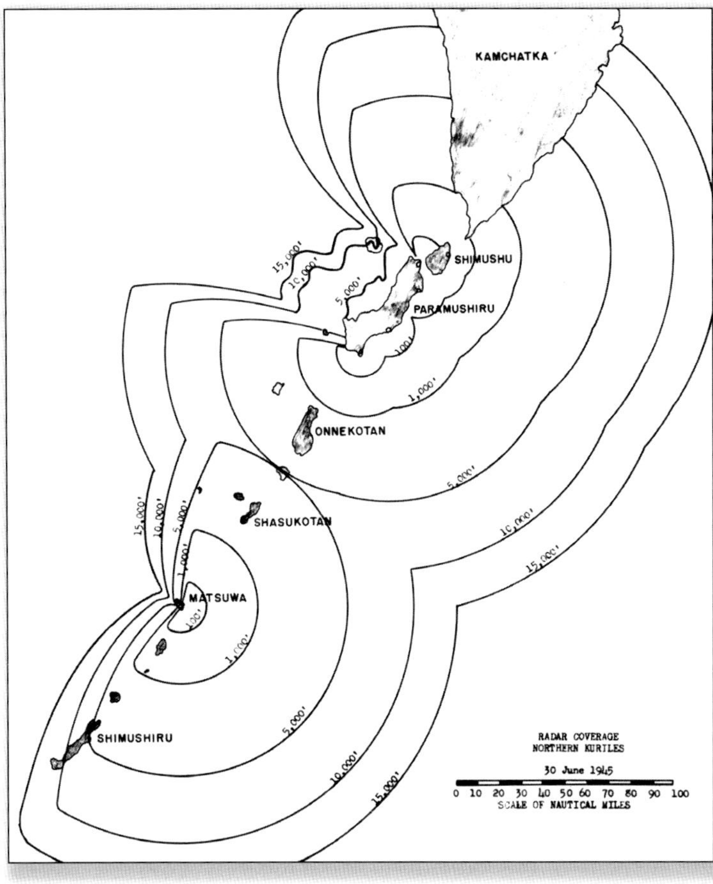

Although radar coverage, derived from Ferret I's search data, was available for the Kuril Islands the USAAF appeared to continue to attack at medium altitude. Only Fleet Air Wing 4 strike missions appeared to be flown at low altitude to slip in under radar coverage. *Ike Skelton Combined Arms Research Library*

Two days later, on 27 April, Ferret '23886 joined seven other B-24s for an attack on Shumushu Island. While six of the Liberators dropped fragmentation bombs on Kataoka Naval Base, a single B-24 attacked the offending radar site at Minami Cape. The role Ferret I played in this mission is unknown, whether it was to take advantage of the Katoaka attack to stimulate Japanese defences or to determine the activity level of the Minami Cape radar before and after the attack. Four radars were detected, a lone Tachi 6 at Minami Cape and

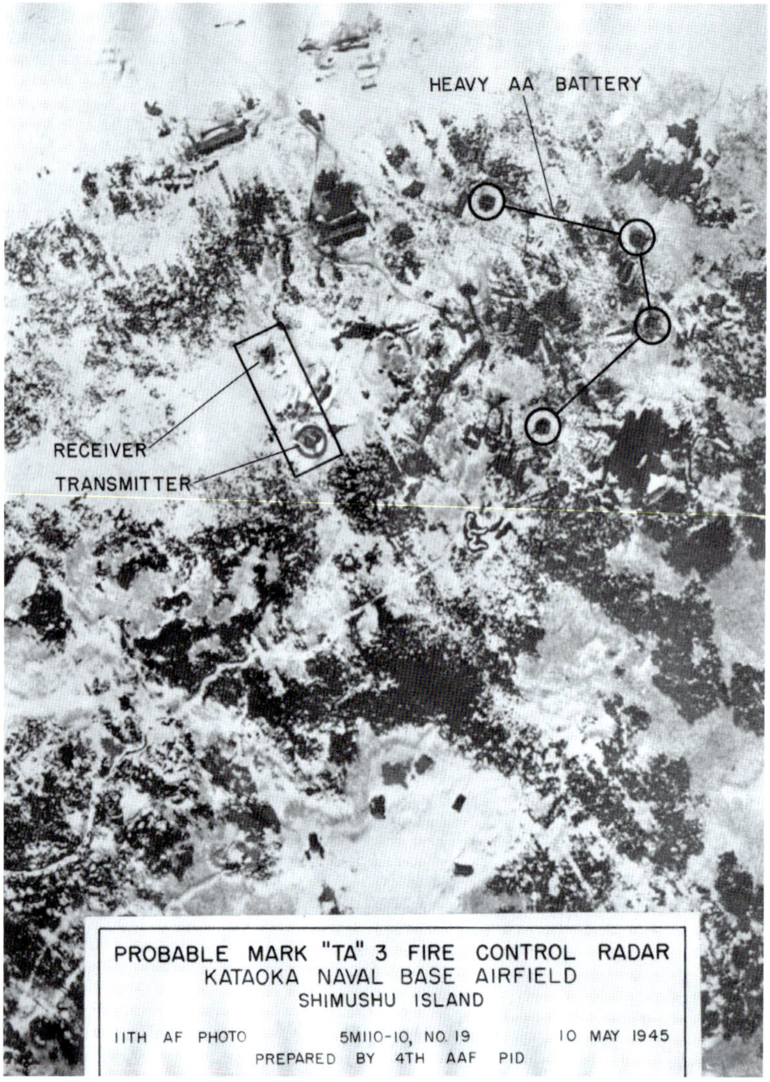

Vertical aerial reconnaissance image of a Tachi 3 radar co-located with an AAA battery near the Kataoka Naval Base on Shumushu Island in the Kuril Island chain, imaged on 10 May 1945. The Tachi 3 at the Kataoka Naval Base proved to be the only gun-laying radar in the Kurils and was noted on many ferret missions. *Ike Skelton Combined Arms Research Library*

Low-level oblique aerial reconnaissance photograph of 'Radar Hill' at Minami Cape, Shumushu Island. Eleventh Air Force staff suspected the site to be 'the heart of the Northern Kurils Air Warning System'. The snow-covered coastal clifftop has what appears to be three Tachi 6 transmitter towers, each annotated with a '1', in this 6 April 1945 photograph. *Ike Skelton Combined Arms Research Library*

Type 2 Mark I Model 1 radars in Paramushiru Strait, northern Shumushu, and at Suribachi.[292] The next day, 28 April, saw VPB-139 attack Cape Minami with four PV-2 Harpoons, an attack delayed from three weeks earlier due to weather. While the Harpoons put rockets into the target area, radar antennas are relatively resilient and the attack appears to have caused minimal damage to the equipment.[293] The Eleventh Air Force and FAW-4 continued to fly missions at a slow rate against the Kuril Islands throughout April.

Eleventh Air Force staff suspected 'Radar Hill' at Minami Cape to be 'the heart of the Northern Kurils Air Warning System' and recommended that it become the primary object of a bombing raid in the near future. Though a total of seven 'radar screens' were identified in imagery during April 1945, the 28th BG did not execute any missions against the offending radar site until later in May.[294] Additional analysis by the staff concluded that gun-laying radars had not yet been definitely identified in the Kurils and no known radar-directed flak had been encountered by bombers.[295] As the Japanese continued to feed their aviation assets into the fight around Okinawa, fighter interceptions against 28th BG strikes were becoming less frequent over the Kurils.

On 5 May ferret '23886 was airborne with its two RCM Observer Lieutenants for a RCM, weather and shipping reconnaissance mission in the Paramushiru Strait. Only one radar was detected, a probable Tachi 6 displaying two separate frequencies. In his post-mission report, Lt Lytle postulated that the Japanese may have been hesitant to bring up their radars due to the FAW-4 attacks on the Cape Minami radar.[296] On 9 May, ferret '23886 took off fifteen minutes after a formation of twelve B-24s lifted off en route to bomb Kataoka Naval Base on Shumushu. Based on the apparent hesitancy of the Japanese to bring their radars up against single aircraft as witnessed on the prior ferret mission, the Eleventh Air Force decided that future RCM missions should be flown in conjunction with strike missions. Lts Lytle and Gluckman flew on the ten-hour flight from Shemya, with Ferret I staying at an altitude of 8,500ft off Paramushiru and Shumushu Islands. The probable Tachi 6 at Cape Tomari on Paramushiru was the first radar detected, a pattern noted by Lytle. It was joined by another probable Tachi 6 radar, the infamous Cape Minami radar. The Tachi 3 fire control radar first noted on 25 April was also observed, its presence correlated to the firing of AAA through cloud cover at the B-24s attacking Kataoka. The offending gun-laying radar was bombed in June and not replaced. Two Type 2 Mark I Model 1 radars were also logged, one being located on southern Paramushiru, as well as a signal at 94 MHz – possibly a Tachi 18.[297]

On 10 May , the Eleventh Air Force and Fleet Air Wing Four executed their largest mission to date. Eight PV-2 Harpoons of VB-139 attacked the Cape Minami radar installation with rockets as a diversion for the main effort, an attack on Japanese shipping.

Twelve B-24s bombed ships at Kataoka naval base and took reconnaissance photos over Paramushiru on the return trip. The Liberators were joined by sixteen Attu-based B-25s that hit shipping between Kashiwabara and Kataoka. The Minami Cape radar attack was determined to be unsuccessful as no rockets were observed to hit the target facility. Heavy AAA fire was encountered by all raiders, knocking out one B-25 and forcing a B-24 and B-25 to land in the USSR. The lost Liberator, B-24D 41-11924 of earlier ferret fame, made a forced landing at Petropavlovsk with all of Lt Kleinke's crew surviving and being interned by the Soviets. By this time the aircraft was once again operating as a bomber and carried no RCM equipment.[298]

The 28th BG returned to Kataoka two more times within the week, with both missions garnering support from Ferret I. On 15 May seven B-24s set out to attack shipping in Kataoka Harbor, fighting through 10/10 cloud cover and a few Japanese fighter aircraft. The RCM Observers aboard ferret '23886 logged five radars including an unknown radar operating at 195 MHz at Tomari Cape, a Type 2 Mark I Model 1 at Suribachi, and a Tachi 6 near Minami Cape. The 18 May sortie was active from a radar standpoint, stimulated by nine B-24s attacking shipping in the Kataoka naval base and Paramushiru Strait. Ferret I's crew logged Type 2 Mark I Model 1 radars at Suribachi and Shiro Iwa, the Tachi 3 fire control radar near Kataoka, and the unknown the 195 MHz signal at Tomari Cape.[299] The next day, eight B-25s went against the seemingly indestructible Tachi 6 radar at Minami Cape and a nearby cannery. Met with intense AAA and enemy fighters, three B-25s were lost.[300]

On 23 May, ferret '23886 flew a short four-hour sortie with seven B-24s radar bombing the Kataoka Naval Base. The ferret flew 15 miles off the Paramushiru and Shumushu Islands, concentrating on the 70 to 320 MHz band, but intermittently searching down to 28 MHz and also the 1000 to 3000 MHz band. A Tachi 6 was recorded as well as two Type 2 Mark I Model 1 radars and a Type 2 Mark I Model 2 radar.[301] The flight tempo continued, buoyed by the good summer weather. On 3 June the Eleventh Air Force and FAW-4 sent out four strike missions. While B-25s and PV-2s attacked shipping, another group of B-25s hit the cannery complex at Masugawa on Suribachi. While this was occurring, eight B-24s attacked the Kataoka Naval Base while the ferret monitored Japanese activity in the area. Six signals were detected, including Type 2 Mark I Model 1 radars at Suribachi and Kurabu and a Tachi 6 near Cape Minami.[302] Similar-sized attacks, without the ferret, took place on 9 and 11 June. On 18 June, six B-24s and two PV-2s conducted anti-shipping patrols and when no targets were found, bombed Tomari Cape and Kataoka Naval Base; during this activity, the ferret was patrolling off the east coast of Paramushiru and noted five radars active but did not detect any new signals.[303]

The missions did not let up in July. On the 10th, FAW-4 flew shipping search sectors from Attu, while four 404th BS B-24s flew shipping search missions off the west coast of Paramushiru and Shumushu and when no targets were found bombed Minami Cape with the aid of radar. Ferret I orbited off Paramushiru and only noted two signals active, including the Minami Cape Tachi 6. On 26 July, the Navy again conducted sector patrol while the 404th BS sent seven B-24s to attack Kataoka with 500lb incendiary cluster bombs. Ferret '23886 flew down the east coast of Shumushu and Paramushiru to Watanabe Cape, then flew across the island to the west coast. After flying along the west side of the island, the ferret flew south between Paramushiru and Shumushu and returned to base.[304] No new signals were detected.

At the end of July, FAW-4 welcomed the PB4Y-2 Privateer to the theatre as VPB-120 and VPB-122 arrived to replace the PV-1s of VPB-131. Privateers were delivered with radar receivers installed, but no reporting from their seven combat missions in the Kurils indicate it saw much use in the north Pacific. 12 August witnessed the last ferret mission by the Eleventh Air Force. Ferret '23886 flew a mission while 404th BS B-24s hit Kataoka Naval Base and Suribachi airfield. Three signals were received and plotted to known radar sites. The next day the 28th BG flew its last bombing mission of the war, as hostilities ceased on 15 August and the US only flew reconnaissance missions against the Kuril Islands. On 9 August, the Soviets invaded Manchuria and on 15 August the Red Army carried out an assault landing on Shumushu Island for the start of their offensive in the Kurils.[305] For the US forces in the far north, it was the birth of a new mission as a hot war transitioned to a cold one. The 404th BS continued to fly reconnaissance missions in the region, keeping tabs on Soviet activity. On 5 September RCM Observer Lt Lytle was scheduled for an engineering flight over Alaid Island, when early in the mission the B-24D he was flying in crashed into an overcast-obscured peak. There were no survivors. After a combined funeral service with his crew mates at the Shemya chapel he was buried in the post cemetery.[306]

Serial Number	Aircraft	First Mission	Last Mission	Total # Ops Missions	Notes	Fate
41-11924	B-24D-CO	20 Jan 45	23 Jan 45	2	Field modified by 11 AF; more akin to an 'ad hoc' ferret	Forced landing at Petropavlovsk, USSR, after Kurils bombing strike on 10 May 1945
41-23886	B-24D-10-CO	29 Mar 45	12 Aug 45	15	Ferret I	Turned in to Alaska Air Depot on 18 Oct 45 for disposition

Chapter 11

The Twentieth Air Force was created with the sole purpose of using the United States Army Air Forces' (USAAF's) most advanced bomber, the Boeing B-29, to conduct a strategic bombing campaign against Japan. Originally composed of the XX Bomber Command (XX BC) based in India, it started a desultory bombing campaign against Japan in mid-1944 but it wasn't until early 1945, after the creation of the Twenty-First Bomber Command (XXI BC) on Saipan and Guam, that the campaign went into high gear.[307] As the XXI BC staff prepared initial plans for its aerial onslaught against the Empire in October 1944 little was known about Japan and its air defences. Precious little data existed on the types of radars employed on Kyushu and Honshu, much less the density of their deployment and details of their command structure. Initial thoughts were to start the XXI BC offensive with heavy radar jamming and chaff, but staff studies disapproved this concept due to the dearth of knowledge about Japan's defensive capabilities. While XX BC would slowly map these radars over the coming months, it provided little comfort to the planners of the XXI BC. That winter they decided they needed a plan to go it alone and map the radar defences themselves.[308]

The IJA was charged with the protection of the Japanese Home Islands; this not only included coastal defences and land forces but also applied to air defence. The air defences of the Home Islands centred on a protective ring of Tachi 6 and Tachi 18 early-warning radars on Honshu and Kyushu with outlying radar posts on the Nanpo Shoto chain of islands that ran between Iwo Jima and the Home Islands that detected incoming bomber strikes and provided the command and control structure advance notice and time to scramble fighters.[309] The Home Islands, excluding Hokkaido, were originally organised into three air defence districts. The size of these districts proved unwieldy as the war progressed and the number of air defence districts eventually reached seven by 1945. Each district had an Information Centre that combined tracking data from radars and ground observers and used the fused air picture to control air defence fighters, supervise anti-aircraft artillery (AAA) operations, and issue civil defence alerts.[310] Although not as developed as its counterpart in Nazi Germany, the Japanese air defence system was still a formidable force that needed to be countered if an extensive bombing campaign against the Home Islands was to take place.

The Japanese air defence system in China and portions of the Home Islands had been mapped by XX Bomber Command's AN/APR-4-equipped B-29s starting in mid-1944 and but this was seen as inadequate for the strategic bombing campaign against Japan. An internal report of the United States Army Strategic Air Forces noted many challenges with using bomber B-29s for radar reconnaissance, listing deficiencies ranging from procedures and training to equipment. In short, dedicated ferret aircraft were needed to support the strategic bombing effort against Japan.[311] While still forming up in Colorado in September 1944, the nascent XXI BC noted the need for an organic flight of ferret aircraft and outlined the requirements in writing for four B-29 ferret aircraft.[312] This requirement worked its way through the administrative wickets into the Reconnaissance Branch of Headquarters, Army Air Forces in Washington and was formally discussed on 19 November in a telephone conversation between Brigadier General Haywood Hansell, XXI BC commander, Major General Millard Harmon, Commander of the Strategic Air Force of the Pacific Ocean Area, and General 'Hap' Arnold. They agreed upon the need for ferret aircraft to assist in the conduct of an effective bombing campaign against Japan by identifying electronic threats and helping in subsequent radar jamming efforts. One ferret aircraft was promised immediately and an additional five ferrets were noted as the necessary force to create a RCM flight assigned to the XXI BC.[313] With leadership in both Washington and at the Twentieth Air Force backing the plan, the staffs started to flesh out the details. The commander of the Army Air Forces, Pacific Ocean Area (AAFPOA) asked Headquarters Twentieth Air Force for assistance in augmenting the

XXI BC's long -range photo reconnaissance squadron, the F-13-equipped 3rd Photo Reconnaissance Squadron (Very Long Range) (3rd PRS), with a flight of RCM reconnaissance aircraft. The Twentieth Air Force responded with an authorisation for four primary and two reserve ferret aircraft with eight flight crews and support personnel as required. Air Staff in Washington had been examining the very heavy reconnaissance aircraft programme and in June 1944 recommended that Very Heavy Reconnaissance Squadrons and their F-13 aircraft not be equipped with ferret equipment as this would detract from the primary mission of imagery reconnaissance.[314] With the B-29/F-13 airframe taken off the table, the USAAF turned to its growing B-24 ferret fleet. Ferret VI, scheduled to depart the Continental United States on 24 December, was seen as the first instalment of this new unit and was to be followed up with five additional ferret aircraft on or about 17 February 1945.[315] The ferret flight, though, was all in the future. With XXI BC commencing bombing operations from its Guam base in November 1944, the command would have to make do with AN/APR-4-equipped B-29 bombers. The XXI BC mirrored the XX BC in radar search operations, outfitting two aircraft in each bomb squadron with search receivers; once again, a shortage of AN/APA-24 antennas restricted the ability on the RCM operators to triangulate and plot the received Japanese radars.[316]

Ferret VI was part of a group of five B-24J ferret aircraft – Ferrets VI, X, XI, XII, and XIII – built as the 'next generation' of ferrets after Ferrets VII and VIII. These aircraft differed from Ferrets VII and VIII by having a larger RCM compartment utilising the entire bomb bay as opposed to only half as found on the earlier ferret aircraft. The RCM suite was upgraded with newer equipment and an updated navigation radar – the SCR-717 – was fitted. Ferret VI, B-24J-195-CO 44-41124, was accepted by the USAAF from Consolidated on 26 June 1944 and was shipped off to the Fairfield Air Depot at Patterson Field, Ohio, for modification into a ferret aircraft, arriving on 16 July. Its assigned flight crew accompanied it through depot work, giving the RCM Observers a chance to see how their equipment was installed into the aircraft and understand their custom-integrated mission gear. After the extensive rework, the newly named Ferret VI was assigned to Eglin Field on 28 October. After crew training and additional work, it transited through Hunter Field, Georgia, en route to its overseas assignment. It finally departed the Continental United States on 5 January 1945 but did not travel far. Ferret VI needed to fly a few training flights in order to perform a complete check of the installed RCM equipment as well as make modifications to the gear based on these flights; Hickam Field, Hawaii, and its co-located Hawaii Air Depot were perfectly suited for the task at hand.[317] In addition to minor modifications to the RCM equipment, Hawaii Air Depot was also tasked with two additional jobs for Ferret VI – theatre modifications and ferret upgrades. While the Depot was able to accommodate the theatre-level modifications such as swapping out the tail turret for twin tail guns, modifying the life raft release mechanism and installing blister windows for the pilots, they could not accommodate the requested ferret modifications. The Depot's schedule was full and these changes would take six weeks and delay departure from Hawaii until mid-March 1945.[318] The ferret changes were deferred until arrival at Guam, but one thing that was accomplished in Hawaii was moving the AN/APA-24 antenna from under the RCM compartment to the position formerly occupied by the belly turret. After calibration flights Ferret VI departed Hickam Field on 21 February and arrived on Guam on the 23rd of the month.[319]

The underside of the starboard aft fuselage of a B-24J/M ferret; AT-38/APR-4 stub antenna at left, clear blister with AT-49/APR-4 mounted on the belly. This is likely B-24J s/n 44-41124 Ferret VI either at Eglin Field or Hickam Field.
Air Force Historical Research Agency via George Cully

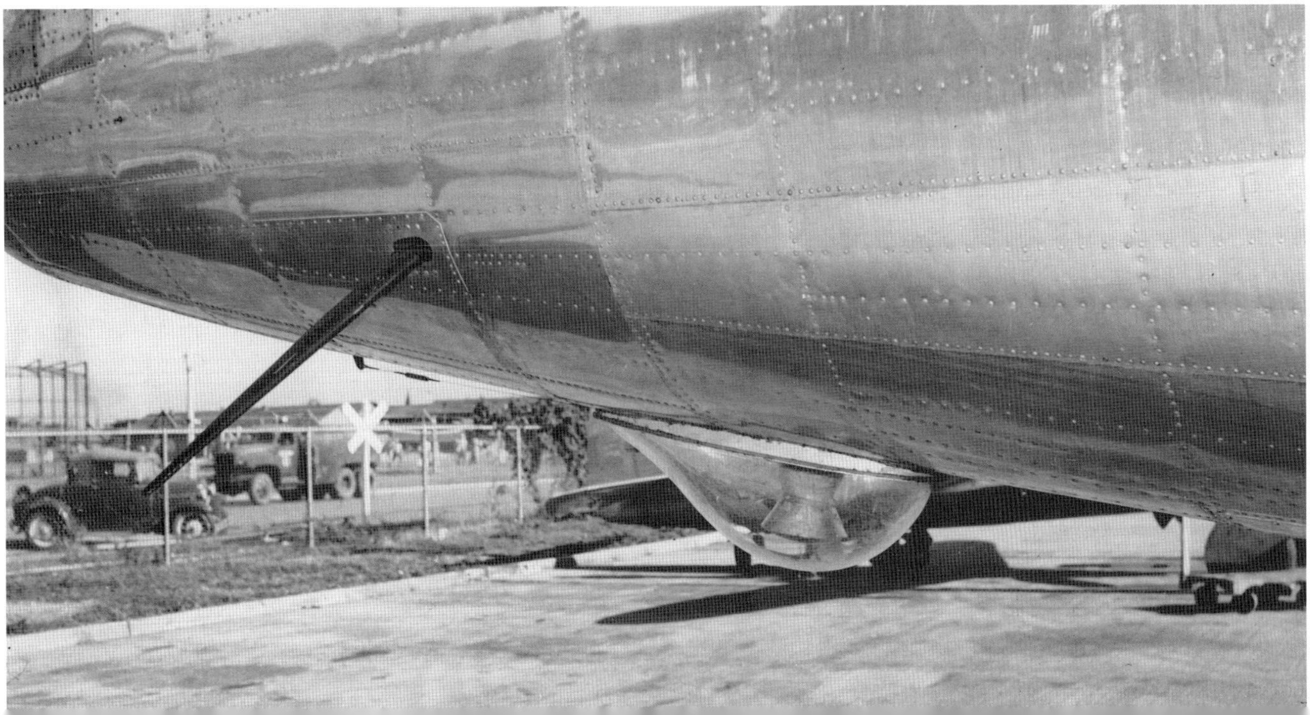

The starboard aft fuselage of a B-24J/M ferret near the waist gunner position with a sealed bomb bay. The AT-38/APR-4 stub antenna at right, the AS-44/APR-5 blister antenna at centre beneath twin lower windows, and the opaque blister with AS-49/APR-4 at left with 'T'-shaped AN/APN-1 peeking out from behind. This is likely B-24J s/n 44-41124 Ferret VI either at Eglin Field or Hickam Field. *Air Force Historical Research Agency via George Cully*

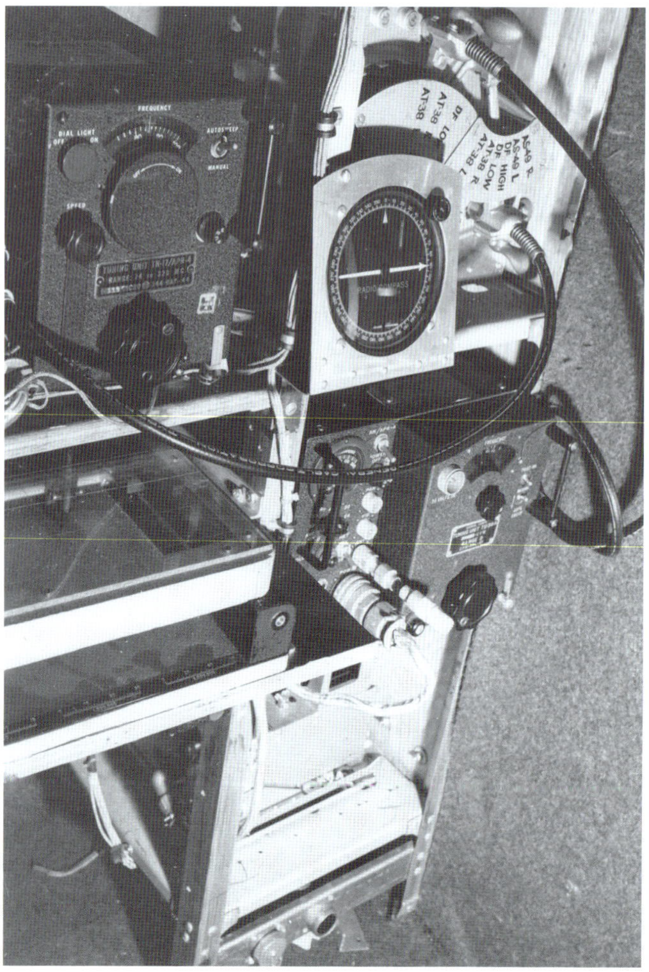

Left: The interior of a B-24J/M ferret showing the rack of equipment in the RCM operator's position in the former bomb bay. Upper left: AN/APR-4 w/ TN-17 tuning unit; upper right: antenna patch panel; middle: radio compass/direction finding indicator; lower left: odograph plotting table slid into rack; lower right: AN/APR-4 w/ TU-56-A tuning unit. This is likely B-24J s/n 44-41124 Ferret VI either at Eglin Field or Hickam Field. *Air Force Historical Research Agency via George Cully*

Below: The interior of a B-24J/M ferret showing the RCM operator's position in the former bomb bay; two rows of equipment with door at left. Top row, L–R: SX-28, an empty bay, vertical arrangement of compass, altimeter, and Magnesyn/flux gate compass indicator. Bottom row, L–R: AN/APR-2, AN/APA-11, AN/APR-4 w/ TN-17. This is likely B-24J s/n 44-41124 Ferret VI either at Eglin Field or Hickam Field. *Air Force Historical Research Agency via George Cully*

The interior of a B-24J/M ferret showing the RCM operator's position in the former bomb bay. Top row, L–R: SX-28, an empty bay, vertical arrangement of compass, altimeter, and Magnesyn/flux gate compass indicator. Middle row, L–R: AN/APR-2, AN/APA-11, AN/APR-4 w/ TN-17, radio compass/direction-finding indicator. Bottom row, L–R: AN/APR-5, clear glass odograph plotting table. This is likely B-24J s/n 44-41124 Ferret VI either at Eglin Field or Hickam Field. *Air Force Historical Research Agency via George Cully*

Back in the US, Headquarters AAF established a requirement for five ferret aircraft of a new design that incorporated the latest RCM equipment and lessons learned from the prior ferret aircraft. To meet the timeline agreed upon in December conversations with XXI BC, the aircraft had to be produced in thirty-five days.[320] Five B-24M-10-CO aircraft produced in late December 1944 were diverted to Fairfield Air Depot, arriving in the first week of January 1945. Air Technical Service Command actually pushed the aircraft through the modification line in a little over three weeks, with four of the new ferrets (Ferrets XIV, XV, XVI and XVIII) arriving at Eglin Field, Florida, for a two-week stay before departing for overseas operations. Somewhere along the line a decision was made to keep Ferret XVII for training at a new ferret training course set up at March Field, California, so only four aircraft departed for Guam in mid-February 1945.[321]

The 8.5 × 5.5ft ferret compartment provided housing for the two RCM operators and their equipment. Racks were mounted along the port side of the fuselage and separate work stations were built for each of the operators. The RCM Observer at the aft end looked for signals up to 300 MHz, while the forward operator scanned for signals above this frequency.

The port lower aft rear fuselage of a B-24J/M ferret with windows added along the lower fuselage side near the ball turret position. AT-38/APR-4 stub antenna at left, AS-44/APR-5 blister antenna at centre under windows, and opaque blister with AS-49/APR-4 at right. This is likely B-24J s/n 44-41124 Ferret VI either at Eglin Field or Hickam Field. *Air Force Historical Research Agency via George Cully*

The B-24M RCM Observers had AN/APA-17 and AN/APA-24 direction-finding equipment and AN/APR-4, AN/APR-5, AN/APR-7 search receivers as well as AN/APA-11 pulse analyser and AN/APA-10 panoramic scope. AN/ARR-5 and AN/ARR-7 receivers able to cover HF and VHF radio communications were also installed. Wire signal recorders rounded out the equipment suite in the bomb bay. Ferret VI had a similar complement of equipment, although it lacked the AN/APA-17 and AN/APA-10. Located above and behind the RCM Observers positions was the radar operator's position. He had access to the SCR-717 radar and AN/APN-1 and SCR-718 radar altimeters.

View of underside of fuselage of a B-24J/M ferret aircraft with a modified AN/APA-24 antenna at centre and 'T'-shaped AN/APN-1 at right. The vertical dipoles of the AN/APN-24 were made into monopoles by retaining the upper portions – which could be drawn up into holes in the fuselage for stowing – and chopping off the bottoms to eliminate a ground clearance problem. Visible is the AN/APN-24 under the RCM compartment; before leaving Hawaii it was moved to the position formerly occupied by the belly turret. This is likely B-24J s/n 44-41124 Ferret VI either at Eglin Field or Hickam Field. *Air Force Historical Research Agency via George Cully*

Below: The top aft fuselage of a B-24J/M ferret. Equipment on the spine of the aircraft was normally confined to friendly communications and includes, from right to left: IFF antenna; SCR-274-4 HF command radio wire strung between insulator on fuselage and port fin; forward mast for radio compass sense/radio range receive horizontal wire antenna; radio compass loop enclosure; feed through insulator for wire antenna strung to starboard fin for high HF/low VHF (SX-28); localiser antenna; aft mast for radio compass sense/radio range receive horizontal wire antenna; and SCR-522 VHF command antenna. This photo is likely B-24J s/n 44-41124 Ferret VI either at Eglin Field or Hickam Field.
Air Force Historical Research Agency via George Cully

The navigator was moved from the nose to the flight deck behind the pilots and had a repeater for the SCR-717 and SCR-718 units and AN/APN-4 precision navigation receivers. The radar operator and navigator worked as a team to precisely plot the location of the aircraft to enable accurate signal plotting by the RCM Observers. To ensure maximum efficiency between these three locations an interphone system connected the RCM Observers with the navigator and radar operator.[322]

The four new B-24M ferret aircraft met up with Ferret VI at Guam, all aircraft arriving within days of each other in late February 1945. Unfortunately, B-24M ferret 44-41985/Ferret XV was lost due to a blown tyre when landing after a training flight shortly after it was delivered to Guam.[323] The remaining four ferret aircraft were assigned to Guam Air Depot for modification work to bring the B-24s up to theatre standards. Some additional work was also carried out on the mission equipment – the AN/APA-24 on the B-24Ms was moved from under the RCM compartment to the position formerly occupied by the belly turret, a modification Ferret VI received at the Hawaiian Air Depot. This movement of the AN/APA-24 allowed antenna heads to be replaced in flight, permitting direction finding over a wider frequency range. The AN/APA-23 recorders were also removed from the ferret and reallocated to the RCM effort in the bomb wings of XXI Bomber Command.[324] Additional work was undertaken on the RCM compartments of the ferrets to address water leaks and carbon monoxide fumes and a compass repeater and altimeter were installed in the radar operator's position.[325] The requested ferret configuration changes that had been originally scheduled to be performed on Ferret VI by the Hawaiian Air Depot were performed by the Guam Air Depot. Originally two aircraft were slated for this modification but with the loss of B-24M ferret 44-41985 only Ferret VI was converted. Since these aircraft were intended to fly mainly at night, most of their defensive armament was removed in order to save weight and increase the aircraft's range. The upper turret, waist guns and nose turret were removed, the ball turret already being removed in Hawaii along with the swapping of twin tail guns for the tail turret. The bombardier's equipment and automatic flight control equipment was removed as well and a C-87 nose section along with 625lb of radio gear were put in the nose. Finally, the window in the RCM compartment was enlarged and the navigator's table expanded. The B-24M ferrets left the Guam Air Depot on 27 April with Ferret VI following almost a month later in the last part of May due to the more extensive modifications required by stripping its turrets.[326]

The 3rd PRS and attached RCM (or R) Flight fell under the control of Twentieth Air Force for the purpose of supporting the strategic bombing campaign against Japan. Day-to-day control of the RCM mission was initially handled by the Countermeasures Air Analysis Center, a unit that reported directly to the Strategic Air Force, Pacific

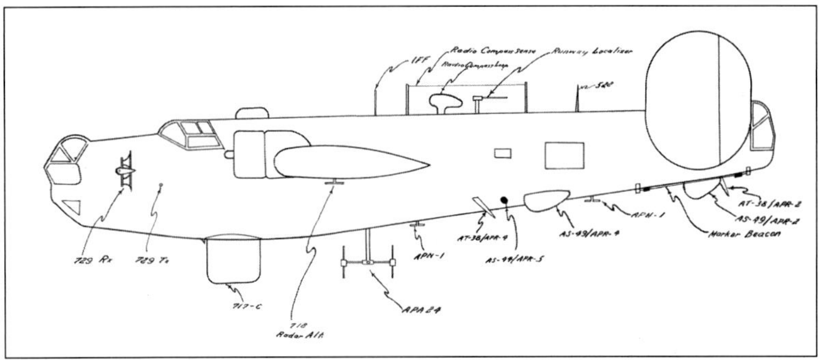

Line drawing of the port fuselage of a B-24J/M ferret depicting antennas and other electronic gear, likely of B-24J s/n 44-41124 Ferret VI prior to deployment. *Air Force Historical Research Agency via George Cully*

Line drawing of top of a B-24J/M ferret aircraft depicting antennas and other electronic gear, likely depicting B-24J s/n 44-41124 Ferret VI prior to deployment. *Air Force Historical Research Agency via George Cully*

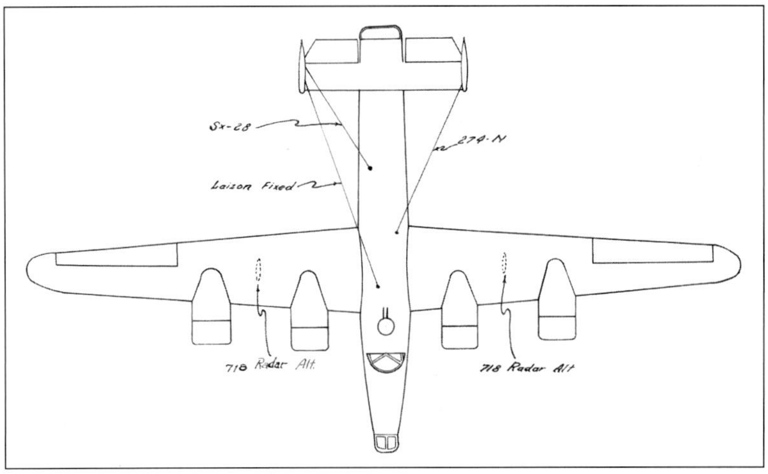

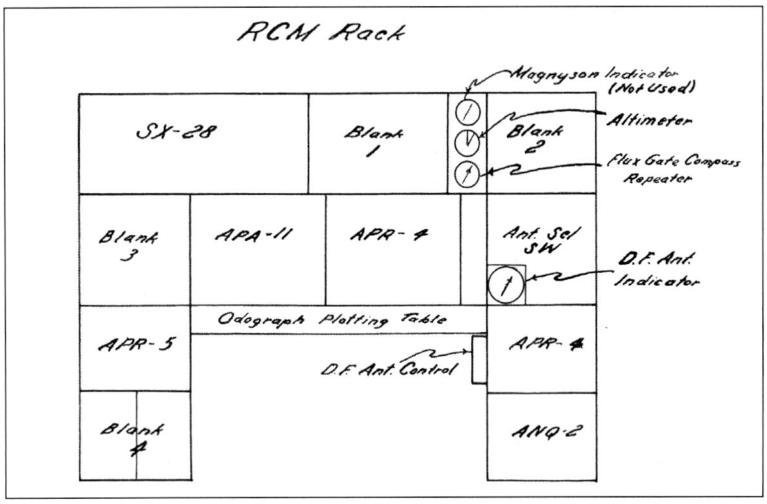

Line drawing of interior electronics rack of a B-24J/M ferret depicting electronic gear, likely depicting B-24J s/n 44-41124 Ferret VI prior to deployment. *Air Force Historical Research Agency via George Cully*

Lt Quevedo poses with his crew next to one of the 3rd PRS Flight R B-24M ferrets. The 3rd PRS did not appear to assign the ferrets to specific crews, but this aircraft is likely B-24M s/n 44-41994, Ferret XVI. Like B-24M s/n 44-41996, Ferret XVIII *Ramp Champ*, its undersides have been painted a dark colour, possibly black. *Joe Riedel via Chuck Varney*

Ocean Area, commanded by the Deputy Commander, Twentieth Air Force. This centre was designed to correlate, analyse and disseminate information on Japanese radars, not only to the XXI BC but also to the Seventh Air Force and US Navy shore-based and aviation RCM activities in the Pacific Ocean Area. In both form and function, it was similar to Section 22.[327] Established in late February 1945 by direction of the Commander in Chief, Pacific Ocean Area, the Countermeasures Air Analysis Center provided collection guidance to the 3rd PRS with respect to missions against Japanese radar sites. A single Quonset hut provided housing for both CAAC staff as well as representatives from each of the Guam-based B-29 wings. In early August the USASTAF HQ recommended the CAAC be reconfigured as the Joint Radar Countermeasures Analysis Group, Pacific, to better incorporate USN actions but it is unlikely this was completed before the end of hostilities.[328] Even with the fine faculties of the CAAC available, the XXI BC needed to know more about Japanese air defence operations than what pure radar reconnaissance could divine for them and for this they turned to intercepting Japanese radio communications.

The initial RCM plan for the XXI BC was drafted in December 1944. Covering radar and radio reconnaissance, the plan emphasised the need to intercept enemy air-ground communications to better understand Japanese fighter direction tactics.[329] The initial concept was to install AN/ARR-5 and BC-348 radio receivers and AN/ANQ-2 voice recorders operated by the RCM observer on one to two B-29 bombers in each squadron, but the programme immediately ran into problems with equipment installation and integration. In addition, the challenge of having non-Japanese speakers trying to sift through radio chatter to determine what was worth recording was also proving to be quite an obstacle. While some minor successes occurred in February 1945 with B-29s recording radio traffic for post-mission translation by Japanese American (Nisei) linguists assigned to the 8th Radio Squadron Mobile (8th RSM), a better solution was required. The preferred answer was an aircraft dedicated to radio reconnaissance with sufficient Japanese linguists and equipment aboard to intercept and translate up to twelve channels of Japanese HF and VHF radio communications. While headquarters worked to develop and field a dedicated platform, the XXI BC turned to the 3rd PRS's new ferret aircraft to provide an interim solution that could operate in both the radio and radar reconnaissance role.[330]

As delivered, the 3rd PRS ferrets were equipped with the AN/ARR-5 and AN/ARR-7 radio receivers. These systems covered the HF and lower VHF frequency range, leaving a linguist to rely upon the ill-suited AN/APR-4 radar receiver to cover the upper VHF spectrum. Guam Air Depot added two voice recorders and two seats in the former navigator's position in the nose to enable two radio search personnel to perform their function.[331] The B-24M ferrets were only able to accommodate two channels of voice intercept without impacting radar search operations, while Ferret VI, the sole B-24J, could handle three voice channels. Even if the requirement was dropped from twelve to four channels for intercept, the mission would still require two ferret aircraft to be flown simultaneously. With only four aircraft on the ramp and each aircraft only capable of flying five missions per month, not enough sorties could be generated to cover the fifteen XXI BC strikes per month. A series of meetings was held and it was determined that the best course of action would be to modify one B-24M ferret for a pure radio intercept role with six channels covered by three Japanese linguist radio intercept operators.[332] The required conversion work could have been performed at the Guam depot, but it is unlikely that it was initiated before the war ended.

For Japanese linguists, the Twentieth Air Force turned to the 8th RSM. Initially, there was concern in having Nisei linguists fly in the B-29 aircraft due to the fact they would be overflying Japan; if the B-29 was shot down there could be dire consequences for this crew member. While some thought was given to training Anglo-Americans to be Japanese linguists, there does not appear to have been much in the way of results from this initiative. The arrival of the ferret aircraft flying a stand-off profile over water opened up the door once again to the use of Nisei linguists.[333] Ten Nisei assigned to the 8th RSM volunteered for flight operations and were trained to operate the AN/ARR-5 and AN/ARR-7 receivers installed on the ferret aircraft.[334] Not only did the linguists remain assigned to the 8th RSM, they continued to receive tasking through their squadron as opposed to the Countermeasures Air Analysis Center tasking that directed the work of the RCM officers. Although an Army Air Forces unit, by mid-1945 the 8th RSM fell under a joint agency for tasking and control. In April 1945 the 8th RSM became the USAAF component of a joint Army-Navy radio exploitation centre, Radio Analysis Group, Forward (RAGFOR). RAGFOR was set up on Guam to exploit Japanese Army and Navy air–ground traffic, using the 8th RSM as one of its intercept arms.[335] With aircraft out of depot, crews in place, and a command and control chain – convoluted as it was – established, the 3rd PRS' Flight R was finally ready to start flying missions.

The XXI BC noted that the crews needed intensive operational and technical training before they could be released to fly against the Home Islands. After emerging from the Guam Air Depot at the end of April, the B-24M ferrets first flew a series of operational check flights and RCM calibration sorties against friendly radars. After the aircraft were declared fit for operations and the crews had a few sorties under their belts they graduated to a series of missions to map Japanese radars on the Nanpo Shoto chain of islands between Iwo Jima and Japan. These sorties were seen as low-threat flights and ideal for Flight R's combat debut.[336]

The first operational mission was flown on 18 May with B-24M ferret 44-41981/Ferret XIV flying a fourteen-and-a-half-hour mission against Haha Jima with the crew of pilot Lt William Marshall. The long transit north from Guam and over Iwo Jima limited '41981 to three hours of circling the target area, prescribing a rectangle approximately 15 miles off the coast. The RCM Observers were able to intercept thirteen signals from Haha Jima and nearby Chichi

Jima, DF'ing five of the signals for plotting. Over the next two weeks, the squadron flew additional DF calibration flights, usually two to three hours in length, to continue to tweak the SIGINT gear. The 3rd PRS' second RCM mission was flown on 24 May to the same locale as Mission #1. Ferret XVI 44-41994 flown by Lt Merlin Harnly's crew was airborne for fourteen and a half hours with tasking to confirm the radars plotted by Mission #1 and gain further data against Chichi Jima. The tempo of operational flights was still low as crews continued to perform calibration and training flights on the other ferret aircraft. This changed in the last week of May when Flight R managed to fly three missions in three days. Ferrets XIV and XVI both flew missions on 29 May, while 44-41996/Ferret XVIII completed a mission on the 31st of the month. While one of the missions on the 29th and the mission on the 31st were back circling Haha Jima, Ferrets XIV's flight on 29 May reached out to Aogashima at the north end of the Nanpo Shoto chain. While a large amount of radar activity was noted, likely in reaction to a B-29 strike hitting Yokohama at the same time, the ferret's AN/APA-24 DF system failed and intercepted radars could not be located. While not confirmed, the B-24M ferret likely staged through Iwo Jima to give it adequate range and endurance to meet mission needs. Flight R's first month of combat ended with Ferret VI returning from the depot.[337] While only five missions were flown, the XXI BC was poised to leap into the world of RCM reconnaissance in June. Trained crews and four ferrets were on hand and results were trickling in – already, Japanese radars plotted by Flight R had their positions confirmed with photography and were passed on to Iwo Jima-based P-51s for destruction.[338]

Map of Japanese radar sites on Chichi Jima Retto produced by the Office of the Director of Communications, Headquarters United States Army Strategic Air Forces, July 1945. The 3rd PRS ferrets routed over this island en route to the Home Islands, providing frequent updates to USAAF knowledge of the island's radars. *Air Force Historical Research Agency via George Cully*

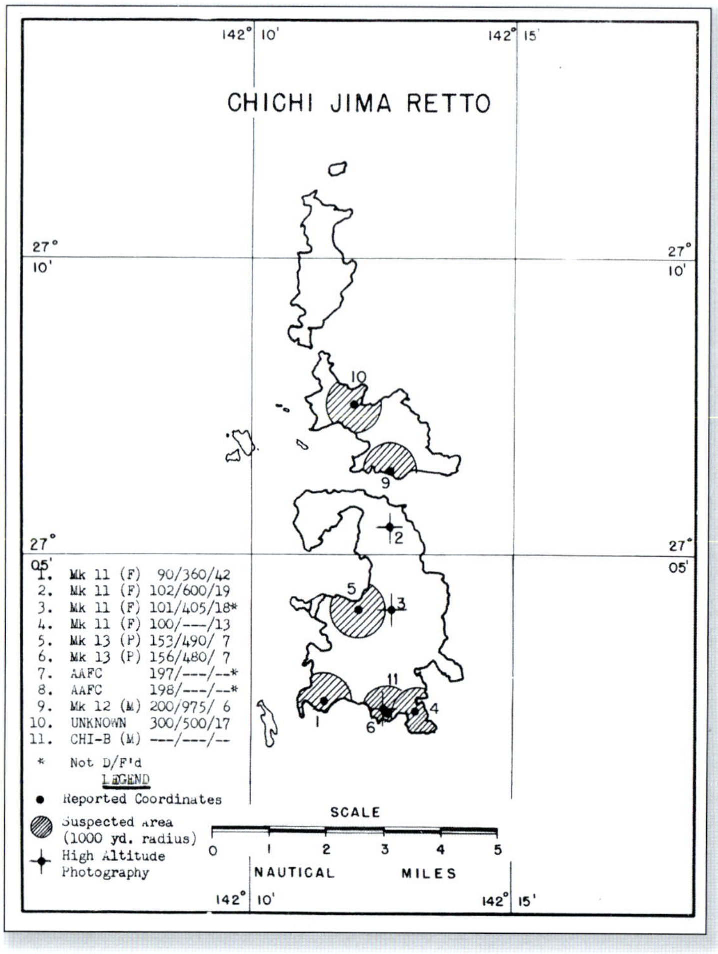

Flight R started out the new month with Mission #6 on 2 June. The mission flew the now familiar track up the Nanpo Shoto, reaching up to Tori Shima to continue the general search for Japanese radars. A lack of activity confirmed the idea that radar reconnaissance missions should be coordinated with B-29 strikes. On the return leg of the flight Ferret XIV landed at Iwo Jima to refuel before continuing back to Guam to complete its near-seventeen-hour mission. The operations tempo continued with missions to Hachijo-Jima, Tori Shima and Aogashima with sorties lasting up to nineteen and a half hours to include the debut combat mission for B-24J Ferret VI. Results varied from mission to mission, with weather impacting collection efforts and all RCM missions still not synched with B-29 strikes. The next series of missions resolved the synchronisation piece. Mission #10 on 9 June flew in conjunction with B-29 strikes against Nagoya, Akashi and Narao, legging up to Aogashima to confirm radar locations and activity in the northern Nanpo Shoto. On 15 June Flight R conducted a more impressive mission set – two ferrets were launched to support a B-29 strike against Osaka. While B-24M Ferret XVI covered the southern Nanpo Shoto chain and orbited near Hachijo-Jima, B-24J Ferret VI flew up to Hachijo-Jima to investigate the northern Nanpo Shoto region. Although results were excellent, Flight R reduced its tempo for the rest of the June by only flying three missions. Mission #13 saw a return to the Aogashima region in conjunction with the 22 June B-29 strikes on Honshu; although radio intercepts were considered excellent, radar reconnaissance was not good due to poor navigation and issues with the AN/APA-24. Mission #14 was a coastal patrol off Honshu the night of 25–26 June with Mission #15 flown on the 26th a carbon copy of Mission #13, this time with good results. Mission #16 on 28 June rounded out flight operations for June. The goal was to update the order of battle in the familiar lower Nanpo Shoto region of Haha Jima and see if radars targeted by Iwo Jima-based P-51s had been taken out of action; the ferret confirmed the radars were still operational.[339] Although June only saw ten missions flown, the flight was preparing for a higher operations tempo by confirming tactics for integration with B-29 strikes and staging through Iwo Jima to enable the overloaded B-24 ferrets to reach the Home Islands of Japan.

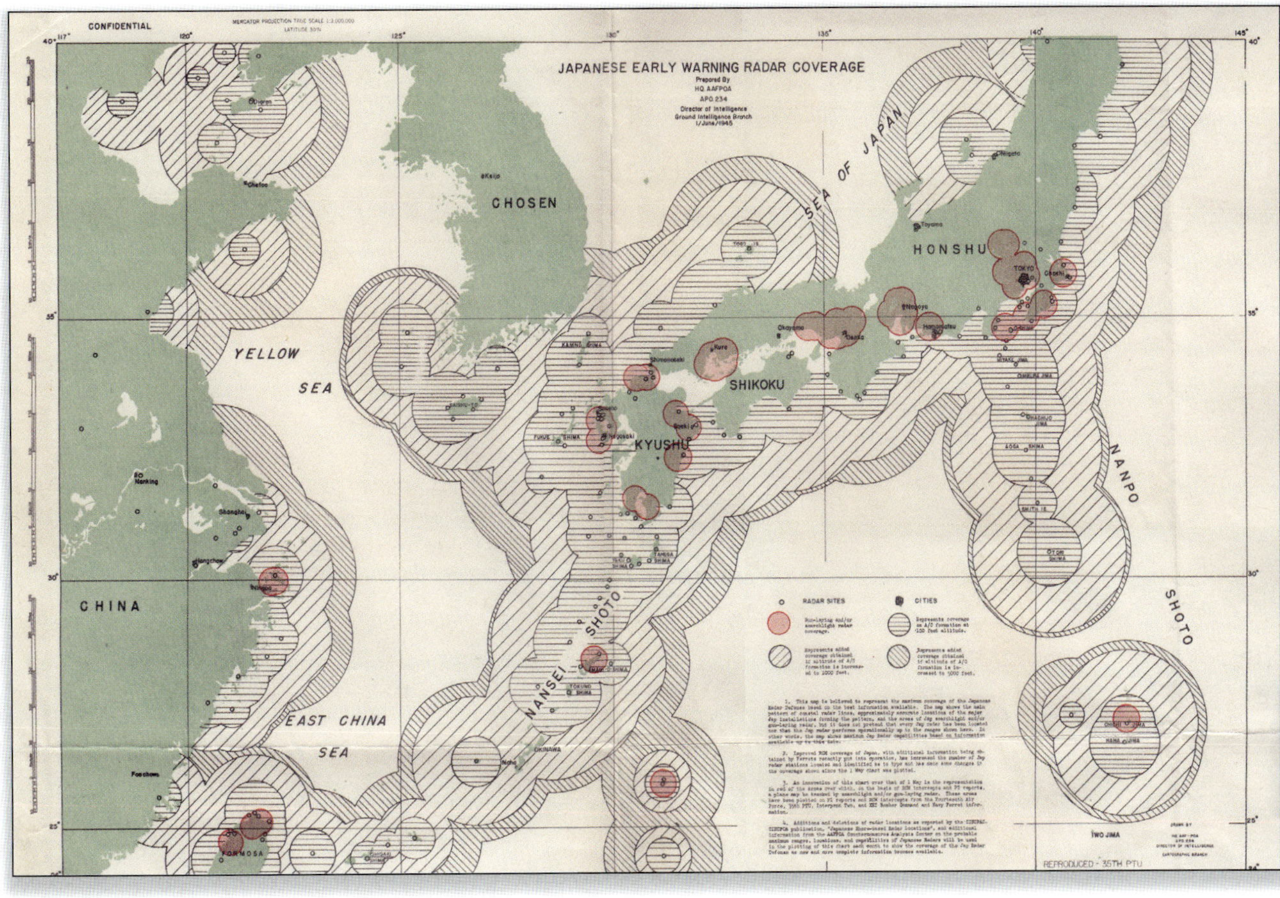

AAF Pacific Ocean Area developed map of the Japanese Home Islands with locations of Japanese radars and rings depicting radar coverage at 100ft, 1,000ft and 5,000ft as well as gun-laying radar coverage in red, 1 June 1945. The 3rd PRS ferrets were critical in providing data with which to construct graphics such as this. *Air Force Historical Research Agency via George Cully*

By the end of June, Flight R's crews were getting comfortable with the missions they were flying and had developed a routine. A typical mission would start with the mission assignment from the CAAC; ferrets were tasked to investigate specific locations – either to fill in gaps of knowledge or confirm suspected radar sites – that were also synchronised with planned XXI BC strikes to ensure the Japanese radars were active. The day of the mission the aircraft and its RCM equipment were checked over by the ground crew before the mission crew arrived. Once the aircraft reached cruising altitude, all the receivers and associated boxes would be rechecked to give time for in-flight maintenance to address any faulty equipment before the aircraft arrived in the target area. If the aircraft was flying north over the Nanpo Shoto, the RCM Observers would verify that incoming radar signals matched the plotted order of battle that by now existed. The work was tedious, mainly scanning through known operating signals and listening for the telltale sound of a scanning radar. Once the ferret arrived at its mission location, the real work started. The RCM Observers listened for radars and once one was found would patch in the AN/APA-17 or AN/APA-24 to get a DF fix on the signal, while at the same time coordinating with the navigator to acquire the exact location of the aircraft. Notes were made on received signals and plots for post-mission analysis. The missions would stretch out to sixteen to twenty hours with a fuel stop at Iwo Jima on the return leg. After landing and maintenance debrief the crews would crawl into their racks for a well-deserved sleep. The next day the RCM Observers would spend four to five hours plotting the DF fixes from the mission and writing up a report on observed radar activity and signals of interest.[340]

Mission #17 flown over 2–3 July saw B-24J Ferret VI fly for eighteen and a half hours off the coasts of Honshu and Shikoku, an operational first for Flight R. Flown in conjunction with a B-29 strike against Minoshima, the mission provided insight into Home Island radio procedures as well as radar deployments. The route of flight was also new for the ferrets, striking out over open water north-west of Iwo Jima as opposed to flying over the islands of the Nanpo Shoto. Mission #18 followed the next day with a flight to the same region to support XXI BC strikes against Shikoku. This sortie was able to uncover the Japanese employment of picket boats for early warning by DF'ing many shipborne radio transmissions and also had one fleeting glance at a

Left forward fuselage of B-24M s/n 44-41996 Ferret XVIII *Ramp Champ* on 7 June 1945. Of note is the black camouflage on the underside of the aircraft and the small radome under the nose housing the spinning AN/APA-17 direction-finding antenna.
Air Force Historical Research Agency via George Cully

Japanese airborne radar carried by a night fighter. Missions #19, 20 and 21 were flown as part of an all-out effort by Flight R to support a 6–7 July strike by 500 B-29s against Chiba, Akashi, Shimizu and Kofu in central and southern Honshu. The ferrets were arrayed in orbits along the southern coast of Honshu, stretching from Wakayama near Shikoku east to Izu shima off Tokyo Bay. All aircraft reported good radar and radio intercepts, although the ferret off Tokyo Bay was not able to locate Japanese radars due to the jamming undertaken by the B-29s and the ferret off Hamatsu had a faulty AN/APA-24 antenna.

Two days later B-24M Ferret XVIII was winging north up the Nanpo Shoto for a mission off Izu shima south of Tokyo Bay, not an optimal placement as the B-29 strikes for the night were west of this location. The AN/APA-24 again failed, reducing mission effectiveness and highlighting the challenges of working with 1940s-era technology. Mission #24 flew on the night of 12–13 July in conjunction with B-29 strikes against Kawasaki, Utsonomiya, and Ichinomiya in eastern Honshu. B-24M Ferret XIV flew north along the familiar Nanpo Shoto to a location along the Honshu coast east of Izu shima to gather good radio and radar intercepts before heading home via Iwo Jima. Four days later Flight R achieved another three-ferret effort to support B-29 strikes against Honshu and Kyushu on the night of 16–17 July. One ferret was positioned off Hamamatsu while the others were positioned off the east coast of Kyushu and the east coast of Shikoku. While B-24J Ferret VI received a fair amount of activity from its location off Hamamatsu, the other ferret aircraft received little to no activity. The placement of a ferret off Shikoku, clearly away from the target areas, was likely to fill in the gaps of radar databases and confirm existing light coverage in this region.[341]

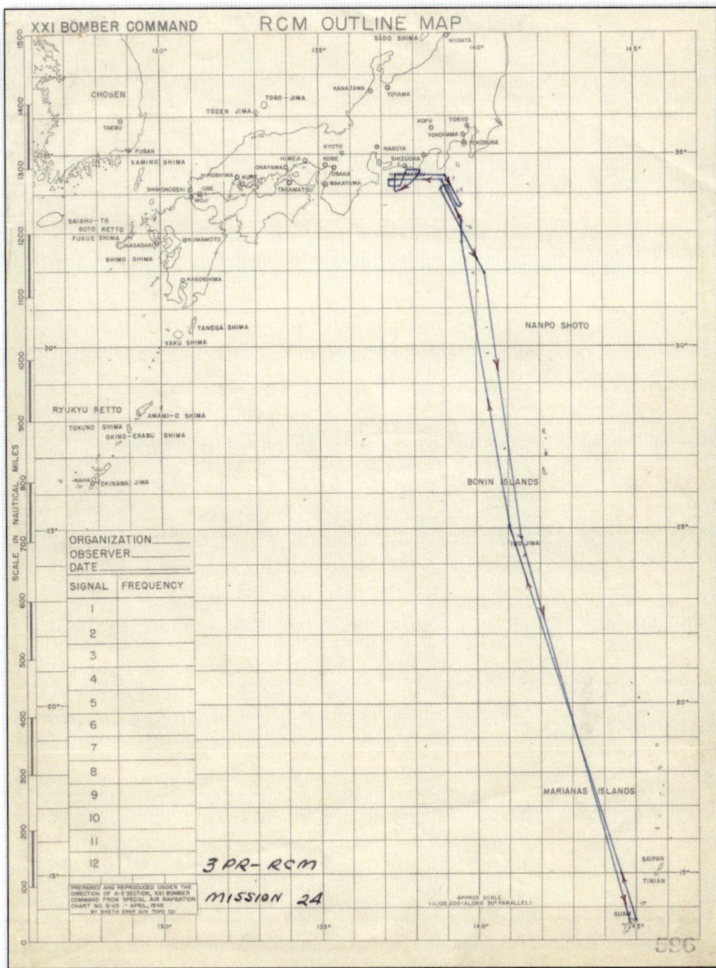

3rd PRS RCM Mission 24 flew on the night of 12–13 July in conjunction with B-29 strikes against Kawasaki, Utsonomiya, and Ichinomiya in eastern Honshu. B-24M Ferret XIV flew north along the familiar Nanpo Shoto to a location along the Honshu coast east of Izu shima to gather good radio and radar intercepts before heading home via Iwo Jima.
Air Force Historical Research Agency via George Cully

The night of 19–20 July witnessed another three-mission surge for Flight R. B-24M Ferrets XIV, XVI and XVIII were dispatched to support B-29 strikes against Chosi, Hitachi and Okazaki. Ferret XIV was positioned off Chosi to support the first two strikes, while Ferret XVI was off Wakayama and Kushimoto and Ferret XVIII was in the Hamamatsu area, both supporting the Okazaki raid. All aircraft received what were now standard radar intercepts and good radio intercepts. The month wrapped up with two more triple-sortie missions – 24 and 29 July. On the 24th the three ferrets took up their now standard orbits off Wakayama, Hamamatsu, Izu shima outside Tokyo Bay to support B-29 strikes on Nagoya, Handa, Takarazuka, Osaka, Tsu and Kawana. The final mission supported B-29 missions flown on the night of 28–29 July against Tsu, Ichinomiya, Ujiyamada, and Ogaki, with two orbits set up in the Nagoya area off Hamamatsu and another outside Tokyo Bay.[342]

Flight R wrapped up its busy week with a single mission off Hamamatsu on 2 August. Ferret VI's mission length, including refuelling at Iwo Jima, stretched out to twenty-five hours to support B-29 strikes against Honshu. Although not optimally placed for what was the Twentieth Air Force's biggest single-day effort, bomber groups en route to northern Honshu likely passed close by. Two missions were flown to support B-29 strikes on 6 August against Ube, Saga, Imabari and Nishinomiya; Ferret XVI set up an orbit off Kyushu, while 44-41981flew off Shikoku. About the time that the ferrets were leaving their mission location off the coast of Japan, three B-29s took off from Tinian on a world-changing atomic mission to Hiroshima. The war was still on, though, and two single missions were flown, one on 8 August off Kyushu and one on the 9th off Shikoku. On 10 August Lt Harnly flew his B-24M Ferret XVI to Guam accompanied by B-24M Ferret XVIII and Ferret VI in preparation for a mission on the 11th but the operation was scrubbed. On 14 August a trio of ferrets was in the air again, this time to support daytime B-29 strikes to Hikari, Osaka and Marifu;

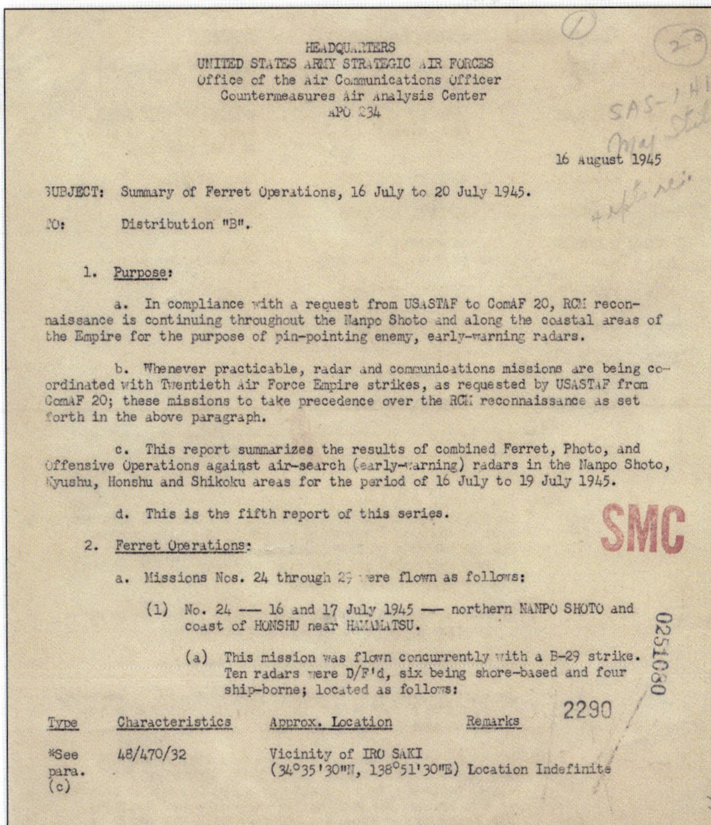
HEADQUARTERS
UNITED STATES ARMY STRATEGIC AIR FORCES
Office of the Air Communications Officer
Countermeasures Air Analysis Center
APO 234

16 August 1945

SUBJECT: Summary of Ferret Operations, 16 July to 20 July 1945.

TO: Distribution "B".

1. Purpose:

a. In compliance with a request from USASTAF to ComAF 20, RCM reconnaissance is continuing throughout the Nanpo Shoto and along the coastal areas of the Empire for the purpose of pin-pointing enemy, early-warning radars.

b. Whenever practicable, radar and communications missions are being co-ordinated with Twentieth Air Force Empire strikes, as requested by USASTAF from ComAF 20; these missions to take precedence over the RCM reconnaissance as set forth in the above paragraph.

c. This report summarizes the results of combined Ferret, Photo, and Offensive Operations against air-search (early-warning) radars in the Nanpo Shoto, Kyushu, Honshu and Shikoku areas for the period of 16 July to 19 July 1945.

d. This is the fifth report of this series.

SMC

2. Ferret Operations:

a. Missions Nos. 24 through 29 were flown as follows:

(1) No. 24 — 16 and 17 July 1945 — northern NANPO SHOTO and coast of HONSHU near HAMAMATSU.

(a) This mission was flown concurrently with a B-29 strike. Ten radars were D/F'd, six being shore-based and four ship-borne; located as follows:

0251080

2290

Type	Characteristics	Approx. Location	Remarks
*See para. (c)	48/470/32	Vicinity of IRO SAKI (34°35'30"N, 138°51'30"E)	Location Indefinite

A ferret mission was not over until its paperwork was complete! The first page for the Summary of Ferret Operations, 16 July to 20 July 1945, outlining 3rd PRS R Flight ferret missions.
Air Force Historical Research Agency via George Cully

Harnly flew his B-24 off Shikoku, Lt Snyder in Ferret XVIII was south of Hamamatsu and Lt Jordan in Ferret VI was east of Tokyo. After completing their mission the crews recovered at Iwo Jima and got some sleep. On 15 August the tired crews flew back to Guam and completed their last combat sorties. For Flight R and the entire USAAF the war was over.[343]

Serial Number	Aircraft	First Mission	Last Mission	Total # Ops Missions	Notes	Fate
44-41124	B-24J-195-CO	7 Jun 45	15 Aug 45	11	Ferret VI	Turned in to RFC, 7 Jun 46
44-41981	B-24M-10-CO	18 May 45	8 Aug 45	11	Ferret XIV	Turned in to RFC, 7 Jun 46
44-41985	B-24M-10-CO	N/A	N/A	N/A	Ferret XV	Lost in training at Guam, March 1945
44-41994	B-24M-10-CO	24 May 45	14 Aug 45	11	Ferret XVI	Returned to US 25 Dec 45; bounced through Garden City, NJ; scrapped Jun 46?
44-41996	B-24M-10-CO	31 May 45	14 Aug 45	9	Ferret XVIII; 'Ramp Champ'	Returned to US 25 Dec 45; bounced through Garden City, NJ; scrapped Jun 46?

Chapter 12

Ferret Production Line

The utility of ferrets for operational purposes had been proven by the early production examples along with the field-modified interim aircraft. Based on this information, the Air Staff directed Wright Field to look into a follow-on production lot of ferrets after the XXI BC aircraft of Project 96978S were built. By late 1944, plans were in place to produce at least eight more ferrets within the coming six months.[344] Two months later, in early February 1945, Air Technical Service Command (ATSC) solidified the new production line in an official memo. Ten ferrets were planned, with the first example scheduled to be completed on 1 May, and four more per month to be completed for the remainder of the year. The basis for these aircraft was the engineering undertaken for Project 96978S, the XXI BC ferrets, as captured in Technical Instruction 2024 Addendums 14 and 27.[345]

Hangar space and manpower limited the production line at Fairfield Air Depot to five aircraft at a time even with personnel on a twelve hours per day, seven day a week work schedule.[346] Four aircraft per month for months on end could not be handled in house by Patterson Field, so instead the USAAF turned to the existing system of modification centres that aided US aircraft production. Modification centres were a result of the American style of producing of aircraft in the Second World War. To expedite aircraft changes required for an export customer or modifications dictated by a combat theatre, the centres were established in January 1942. About twenty were opened during the war, though not all were in operation at the same time. The centres started out as repair and maintenance facilities for the nation's major airlines, but eventually they grew into dedicated factories. This growing mass of production sites was managed by the Production Division at Wright Field. Two of the modification facilities were set aside in late 1944 to handle rush orders – United Cheyenne (Wyoming) and Bechtel-McCone-Parsons Birmingham (Alabama) – and ATSC chose the former to establish a ferret production line.[347] Engineering drawings, wiring diagrams and photographs were sent to Cheyenne from ATSC's Systems Engineering Laboratory. An aircraft was set aside at the modification centre as a prototype ferret to verify the plans worked in the real world.[348] This Cheyenne model ferret was started in late March and completed by May 1945. Minor equipment changes based on experience from the field continued to trickle in from Air Staff even as the production line started.[349] By mid-May the requirement for production at Cheyenne had grown to fifteen ferrets.[350]

The USAAF turned to the United Cheyenne Modification Centre for a ferret production line in early 1945. Building No. 101 of the Modification Centre survives at Cheyenne Airport, Wyoming. *US National Archives*

The Final Deliveries

Just when the ferret production line was finally established and running at full steam the war started to change. The surrender of Nazi Germany and the acceleration of the war in the Pacific wreaked havoc on the ATSC production planners in Ohio. The last production series was continually in a state of flux, with projects being added, cancelled, and updated in the last few months of the Second World War. Records indicate at least two domestic and seven overseas projects were carried on the books at one time or another. The two domestic projects delivered three ferrets from Cheyenne to the Fourth Air Force for service at the RCM Reconnaissance Training Programme at March Field where Ferrets XVII and 0 were stationed. The first aircraft arrived in California in June 1945, with two following in July.[351]

The overseas projects can be divided into two groups – theatre-level requirements and strategic requirements. Theatre requirements were associated with numbered air forces and aligned to support their RCM needs within their areas of responsibility. The existing pattern in theatres had been to control RCM activities at the numbered air force level with ferret aircraft administratively assigned to a bomb group or squadron. With the Eleventh Air Force in Alaska and the Tenth and Fourteenth Air Forces in the CBI theatre this continued until the end of the war and replacements for existing production or theatre-built ferrets were programmed for delivery. Project 97047S was a high-priority production of a single ferret to replace Ferret I in Alaska supporting Eleventh Air Force operations in the Aleutians. Project 94260-R was the production of two ferrets for the Tenth Air Force with Project 94224S two ferrets likely intended for the Fourteenth Air Force. Projects 94260-R and 94224S were both cancelled by late May 1945, with Project 97047S delivered after the end of hostilities. Strategic requirements were associated with the strategic bombing campaign against Japan. The Twentieth Air Force had the RCM flight of the 3rd PRS; a similar arrangement was intended for the Eighth Air Force, en route to the Pacific theatre at the end of the war. This new unit, though, needed specialised ferret training.

Training

In March 1945 the USAAF finally formalised ferret crew training with an official course. Requirements for the course were outlined in a 7 March 1945 directive from HQS AAF. Since the ferrets were going exclusively to the Pacific theatre, it made sense to align the course with existing Pacific-oriented training. The 420th AAF Base Unit at March Field, California, assigned to the Fourth Air Force, provided Pacific theatre-oriented B-24 training unit for aircrew assigned to the AAF Pacific Ocean Areas. Crews would arrive from Air Training Command (ATC) B-24 training and get additional navigation training, training on tactics such as open ocean reconnaissance, and orientation on Pacific theatre-specific modifications to the B-24. Established as Section V within 420th AAF Base Unit, the ferret training programme was broken into flying and ground segments and led by Maj. James McElhone, formerly of the 16th RS. B-24 crews graduating from the 420th AAF Base Unit and destined for ferret training had their bombardier and three gunners replaced by two 748s (Aircraft Mechanic Gunner), two 7888s (RCM Observers), and one 0142 (Radar Observer) to make a new-eleven man crew. The initial plan for the ferret course was to run three two-month courses, then transition to a four-month course. The first ferret aircraft was to arrive the end of February, the second mid-March, and a third the first of April but by the time training started on 1 April only Ferret XVII was in place, arriving at March Field sometime during the month prior. Fourth Air Force engaged Washington to expedite delivery of equipment for ground simulators to allow training on specific pieces of RCM equipment.[352]

The first ferret course started on 1 April with five crews who graduated from the 18 March B-24 class. Additional instructor cadre were assigned after the course had already started. The maximum capacity of the training was ten ferret crews (two classes), using Ferret XVII and three standard B-24s for the flying curriculum. Initial training centred on making the individual crew positions work together; RCM officers who arrived knowing about individual equipment sets now needed to know how to work as part of a crew with their pilot, navigator, and other crew members. Flying training was set at a minimum of eight missions, including flights along the US west coast from San Diego to Seattle to plot US Army radar sites as well as long-duration, night, over-water missions. The Ferret Ground School focused on equipment operation, to include the AN/APR-4; AN/APR-5A; AN/APR-7; AN/ARR-5; AN/ARR-7; AN/APA-11; AN/APA-24; AN/APA-17; and AN/ANQ-1 and AN/APA-23 recorders, with many of the instructors former members of the 16th RS. Radar Observers were given additional training on the SCR-717 and SCR-729 radars.[353]

Training expanded with a second set of five crews starting the next class on 25 April. Ground trainers were also completed, including a mock-up of a B-24 fuselage with RCM equipment installed. On 12 May, Ferret XVII B-24M s/n 44-41995 crashed on a training flight with Crew 505 on a long-range, over-water training mission up to Oregon. There were no survivors among the crew of eleven. Training ground to a halt without having a ferret aircraft for crews, with the course that started on 1 April and scheduled for graduation on 25 May on hold; a waiver allowed the remaining four crews to graduate with the training they had already completed. A request was made for four ferret aircraft to the Continental Air Force, which replied 'several ferret aircraft would be available at the end of May'. By the end of May the Cheyenne production line only had one ferret available, Section V dispatching a crew from March Field via C-47 on 31 May to retrieve Ferret B-24M s/n 44-51282. In the interim, two SCR 717 radar-equipped B-24Js on base were made available for the course. Ferret '282 arrived from Cheyenne on 3 June, followed on 7 June by B-24J s/n 44-40225 Ferret 0 from Eglin. With the transition to very heavy training (initially B-32, then B-29) at March Field, it was anticipated that B-24 ferret training could move to a base that was continuing with B-24 training.[354]

Four new crews started training on 25 May. In June 1945 two ferret crews went to Salinas, California, for overseas shipment. They retrieved two new B-24M ferrets from Cheyenne and set out to join the 20th RS in the Pacific, leaving eleven ferret crews at March Field. That month most of March Field's B-24s transferred to other bases including Gowen Field, Idaho, the new B-24 training base for Pacific theatre crews, leaving behind the two ferret B-24s along with the two radar-equipped B-24Js. The decision was made to keep ferret training at March Field due to the terrain and its proximity to coast to allow work with US Army radars as well as overwater flights. The ferret training was assigned to the 474th Base Unit on 1 July 1945, remaining under the Fourth Air Force while the March Field B-29s were aligned under the Second Air Force. A reduced class of two crews started ferret training on 25 June.[355]

On 18 July five crews arrived at March Field after graduating from Pacific theatre orientation training at Gowen Field and started ferret training. The following week two B-24M ferrets arrived from Cheyenne, s/n 44-51802 and s/n 44-51356, bringing the ferret training fleet up to four ferret B-24s and two radar-equipped B-24Js. In early August six partially trained crews of the RCM Flight, 1st PRS arrived from Salina Field, Kansas, for a three-week training course. A quick review of their experience by the school staff revealed they needed the full two-month training course.[356]

B-24M-30-FO s/n 44-51802 arrived at March Field from Cheyenne in late July 1945 to assist in the training. By the end of the war the ferret training fleet at March Field had four ferret B-24s and two radar-equipped B-24Js. *Chuck Varney*

1 PRS

The final requirement for new ferrets was to support the strategic war against Japan. Similar in form and function to the 3rd PRS, the 1st Photo Reconnaissance Squadron, Very Heavy, was training in the US on the F-13 before deploying to the Pacific to support the XX Bomber Command of the Eighth Air Force. The Eighth Air Force, under the command of Gen. Jimmy Doolittle, was in the process of redeploying to the Pacific Theatre from Europe and re-equipping with B-29 bombers to aid the XXI Bomber Command in the strategic bombing campaign against Japan. In February 1945 the formal requirement was identified for a RCM flight for the 1st PRS equipped with four aircraft with two

Order DOM 126-B covered the production of three ferrets for training with the Fourth Air Force. B-24M-25-FO s/n 44-51356, along with Ferret XVII and B-24M s/n 44-51282, constituted this order. While Ferret XVII was built in Ohio and Florida, the other two ferrets were built at the new production line at the Cheyenne Modification Centre. *C. Walker via Chuck Varney*

reserves. While it was originally planned to use experienced personnel from the disbanding 16th RS (H), this apparently did not take place.[357] Although the 1st PRS had organised its new RCM flight in June as planned, records do not indicate that any aircraft were actually delivered to the squadron by the promised June delivery date.[358] The 1st PRS F-13s deployed to Okinawa in September 1945, leaving the RCM Flight back at March Field.[359]

Ferret C-1 – Pathway to the Future

Back in the US, a dedicated COMINT reconnaissance aircraft was initially discussed in October 1944. By early December, Air Staff ordered ATSC to modify a B-24J into a COMINT ferret dubbed 'C-1' that incorporated radio receivers and three operators into the rear bomb bay of the aircraft in an arrangement used by Ferrets XIV–XVIII. Although the radar ferrets had priority in engineering, as soon as their development work was done the C-1 was to be next in line.[360] Air Staff had initially directed six B-24s be diverted from radar ferrets to C-1 COMINT ferrets in late March 1945, but for unknown reasons within two weeks the order was reversed and only Ferret C-1 was produced.[361]

C-1 was a joint development of ATSC at Wright Field and Bell Telephone Laboratories, Inc. B-24M s/n 44-42106, accepted by the USAAF on 27 December 1944, was used as a starting point. The bomber made its way to Patterson Field in January and was shifted around Wright Field for a few months before work began in earnest in April 1945. Within three months it was completed and delivered to Eglin Field on 23 July 1945.[362] C-1 was designed to search between .55 and 300 MHz. The rear bomb bay was converted to house equipment, with positions for three operators each equipped with a search receiver and recording attachment for automatically scanning a band of frequencies, a manually operated search receiver, and two voice recorders. Panoramic receivers and direction-finding equipment for 50 to 250 MHz rounded out the fit. Three radio receivers were required to cover the desired frequency range, each with its own antenna. In order to save time, standard communications equipment in inventory was used.[363]

FEAF was initially lukewarm to the idea of airborne COMINT capability. By early 1945 the Fifth Air Force was encountering few Japanese fighters and their VHF radio communications, the primary target of an COMINT airborne platform and its added capability when compared to the HF intercept undertaken by the terrestrial 1st RSM linguists.[364] As planning neared for the invasion of Japan and the FEAF started to look at the air defences of the Home Islands, the Fifth Air Force showed renewed interest in the concept.[365] Strategic forces, already battling the Home Island air defences, had addressed this need through modifying their existing radar ferret fleet (see Chapter 11). With Japan's surrender announcement on 15 August the need for a dedicated airborne COMINT platform disappeared and by the end of August the FEAF recommended cancelling Project 96974-S/Ferret C-1.[366] Ferret C-1 never deployed overseas and ended up at the AAF Centre at Orlando, Florida, with testing scheduled in December 1945 to verify equipment installation planned for a B-29 aircraft.[367]

The End – and the Beginning

Japan's surrender on 15 August 1945 brought air combat in the Pacific to a sudden halt. Two weeks later, on 29 August, the Air Staff cancelled all B-24 ferret production.[368] Although there was some initial planning to develop a ferret variant of the B-32, little evidence has been found that it went beyond the design stage.[369] The USAAF war machine, operating with almost four years of inertia, took a while to wind down. Training at March Field continued more out of momentum than for any stated need as the Army struggled to demobilise personnel rapidly. In six months, the formal ferret training had produced twenty-six crews; one was lost in the crash of Ferret XVII in May 1945, nine were sent overseas, and sixteen were awaiting orders at end of the war.[370] One of the crews went to Salinas in September to retrieve a ferret bound for Alaska, the last of the B-24 ferrets to see active service. The 474th Air Base Unit concluded flying training on 2 October 1945. The four B-24 ferrets remained at March Field until they flew to Garden City Field, Kansas, for storage on 3 March 1946.

Completed ferrets still in the US were likely flown into storage at one of the many aircraft storage sites set up in 1945. Overseas ferrets slowly returned to the US as their squadrons were stood down. The four 20th RS ferrets returned at the end of the 1945, with Ferrets XI–XIII all being declared excess in November 1945; Ferret X lasted until January 1946. The 3rd PRS ferrets returned to the US in late December and were turned over to the Reconstruction Finance Corporation for disposition in June 1946. Although the USAAF was closing down most of its ferret operations, Alaska appeared to be the outlier.

The RCM section of the 404th BS was slowly consolidated. The five enlisted RCM mechanics were formally assigned to the squadron when the 8th Signal Maintenance Team, Advanced Command Post, HQ Eleventh Air Force ,was dis-established in October 1945. On 17 October 1945 new-build ferret B-24M-30-FO s/n 44-51784 arrived from Salinas via San Francisco and was assigned to the 404th BS to replace Ferret 1, B-24D 41-23886. The new aircraft was expected to arrive at Shemya in early November. On 18 October, long-serving '23886 and the other remaining B-24Ds in the squadron were transferred to the Alaska Air Depot at Elmendorf Field for storage and further disposition. The B-24M ferret continued where

Ferret 1 left off, joining other 404th BS bombers flying maritime missions in the far north to monitor Soviet activity. Unfortunately, '51784 would not lead the charmed life of its predecessor as it crashed at Shemya due to heavy fog on 16 June 1946 with only three survivors.[371] The last B-24 ferret mission had been flown.

Serial Number	Aircraft	First Mission	Last Mission	Total # Ops Missions	Notes	Fate
44-41995	B-24M-10-CO	N/A	N/A	N/A	Ferret XVII; training, March Field, CA	Lost on training flight in CA, 12 May 45
44-40255	B-24J-150-CO	N/A	N/A	N/A	Ferret 0; training, March Field, CA	Turned in to 'Long Bch ATC', 13 Jun 46
44-42106	B-24M-15-CO	N/A	N/A	N/A	Ferret C-1; stayed at Eglin Field, FL	Turned in to RFC, 3 Jun 46
44-51802	B-24M-30-FO	N/A	N/A	N/A	Training, March Field, CA	Turned in to RFC, 21 May 46
44-51356	B-24M-25-FO	N/A	N/A	N/A	Training, March Field, CA	Turned in to RFC, 1 Jun 46
44-51282	B-24M-30-FO	N/A	N/A		Training, March Field, CA	Turned in to RFC, 18 May 46
44-51784	B-24M-30-FO	Oct 45?	16 Jun 46	Unk	Arrived at Shemya, AK, for assignment to 404 BS, 17 Oct 45	Crashed at Shemya Island, Alaska, due to heavy fog 16 Jun 46. Three survivors.

Chapter 13

After the end of hostilities, the B-24 was deemed obsolete and mass scrapping of the Second World War fleet had commenced; by 1947, only seven Liberators were still on strength with the USAAF. The sound of gunfire from the Second World War had barely quieted when reconnaissance activities against the Soviet Union started to tick upward, as proven by the tasking of new-build ferret B-24M-30-FO '51784 in Alaska. Unfortunately, the SIGINT effort was still managed along the lines of the numbered air force-centric approach from the prior war. USAF forces in Europe modified photo mapping B-17s to fly SIGINT missions against the Soviets in the Baltic region. This activity drove the Aircraft Radio Laboratory at Wright Field to modify a B-29 into a 'ferret' radar reconnaissance aircraft in early 1947. Stripped of armament and with electronic gear and six operators in the fuselage aft of the bomb bay, the aircraft departed for Alaska on 17 May 1947. After flying eight operational missions against the Soviet Chukotski Peninsula the aircraft returned to the US, then deployed to West Germany in September to fly a mission along the Berlin corridor.[372]

The prototype B-29 ferret provided proof of concept for a new breed of SIGINT aircraft, and after a few tweaks in the design in late 1947 conversion of ten stored B-29 aircraft into RB-29AE ferret aircraft commenced in early 1948.[373] Not all modifications to the RB-29s came from manufacturers or Wright Field. Similar to the field-modified ferrets from the Second World War,

Following a B-29 ferret proof of concept, design work was completed in late 1947 and conversion of ten stored B-29 aircraft into RB-29AE ferret aircraft commenced in early 1948. These aircraft saw use with Strategic Air Command until 1953. A 324th SRS flight crew poses with RB-29AE ferret aircraft s/n 44-62286 in June 1950. *Air Force Historical Research Agency via George Cully*

theatre forces built their own ferrets to provide a capability that Washington was slow in providing. In August 1947 the 46th RS in Alaska modified two of their F-13 photo reconnaissance B-29s to carry SIGINT gear and two RCM Observers in the aft pressurised section. In late 1948 Far East Air Forces, desiring a SIGINT capability for the 31st RS as well, modified two squadron RB-29A aircraft into SIGINT birds at the Japan Air Material Area Depot at Tachikawa, Japan. Not one to miss out, European Command activated its own special reconnaissance unit, the 7499th Squadron, and flew theatre-modified RB-17s as ferrets.[374]

The Second World War's Twentieth Air Force turned out to be the progenitor of Cold War reconnaissance, Strategic Air Command (SAC) eventually taking charge of USAF airborne SIGINT assets and employing them in a manner seen over Japan in 1945. In its short six-month existence, Flight R of the 3rd PRS was assigned four of the most advanced electronic reconnaissance aircraft available to the USAAF and flew forty-three combat sorties. These sorties – many ranging up to twenty hours and including refuelling stops en route – supported the Twentieth Air Force's strategic bombing campaign against Japan by effectively locating and characterising Japanese Army radars for subsequent jamming or destruction. In addition,

The RB-50G replaced the RB-29AE for ferret operations within Strategic Air Command. Fifteen RB-50B photo reconnaissance aircraft were sent to Boeing for conversion to RB-50Gs, with the first three aircraft arriving at the 343rd SRS in July 1951. RB-50G s/n 47-151 was one of this group, specifically designed for the worldwide signals intelligence mission. *Jack Morris via George Cully*

Strategic Air Command SIGINT transitioned to the jet age with the RB-47H, with the first aircraft delivered in August 1955. A total of thirty-two RB-47H models were built for electronic intelligence missions, with three additional airframes as the specialised ERB-47H. The bomb bay was replaced by a pressurised compartment, which accommodated three Electronic Warfare Officers on the RB-47H and two on the ERB-47H. RB-47H s/n 53-4296 is parked on the ramp at Offutt AFB, Nebraska, in June 1967. *US National Archives*

Flight R was the first unit in the USAAF to routinely fly with linguists as airborne radio intercept operators. When the Cold War turned hot over Korea, SAC 31st SRS RB-29 SIGINT aircraft accompanied bomber strikes over North Korean territory to look for new radars. When the second hot war in Asia started the following decade SAC RC-135M SIGINT aircraft performed a similar function, plotting radars and listening in on enemy radio communications.

While the number of ferret aircraft built during the war was small compared to total bomber production, their impact is still being felt today. Through their reconnaissance missions, the USAAF learned how to conduct warfare in the electromagnetic spectrum and increase their understanding of adversary radar systems. Techniques were developed and personnel were trained on how to task, collect and analyse enemy communications and radar systems – all processes that are still in use today. In addition, airmen learned how to rapidly field new technology and modify it in the field – a predecessor to the quick reaction capabilities currently used by contemporary SIGINT units. What is old is new and forever young in the world of airborne reconnaissance.

Soon a larger airframe with more capacity was required to replace the RB-47H. Three KC-135A-II Office Boy aircraft were delivered in 1962 and soon upgraded to the RC-135D Rivet Brass configuration. The RC-135M was the result of a 1965 requirement for additional Office Boy aircraft. Six C-135Bs were converted into RC-135M Rivet Card aircraft with delivery starting in 1967. RC-135M s/n 62-4132 is shown at the Greenville, Texas, facility used to upgrade the aircraft. The aircraft were modified over the ensuing fifty years and still fly as part of the current RC-135 fleet. *Big Safari Programme Office, Greenville, Texas, via John Reynolds*

Notes

1 Director of Training, Boca Raton Army Air Field. RCM Instruction Manual. March 1944. Air Force Historical Research Agency, IRIS 169984, Maxwell AFB, AL.; Director for Training & Operations, Boca Raton Army Air Field. The Story of Radar. November 1944. Located in History of Boca Raton Field – 1 November 1944–31 December 1944. Documents 79–141. No date. Air Force Historical Research Agency, IRIS 169935, Maxwell AFB, AL.

2 Harry Von Kroge, *GEMA: Birthplace of German Radar and Sonar* (Bristol: Institute of Physics Publishing, 1998)

3 Yasuzo Nakagawa, Japanese Radar and Related Weapons of World War II (Aegean Park Press: Laguna Hills, CA, 1997), pp.10–16.

4 Nakagawa, pp.24–29.

5 2D & 3D Operations Analysis Section, Far East Air Force. A Short Survey of Japanese Radar, Volume I, 20 November 1945; Air Force Historical Research Agency, 720.310A V.1, Maxwell AFB, AL., p.11.

6 2D & 3D Operations Analysis Section, Far East Air Force. A Short Survey of Japanese Radar, Volume II, 20 November 1945; Air Force Historical Research Agency, 720.310A V.2, Maxwell AFB, AL., pp.5–15.

7 A Short Survey of Japanese Radar, Volume I, pp.1–8.

8 A Short Survey of Japanese Radar, Volume I, pp.14–15.

9 David Zimmerman, *Britain's Shield* (Stroud: Sutton Publishing Company, 2001).

10 Sean Swords, *Technical History of the Beginnings of Radar* (London: P. Peregrinus on behalf of the Institution of Electrical Engineers, 1986), pp.101–115.

11 Arthur Vieweger, 'Development of Radar SCR-270,' *Radar Reliability Newsletter* (Dec. 1960, Jan. 1961): p.555. Historical Electronics Museum Archive, Baltimore, Md.

12 Swords, pp.115–16.

13 Vieweger, p.558.

14 US Congress, *Hearings before the Joint Committee on the Investigation of the Pearl Harbor Attack* (Washington, D.C.: U.S. GPO, 1946), 27:358.

15 George Thompson and Dixie Harris, *The Signal Corps: The Outcome (Mid-1943 Through 1945),* (Washington: US Government Printing Office, 1991), pp.306–7.

16 Assistant Chief of Air Staff, Operations, Commitments & Requirements (Air Communications Division). Memorandum to Chief Signal Officer, War Department. 1 Sept 1943. Subject: Development of RC-164. File 413.44-R, Box 627, Entry 294 – Classified Central Decimal Files, RG 18, National Archives; Dulany Terrett, *The Signal Corps: The Emergency (To December 1941),* (Washington: US Government Printing Office, 1994), p.28.

17 Thompson and Harris, pp.306–7.

18 George Thompson, Dixie Harris, Pauline Oakes and Dulany Terrett, *The Signal Corps: The Test (December 1941 to July 1943),* (Washington: US Government Printing Office, 1957), p.85.

19 Thompson and Harris, pp.435–7.

20 Historical Branch, Army Air Forces Proving Ground Command. History of the Army Air Forces Proving Ground Command, Part I – Historical Outline. 30 Jan 1945. Air Force Historical Research Agency, IRIS 155425, Maxwell AFB, AL.

21 Historical Branch, Army Air Forces Proving Ground Command. History of the Army Air Forces Proving Ground Command, Part I – Historical Outline. 30 Jan 1945. Air Force Historical Research Agency, IRIS 155425, Maxwell AFB, AL.; Thompson and Harris, p.308.

22 Terrett, p.173.

23 Thompson and Harris, p.305.

24 Thompson and Harris, p.302.

25 Monroe Singer, 'Harvard Radio Research Lab Developed Countermeasures Against Enemy Defences', 30 November 1945, Harvard Crimson.

[26] Alfred Price, *The History of US Electronic Warfare, Volume I,* (Washington: Association of Old Crows, 1984), pp.36, 52–53.

[27] Headquarters, 16th Reconnaissance Squadron (H) Sp. History, May–Sept 1943. N.d. Air Force Historical Research Agency, SQ-RCN-16-HI, May–Sep 43/IRIS 66538, Maxwell AFB, AL.

[28] Base Historical Officer, Boca Raton Army Air Field. History of Boca Raton Army Air Field, Boca Raton, Florida (3501st Base Unit, Tech. School), 1 March 1945–30 April 1945. No date. Air Force Historical Research Agency, IRIS 169941, Maxwell AFB, AL.

[29] Base Historical Officer, Boca Raton Army Air Field. History of Boca Raton Army Air Field, Boca Raton, Florida (3501st Base Unit), 1 January 1945–28 February 1945. No date. Air Force Historical Research Agency, IRIS 169937, Maxwell AFB, AL; Historical Programme, Technical Training Command. History of Boca Raton Field – 1 March 1944–30 April 1944, Appendix B – Academic Department Courses and Syllabi. No date. Air Force Historical Research Agency, IRIS 169917, Maxwell AFB, AL.

[30] Base Historical Officer, Boca Raton Field. History of Boca Raton Field – 1 May 1944–30 June 1944, Appendix B, Documents (Radar Training Program). No date. Air Force Historical Research Agency, IRIS 169923, Maxwell AFB, AL.

[31] Base Historical Officer, Boca Raton Field. History of Boca Raton Field – 1 May 1944–30 June 1944, Appendix B, Documents (Radar Training Program). No date. Air Force Historical Research Agency, IRIS 169923, Maxwell AFB, AL.; Base Historical Officer, Boca Raton Field. History of Boca Raton Field – 1 July 1944–31 August 1944, Volume 2. No date. Air Force Historical Research Agency, IRIS 169926, Maxwell AFB, AL.; Base Historical Officer, Boca Raton Field. History of Boca Raton Field – 1 July 1944–31 August 1944, Appendix B, Documents (Radar Training). No date. Air Force Historical Research Agency, IRIS 169927, Maxwell AFB, AL.; Base Historical Officer, Boca Raton Field. History of Boca Raton Field – 1 September 1944–31 October 1944. No date. Air Force Historical Research Agency, IRIS 169928, Maxwell AFB, AL.

[32] Base Historical Officer, Boca Raton Field. History of Boca Raton Field – 1 September 1944–31 October 1944. No date. Air Force Historical Research Agency, IRIS 169928, Maxwell AFB, AL., Base Historical Officer, Boca Raton Field. History of Boca Raton Field – 1 November 1944–31 December 1944. No date. Air Force Historical Research Agency, IRIS 169933, Maxwell AFB, AL.; Base Historical Officer, Boca Raton Army Air Field. History of Boca Raton Army Air Field, Boca Raton, Florida (3501st Base Unit), 1 January 1945–28 February 1945, Volume 2 – Documents. No date. Air Force Historical Research Agency, IRIS 169938, Maxwell AFB, AL.; Base Historical Officer, Boca Raton Army Air Field. History of Boca Raton Army Air Field, Boca Raton, Florida (3501st Base Unit, Tech. School), 1 March 1945–30 April 1945. No date. Air Force Historical Research Agency, IRIS 169941, Maxwell AFB, AL.

[33] Base Historical Officer, Boca Raton Army Air Field. History of Boca Raton Army Air Field, Boca Raton, Florida (3501st Base Unit, Tech. School), 1 March 1945–30 April 1945. No date. Air Force Historical Research Agency, IRIS 169941, Maxwell AFB, AL.; Base Historical Officer, Boca Raton Army Air Field. History of Boca Raton Army Air Field (3501st Base Unit, Tech. School), Boca Raton, Florida, 1 May 1945–30 June 1945. No date. Air Force Historical Research Agency, IRIS 169944, Maxwell AFB, AL.

[34] Base Historical Officer, Boca Raton Army Air Field. History of Boca Raton Army Air Field (3501st Base Unit, Tech. School), Boca Raton, Florida, 1 May 1945–30 June 1945. No date. Air Force Historical Research Agency, IRIS 169944, Maxwell AFB, AL.; Base Historical Officer, Boca Raton Army Air Field. History of Boca Raton Army Air Field, 3501st AAF Base Unit (Tech Sch – Radar), Boca Raton, Florida, 1 July 1945–31 August 1945. No date. Air Force Historical Research Agency, IRIS 169946, Maxwell AFB, AL.; Base Historical Officer, Boca Raton Army Air Field. History of Boca Raton Army Air Field, 3501st AAF Base Unit (Tech Sch – Radar), Boca Raton, Florida, 1 September 1945–31 October 1945. No date. Air Force Historical Research Agency, IRIS 169948, Maxwell AFB, AL.

[35] Director of Training, Boca Raton Army Air Field. RCM Instruction Manual. March 1944. Air Force Historical Research Agency, IRIS 169984, Maxwell AFB, AL.; Director for Training & Operations, Boca Raton Army Air Field. The Story of Radar. November 1944. Located in History of Boca Raton Field – 1 November 1944–31 December 1944. Documents 79–141. No date. Air Force Historical Research Agency, IRIS 169935, Maxwell AFB, AL.

[36] Martin Streetly, *Confound & Destroy* (London: Janes Publishing Company, Ltd, 1978), pp.19–20.

[37] Martin Streetly, *The Aircraft of 100 Group* (London: Robert Hale, 1984), pp.21–22.

[38] Headquarters, U.S. Strategic Bombing Survey (Pacific). Interrogation No. 491, Subject: Army Radar: Operations and Tactics. 4 Dec 1945; Air Force Historical Research Agency, 137.73-15, Maxwell AFB, AL.

[39] 2D & 3D Operations Analysis Section, Far East Air Force. A Short Survey of Japanese Radar, Volume I, 20 November 1945; Air Force Historical Research Agency, 720.310A V.1, Maxwell AFB, AL., p.14; the GHQ SWPA February 1945 order of battle (see AFHRA IRIS 00254218 listed below) references a 'Mk 'CHI" radar; this is undoubtedly the IJA Tachi-6 radar due to a reference to its bi-static nature and similar frequency range. Office of the Chief Signal Officer, Section 22, General Headquarters, Southwest Pacific Area. Monthly Statement – Japanese Radar & Radio Activities in the Southwest Pacific Area. 9 February 1945, p.30. Air Force Historical Research Agency, 710.654A/IRIS 00254218, Maxwell AFB, AL. Similarly, the 'Mk "B"' radar parametrically fits the Tachi-7; see Office of the Chief Signal Officer, Section 22, General Headquarters, Southwest Pacific Area. Current Statement – No. 0248. 15 December 1944, p.1. Air Force Historical Research Agency, 710.654B/IRIS 00254219, Maxwell AFB, AL.

[40] Department of Scientific and Industrial Research, *World War 2 Narratives. No. 3 Radar* (Wellington, NZ: July 1948), p.547. Archives New Zealand, AAOQ W3424 16.

[41] Craig Bellamy, *The Beginnings of the Secret Australian Radar Countermeasures Unit during the Pacific War*, Thesis submitted in fulfillment of Doctor of Philosophy, Charles Darwin University, February 2020.

[42] Bellamy, *Beginnings*; See Bruce Gamble, *Kangaroo Squadron* (New York: Da Capo Pres, 2018) for more details on the 435th BS; Commanding Officer, H.M.A.S. 'RUSHCUTTER'. Table of R.C.M. Equipment – Record of Fittings. No date. Australian War Memorial Records AWM 79 609/13 'R.C.M. Equipment' (Department of Navy file). Sourced courtesy of Craig Bellamy.

[43] Alfred Price, *The History of US Electronic Warfare, Volume I,* (Washington: Association of Old Crows, 1984), pp.47–49.

[44] Bellamy, *Beginnings.*

[45] Bellamy, *Beginnings*; Commanding Officer, H.M.A.S. 'RUSHCUTTER'. Table of R.C.M. Equipment – Record of Fittings. No date. Australian War Memorial Records AWM 79 609/13 'R.C.M. Equipment' (Department of Navy file). Sourced courtesy of Craig Bellamy.

[46] Bellamy, *Beginnings.*

[47] Department of Scientific and Industrial Research, *World War 2 Narratives. No. 3 Radar* (Wellington, NZ: July 1948), p.547. Archives New Zealand, AAOQ W3424 16.

[48] Dick Dakeyne, Radar Gunner (Coolalinga, Northern Territory: David M. Welch, 2014), pp.35–37; Commander, HMAS 'Rushcutter'. Enclosure to 'Rushcutter' 963/2/20 to The Secretary, Naval Board, Melbourne. 23 February 1943. Australian War Memorial Records (Department of Navy AWM 79 File 609.13); 380th Bomb Group. History, April 1945. 1945. Air Force Historical Research Agency, IRIS 86281, GP-380-HI (Bomb), Apr 45, Maxwell AFB, AL.; Bellamy, *Beginnings*, p.189.

[49] 380th Bomb Group. History, April 1945. 1945. Air Force Historical Research Agency, IRIS 86281, GP-380-HI (Bomb), Apr 45, Maxwell AFB, AL.

[50] Bellamy, *Beginnings*, pp.189, 323–329.

General Headquarters, Southwest Pacific Area. Message to War Department, Adjutant General. No subject. Signal Corps No. Q4546, Staff No. C-5107. 26 August 1943. Box 2064, Entry UD-UP 271 – Outgoing Messages from GHQ to War Department, RG 496, National Archives; Bellamy, *Beginnings*, p.207.

[52] Assistant Chief of Air Staff, Materiel, Maintenance and Distribution. Memorandum to CG, Material Command, Wright Field. 25 September 1943. Subject: Installation of RCM Equipment in Ferrets VII and VIII. 452.1 – CONSOLIDATED B-24 FERRET 1943-44-45 Folder, Box 2713, Entry – Sarah Clark (Central Decimal File), RG 342, National Archives.

[53] Stetson Conn, Rose Engelman, and Byron Fairchild. The United States Army in World War II: Guarding the United States and Its Outposts. (Washington: Center for Military History, 2000), pp.223–265.

[54] Assistant Chief of Staff, G-2, Western Defence Command and Fourth Army. Intelligence Memorandum No. 8, Final Report of Reduction and Occupation of Attu from the Combat Intelligence Point of View. 9 August 1943. Combined Arms Research Library, D769.87.A4F56; Air Intelligence Group, Division of Naval Intelligence, Office of the Chief of Naval Operations, Navy Department. Supplement to Photographic Intelligence Center Report – Japanese Electronics. March 1945. OPNAV – 16 – VP101. Combined Arms Research Library, call no. N10405-B; U.S. Army Air Forces. Second Partial Report of AFRDB Alaska Inspection – Conduct of Aleutian Campaign. 27 November 1942. Air Force Historical Research Agency, IRIS 203747, Maxwell AFB, AL.

[55] Headquarters, Eleventh Air Force. Air Intelligence, North Pacific Area No. 4, 13 Nov 44 to 31 Dec 44. 1 January 1945. Air Force Historical Research Agency, IRIS 203762, Maxwell AFB, AL., Advanced Intelligence Center, North Pacific Area. Aviation Intelligence Summary Aleutian Area, 24 to 31 January 1943. No date. Air Force Historical Research Agency, IRIS 203732, Maxwell AFB, AL.

[56] Alfred Price, *The History of US Electronic Warfare, Volume I,* (Washington: Association of Old Crows, 1984), pp.36, 52–53.

[57] Price, pp.52–55; 'The Work of the Ferrets,' Radar, Issue 8, 28 Feb 1945, Radiation Laboratory, Massachusetts Institute of Technology; reprinted March 1985 Product Support Department, Ferranti Defence Systems Limited

[58] Headquarters Eleventh Air Force. Memorandum to Commanding General, Army Air Forces, Attn: AFREC. 9 Sept 1943. Subject: Radar Interrogation Report. File 413.44-R, Box 627, Entry 294 – Classified Central Decimal Files, RG 18, National Archives.

[59] Assistant Chief of Staff, G-2, Western Defence Command and Fourth Army. Intelligence Memorandum No. 8, Final Report of Reduction and Occupation of Attu from the Combat Intelligence Point of View. 9 August 1943. Combined Arms Research Library, D769.87.A4F56.

[60] Headquarters, Eleventh Air Force. Air Intelligence, North Pacific Area No. 12, 1 Aug 45 to 31 Aug 45. 1 September 1945. Air Force Historical Research Agency, IRIS 203770, Maxwell AFB, AL.

[61] Office of the Assistant Chief of Staff, A-2, Field Headquarters, Eleventh Air Force. Intelligence Summary for 4 August 1943. No date. Air Force Historical Research Agency, IRIS 203732, Maxwell AFB, AL.; Headquarters Eleventh Air Force. Memorandum to Commanding General, Army Air Forces, Attn: AFREC. 9 Sept 1943. Subject: Radar Interrogation Report. File 413.44-R, Box 627, Entry 294 – Classified Central Decimal Files, RG 18, National Archives.

[62] Headquarters Eleventh Air Force. Memorandum to Commanding General, Army Air Forces, Attn: AFREC. 9 Sept 1943. Subject: Radar Interrogation Report. File 413.44-R, Box 627, Entry 294 – Classified Central Decimal Files, RG 18, National Archives; Headquarters, Eleventh Air Force. Air Intelligence, North Pacific Area No. 4, 13 Nov 44 to 31 Dec 44. 1 January 1945. Air Force Historical Research Agency, IRIS 203762, Maxwell AFB, AL.

[63] Headquarters Eleventh Air Force. Memorandum to Commanding General, Army Air Forces, Attn: AFREC. 9 Sept 1943. Subject: Radar Interrogation Report. File 413.44-R, Box 627, Entry 294 – Classified Central Decimal Files, RG 18, National Archives; 36th Bomb Squadron. Histories, February 1940 – November 1944. Air Force Historical Research Agency, IRIS 43935, Maxwell AFB, AL.

[64] Office of the Assistant Chief of Staff, A-2, Field Headquarters, Eleventh Air Force. Kiska Island – Special Bomb Damage Report. 13 September 1943. Air Force Historical Research Agency, IRIS 203788, Maxwell AFB, AL.

[65] Headquarters, Eleventh Air Force. Air Intelligence, North Pacific Area No. 12, 1 Aug 45 to 31 Aug 45. September 1, 1945. Air Force Historical Research Agency, IRIS 203770, Maxwell AFB, AL.

[66] Stetson Conn et al, pp.299–300.

[67] 404th Bombardment Squadron. History of the 404th Bombardment Squadron (H), 14–15 January 1941 to 1 January 1944. 14 June 1944. Air Force Historical Research Agency, IRIS 46330, Maxwell AFB, AL.

[68] Headquarters, Eleventh Air Force. Air Intelligence, North Pacific Area No. 12, 1 Aug 45 to 31 Aug 45. 1 September 1945. Air Force Historical Research Agency, IRIS 203770, Maxwell AFB, AL.

[69] Individual Aircraft Data Card for B-24D 41-23941. Air Force Historical Research Agency, Maxwell AFB, AL.

[70] Charles Scrivner. Empire Express (Temple City: Historical Aviation Album, 1976), pp.13–40.

[71] Historical Branch, Army Air Forces Proving Ground Command. History of the Army Air Forces Proving Ground Command, Part I – Historical Outline. 30 Jan 1945. Air Force Historical Research Agency, IRIS 155425, Maxwell AFB, AL.

Price, p.71; Headquarters, 16th Reconnaissance Squadron. Unit History, 17 May 1943–26 September 1943. N.d. Air Force Historical Research Agency, SQ-RCN-16-HI, May-Sep 43/IRIS 66538, Maxwell AFB, AL.

[73] Air Communications Officer, Equipment Division, Air Staff. Headquarters Army Air Force Routing and Record Slip to Assistant Chief, Air Staff, MM&D, Supply and Maintenance Branch. No subject. 13 November 1943. Unknown RG, received from another researcher, declass nomenclature NND730061, National Archives; Headquarters, Eleventh Air Force. Air Intelligence, North Pacific Area No. 12, 1 Aug 45 to 31 Aug 45. September 1, 1945. Air Force Historical Research Agency, IRIS 203770, Maxwell AFB, AL.

[74] Martin Streetly. *The Aircraft of 100 Group* (London: Robert Hale, 1984), pp.21–23.

[75] George Thompson and Dixie Harris, The Signal Corps: The Outcome (Mid-1943 Through 1945) (Washington: US Government Printing Office, 1991), p.308.

[76] Headquarters, 16th Reconnaissance Squadron (H) Sp. History, May–Sept 1943. N.d. Air Force Historical Research Agency, SQ-RCN-16-HI, May–Sep 43/IRIS 66538, Maxwell AFB, AL.

[77] Headquarters, 16th Reconnaissance Squadron (H) Sp. History, May–Sept 1943. N.d. Air Force Historical Research Agency, SQ-RCN-16-HI, May–Sep 43/IRIS 66538, Maxwell AFB, AL.

[78] Headquarters, 16th Reconnaissance Squadron (H) Sp. History, May–Sept 1943. N.d. Air Force Historical Research Agency, SQ-RCN-16-HI, May–Sep 43/IRIS 66538, Maxwell AFB, AL.

[79] Price, pp.72-73.

[80] Headquarters, 16th Reconnaissance Squadron (H) Sp. History, May–Sept 1943. N.d. Air Force Historical Research Agency, SQ-RCN-16-HI, May–Sep 43/IRIS 66538, Maxwell AFB, AL.

[81] Headquarters, 16th Reconnaissance Squadron (H) Sp. History, May–Sept 1943. N.d. Air Force Historical Research Agency, SQ-RCN-16-HI, May–Sep 43/IRIS 66538, Maxwell AFB, AL.

[82] Norman Weed. 'Ferrets', Friends Journal, Vol. 29 No. 3, Fall 2006, Air Force Museum Foundation, pp.40–43.

[83] Headquarters, 16th Reconnaissance Squadron (H) Sp. History, May–Sept 1943. N.d. Air Force Historical Research Agency, SQ-RCN-16-HI, May–Sep 43/IRIS 66538, Maxwell AFB, AL.; Headquarters, 16th Reconnaissance Squadron (H) Sp. History, Sep–Oct 1943. N.d. Air Force Historical Research Agency, IRIS 66539, Maxwell AFB, AL.; Headquarters, 16th Reconnaissance Squadron (H) Sp. History, Nov–Dec 1943. N.d. Air Force Historical Research Agency, IRIS 66540, Maxwell AFB, AL.

[84] Headquarters, 16th Reconnaissance Squadron (H) Sp. History, Sep–Oct 1943. N.d. Air Force Historical Research Agency, IRIS 66539, Maxwell AFB, AL.

[85] Headquarters, 16th Reconnaissance Squadron (H) Sp. History, May–Sep 1943. N.d. Air Force Historical Research Agency, SQ-RCN-16-HI, May–Sep 43/IRIS 66538, Maxwell AFB, AL.

[86] Headquarters, 16th Reconnaissance Squadron (H) Sp. History, May–Sept 1943. N.d. Air Force Historical Research Agency, SQ-RCN-16-HI, May–Sep 43/IRIS 66538, Maxwell AFB, AL.

[87] Headquarters, 16th Reconnaissance Squadron (H) Sp. History, Sep–Oct 1943. N.d. Air Force Historical Research Agency, IRIS 66539, Maxwell AFB, AL.

[88] Headquarters, 16th Reconnaissance Squadron (H) Sp. History, Nov–Dec 1943. N.d. Air Force Historical Research Agency, IRIS 66540, Maxwell AFB, AL.

[89] Headquarters, 16th Reconnaissance Squadron (H) Sp. History, Sep–Oct 1943. N.d. Air Force Historical Research Agency, IRIS 66539, Maxwell AFB, AL.; Headquarters, 16th Reconnaissance Squadron (H) Sp. History, Nov–Dec 1943. N.d. Air Force Historical Research Agency, IRIS 66540, Maxwell AFB, AL.

[90] Headquarters, 16th Reconnaissance Squadron (H) Sp. History, Sep–Oct 1943. N.d. Air Force Historical Research Agency, IRIS 66539, Maxwell AFB, AL.; Headquarters, 16th Reconnaissance Squadron (H) Sp. History, Nov–Dec 1943. N.d. Air Force Historical Research Agency, IRIS 66540, Maxwell AFB, AL.

[91] Headquarters, 16th Reconnaissance Squadron (H) Sp. History, Sep–Oct 1943. N.d. Air Force Historical Research Agency, IRIS 66539, Maxwell AFB, AL.; Headquarters, 16th Reconnaissance Squadron (H) Sp. History, Nov–Dec 1943. N.d. Air Force Historical Research Agency, IRIS 66540, Maxwell AFB, AL.

[92] Headquarters, 16th Reconnaissance Squadron (H) Sp. History, Sep–Oct 1943. N.d. Air Force Historical Research Agency, IRIS 66539, Maxwell AFB, AL.; Headquarters, 16th Reconnaissance Squadron. War Diary, Sep–Oct 1943. N.d. Air Force Historical Research Agency, SQ-RCN-16-HI, Sep–Oct 43/IRIS 66537, Maxwell AFB, AL

[93] Headquarters, 16th Reconnaissance Squadron (H) Sp. History, Nov–Dec 1943. N.d. Air Force Historical Research Agency, IRIS 66540, Maxwell AFB, AL.

[94] Headquarters, 16th Reconnaissance Squadron (H) Sp. History, Sep–Oct 1943. N.d. Air Force Historical Research Agency, IRIS 66539, Maxwell AFB, AL.

[95] Headquarters, 16th Reconnaissance Squadron (H) Sp. History, Nov–Dec 1943. N.d. Air Force Historical Research Agency, IRIS 66540, Maxwell AFB, AL.

[96] Headquarters, 16th Reconnaissance Squadron (H) Sp. History, Nov–Dec 1943. N.d. Air Force Historical Research Agency, IRIS 66540, Maxwell AFB, AL.

[97] Headquarters, 16th Reconnaissance Squadron (H) Sp. History, Nov–Dec 1943. N.d. Air Force Historical Research Agency, IRIS 66540, Maxwell AFB, AL.

[98] Headquarters, 16th Reconnaissance Squadron (H) Sp. History, Jan–Feb 1944. N.d. Air Force Historical Research Agency, IRIS 66541, Maxwell AFB, AL.

[99] Headquarters, 16th Reconnaissance Squadron (H) Sp. History, Jan–Feb 44. N.d. Air Force Historical Research Agency, IRIS 66541, Maxwell AFB, AL.; Headquarters, 16th Reconnaissance Squadron (H) Sp. History, Mar–Apr 44. N.d. Air Force Historical Research Agency, IRIS 66542, Maxwell AFB, AL.

[100] Headquarters, 16th Reconnaissance Squadron (H) Sp. History, Mar–Apr 44. N.d. Air Force Historical Research Agency, IRIS 66542, Maxwell AFB, AL.

[101] Headquarters, 16th Reconnaissance Squadron (H) Sp. History, Mar–Apr 44. N.d. Air Force Historical Research Agency, IRIS 66542, Maxwell AFB, AL.

[102] Headquarters, 16th Reconnaissance Squadron (H) Sp. History, May–Jun 44. N.d. Air Force Historical Research Agency, IRIS 66543, Maxwell AFB, AL.

[103] Headquarters, 16th Reconnaissance Squadron (H) Sp. History, May–Jun 44. N.d. Air Force Historical Research Agency, IRIS 66543, Maxwell AFB, AL.

[104] Headquarters, 16th Reconnaissance Squadron (H) Sp. History, May–Jun 44. N.d. Air Force Historical Research Agency, IRIS 66543, Maxwell AFB, AL.

[105] Headquarters, 16th Reconnaissance Squadron (H) Sp. History, May–Jun 44. N.d. Air Force Historical Research Agency, IRIS 66543, Maxwell AFB, AL.

[106] Headquarters, 16th Reconnaissance Squadron. History, Jul–Aug 1944. N.d. Air Force Historical Research Agency, SQ-RCN-16-HI, Jul–Aug 44/IRIS 66544, Maxwell AFB, AL.

[107] Headquarters, 16th Reconnaissance Squadron. History, Jul–Aug 1944. N.d. Air Force Historical Research Agency, SQ-RCN-16-HI, Jul–Aug 44/IRIS 66544, Maxwell AFB, AL.

[108] Headquarters, 16th Reconnaissance Squadron. History, Jul–Aug 1944. N.d. Air Force Historical Research Agency, SQ-RCN-16-HI, Jul–Aug 44/IRIS 66544, Maxwell AFB, AL.

[109] Headquarters, 16th Reconnaissance Squadron. History, Jul–Aug 1944. N.d. Air Force Historical Research Agency, SQ-RCN-16-HI, Jul–Aug 44/IRIS 66544, Maxwell AFB, AL.

[110] Headquarters, 16th Reconnaissance Squadron. War Diary, Sep–Dec 1944. N.d. Air Force Historical Research Agency, SQ-RCN-16-HI, Sep–Dec 44/IRIS 66545, Maxwell AFB, AL.

[111] Headquarters, 16th Reconnaissance Squadron. War Diary, Sep–Dec 1944. N.d. Air Force Historical Research Agency, SQ-RCN-16-HI, Sep-Dec 44/IRIS 66545, Maxwell AFB, AL.

[112] Headquarters, 16th Reconnaissance Squadron. War Diary, Sep–Dec 1944. N.d. Air Force Historical Research Agency, SQ-RCN-16-HI, Sep–Dec 44/IRIS 66545, Maxwell AFB, AL.

[113] Headquarters, 16th Reconnaissance Squadron. War Diary, Sep–Dec 1944. N.d. Air Force Historical Research Agency, SQ-RCN-16-HI, Sep–Dec 44/IRIS 66545, Maxwell AFB, AL.

[114] Assistant Chief of Air Staff, Materiel, Maintenance and Distribution. Memorandum to CG, Material Command, Wright Field. 25 September 1943. Subject: Installation of RCM Equipment in Ferrets VII and VIII. 452.1 – CONSOLIDATED B-24 FERRET 1943-44-45 Folder, Box 2713, Entry – Sarah Clark (Central Decimal File), RG 342, National Archives

[115] History Support Office, Aeronautical Systems Command, 'Splendid Vision, Unswerving Purpose,: 2002 AF History and Museums Programme, pp.95–96.

[116] General Headquarters, Southwest Pacific Area. Message to War Department, Adjutant General. Subject: Ferret Installation. Signal Corps No. Q4478, Staff No. C-7470. 4 November 1943. Box 2065, Entry UD-UP 271 – Outgoing Messages from GHQ to War Department, RG 496, National Archives; General Headquarters, Southwest Pacific Area. Message to War Department, Adjutant General. Subject: SCR Fittings in Ferrets. Signal Corps No. Q54, Staff No. C-7713. 11 November 1943. Box 2065, Entry UD-UP 271 – Outgoing Messages from GHQ to War Department, RG 496, National Archives.

[117] Price, p.139; Individual Aircraft Data Card for 42-63991 and 42-64045, AFHRA.

[118] General Headquarters, Southwest Pacific Area. Message to War Department, Commanding General, Army Air Force. No subject. Signal Corps No. Q4542, Staff No. C-5079. 25 August 1943. Box 2064, Entry UD-UP 271 – Outgoing Messages from GHQ to War Department, RG 496, National Archives; General Headquarters, Southwest Pacific Area. Message to War Department, Adjutant General. No subject. Signal Corps No. Q4966, Staff No. C-5259. 31 August 1943. Box 2064, Entry UD-UP 271 – Outgoing Messages from GHQ to War Department, RG 496, National Archives.

[119] General Headquarters, Southwest Pacific Area. Message to War Department, Adjutant General. Subject: RCM Officers. Signal Corps No. Q1162, Staff No. C-8314. 28 November 1943. Box 2065, Entry UD-UP 271 – Outgoing Messages from GHQ to War Department, RG 496, National Archives.

[120] Office of the Chief Signal Officer, General Headquarters, Southwest Pacific Area. Memorandum to Chief Signal Officer, War Department, Washington. 28 February 1944. Subject: Radar Counter Measures in the Southwest Pacific Area. SWPA RCM #1 1 of 2 Folder, Box 1489, Entry – Classified Central Decimal Files, RG 111, National Archives.

[121] Office of the Chief Signal Officer, Stock Control Branch, War Department. Material Requirements for Section 22, OCSigO, GHQ, SWPA. 22 February 1944. SWPA RCM #1 2 of 2 Folder, Box 1489, Entry – Classified Central Decimal Files, RG 111, National Archives.

[122] General Headquarters, Southwest Pacific Area. Message to War Department, Adjutant General. Subject: Personnel for Ferret Aircraft. Signal Corps No. Q1916, Staff No. C-6161. 29 September 1943. Box 2064, Entry UD-UP 271 – Outgoing Messages from GHQ to War Department, RG 496, National Archives; General Headquarters, Southwest Pacific Area. Message to War Department, Adjutant General. Subject: Ferret Aircraft. Signal Corps No. Q4472, Staff No. C-74450. 4 November 1943. Box 2065, Entry UD-UP 271 – Outgoing Messages from GHQ to War Department, RG 496, National Archives.

[123] General Headquarters, Southwest Pacific Area. Message to War Department, Adjutant General. No subject. Signal Corps No. Q2711, Staff No. C-6492. 4 October 1943. Box 2065, Entry UD-UP 271 – Outgoing Messages from GHQ to War Department, RG 496, National Archives.

[124] 63rd Bombardment Squadron (H). History, February 1944. 1 March 1944. IRIS 44204, Air Force Historical Research Agency, Maxwell AFB, AL.; 63rd Bombardment Squadron (H). History, March 1944. 1 April 1944. IRIS 44205, Air Force Historical Research Agency, Maxwell AFB, AL.

[125] Reports on Ferret Flights No. 22–27, 10–16 March 1944. Air Force Historical Research Agency, IRIS 0064630, Maxwell AFB, AL.; George Kenney. *General Kenney Reports* (Washington: Government Printing Office, 1997), p.277.

[126] United States Strategic Bombing Survey (Pacific). The Allied Campaign Against Rabaul. (Washington: 1946), pp.15–17, 28.

[127] Office of the Chief Signal Officer, General Headquarters, Southwest Pacific Area. Memorandum to Chief Signal Officer, War Department, Washington. 28 February 1944. Subject: Radar Counter Measures in the Southwest Pacific Area. SWPA RCM #1 1 of 2 Folder, Box 1489, Entry – Classified Central Decimal Files, RG 111, National Archives; General Headquarters, Southwest Pacific Area. Message to War Department, CG AAF (To Arnold for Jackson). Subject: Radar Shipment. Signal Corps No. Q518, Staff No. C-1120. 30 January 1944. Box 2066, Entry UD-UP 271 – Outgoing Messages from GHQ to War Department, RG 496, National Archives.

[128] Section 22, General Headquarters Southwest Pacific Area. Report No. OWW-7, Radars Located by Ferrets in Northwest Area of SWPA, 5 April 1944 and Report No. OWW-6, Ferret Operations, 24 April 1944. Both at Air Force Historical Research Agency, 178.46-188/IRIS 00132153, Maxwell AFB, AL.

[129] General Headquarters, Southwest Pacific Area. Memorandum to Commanding General, Army Air Forces; Attention: Air Communications Section. Subject: Ferret Installations. 2 June 1944. Air Force Historical Research Agency, 710.84-1, Jun 44, Maxwell AFB, AL.; Office of the Chief Signal Officer, Army Service Forces. Memorandum to Commanding General, SWPA – Attn: Chief Signal Officer. 8 April 1944. Subject: Radar Counter Measures in the Southwest Pacific Area. SWPA RCM #1 2 of 2 Folder, Box 1489, Entry – Classified Central Decimal Files, RG 111, National Archives; Section 22, General Headquarters Southwest Pacific Area. Report No. OWW-6, Ferret Operations. 24 April 1944. Air Force Historical Research Agency, 178.46-188/IRIS 00132153, Maxwell AFB, AL.

[130] Section 22, General Headquarters Southwest Pacific Area. Report on Ferret Flight No. 63, Aug 6, 1944; Section 22, General Headquarters Southwest Pacific Area. Report on Ferret Flight No. 64, 7–8 Aug 1944; Section 22, General Headquarters Southwest Pacific Area. Report on Ferret Flight No. 65, 9–10 Aug 1944. All Air Force Historical Research Agency, IRIS 132100, Maxwell AFB, AL.; http://380th.org/HISTORY/partV-intro.html, accessed 7 August 2021.

[131] Office of Scientific Research and Development, National Defence Research Committee, *Summary Technical Report of Division 15, NDRC, Volume 1. Radio Countermeasures* (Washington, DC: 1946), p.348.

[132] Office of Scientific Research and Development, National Defence Research Committee, *Summary Technical Report of Division 15, NDRC, Volume 1. Radio Countermeasures* (Washington, DC: 1946), p.320; Alfred Price, The History of US Electronic Warfare, Volume I, (Washington: Association of Old Crows, 1984), pp.133–137.

[133] Office of Scientific Research and Development, National Defence Research Committee, *Summary Technical Report of Division 15, NDRC, Volume 1. Radio Countermeasures* (Washington, DC: 1946), p.320.

[134] Office of Scientific Research and Development, National Defence Research Committee, *Summary Technical Report of Division 15, NDRC, Volume 1. Radio Countermeasures* (Washington, DC: 1946), p.348; Alfred Price, The History of US Electronic Warfare, Volume I, (Washington: Association of Old Crows, 1984), pp.146–147.

[135] Streetly, Martin. Confound & Destroy: 100 Group and the Bomber Support Campaign (London: Jane's Publishing, 1978), pp.35–40.

[136] Streetly, pp.35–40.

[137] 36th Bomb Squadron. Histories, February 1940–November 1944. Air Force Historical Research Agency, IRIS 43935-41, SQ-BOMB-36-HI, Maxwell AFB, AL.

[138] First Proving Ground Electronics Unit. Project No. 13, Countermeasures Programme. 7 December 1943. Air Force Historical Research Agency, IRIS 156538, Maxwell AFB, AL.

[139] Headquarters, United States Army Air Forces in the United Kingdom (USAAFUK). Memorandum to Commanding General, USAAFUK. Subject: Proposal for RCM Organisation of USAAFUK. 27 November 1943; Headquarters, United States Strategic Air Forces in Europe. Memorandum to Major Guillou. No subject. 17 January 1945; Signal Communications Officer, Eighth Air Force. Carrier Sheet to Director of Operations, Eighth Air Force. Subject: 803rd Squadron, 100th Group. 27 June 1944; all located in file United States Strategic Air Forces in Europe, 1943–1945, Electronic Warfare. Air Force Historical Research Agency, IRIS 218333, Maxwell AFB, AL. 36th Bomb Squadron. History, 36th Bombardment Squadron (H) RCM, 13 to 31 August 1944. Air Force Historical Research Agency, IRIS 43938, SQ-BOMB-36-HI, Maxwell AFB, AL.

[140] Headquarters, United States Strategic Air Forces in Europe. Review of Correspondence on RCM Squadron. 17 October 1944; Headquarters, United States Strategic Air Forces in Europe. Memorandum to Major Guillou. No subject. 17 January 1945. Both located in file United States Strategic Air Forces in Europe, 1943–1945, Electronic Warfare. Air Force Historical Research Agency, IRIS 218333, Maxwell AFB, AL; 36th Bomb Squadron. History, 36th Bombardment Squadron (H) RCM, 13 August 44 to 31 August 44. Air Force Historical Research Agency, IRIS 43938, SQ-BOMB-36-HI, Maxwell AFB, AL.

[141] 36th Bomb Squadron. History, 36th Bombardment Squadron (H) RCM, 13 August 44 to 31 August 44. Air Force Historical Research Agency, IRIS 43938, SQ-BOMB-36-HI, Maxwell AFB, AL.

[142] 36th Bomb Squadron. History, 36th Bombardment Squadron (H) RCM, 13 August 44 to 31 August 44. Air Force Historical Research Agency, IRIS 43938, SQ-BOMB-36-HI, Maxwell AFB, AL.

[143] Headquarters, United States Army Air Forces in the United Kingdom (USAAFUK). Memorandum to Commanding General, USAAFUK. Subject: Proposal for RCM Organisation of USAAFUK. 27 November 1943. Located in file United States Strategic Air Forces in Europe, 1943–1945, Electronic Warfare. Air Force Historical Research Agency, IRIS 218333, Maxwell AFB, AL.

[144] 36th Bomb Squadron. History, 36th Bombardment Squadron (H) RCM, 13 August 44 to 31 August 44. Air Force Historical Research Agency, IRIS 43938, Maxwell AFB, AL.; 36th Bombardment Squadron (H) RCM. History, 1 Sep 1944 to 30 Sep 1944. Air Force Historical Research Agency, IRIS 43939, Maxwell AFB, AL.

[145] 36th Bombardment Squadron (H) RCM. History, 1 Sep 1944 to 30 Sep 1944. Air Force Historical Research Agency, IRIS 43939, Maxwell AFB, AL.; 36th Bombardment Squadron (H) RCM. History, 1 Oct 1944 to 31 Oct 1944. Air Force Historical Research Agency, IRIS 43940, Maxwell AFB, AL.

[146] 36th Bombardment Squadron (H) RCM. History, 1 Dec 1944 to 31 Dec 1944. Air Force Historical Research Agency, IRIS 43942, Maxwell AFB, AL.; 36th Bombardment Squadron (H) RCM. History, 1 Jan 1945 to 31 Jan 1945. Air Force Historical Research Agency, IRIS 43943, Maxwell AFB, AL.

[147] Headquarters, Eighth Air Force. Message to Commanding General, US Strategic Air Forces in Europe. No Subject. 25 July 1944. Located in file United States Strategic Air Forces in Europe, 1943–1945, Electronic Warfare. Air Force Historical Research Agency, IRIS 218333, Maxwell AFB, AL.

[148] 36th Bombardment Squadron (H) RCM. History, 1 Dec 1944 to 31 Dec 1944. Air Force Historical Research Agency, IRIS 43942, Maxwell AFB, AL.; 36th Bombardment Squadron (H) RCM. History, 1 Jan 1945 to 31 Jan 1945. Air Force Historical Research Agency, IRIS 43943, Maxwell AFB, AL.

[149] Lt. Gen. Jimmy Doolittle, Commander, Eighth Air Force. Message to Officer Commanding, US Strategic Air Forces in Europe. No Subject. 11 October 1944; Technical Liaison Division (RCM), Office of the Chief Signal Officer, Headquarters US Strategic Air Forces in Europe. Air Force RCM Bulletin No. 16, 16 December to 31 December 1944. 22 January 1945. Both located in file United States Strategic Air Forces in Europe, 1943–1945, Electronic Warfare. Air Force Historical Research Agency, IRIS 218333, Maxwell AFB, AL.

[150] Tyler Morton, 'Linguists Get Their Wings: Airborne Voice Intercept Operators in World War II', Air Power History, Fall 2019, pp.21–28.

[151] Morton, 'Linguists Get Their Wings: Airborne Voice Intercept Operators in World War II'.

[152] 36th Bombardment Squadron (H) RCM. History, 1 Jan 1945 to 31 Jan 1945. Air Force Historical Research Agency, IRIS 43943, Maxwell AFB, AL; 36th Bombardment Squadron (H) RCM. History, 1 Feb 1945 to 28 Feb 1945. Air Force Historical Research Agency, IRIS 43944, Maxwell AFB, AL.

[153] 36th Bombardment Squadron (H) RCM. History, 1 Jan 1945 to 31 Jan 1945. Air Force Historical Research Agency, IRIS 43943, Maxwell AFB, AL.

[154] Commanding General, Eighth Air Force. Memorandum to Commanding General, 1st Air Division. Subject: RCM Programme for 36th Bomb Sq (RCM). 3 February 1945. Located in file United States Strategic Air Forces in Europe, 1943–1945, Electronic Warfare. Air Force Historical Research Agency, IRIS 218333, Maxwell AFB, AL.

[155] Streetly, p.82.

[156] Headquarters, United States Strategic Air Forces in Europe. Memorandum to Commanding General, Army Air Forces. Subject: Future RCM Programme for Heavy Bombers. 1 March 1945. Located in file United States Strategic Air Forces in Europe, 1943–1945, Electronic Warfare. Air Force Historical Research Agency, IRIS 218333, Maxwell AFB, AL.

[157] 36th Bombardment Squadron (H) RCM. History, 1 Feb 1945 to 28 Feb 1945. Air Force Historical Research Agency, IRIS 43944, Maxwell AFB, AL.

[158] 36th Bombardment Squadron (H) RCM. History, 1 March 1945 to 31 March 1945. Air Force Historical Research Agency, IRIS 43945, Maxwell AFB, AL.

[159] 36th Bombardment Squadron (H) RCM. History, 1 March 1945 to 31 March 1945. Air Force Historical Research Agency, IRIS 43945, Maxwell AFB, AL.

[160] Technical Liaison Division (RCM), Office of the Chief Signal Officer, Headquarters US Strategic Air Forces in Europe. Air Force RCM Bulletin No. 19, 1 February to 28 February 1945. March 1945. Located in file United States Strategic Air Forces in Europe, 1943–1945, Electronic Warfare. Air Force Historical Research Agency, IRIS 218333, Maxwell AFB, AL.

[161] Headquarters, United States Strategic Air Forces in Europe. Memorandum to Director of Operations, United States Strategic Air Forces in Europe. Subject: P-38 'Droop Snoot' Search Aircraft. No date, assessed January–February 1945. Located in file United States Strategic Air Forces in Europe, 1943–1945, Electronic Warfare. Air Force Historical Research Agency, IRIS 218333, Maxwell AFB, AL.

[162] 36th Bombardment Squadron (H) RCM. History, 1 March 1945 to 31 March 1945. Air Force Historical Research Agency, IRIS 43945, Maxwell AFB, AL

[163] 36th Bombardment Squadron (H) RCM. History, 1 April 1945 to 30 April 1945. Air Force Historical Research Agency, IRIS 43946, Maxwell AFB, AL.

[164] 36th Bombardment Squadron (H) RCM. History, 1 May 1945 to 31 May 1945. Air Force Historical Research Agency, IRIS 43947, Maxwell AFB, AL

[165] Commander-in-Chief, Southwest Pacific Area. Message to Chief of Staff, War Department. 26 February 1945. No subject. Box 852, Entry 184/Top Secret General Corr., RG 496, National Archives.

[166] Assistant Chief of Air Staff, Materiel, Maintenance and Distribution. Memorandum to CG, Material Command, Wright Field. 23 March 1944. Subject: Ferrets X and XI, Project Number 96508R. 452.1 – CONSOLIDATED B-24 FERRET 1943-44-45 Folder, Box 2713, Entry – Sarah Clark (Central Decimal File), RG 342, National Archives.

[167] General Headquarters, Southwest Pacific Area. Message to War Department, Adjutant General. No subject. Signal Corps No. Q1700, Staff No. C-6084. 27 September 1943. Box 2064, Entry UD-UP 271 – Outgoing Messages from GHQ to War Department, RG 496, National Archives.

[168] General Headquarters, Southwest Pacific Area. Message to Commanding General, Far East Air Forces. 13 September 1944. Subject: Radars in Halmahera and Morotai. Box 850, Entry 184/Top Secret General Correspondence, RG 496, National Archives.

[169] Office of Scientific Research and Development, National Defence Research Committee, *Summary Technical Report of Division 15, NDRC, Volume 1. Radio Countermeasures* (Washington, DC: 1946), p.349.

[170] Joint Electronic Information Agency. Report No. 6229, Radio Countermeasures in Southwest Pacific Area. 6 September 1944. Air Force Historical Research Agency, 706.906, Jan–Mar 45/Frame 1650, Reel A7182, Maxwell AFB, AL.

[171] Office of Scientific Research and Development, National Defence Research Committee, *Summary Technical Report of Division 15, NDRC, Volume 1. Radio Countermeasures* (Washington, DC: 1946), p.349.

[172] Office of the Air Force Commander, Headquarters Seventh Air Force, APO 244. Memorandum to Distribution. 19 November 1944. Subject: General Programme for Radar and Radio Reconnaissance in the Seventh Air Force. IRIS 259960, 740.907 Aug 1944–Apr 1945, Air Force Historical Research Agency, Maxwell AFB, AL.

[173] Department of Scientific and Industrial Research, *World War 2 Narratives. No. 3 Radar* (Wellington, NZ: July 1948), p.547. Archives New Zealand, AAOQ W3424 16.

[174] Office of the Chief Signal Officer, Section 22, General Headquarters Southwest Pacific Area. Current Statement 259. 14 January 1945. Found in: RAAF Command Headquarters – RCM [Radio Counter Measure] Current Statements – Section 22, Series number A11093, Control symbol 676/4A11 PART 7, Barcode 1120657, National Archives of Australia.

[175] Office of the Chief Signal Officer, Section 22, General Headquarters, Southwest Pacific Area. Monthly Statement – Japanese Radar & Radio Activities in the Southwest Pacific Area. 9 February 1945, p.34. Air Force Historical Research Agency, 710.654A/IRIS 00254218, Maxwell AFB, AL.; U.S. Congress, *Hearings before the Joint Committee on the Investigation of the Pearl Harbor Attack* (Washington, D.C.: U. S. Government Printing Office, 1946), 18:3013; Dulany Terrett, *The Signal Corps: The Emergency* (Washington, D.C.: US Government Printing Office, 1956), pp.304–305. The February 1945 is found in tabular format in the 9 February 1945 Monthly Statement on Japanese Radar & Radio Activities in the Southwest Pacific Area.

[176] Royal Australian Navy. Monthly Naval Review, A.C.B. 0254/44. November 1944, pp.9–11. www.navy.gov.au/media-room/publications, accessed 7 Jan 2017.; Ed Simmonds and Norm Smith, *Echoes Over the Pacific: An overview of Allied Air Warning Radar in the Pacific from Pearl Harbor to the Philippines Campaign* (E.W. & E. Simmonds, 1995), p.235; Dr S. Nakajima, 'The history of Japanese radar development to 1945,' found in *Radar Development to 1945* (IEE Radar, Sonar, Navigation and Avionics Series 2, Russell Burns (Editor); Inspec/IEE, revised edition February 1989).

[177] Air Evaluation Board, Southwest Pacific Area. Report No. 18, Reconnaissance Aviation in the Southwest Pacific Area. 22 April 1946, pp.24–6. IRIS 114060, Air Force Historical Research Agency, Maxwell AFB, AL.

[178] Bob Unwin. Letter to Ed Simmonds. 12 December 1994. AG-989/003, Hocken's Archives, University of Otago, New Zealand; Obituary for Bob Unwin. 19 February 1996, Wanaka Sun.

[179] Field Unit 13, Section 22, GHQ, Headquarters Thirteenth Air Force, A-3 Section. Memorandum to Assistant Director, Section 22, GHQ SWPA, APO 500. 26 December 1944. Subject: Change of Address of Field Unit 13. Reel A7671, Frame 465, Air Force Historical Research Agency, Maxwell AFB, AL.; Department of Scientific and Industrial Research, *World War 2 Narratives. No. 3 Radar* (Wellington, NZ: July 1948), pp.535, 546. Archives New Zealand, AAOQ W3424 16; Field Unit 13, Section 22, GHQ, 868th Bombardment Squadron (H). Booklet of radar plots. 27 November 1944. Air Force Historical Research Agency, Maxwell AFB, AL, SQ-BOMB-868-Su Reel. Located on Reel A0670, Frame 599.

[180] Office of Scientific Research and Development, National Defence Research Committee, *Summary Technical Report of Division 15, NDRC, Volume 1. Radio Countermeasures* (Washington, DC: 1946), p.349.

[181] Adjutant General, General Headquarters, Southwest Pacific Area. Memorandum to Commander, Allied Air Forces, Southwest Pacific Area. No subject. 30 October 1944. Air Force Historical Research Agency, 730.903-2, 5th AF Radar & Radio Security, Nov 44 – Mar 45, Maxwell AFB, AL.; 380th Bomb Group. History, April 1945. 1945. Air Force Historical Research Agency, IRIS 86281, GP-380-HI (Bomb), Apr 45, Maxwell AFB, AL.

[182] Office of Scientific Research and Development, National Defence Research Committee, *Summary Technical Report of Division 15, NDRC, Volume 1. Radio Countermeasures* (Washington, DC: 1946), p.321.

[183] 868th Bombardment Squadron. Special Report on Mission No. 868-381, 2–3 November 1944; 3 November 1944; Section 22 Field Unit 13 Det. Report on RCM Mission #22. 7 November 1944; IRIS 50367, SQ-BOMB-868-Su, Microfilm Reel A0670, Frames 746–758, Air Force Historical Research Agency, Maxwell AFB, AL.

[184] Chief Signal office, GHQ SWPA. Classified Message to the Chief Signal Officer, Army Service Forc.es. 1 October 1944. SWPA RCM #1 1 of 2 Folder, Box 1488, Entry – Classified Central Decimal Files, RG 111, National Archives; Signal Corps Liaison Office, Radio Research Laboratory. Memorandum to Office of the Chief Signal Officer, Army Service Forces. 16 October 1944. Subject: C-1900, Tail. SWPA RCM #1 1 of 2 Folder, Box 1488, Entry – Classified Central Decimal Files, RG 111, National Archives.

[185] Field Unit 13, Section 22, General Headquarters Southwest Pacific Area. Memorandum on Special RCM missions in cooperation with Thirteenth Fighter Command, 1 Dec 1944. Air Force Historical Research Agency, Maxwell AFB, AL, 750.907; located on Reel A7671, Frame 526.

[186] 100th Bomb Squadron. Historical Records and Histories of Organisation. 1 January 1945, p.4; narrative mission reports for 14 and 17 December 1944. IRIS 45024, Air Force Historical Research Agency, Maxwell AFB, AL.

[187] Office of the Intelligence Officer, Headquarters XIII Fighter Command. Memorandum on Armed Ferret Mission for 19 December 1944, 18 Dec 1944. Air Force Historical Research Agency, Maxwell AFB, AL, 750.907; located on Reel A7671, Frame 485.

[188] Headquarters XIII Fighter Command. Armed Ferret Mission for 28 December 1944. 27 December 1944. Air Force Historical Research Agency, Maxwell AFB, AL, 750.907; located on Reel A7671, Frame 532.

[189] 100th Bomb Squadron. Historical Records and Histories of Organisation. 1 March 1945, Final Mission Report No. 266. IRIS 45026, Air Force Historical Research Agency, Maxwell AFB, AL.

[190] Office of the Intelligence Officer, Headquarters XIII Fighter Command. Memorandum on Armed Ferret Mission.

[191] 100th Bomb Squadron. Historical Records and Histories of Organisation. 1 February 1945, p.3. IRIS 45025, Air Force Historical Research Agency, Maxwell AFB, AL; Field Unit 13, Section 22, GHQ. RCM Mission Report #53 (100th Bomb Squadron – B-25 Aircraft). 6 February 1945. Air Force Historical Research Agency, Maxwell AFB, AL, 750.907; located on Reel A7671, Frame 720.

[192] Section 22 Field Unit 13 Det. Report on Ferret Flight #38 on 15 February 1945, and Flight #39 on 16 February 1945. 17 February 1945. Air Force Historical Research Agency, Maxwell AFB, AL, 750.907; located on Reel A7671, Frame 823; Headquarters, 42nd Bomb Group. Standard Mission Report for Mission No. 42-1119. 16 February 1945. Air Force Historical Research Agency, Maxwell AFB, AL, 750.907; located on Reel A7671, Frame 828.

[193] Office of Scientific Research and Development, National Defence Research Committee, *Summary Technical Report of Division 15, NDRC, Volume 1. Radio Countermeasures* (Washington, DC: 1946), p.348.

[194] Headquarters XIII Bomber Command, APO #719-2. Informal Action Sheet. No date (estimate 22 December 1944). Subject: Jolo Island Radar. Air Force Historical Research Agency, Maxwell AFB, AL, 750.907; located on Reel A7671, Frame 478 .

[195] Department of Scientific and Industrial Research, *World War 2 Narratives. No. 3 Radar* (Wellington, NZ: July 1948), p.549. Archives New Zealand, AAOQ W3424 16.

[196] Field Unit 13, Section 22 GHQ. RCM Mission Report #57. 8 March 1945. Air Force Historical Research Agency, Maxwell AFB, AL, 750.907; located on Reel A7671, Frame 839; Field Unit 13, Section 22 GHQ. RCM Mission Report #68. 12 April 1945. Air Force Historical Research Agency, Maxwell AFB, AL, 750.907; located on Reel A7671, Frame 985; Field Unit 13, Section 22 GHQ. RCM Log Sheet. 10 April 1945. Air Force Historical Research Agency, Maxwell AFB, AL, 750.907; located on Reel A7671, Frame 985; Office of Scientific Research and Development, National Defence Research Committee, *Summary Technical Report of Division 15, NDRC, Volume 1. Radio Countermeasures* (Washington, DC: 1946), p.348.

[197] Field Unit 13, Section 22 GHQ. RCM Mission Report #78, 1 May 1945; Air Force Historical Research Agency, Maxwell AFB, AL, 750.907; located on Reel A7671, Frame 1216.

[198] Field Unit 13, Section 22 GHQ. RCM Mission Report #79. 3 May 1945. Air Force Historical Research Agency, Maxwell AFB, AL, 750.907; located on Reel A7671, Frame 1245; 868th Bombardment Squadron. Standard Mission Report, mission no. 868-626. 29 April 1945. Air Force Historical Research Agency, Maxwell AFB, AL, 750.907; located on Reel A7671, Frame 1251.

[199] Alan Carey, Consolidated PB4Y-2 Privateer (Schiffer Military History: Atglen, PA, 2005), pp.91–94.

[200] Field Unit 15, Section 22. Memorandum to O.I.C. Section 22, Rear Echelon. 4 June 1945. Subject: Monthly Report – May; Field Unit 15, Section 22. Memorandum to GHQ, SWPA, O.C. Sig. O., Section 22. 3 July 1945. Subject: Monthly Report – June. Both located in RAAF Command Headquarters - RCM [Radio Counter Measure] – Search equipped strike aeroplanes – Reports. Series number A11093, Control symbol 676/4A8, Barcode 3081754, National Archives of Australia.

[201] 'The Jap Radar Net', Radar, Issue 8, 28 Feb 1945, Radiation Laboratory, Massachusetts Institute of Technology; reprinted March 1985 Product Support Department, Ferranti Defence Systems Limited; Price, p.217; Alfred Price, *The History of US Electronic Warfare, Volume 1*, (Washington: Association of Old Crows, 1984), pp.152–160.

[202] Alfred Price. Interview of Joseph M. Pettit for History of U.S. Electronic Warfare. No date, *circa* 1980. MS387, Joseph M. Pettit Diary and Interview Transcript, Archives and Special Collections, Library, Georgia Institute of Technology.

[203] Steve Birdsall, *Log of the Liberators*, (Garden City: Doubleday and Company, 1973), pp.163–177.

[204] Joseph M. Pettit. Diary and research notebook. 13 April–19 August 1944. MS387, Joseph M. Pettit Diary and Interview Transcript, Archives and Special Collections, Library, Georgia Institute of Technology.

[205] Pettit diary.

[206] Price, pp.160–163; March Field. History of March Field, 1 April 1945 to 30 April 1945. No date. Air Force Historical Research Agency, IRIS 175043, Maxwell AFB, AL.; Lloyd, pp.89–90; 375th Bombardment Squadron. Unit Journal, August 1944–October 1945. N.d.. Air Force Historical Research Agency, IRIS 45919, Maxwell AFB, AL.; Pettit diary.

[207] Roger Cook, 'Charles Beard's Story: Radar Counter Measures in the CBI Theatre', online webpage contained within China-Burma-India webpage, available at: www.cbi-theatre.com/radar/radar_cbi.html, accessed 8 Dec 2020.

[208] 436th Bombardment Squadron. Unit Historical Report, October 1944. N.d.. Air Force Historical Research Agency, IRIS 46822, Maxwell AFB, AL.; 375th Bombardment Squadron. Unit Journal, August 1944–October 1945. N.d.. Air Force Historical Research Agency, IRIS 45919, Maxwell AFB, AL.

[209] Alwyn Lloyd, *Liberator: America's Global Bomber*, (Missoula: Pictorial Histories Publishing, 1993), pp.89–90; Carroll Glines, *Chennault's Forgotten Warriors*, (Atglen: Schiffer Publishing, 1995), p.150.

[210] 375th Bombardment Squadron. Ferret Mission Reports, September–November 1944. N.d.. Air Force Historical Research Agency, IRIS 45922, Maxwell AFB, AL.

[211] 375th Bombardment Squadron. Ferret Mission Reports, September–November 1944. N.d.. Air Force Historical Research Agency, IRIS 45922, Maxwell AFB, AL.

[212] Headquarters XX Bomber Command. Memorandum to Air Communications Officer, HQ, AAF, Washington, D.C. 7 October 1944. Subject: Weekly RCM Newsletter No. 18, 26 September–7 October 1944. Air Force Historical Research Agency, IRIS 132054, Maxwell AFB, AL.

[213] Headquarters 375th Bombardment Squadron. Memorandum to Air Communications Officer, HQ, AAF, Washington, D.C. 8 December 1944. Subject: China RCM Newsletter No. 5, 29 November 1944. Air Force Historical Research Agency, IRIS 258503, Maxwell AFB, AL.; 375th Bombardment Squadron. Unit Journal, August 1944–December 1945. N.d.. Air Force Historical Research Agency, IRIS 45919, Maxwell AFB, AL.; 375th Bombardment Squadron. Weekly Status and Operations Reports, March 1943–July 1945. N.d.. Air Force Historical Research Agency, IRIS 45921, Maxwell AFB, AL; 375th Bombardment Squadron. Ferret Mission Reports, September–November 1944. N.d.. Air Force Historical Research Agency, IRIS 45922, Maxwell AFB, AL.

[214] Headquarters 375th Bombardment Squadron. Memorandum to Air Communications Officer, HQ, AAF, Washington, D.C. 8 December 1944. Subject: China RCM Newsletter No. 5, 29 November 1944. Air Force Historical Research Agency, IRIS 258503, Maxwell AFB, AL.; Price, p.215.

[215] 436 Bombardment Squadron. Squadron History for November 1944. 1 Dec 1944; IRIS 46823, Air Force Historical Research Agency, Maxwell AFB, AL; 436 Bombardment Squadron. Memorandum to Commanding General, 10th Air Force. Subject: Report on Ferret Mission No. 2. 11 November 1944; IRIS 131967, Air Force Historical Research Agency, Maxwell AFB, AL; Headquarters, Army Air Forces India-Burma Theatre. Report on Ferret Mission No. 4, 20 Nov 1944. N.d.; IRIS 266814, Air Force Historical Research Agency, Maxwell AFB, AL.

[216] Headquarters, Army Air Forces India-Burma Theatre. Report on Ferret Mission No. 6 – 1 December 1944. 6 Dec 1944; Air Force Historical Research Agency, IRIS 258503/730.903-2, 5th AF Radar & Radio Security, Nov 44–May 45, Maxwell AFB, AL; 436 Bombardment Squadron. Squadron History for December 1944. 1 Jan 1945; IRIS 46824, Air Force Historical Research Agency, Maxwell AFB, AL; Headquarters 375th Bombardment Squadron. Memorandum to Air Communications Officer, HQ, AAF, Washington, D.C. 8 December 1944. Subject: China RCM Newsletter No. 5, 29 November 1944. Air Force Historical Research Agency, IRIS 258503, Maxwell AFB, AL.; Headquarters, Army Air Forces India-Burma Theatre. Report on Ferret Mission No, 5, 27–28 Nov 1944. 6 Dec 44. IRIS 266815, Air Force Historical Research Agency, Maxwell AFB, AL.; Headquarters, Army Air Forces India-Burma Theatre. Report on Ferret Mission No. 13, 29 Dec Nov 1944; IRIS 266816, Air Force Historical Research Agency, Maxwell AFB, AL.

[217] 375th Bombardment Squadron. Unit Journal, August 1944–October 1945. N.d.. Air Force Historical Research Agency, IRIS 45919, Maxwell AFB, AL.

[218] 375th Bombardment Squadron. Unit Journal, August 1944–October 1945. N.d.. Air Force Historical Research Agency, IRIS 45919, Maxwell AFB, AL.

[219] China Theatre Ferret Project. Headquarters, 373rd Bombardment Squadron (H), AAF. Report on Ferret Mission No. 35. 21 March 1945. IRIS 45913, Air Force Historical Research Agency, Maxwell AFB, AL.

[220] 373rd Bombardment Squadron. Flight Operational Intelligence Reports, February–May 1945. N.d.. Air Force Historical Research Agency, IRIS 45913-4, Maxwell AFB, AL.

[221] 436th Bombardment Squadron. Squadron History for April 1945. N.d.. Air Force Historical Research Agency, IRIS 46828, Maxwell AFB, AL.; Office of the Communications Officer, Headquarters Army Air Forces, India Burma Theatre. AAF Ferret Project Summary of Missions 14–30. 16 April 1945. Air Force Historical Research Agency, IRIS 266817, Maxwell AFB, AL.

[222] Commander, Far East Air Forces. Message to Commander, Fifth Air Force. 21 June 1945. Cite: A 72430. Air Force Historical Research Agency, IRIS 258504, Maxwell AFB, AL.

[223] Martin Streetly, *The Aircraft of 100 Group*, (London: Robert Hale Ltd, 1984), pp.31, 92; Price, p.153; R.G. Quirk, *'The Special Flight:' Liberator Operations on Radar Countermeasure With 160 Squadron, 159 Squadron and 1431 Flight, SEAC January, 1944 to October, 1945*, (unpublished manuscript, March 2002); available at: http://www.rquirk.com/splflt/draft.pdf, accessed 6 July 2021.

[224] Office of Scientific Research and Development, National Defence Research Committee, *Summary Technical Report of Division 15, NDRC, Volume 1. Radio Countermeasures* (Washington, DC: 1946), p.348.

[225] 63rd Bombardment Squadron (H). History, September 1944. 30 September 1944. IRIS 44211, Air Force Historical Research Agency, Maxwell AFB, AL.

[226] Section 22, General Headquarters Southwest Pacific Area. Report on Ferret Flight No. 81, 13–14 Sep,1944 and Report on Ferret Flight No. 82, 15 Sep 1944. 178.46-171, IRIS 132136-7, Air Force Historical Research Agency, Maxwell AFB, AL.

[227] Section 22, General Headquarters Southwest Pacific Area. Report on Ferret Flight No. 84, 26–27 Sep 1944; Report on Ferret Flight No. 85, 27–28 Sep 1944; Report on Ferret Flight No. 86, 27 Sep 1944; Report on Ferret Flight No. 87, 28–29 Sep 1944. 178.46-171, IRIS 132093, 132138, Air Force Historical Research Agency, Maxwell AFB, AL.; 63rd Bombardment Squadron (H). History, September 1944. 30 September 1944. IRIS 44211, Air Force Historical Research Agency, Maxwell AFB, AL.

[228] 63rd Bombardment Squadron (H). History, March 1945. No date. IRIS 44216, Air Force Historical Research Agency, Maxwell AFB, AL.

[229] 63rd Bombardment Squadron (H). History, October 1944. 31 October 1944; 63rd Bombardment Squadron (H). History, November 1944. 30 November 1944; 63rd Bombardment Squadron (H). History, December 1944. No date;. IRIS 44212-14, Air Force Historical Research Agency, Maxwell AFB, AL.

[230] Communications Officer, Fifth Air Force. Memorandum to Chief of Staff, A-2, A-3, Fifth Air Force. No subject. 9 February 1945. Air Force Historical Research Agency, IRIS 258503/730.903-2, 5th AF Radar & Radio Security, Nov 44–Mar 45, Maxwell AFB, AL.; Air Evaluation Board, Southwest Pacific Area. Report No. 18, Reconnaissance Aviation in the Southwest Pacific Area. 22 April 1946, p.4. IRIS 114060, Air Force Historical Research Agency, Maxwell AFB, AL.

[231] 63rd Bombardment Squadron (H). History, March 1945. No date. IRIS 44216, Air Force Historical Research Agency, Maxwell AFB, AL.

[232] Joint Electronic Information Agency. Report No. 6229, Radio Countermeasures in Southwest Pacific Area. 6 September 1944. Air Force Historical Research Agency, 706.906, Jan–Mar 45/Frame 1650, Reel A7182, Maxwell AFB, AL.; Office of Scientific Research and Development, National Defence Research Committee, *Summary Technical Report of Division 15, NDRC, Volume 1. Radio Countermeasures* (Washington, DC: 1946), p.349.

[233] Section 22, General Headquarters Southwest Pacific Area. Report on Ferret Flight No. 116, 4–5 Jan 1945. IRIS 132017, 178.46-52, Air Force Historical Research Agency, Maxwell AFB, AL.; 63rd Bombardment Squadron (H). History, January 1945. No date. IRIS 44215, Air Force Historical Research Agency, Maxwell AFB, AL.; Section 22, General Headquarters Southwest Pacific Area; Report on Ferret Flight No. 115, 30–31 Dec 1944. IRIS 132133, 178.46-168, Air Force Historical Research Agency, Maxwell AFB, AL.; Office of Scientific Research and Development, National Defence Research Committee, *Summary Technical Report of Division 15, NDRC, Volume 1. Radio Countermeasures* (Washington, DC: 1946), p.349; Communications Officer, Fifth Air Force. Memorandum to Chief of Staff, A-2, A-3, Fifth Air Force. No subject. 9 February 1945. Air Force Historical Research Agency, 730.903-2, 5th AF Radar & Radio Security, Nov 44–Mar 45, Maxwell AFB, AL.; Air Evaluation Board, Southwest Pacific Area. Report No. 18, Reconnaissance Aviation in the Southwest Pacific Area. 22 April 1946, p.4. IRIS 114060, Air Force Historical Research Agency, Maxwell AFB, AL.

[234] Communications Officer, Fifth Air Force. Memorandum to Chief of Staff, A-2, A-3, Fifth Air Force. No subject. 9 February 1945. Air Force Historical Research Agency, IRIS 258503/730.903-2, 5th AF Radar & Radio Security, Nov 44–May 45, Maxwell AFB, AL.

[235] Office of Scientific Research and Development, National Defence Research Committee, *Summary Technical Report of Division 15, NDRC, Volume 1. Radio Countermeasures* (Washington, DC: 1946), pp.348–9; Report on Ferret Flight No. 118, 15–16 Jan 1945. IRIS 132094, 178.46-129, Air Force Historical Research Agency, Maxwell AFB, AL.

[236] 63rd Bombardment Squadron (H). History, March 1945. No date. IRIS 44216, Air Force Historical Research Agency, Maxwell AFB, AL.

[237] Assistant Chief of Air Staff, Materiel, Maintenance and Distribution. Memorandum to CG, Material Command, Wright Field. 28 January 1944. Subject: Ferrets IX Installation. 452.1 – CONSOLIDATED B-24 FERRET 1943-44-45 Folder, Box 2713, Entry – Sarah Clark (Central Decimal File), RG 342, National Archives.

[238] Assistant Chief of Air Staff, Materiel, Maintenance and Distribution. Memorandum to CG, Material Command, Wright Field. 23 March 1944. Subject: Ferrets X and XI, Project Number 96508R. 452.1 – CONSOLIDATED B-24 FERRET 1943-44-45 Folder, Box 2713, Entry – Sarah Clark (Central Decimal File), RG 342, National Archives

[239] Charles Beard's Story – Radar Counter Measures in the CBI Theatre; 7th Bombardment Group/Wing, 1918–1995; Robert Dorr, p.183.

[240] Maintenance Division, AAF Air Technical Service Command, Wright Field. Memorandum to Assistant Chief of Air Staff, Materials and Services. 6 November 1944. Subject: Ferret XI; Assistant Chief of Air Staff, Materials and Services. Memorandum to Director, AAF Air Technical Service Command, Wright Field. 15 December 1944. Subject: Unsatisfactory Installation of Communications Equipment in Ferrets VI and X; both filed in Folder 452.1 – CONSOLIDATED B-24 FERRET 1943-44-45, Box 2713, Entry – Sarah Clark (Central Decimal File), RG 342, National Archives

[241] Assistant Chief of Air Staff, Materials and Services. Memorandum to Director, AAF Air Technical Service Command, Wright Field. 15 December 1944. Subject: Unsatisfactory installation of Communications Equipment in Ferrets VI and X. Folder 452.1 – CONSOLIDATED B-24 FERRET 1943-44-45, Box 2713, Entry – Sarah Clark

[242] Section 22, General Headquarters Southwest Pacific Area. Report on Ferret Flight No. 120, 8 Feb 1945; Report on Ferret Flight No. 122, 16–17 Feb 1945; Report on Ferret Flight No. 124, 25–26 Feb 1945. 178.46-174/IRIS 132139, 178.46-175/IRIS 132140, 178.46-10/IRIS 131975, Air Force Historical Research Agency, Maxwell AFB, AL.

[243] Section 22, General Headquarters Southwest Pacific Area. Report on Ferret Flight No. 125, 3–4 Mar 1945; Report on Ferret Flight No. 126, 5–6 Mar 1945; Report on Ferret Flight No. 127, 8–9 Mar 1945; Report on Ferret Flight No. 133, 8–9 Apr 1945; Report on Ferret Flight No. 135, 18–19 Apr 1945; Report on Ferret Flight No. 136, 20–21 Apr 1945; Report on Ferret Flight No. 137, 22–23 Apr 1945; Report on Ferret Flight No. 138, 26–27 Apr 1945; Report on Ferret Flight No. 139, 29–30 Apr 1945. 178.46-20/IRIS 131985, 178.46-6/IRIS 131971, 178.46-7/IRIS 131973, 178.46-134/IRIS 132099, 178.46-133/IRIS 132098, 178.46-132/IRIS 132097, 178.46-131/IRIS 132096, 178.46-130/IRIS 132095, 178.46-127/IRIS 132092. Air Force Historical Research Agency, Maxwell AFB, AL.

[244] Communications Officer, Fifth Air Force. Memorandum to Chief of Staff, A-2, A-3, Fifth Air Force. No subject. 9 February 1945. Air Force Historical Research Agency, 730.903-2, 5th AF Radar & Radio Security, Nov 44–Mar 45, Maxwell AFB, AL.; Air Evaluation Board, Southwest Pacific Area. Report No. 18, Reconnaissance Aviation in the Southwest Pacific Area. 22 April 1946, p.4. IRIS 114060, Air Force Historical Research Agency, Maxwell AFB, AL.

[245] Communications Officer, Fifth Air Force. Memorandum to Chief of Staff, A-2, A-3, Fifth Air Force. No subject. 9 February 1945; Headquarters, V Bomber Command. Memorandum to Commanding General, Fifth Air Force. Subject: Radar Countermeasures for Heavy Bomb Group. 19 February 1945. Both in 730.903-2, 5th AF Radar & Radio Security, Nov 44–Mar 45, Air Force Historical Research Agency, Maxwell AFB, AL.

[246] Communications Officer, Fifth Air Force. Memorandum to Chief of Staff, A-2, A-3, Fifth Air Force. No subject. 9 February 1945. Air Force Historical Research Agency, 730.903-2, 5th AF Radar & Radio Security, Nov 44–Mar 45, Maxwell AFB, AL.

[247] Communications Officer, Fifth Air Force. Check Sheet to A-3 (ATT Col Allison), Fifth Air Force. No subject. 24 May 1945. Air Force Historical Research Agency, 730.903-2, 5th AF Radar & Radio Security, Nov 44–Mar 45, Maxwell AFB, AL.

[248] Headquarters, Far East Air Forces. Memorandum to Commanding General, Fifth Air Force. No subject. 14 April 1945. Air Force Historical Research Agency, 730.903-2, 5th AF Radar & Radio Security, Nov 44–Mar 45, Maxwell AFB, AL; Radio Message. From 8GN 242115/I, To 4TO, No subject. No date. Air Force Historical Research Agency, 730.903-2, 5th AF Radar & Radio Security, Nov 44–Mar 45, Maxwell AFB, AL.

[249] 380th Bomb Group. History, May 1945. 1945. Air Force Historical Research Agency, IRIS 86282, GP-380-HI (Bomb), May 45, Maxwell AFB, AL; 380th Bomb Group. History, April 1945. 1945, p.29. Air Force Historical Research Agency, IRIS 86281, GP-380-HI (Bomb), Apr 45, Maxwell AFB, AL.; V Bomber Command (?). Draft Standard Operating Procedure for RCM Section in a Heavy Bomb Group. No date, likely April 1945. Air Force Historical Research Agency, 730.903-2, 5th AF Radar & Radio Security, Nov 44–Mar 45, Maxwell AFB, AL.

[250] Headquarters, Far East Air Forces. Memorandum to Commanding General, Fifth Air Force. No subject. 14 April 1945. Air Force Historical Research Agency, 730.903-2, 5th AF Radar & Radio Security, Nov 44–Mar 45, Maxwell AFB, AL; Radio Message. From 8GN 242115/I, To 4TO, No subject. No date. Air Force Historical Research Agency, IRIS 258503/730.903-2, 5th AF Radar & Radio Security, Nov 44–May 45, Maxwell AFB, AL.

[251] Air Commo (?). Summary for Chief of Staff, Fifth Air Force. No Subject. 16 May 1945. Air Force Historical Research Agency, IRIS 258503/730.903-2, 5th AF Radar & Radio Security, Nov 44–May 45, Maxwell AFB, AL.; Radio Message. From VAF to VBC, No subject. No date. Air Force Historical Research Agency, 730.903-2, 5th AF Radar & Radio Security, Nov 44–Mar 45, Maxwell AFB, AL.

[252] The Adjutant General's Office, War Department. Memorandum to Commander-in-Chief, Southwest Pacific Area. Subject: Redesignation and Reorganisation of the 20th Combat Mapping Squadron. 10 May 1945; Headquarters, Far East Air Forces. General Orders No. 876. 25 May 1945. Both Air Force Historical Research Agency, IRIS 258504, Maxwell AFB, AL.

[253] Section 22, General Headquarters Southwest Pacific Area. Report on Ferret Flight No. 140, 2–3 May 1945; Report on Ferret Flight No. 141, 5–6 May 1945; Report on Ferret Flight No. 142, 8–9 May 1945; Report on Ferret Flight No. 143, 11–12 May 1945; Report on Ferret Flight No. 144, 15–16 May 1945; Report on Ferret Flight No. 145, 18–19 May 1945; Report on Ferret Flight No. 146, 21–22 May 1945; Report on Ferret Flight No. 148, 25–26 May 1945. IRIS 132002/178.46-38, IRIS 131974/178.46-9, IRIS 132141/178.46-176, IRIS 132015/178.46-50, IRIS 132022/178.46-57, IRIS 132021/178.46-56, IRIS 131988/178.46-23, 131987/178.46-22, Air Force Historical Research Agency, Maxwell AFB, AL.

[254] War Department, Chief, Material Division, Office of the Assistant Chief of Air Staff, Material and Services. Memorandum to Commanding General, Air Technical Service Command. Subject: Status of Radar Ferrets in FEAF. 8 August 1945. 452.1 – CONSOLIDATED B-24 FERRET 1943-44-45 Folder, Box 2713, Entry – Sarah Clark (Central Decimal File), RG 342, National Archives; Commander, Fifth Bomber Command. Message to Commander, Fifth Air Force. 30 May 1945. Air Force Historical Research Agency, IRIS 258503, Maxwell AFB, AL.

[255] 63rd Bombardment Squadron (H). History, June 1945. No date. IRIS 44220, Air Force Historical Research Agency, Maxwell AFB, AL.

[256] Headquarters, Far East Air Forces. Memorandum to Commanding General, Fifth Air Force. No subject. 15 June 1945. IRIS 258504/730.903-2, 5th AF Radar & Radio Security, Jun-Jul 45, Air Force Historical Research Agency, Maxwell AFB, AL.

[257] Headquarters, V Bomber Command. Memorandum to Section 22 GHQ (Attn Dr. Sutro), Commanding General, Far East Air Forces (Attn RCM Officer), Commanding General, Fifth Air Force (Attn RCM Officer). Subject: Use of Ferrets from 14th Air Force. 4 June 1945. Air Force Historical Research Agency, 730.903-2, 5th AF Radar & Radio Security, Nov 44–Mar 45, Maxwell AFB, AL.

[258] Commander, Far East Air Forces. Message to Commander, Fifth Air Force. 21 June 1945. Cite: A 72430. Air Force Historical Research Agency, IRIS 258504, Maxwell AFB, AL.

[259] Headquarters, Fifth Air Force. Memorandum to Commanding General, V Bomber Command and Commanding Officer, 91st Recce Wing. Subject: Ferret RCM Reconnaissance. 2 July 1945. Air Force Historical Research Agency, 730.903-2, 5th AF Radar & Radio Security, Nov 44–Mar 45, Maxwell AFB, AL.

[260] Headquarters, Fifth Air Force. Memorandum to Commanding Officer, 91st Recce Wing. Subject: Ferret Flights. 30 June 1945. Air Force Historical Research Agency, 730.903-2, 5th AF Radar & Radio Security, Nov 44–Mar 45, Maxwell AFB, AL.

[261] Headquarters, V Bomber Command. Memorandum to Commanding General, Fifth Air Force. 30 June 1945. Subject: RCM Receivers and Equipment. Air Force Historical Research Agency, IRIS 258504, Maxwell AFB, AL.

[262] General Headquarters, U.S. Army Forces in the Pacific. Staff Study Operations: Olympic. 1st Edition, 28 May 1945. D767.25.K9U6, Joint Forces Staff College Library.

[263] Office of Scientific Research and Development, National Defence Research Committee, Summary Technical Report of Division 15, NDRC, Volume 1. Radio Countermeasures (Washington, DC: 1946), p.359.

[264] Headquarters, Fifth Air Force. Memorandum to Commanding General, V Bomber Command and CO's, 1st RSM and 91st Recce Wing. No subject. 6 July 1945. Air Force Historical Research Agency, 730.903-2, 5th AF Radar & Radio Security, Nov 44–Mar 45, Maxwell AFB, AL.; Countermeasures Air Analysis Center, Office of the Director of Communications, Headquarters, Army Air Forces, Pacific Ocean Areas. Memorandum to Distribution 'A'. Subject: Jamming of Gun-Laying Radars by the XXI Bomber Command. 18 June 1945. Air Force Historical Research Agency, 730.907, 5th AF RCM Reports, May–June 1945, Maxwell AFB, AL; Air Evaluation Board, Southwest Pacific Area. Report No. 18, Reconnaissance Aviation in the Southwest Pacific Area. 22 April 1946, p.30. IRIS 114060, Air Force Historical Research Agency, Maxwell AFB, AL.

[265] 20th Combat Mapping Squadron. Unit Historical Report, July 1945. N.d. IRIS 65351, Sq-photo-20-hi, Jul 45, Air Force Historical Research Agency, Maxwell AFB, AL.

[266] 43rd Bomb Group. RCM Mission Reports, May–August 1945. 1945. Air Force Historical Research Agency, IRIS 79888, GP-43-SU-OP, 30 Apr 45–13 Aug 45, Maxwell AFB, AL.

[267] 20th Combat Mapping Squadron. Unit Historical Report, August 1945. N.d. IRIS 65352, Sq-photo-20-hi, Aug 45, Air Force Historical Research Agency, Maxwell AFB, AL.

[268] 20th Combat Mapping Squadron. Unit Historical Report, July 1945. N.d. IRIS 65351, Sq-photo-20-hi, Jul 45, Air Force Historical Research Agency, Maxwell AFB, AL; 20th Combat Mapping Squadron. Unit Historical Report, August 1945. N.d., p.18. IRIS 65352, Sq-photo-20-hi, Aug 45, Air Force Historical Research Agency, Maxwell AFB, AL.

[269] Office of the Commanding General, Headquarters Alaskan Department. Memorandum to Commanding General, Eleventh Air Force. Subject: Letter of Instructions on Projects 2022, 2023 and 2024. April 27, 1944. Air Force Historical Research Agency, IRIS 202602, Maxwell AFB, AL.

[270] Headquarters, Eleventh Air Force. Annex F to ComNorPac OpOrder 8-44: Paramushiru To, Karabu Saki. 1 July 1944. Air Force Historical Research Agency, IRIS 203777, Maxwell AFB, AL.

[271] Headquarters, Eleventh Air Force. Annex F to ComNorPac OpOrder 8-44: Paramushiru To, Karabu Saki. 1 July 1944. Air Force Historical Research Agency, IRIS 203777, Maxwell AFB, AL.; Headquarters, Eleventh Air Force. Air Intelligence, North Pacific Area No. 4, 13 Nov 44 to 31 Dec 44. 1 January 1945. Air Force Historical Research Agency, IRIS 203762, Maxwell AFB, AL.

[272] Headquarters, Eleventh Air Force. Air Intelligence, North Pacific Area No. 5, 1 Jan 45 to 31 Jan 45. 1 February 1945. Air Force Historical Research Agency, IRIS 203763, Maxwell AFB, AL.

[273] Kit Carter and Robert Mueller, *Combat Chronology 1941–1945* (Washington: Center for Air Force History, 1991), p.316.

[274] 2nd Photo Charting Squadron. History of Flight 'A' 2d Photo Charting Squadron Aleutian Islands, 7 April 1944 to 30 September 1944. N.d. Air Force Historical Research Agency, IRIS 64565, Maxwell AFB, AL.

[275] Headquarters, Eleventh Air Force. Air Intelligence, North Pacific Area No. 4, 13 Nov 44 to 31 Dec 44. 1 January 1945. Air Force Historical Research Agency, IRIS 203762, Maxwell AFB, AL; Headquarters, Eleventh Air Force. Air Intelligence, North Pacific Area No. 3, 13 Oct 44 to 12 Nov 44. 12 November 1944. Air Force Historical Research Agency, IRIS 203761, Maxwell AFB, AL.

[276] Headquarters, Eleventh Air Force. Air Intelligence, North Pacific Area No. 4, 13 Nov 44 to 31 Dec 44. 1 January 1945. Air Force Historical Research Agency, IRIS 203762, Maxwell AFB, AL.

[277] Commander in Chief, U.S. Pacific fleet, diary for the month of August 1944. 12 September 1944. Combined Arms Research Library, N10277; Charles Scrivner. *Empire Express* (Temple City: Historical Aviation Album, 1976), pp.13–40; Carter and Mueller, pp.400–585.

[278] Headquarters, Eleventh Air Force. Air Intelligence, North Pacific Area No. 2, 16 Sep 44 to 12 Oct 44. 15 October 1944. Air Force Historical Research Agency, IRIS 203761, Maxwell AFB, AL.

[279] Commander, Fifth Fleet. Operations Plan No. 13-44. 3 January 1945. Combined Arms Research Library, call no. N7727.

[280] 28th Bombardment Group. History of the 28th Bombardment Group (Composite), 1 September 1944 to 30 September 1944. 27 October 1944. Air Force Historical Research Agency, IRIS 79224, Maxwell AFB, AL.

[281] Headquarters, Eleventh Air Force. Air Intelligence, North Pacific Area No. 12, 1 Aug 45 to 31 Aug 45. 1 September 1945. Air Force Historical Research Agency, IRIS 203770, Maxwell AFB, AL.; 404th Bombardment Squadron. History of the 404th Bombardment Squadron (H), 1 October 1944 to 31 October 1944. 15 November 1944. Air Force Historical Research Agency, IRIS 46338, Maxwell AFB, AL; 404th Bombardment Squadron. History of the 404th Bombardment Squadron (H), 1 November 1944 to 30 November 1944. 15 December 1944. Air Force Historical Research Agency, IRIS 46339, Maxwell AFB, AL; 404th Bombardment Squadron. History of the 404th Bombardment Squadron (H), 1 December 1944 to 31 December 1944. 15 January 1945. Air Force Historical Research Agency, IRIS 46340, Maxwell AFB, AL.

[282] 404th Bombardment Squadron. History of the 404th Bombardment Squadron (H), 1 to 31 January 31 1945. 15 February 1945. Air Force Historical Research Agency, IRIS 46342, Maxwell AFB, AL; 404th Bombardment Squadron. History of the 404th Bombardment Squadron (H), 1 February 1945 to 28 February 1945. 15 March 1945. Air Force Historical Research Agency, IRIS 46342, Maxwell AFB, AL; USAAF Aircraft data cards for B-24D s/n 41-23886; Air Force Historical Research Agency, Maxwell AFB, AL.

[283] 404 Bombardment Squadron. Report on Ferret Mission #1, 20 Jan 1945 to signal officer, Eleventh Air Force; Air Force Historical Research Agency, 178.46-164, Maxwell AFB, AL.; Headquarters, Eleventh Air Force. Air Intelligence, North Pacific Area No. 5, 1 Jan 45 to 31 Jan 45. 1 February 1945. Air Force Historical Research Agency, IRIS 203763, Maxwell AFB, AL.

[284] 404 Bombardment Squadron. Report on Ferret Mission #2, 24 Jan 1945 to signal officer, Eleventh Air Force; Air Force Historical Research Agency, 178.46-166, Maxwell AFB, AL.

[285] 404th Bombardment Squadron. History of the 404th Bombardment Squadron (H), 1 to 31 January 1945. 15 February 1945. Air Force Historical Research Agency, IRIS 46342, Maxwell AFB, AL; 404th Bombardment Squadron. History of the 404th Bombardment Squadron (H), 1 February 1945 to 28 February 1945. 15 March 1945. Air Force Historical Research Agency, IRIS 46342, Maxwell AFB, AL.

[286] Commander in Chief, U.S. Pacific fleet, diary for 27 Jan–28 Feb 45. 5 July 1945. Combined Arms Research Library, N10277.

[287] VPB-131. War Diary, 6 March 1943–2 September 1945. Micro Serial Number 157984, Reel A2077, NARA ID 4697018, World War II War Diaries, Other Operational Records and Histories, 1942–1946, RG 38, National Archives; VPB-136. War Diary, 1 March 1943–31 December 1944. Micro Serial Number 157989, Reel A2077, NARA ID 4697018, World War II War Diaries, Other Operational Records and Histories, 1942–1946, RG 38, National Archives.

[288] 404th Bombardment Squadron. History of the 404th Bombardment Squadron (H), 1 March 1945 to 31 March 1945. 15 April 1945. Air Force Historical Research Agency, IRIS 46343, Maxwell AFB, AL.

[289] 404 Bombardment Squadron. Report on Ferret Mission #3, 31 March 1945 to signal officer, Eleventh Air Force; Air Force Historical Research Agency, 178.46-167, Maxwell AFB, AL.

[290] Headquarters, Eleventh Air Force. Air Intelligence, North Pacific Area No. 7, 1 Mar 45 to 30 Mar 45. 1 April 1945. Air Force Historical Research Agency, IRIS 203765, Maxwell AFB, AL.; 404th Bombardment Squadron. History of the 404th Bombardment Squadron (H), 1 April 1945 to 30 April 1945. 15 May 1945. Air Force Historical Research Agency, IRIS 46344, Maxwell AFB, AL.

[291] Headquarters, Eleventh Air Force. Air Intelligence North Pacific Area No. 8. 1 May 1945. Combined Arms Research Library, call no. N8806; Kit Carter and Robert Mueller. The Army Air Forces in World War II: Combat Chronology (Washington: Office of Air Force History, GPO, 1991), pp.669, 672, 678; 28th Bombardment Group. History of the 28th Bombardment Group (Composite), 1 April 1945 to 30 April 1945. 19 May 1945. Air Force Historical Research Agency, IRIS 79231, Maxwell AFB, AL.

[292] 404 Bombardment Squadron. Report on Ferret Mission #6, 30 April 1945 to signal officer, Eleventh Air Force; Air Force Historical Research Agency, 178.46-136, Maxwell AFB, AL.

[293] Carter and Mueller, pp.689; 28th Bombardment Group. History of the 28th Bombardment Group (Composite), 1 April 1945 to 30 April 1945. 19 May 1945. Air Force Historical Research Agency, IRIS 79231, Maxwell AFB, AL.

[294] VPB-139. Aircraft Action Report No. 1. 6 April 1945. Micro Serial Number 116395, Reel A1527; VPB-139. Aircraft Action Report No. 4. 28 April 1945.Micro Serial Number 120047, Reel A1577; both NARA ID 4697018, World War II War Diaries, Other Operational Records and Histories, 1942–1946, RG 38, National Archives.

[295] Headquarters, Eleventh Air Force. Air Intelligence, North Pacific Area No. 8, 1 Apr 45 to 30 Apr 45. 1 May 1945. Air Force Historical Research Agency, IRIS 203766, Maxwell AFB, AL; 28th Bombardment Group. History of the 28th Bombardment Group (Composite), 1 April 1945 to 30 April 1945. 19 May 1945. Air Force Historical Research Agency, IRIS 79231, Maxwell AFB, AL.

[296] Headquarters, Eleventh Air Force. Air Intelligence, North Pacific Area No. 8, 1 Apr 45 to 30 Apr 45. 1 May 1945. Air Force Historical Research Agency, IRIS 203766, Maxwell AFB, AL.

[297] 404 Bombardment Squadron. Report on Ferret Mission #8, 7 May 1945 to signal officer, Eleventh Air Force; Air Force Historical Research Agency, 178.46-137, Maxwell AFB, AL.

[298] 404 Bombardment Squadron. Report on Ferret Mission #9, 11 May 1945 to Commanding General, Eleventh Air Force; Air Force Historical Research Agency, 178.46-169, Maxwell AFB, AL.; Headquarters, Eleventh Air Force. Air Intelligence, North Pacific Area No. 8, 1 Apr 45 to 30 Apr 45. 1 May 1945. Air Force Historical Research Agency, IRIS 203766, Maxwell AFB, AL.

[299] Carter and Mueller, pp.698; Missing Air Crew Reports for USAAF aircraft serial number 41-11924. 10 May 1945. Serial number 41-11924, Report Number 11410, Publication Number M1380, NARA ID 305256, Records of the Office of the Quartermaster General, RG 92, National Archives; VPB-139. Aircraft Action Report No. 6. 10 May 1945. Micro Serial Number 121118, Reel A1592, NARA ID 4697018, World War II War Diaries, Other Operational Records and Histories, 1942–1946, RG 38, National Archives.

[300] 28th Bombardment Group. History of the 28th Bombardment Group (Composite), 1 May 1945 to 31 May 1945. 15 June 1945. Air Force Historical Research Agency, IRIS 79232, Maxwell AFB, AL.

[301] Headquarters, Eleventh Air Force. Air Intelligence North Pacific Area No. 9. 1 June 1945. Combined Arms Research Library, call no. N8806; Carter and Mueller, pp.700, 702.

[302] 404 Bombardment Squadron. Report on Ferret Mission #12, 26 May 1945 to Commanding General, Eleventh Air Force; Air Force Historical Research Agency, 178.46-14, Maxwell AFB, AL.

[303] 28th Bombardment Group. History of the 28th Bombardment Group (Composite), 1 June 1945 to 30 June 1945. 10 July 1945. Air Force Historical Research Agency, IRIS 79233, Maxwell AFB, AL.

[304] Headquarters, Eleventh Air Force. Air Intelligence North Pacific Area No. 10. 1 July 1945. Combined Arms Research Library, call no. N8806; Carter and Mueller, pp.708, 711–12, 714; COMNORPACFOR. War Diary, 1 June – 30 June 1945. Serial Number 00240, Reel A1722, NARA ID 4697018, World War II War Diaries, Other Operational Records and Histories, 1942–1946, RG 38, National Archives.

[305] COMNORPACFOR. War Diary, 1 July–31 July 1945. Micro Serial Number 136595, Reel A1797, NARA ID 4697018, World War II War Diaries, Other Operational Records and Histories, 1942–1946, RG 38, National Archives; Headquarters, Eleventh Air Force. Air Intelligence North Pacific Area No. 11. 1 August 1945. Combined Arms Research Library, call no. N8806; Carter and Mueller, pp.724, 731, 733.

[306] Headquarters, Eleventh Air Force. Air Intelligence North Pacific Area No. 12. 1 September 1945. Combined Arms Research Library, call no. N8806; Carter and Mueller, pp.738–9.

[307] 404th Bombardment Squadron. History of the 404th Bombardment Squadron (H), 1 September 1945 to 30 September 1945. 17 October 1945. Air Force Historical Research Agency, IRIS 46349, Maxwell AFB, AL

[308] Alvin Coox, *Strategic Bombing in the Pacific*, 1942–1945 in R. Cargill Hall, *Case Studies in Strategic Bombardment*, 1998, Government Printing Office, pp.275–299.

[309] Headquarters, Twentieth Air Force. Monograph I – RCM Reconnaissance and Countermeasures, 24 November 1944–1 June 1945, p.2. August 1945. Air Force Historical Research Agency, 762.041-2, Maxwell AFB, AL.

[310] Military Intelligence Division, War Department. RATEL No. 11, Japanese Radar Locations. 20 July 1945. Air Force Historical Research Agency, 170.227G-11, Maxwell AFB, AL.

[311] 2D & 3D Operations Analysis Section, Far East Air Force. A Short Survey of Japanese Radar, Volume IV, November 20, 1945; Air Force Historical Research Agency, 720.310A V.4, Maxwell AFB, AL, p.28.

[312] Office of the Air Communications, Headquarters United States Army Strategic Air Forces. Summary of RCM Activities in XXI Bomber Command, Period 18 December 1944 to March 31, 1945, pp.1–9. Air Force Historical Research Agency, 703.907

[313] Office of Communications Officer, Headquarters XXI Bomber Command, Memorandum to A-3 Section, no subject, dated 6 November 1944. Filed in Monograph II – RCM Reconnaissance and Countermeasures, 24 November 1944–1 June 1945. August 1945. Air Force Historical Research Agency, 762.041-2, Maxwell AFB, AL.

[314] TELECON Message FL 19-1 192005ZNovember 1944, from Harmon to Hansell to Arnold/Norstad. Filed in Monograph II – RCM Reconnaissance and Countermeasures, 24 November 1944–1 June 1945. August 1945. Air Force Historical Research Agency, 762.041-2, Maxwell AFB, AL.

[315] Assistant Chief of Air Staff, Operations, Commitments & Requirements (Requirements Division). Memorandum to Assistant Chief of Air Staff, Operations, Commitments & Requirements (Attention: Chief of Staff, XX Air Force). 22 June 1944. Subject: Ferret Radar Equipment in Very Heavy Reconnaissance Aircraft. File 413.44-R, Box 631, Entry 294 – Classified Central Decimal Files, RG 18, National Archives.

[316] Telecon Message No. H-13-3, COMAF 20 to DEPCOMAF 20, subject: Ferrets, 13 December 1944. Air Force Historical Research Agency, SQ – PHOTO – 3 – SU – OP – S, Mar–Aug 1945.

[317] Headquarters, XXI BC. Central Pacific Newsletter No. 2, 6 January 1945. Filed in Monograph II – RCM Reconnaissance and Countermeasures, 24 November 1944–1 June 1945. August 1945. Air Force Historical Research Agency, 762.041-2, Maxwell AFB, AL.

[318] Individual Aircraft Data Card for 44-41124, AFHRA; Memorandum from Director of Communications to Deputy Chief of Operations, subject: Ferret Aircraft, dated 31 December 1944. Air Force Historical Research Agency, SQ – PHOTO – 3 – SU – OP – S, Mar–Aug 1945.

[319] Army Air Forces Air Depot, APO #953, Routing and Record Sheet for Modification of B-24J #44-41124 (Ferret), 1 February 1945. Air Force Historical Research Agency, SQ – PHOTO – 3 – SU – OP – S, Mar–Aug 1945. IRIS 64754.

[320] Joe Riedel via Chuck Varney, e-mail, 25 July 2009.

[321] 'The Search for Jap Radar', Radar, Issue 10, 30 June 1945, Radiation Laboratory, Massachusetts Institute of Technology; reprinted March 1985 Product Support Department, Ferranti Defence Systems Limited.

[322] Individual Aircraft Data Card for 44-41981, 44-41985, 44-41994, 44-41995, 44-41996, AFHRA

[323] 'The Search for Jap Radar', Radar, Issue 10, 30 June 1945, Radiation Laboratory, Massachusetts Institute of Technology; reprinted March 1985 Product Support Department, Ferranti Defence Systems Limited.

[324] 'The Search for Jap Radar', Radar, Issue 10, 30 June 1945, Radiation Laboratory, Massachusetts Institute of Technology; reprinted March 1985 Product Support Department, Ferranti Defence Systems Limited.

[325] Headquarters, XXI BC. Central Pacific Newsletter No. 6, 10 March 1945. Filed in Monograph II – RCM Reconnaissance and Countermeasures, 24 November 1944–1 June 1945. August 1945. Air Force Historical Research Agency, 762.041-2, IRIS 263220, Maxwell AFB, AL.

[326] Headquarters, XXI BC. Central Pacific Newsletter No. 8, 12 April 1945. Filed in Monograph II – RCM Reconnaissance and Countermeasures, 24 November 1944–1 June 1945. August 1945. Air Force Historical Research Agency, 762.041-2, Maxwell AFB, AL. There is some discussion on additional reasons for removal of the nose and upper turrets on Ferret VI. When transiting through Hickam Field, the Hawaii Air Depot voiced concern on the overloading of the aircraft and recommended removal of these weapons to bring it back into weight tolerances. This concern was not voiced by Guam Air Depot; curiously, the B-24M ferrets were just as heavy as B-24J Ferret VI and no concerns have been found about their 'overloading'. See Army Air Forces Air Depot, APO #953, Informal Action Sheet, Subject: Modification of Ferret 6, 17 January 1945. Air Force Historical Research Agency, SQ – PHOTO – 3 – SU – OP – S, Mar – Aug 1945 for discussion on Ferret VI and weight.

[327] Headquarters, XXI BC. Central Pacific Newsletter No. 9, 4 May 1945; Headquarters, XXI BC. Radar, RCM and Radio Newsletter No. 11, 28 May 1945. Filed in Monograph II – RCM Reconnaissance and Countermeasures, 24 November 1944–1 June 1945. August 1945. 762.041-2, IRIS 263220. Air Force Historical Research Agency, Maxwell AFB, AL.; Army Air Forces Air Depot, APO #953, Routing and Record Sheet for Modification of B-24J #44-41124 (Ferret), 1 February 1945. SQ – PHOTO – 3 – SU – OP – S, Mar–Aug 1945. IRIS 64754, Air Force Historical Research Agency, Maxwell AFB, AL.

[328] Countermeasures Analysis Center, Headquarters Strategic Air Forces Pacific Ocean Area. Report No. 1 to Assistant Director, Section 22, GHQ, SWPA, APO 500, 29 March 1945. Air Force Historical Research Agency, SQ – PHOTO – 3 – SU – OP – S, Mar–Aug 1945.

[329] Office of the Deputy Commander, Headquarters Strategic Air Forces Pacific Ocean Area, memorandum to Commander in Chief, US Pacific Fleet, subject: Formation of Joint Radar Countermeasures Analysis Group, Pacific, Aug 4 1945. Air Force Historical Research Agency, SQ – PHOTO – 3 – SU – OP – S, Mar–Aug 1945.

[330] Headquarters, XXI BC. Central Pacific Newsletter No. 1, 27 December 1944. Filed in Monograph II – RCM Reconnaissance and Countermeasures, 24 November 1944–1 June 1945. August 1945. Air Force Historical Research Agency, 762.041-2, Maxwell AFB, AL.

[331] Office of the Air Communications, Headquarters United States Army Strategic Air Forces. Summary of RCM Activities in XXI Bomber Command, Period 18 December 1944 to 31 March 1945, pp.9–11. Air Force Historical Research Agency, 703.907.

[332] Office of the Communications Officer, Headquarters, XXI BC. Memorandum to Deputy Chief of Staff for Operations, subject: RCM Ferret Aircraft, dated 25 February 1945. Filed in Monograph II – RCM Reconnaissance and Countermeasures, 24 November 1944–1 June 1945. August 1945. Air Force Historical Research Agency, 762.041-2, Maxwell AFB, AL.; Larry Tart and Robert Keefe, *The Price of Vigilance: Attacks on American Surveillance Flights* (NY: Ballantine Books, 2001), pp.170–171.

[333] Electronic Warfare Section, Office of the Director of Communications, Headquarters United States Army Strategic Air Forces. Memo to Chief, Electronics Section, HQ United States Army Strategic Air Forces, Office of the Director of Communications dated 19 July 1945 with the topic 'Conversion of RCM Ferret A/C for Communications Monitoring Operations. Air Force Historical Research Agency, SQ – PHOTO – 3 – SU – OP – S, Mar–Aug 1945.

[334] Headquarters, XXI BC. Central Pacific Newsletter No. 2, 6 January 1945. Filed in Monograph II – RCM Reconnaissance and Countermeasures, 24 November 1944–1 June 1945. August 1945. Air Force Historical Research Agency, 762.041-2, Maxwell AFB, AL.

[335] Tart and Keefe, pp.170–171.

[336] John Patrick Finnegan, *Military Intelligence, Army Lineage Series*, Center for Military History (Washington, DC: 1998), p.93.

[337] Office of the Communications Officer, Headquarters, XXI BC. Memorandum to Deputy Chief of Staff for Operations, subject: RCM Ferret Aircraft, dated 25 February 1945; Headquarters, XXI BC. Central Pacific Newsletter No. 9, 4 May 1945; Both filed in Monograph II – RCM Reconnaissance and Countermeasures, 24 November 1944–1 June 1945. August 1945. Air Force Historical Research Agency, 762.041-2, Maxwell AFB, AL.

[338] Headquarters, XXI BC. Central Pacific Newsletter No. 11, 31 May 1945. Filed in Monograph II – RCM Reconnaissance and Countermeasures, 24 November 1944–1 June 1945. August 1945. Air Force Historical Research Agency, 762.041-2, Maxwell AFB, AL; flight records of Lt Merlin Harnly, February–August 1945, Jim Stewart via Chuck Varney; 3rd PRS Flight R weekly operational summaries, Jim Stewart via Chuck Varney; 3rd PRS RCM Reconnaissance mission summaries for Missions 1-5, Air Force Historical Research Agency, SQ – PHOTO – 3 – SU – OP – S, Mar–Aug 1945.

[339] Headquarters, Twentieth Air Force. Monograph I – RCM Reconnaissance and Countermeasures, 24 November 1944–1 June 1945, p.6. August 1945. Air Force Historical Research Agency, 762.041-2, Maxwell AFB, AL.

[340] Flight records of Lt Merlin Harnly, February–August 1945, Jim Stewart via Chuck Varney; 3rd PRS Flight R weekly operational summaries, Jim Stewart via Chuck Varney; 3rd PRS RCM Reconnaissance mission summaries for Missions 6–16, Air Force Historical Research Agency, SQ – PHOTO – 3 – SU – OP – S, Mar–Aug 1945.

[341] E-mail correspondence between Joe Riedel, 3rd PRS Flight R RCM operator, and Chuck Varney, 5 Sep 2009.

[342] 3rd PRS Flight R weekly operational summaries, Jim Stewart via Chuck Varney; 3rd PRS RCM Reconnaissance mission summaries for Missions 6–16, Air Force Historical Research Agency, SQ – PHOTO – 3 – SU – OP – S, Mar–Aug 1945; Office of the Director of Communications, Headquarters United States Army Strategic Air Forces. Summary of Ferret Operations, 16 July to 20 July 1945. Air Force Historical Research Agency, 703.907, Maxwell AFB, AL.

[343] 3rd PRS Flight R weekly operational summaries, Jim Stewart via Chuck Varney; Office of the Director of Communications, Headquarters United States Army Strategic Air Forces. Summary of Ferret Operations, 16 July to 20 July 1945. Air Force Historical Research Agency, 703.907, Maxwell AFB, AL.

[344] Flight records of Lt Merlin Harnly, February–August 1945, Jim Stewart via Chuck Varney; 3rd PRS Flight R weekly operational summaries, Jim Stewart via Chuck Varney.

[345] Air Technical Service Command Technical Instruction TI-2024, Addendum 14, 12 Dec 44 – located in Folder 452.1 – CONSOLIDATED B-24 FERRET 1943-44-45, Box 2713, Entry – Sarah Clark (Central Decimal File), RG 342, National Archives.

[346] Air Technical Service Command Technical Instruction TI-2024, Addendum 36, 21 Feb 45 – located in Folder 452.1 – CONSOLIDATED B-24 FERRET 1943-44-45, Box 2713, Entry – Sarah Clark (Central Decimal File), RG 342, National Archives.

[347] Director, AAF Air Technical Service Command, Wright Field. Memorandum to Commanding General, AAF Attn: AFTMA-2F/7. 13 January 1945. Subject: Ferret Project – DP-516 – Report 2. Folder 452.1 – CONSOLIDATED B-24 FERRET 1943-44-45, Box 2713, Entry – Sarah Clark (Central Decimal File), RG 342, National Archives.

[348] Holley, Irving. Buying Aircraft: Material Procurement for the Army Air Forces. Government Printing Office, 1989. Pages 529-533.

[349] Army Air Forces Technical Service Command (Procurement Division). Memorandum to the Army Air Forces Plant Representative, United-Cheyenne Modification Center. 10 March 1945. Subject: Ferret Modification. Ferret Airplane decimal 452.1 Folder, Box 2697, Entry – Sarah Clark (Central Decimal File), RG 342, National Archives.

[350] Assistant Chief of Air Staff, Materials and Services. Memorandum to Director, AAF Air Technical Service Command, Wright Field. 7 May 1945. Subject: Revision of Equipment for B-24 Radar Ferrets. Folder 452.1 – CONSOLIDATED B-24 FERRET 1943-44-45, Box 2713, Entry – Sarah Clark (Central Decimal File), RG 342, National Archives.

[351] Air Technical Service Command Technical Instruction TI-2024, Addendum 66, 19 May 1945; Air Technical Service Command Technical Instruction TI-2024, Addendum 72, 28 May 1945; both located in Folder 452.1 – CONSOLIDATED B-24 FERRET 1943-44-45, Box 2713, Entry – Sarah Clark (Central Decimal File), RG 342, National Archives.

[352] Individual Aircraft Data Card for 44-51802, 44-51356, AFHRA.

[353] March Field. History of March Field, 1 March 1945 to 31 March 1945. No date. Air Force Historical Research Agency, IRIS 175042, Maxwell AFB, AL.

[354] March Field. History of March Field, 1 April 1945 to 30 April 1945. No date. Air Force Historical Research Agency, IRIS 175043, Maxwell AFB, AL.

[355] March Field. History of March Field, 1 May 1945 to 31 May 1945. No date. Air Force Historical Research Agency, IRIS 175043, Maxwell AFB, AL.

[356] March Field. History of March Field, 1 June 1945 to 30 June 1945. No date. Air Force Historical Research Agency, IRIS 175044, Maxwell AFB, AL.

[357] March Field. Histories of March Field, 1 July 1945 to 31 July 1945, 1 August 1945 to 31 August 1945, and 1 September 1945 to 5 October 1945. No date. Air Force Historical Research Agency, IRIS 175045-8, Maxwell AFB, AL.

[358] Assistant Chief of Air Staff, Operations, Commitments and Requirements. Memorandum to Assistant Chief of Air Staff, Operations, Commitments and Requirements, Commitments Division. 18 February 1945. Subject: Ferret Aircraft for the 1st Photo Reconnaissance Squadron, VH. Air Force Historical Research Agency, 143.03-2.

[359] 1st Photographic Reconnaissance Squadron (VH). Unit Historical Report, June 1945. N.d.. Air Force Historical Research Agency, Sq-photo-1-hi, Jun 45, Maxwell AFB, AL.

[360] 1st Photographic Reconnaissance Squadron (VH). Unit Historical Report, November–December 1945. N.d.. Air Force Historical Research Agency, IRIS 64544, Maxwell AFB, AL.

[361] Assistant Chief of Air Staff, Materials and Services. Memorandum to Director, AAF Air Technical Service Command, Wright Field. 8 December 1944. Subject: Modification of B-24J Airplane on Project 96974-S to C-1 Ferret. 452.1 – CONSOLIDATED B-24 FERRET 1943-44-45 Folder, Box 2713, Entry – Sarah Clark (Central Decimal File), RG 342, National Archives.

[362] Assistant Chief of Air Staff, Materials and Services. Memorandum to Director, AAF Air Technical Service Command, Wright Field. 28 March 1945. Subject: Modification of B-24 Ferret Type Aircraft; Assistant Chief of Air Staff, Materials and Services. Memorandum to Director, AAF Air Technical Service Command, Wright Field. 14 April 1945. Subject: Modification of B-24 Ferret Type Aircraft; both in Folder 452.1 – CONSOLIDATED B-24 FERRET 1943-44-45, Box 2713, Entry – Sarah Clark (Central Decimal File), RG 342, National Archives

[363] Individual Aircraft Data Card for 44-42106, AFHRA.

[364] Vannevar Bush and James Conant. Summary Technical Report of Division 15, NRDC – Volume 1, Radio Countermeasures. (National Defence Research Committee – Washington, 1946), p.150.

[365] Communications Office, Fifth Air Force. Memorandum to Colonel Tyler (nfi). No subject. 15 April 1945. Air Force Historical Research Agency, IRIS 258503 730.903-2, 5th AF Radar & Radio Security, Nov 44–May 45, Maxwell AFB, AL.

[366] Headquarters, Fifth Air Force. Memorandum to Commanding General, V Bomber Command and CO's, 1st RSM and 91st Recce Wing. No subject. 6 July 1945. Air Force Historical Research Agency, IRIS 258504, 730.903-2, 5th AF Radar & Radio Security, Jun–Jul 45, Maxwell AFB, AL.

[367] Commanding General, Far East Air Forces, Manila, Philippines. Message to War Department, information to Commanding General, Air Technical Service Command, Wright Field, Dayton, Ohio, and Commanding General, Pacific Air Technical Service Command, Oakland, California. No subject. Signal Corps No. AX 84449 GC. 27 August 1945. Unknown record group or file, National Archives – received scan from Trent Telenko.

[368] Engineering Division, ATSC. Memorandum to Commanding General, AAF Center, Orlando, FL. 5 December 1945. Subject: Ferret C-1 Installation. Folder 452.1 – CONSOLIDATED B-24 FERRET 1943-44-45, Box 2713, Entry – Sarah Clark (Central Decimal File), RG 342, National Archives.

[369] Assistant Chief of Air Staff, AS-4. Memorandum to Commanding General, Air Technical Service Command, Wright Field. 29 August 1945. Subject: Radar Ferret Modifications. Folder 452.1 – CONSOLIDATED B-24 FERRET 1943-44-45, Box 2713, Entry – Sarah Clark (Central Decimal File), RG 342, National Archives

[370] Radar No. 10, p.10.

[371] March Field. Histories of March Field, 1 July 1945 to 31 July 1945, 1 August 1945 to 31 August 1945, and 1 September 1945 to 5 October 1945. No date. Air Force Historical Research Agency, IRIS 175045-8, Maxwell AFB, AL.

[372] 404th Bombardment Squadron. History of the 404th Bombardment Squadron (H), 1 October 1945 to 31 October 1945. 15 November 1945. Air Force Historical Research Agency, IRIS 46350, Maxwell AFB, AL.

[373] Lloyd, p.68; CINC Far East Command. Message to the JCS. 111205Z Dec 1951. RG 218, National Archives; Assistant Chief of Air Staff-2. Staff Memorandum to AC/AS-5 and AC/AS-2. Box 39, Entry 214, Intel General File, Jun 45–Dec 54, RG 341, National Archives; Alfred Price, *The History of US Electronic Warfare, Volume 2* (Washington: The Association of Old Crows, 1989), p.40.

[374] Director of Research & Development, Office of the Deputy Chief of Staff, Materiel. Memorandum to CG, Air Material Command. 20 November 1947. Box 3684, Entry P-26, Sarah Clark, RG 342, National Archives.

[375] Price, pp.40–44; Commanding General, Alaska Air Command. Cable to Air Staff. 16 August 1947. Box 39, Entry 214, Intel General File, Jun 45–Dec 54, RG 341, National Archives; 31 SRS, Photo. Unit Historical Report, 1 April through 31 August 1949. AFHRA, SQ-RCN-31-HI.

APPENDIX I
Aircraft

Production Ferrets

Ferret No.	Tail No	Aircraft Model	Project # (Note 1)	Arrive Fairfield Depot	Arrive Eglin Field	Depart CONUS	Assignment	Nose Art	Fate
None	41-23941	B-24D-10-CO			Wright Field – Nov 42	Feb 43	404 BS, 11 AF	Little Buck	8 Oct 45 – RFC Walnut Ridge
I	41-23886	B-24D-CO			Nov 43	Mar 45	404 BS, 11 AF	Little Girl	Turned in to Alaska Air Depot 18 Oct 45
II	Unknown	B-24?			Late 42?	N/A	Retained at Eglin Field		
III	42-29644	B-17F-50-DL				22 Apr 43	16 RS	Archangel	14 Dec 45 – RFC Walnut Ridge
IV	42-29881	B-17F-75-BO	92144R			20 Jun 43	16 RS		3 Nov 45 – RFC Walnut Ridge
V	42-3055	B-17F-20-DL				20 Jun 43	16 RS	The Pointer	30 Nov 45 – RFC
VI (originally XI #1)	44-41124	B-24J-195-CO	96508R, DOM 124C, 96737-S	16 Jul 44	28 Oct 44	5 Jan 45	3 PRS, 20 AF		7 June 46 RFC
VII	42-63991	B-24D-20-CF				22 Dec 43	Section 22 (63 BS/380 BG)	The Duchess of Paducah	Salvaged 31 May 45, stricken 1 Aug 45
VIII	42-64045	B-24D-20-CF	96288R		23 Sep 43	Dec 43	Section 22 (63 BS/380 BG)	Atom Smasher	Crash landing at Angaur Island, Palau Dec 44
IX	Uknown	B-24D?	96528R		Jan 44?		Originally destined for SWPA; kept at Eglin Field		
X	44-41076	B-24J-195-CO	96508R, DOM 124C	17 Jul 44	26 Oct 44	20 Jan 45	Section 22 (63 BS)/20 RS		Kingman, AZ 13 Dec 45; declared excess 14 Jan 46
XI #2	44-40943	B-24J-185-CO	96508R, DOM 124C, 96727R, 96978	23 Aug 44	25 Jan 45	4 Mar 45	Section 22 (63 BS)/20 RS		Declared excess 1 Nov 45
XII	44-40815	B-24J-180-CO	90754S?, DOM 124C	3 Jun 44	30 Jul 44	30 Sep 44	7 BG, 10 AF/20 RS	Alec Tronix	Declared excess 30 Nov 45
XIII	44-40817	B-24J-180-CO	90754S?, DOM 124C	3 Jun 44	30 Jul 44	30 Sep 44	308 BG, 14 AF/20 RS	Rovin' Lady	Declared excess 27 Nov 45
XIV	44-41981	B-24M-10-CO	96978S, DOM 124C, 98224-S	1 Jan 45	26 Jan 45	Feb 45	3 PRS, 20 AF		7 Jun 46 RFC
XV	44-41985	B-24M-10-CO	96978S, 98224-S	2 Jan 45	25 Jan 45	Feb 45	3 PRS, 20 AF		Lost in training at Guam, Mar 45
XVI	44-41994	B-24M-10-CO	96978S, DOM 124C, 98224-S	2 Jan 45	25 Jan 45	Feb 45	3 PRS, 20 AF		Scrapped Jun 46?

Ferret No.	Tail No	Aircraft Model	Project # (Note 1)	Arrive Fairfield Depot	Arrive Eglin Field	Depart CONUS	Assignment	Nose Art	Fate
XVII	44-41995	B-24M-10-CO	96978S, DOM 124C, 98224-S	4 Jan 45	11 Mar 45	N/A	March Field		Lost on training flight in CA, 12 May 45
XVIII	44-41996	B-24M-10-CO	96978S, DOM 124C, 98224-S	4 Jan 45	26 Jan 45	Feb 45	3 PRS, 20 AF	Ramp Champ	Scrapped Jun 46?
0	44-40225	B-24J-150-CO	DOM 129-B, 96528R	20 Jan 45	18 Apr 45	N/A	Eglin Field; to March Field 7 Jun 45		Turned in to 'Long Bch ATC', 13 Jun 46
C-1	44-42106	B-24M-15-CO	96974-S, DOM 110C	2 Jan 45	23 Jul 45	N/A	Eglin Field		Turned in to RFC, 3 Jun 46
Unknown	Unknown	B-24M-25/30?	97078-R?			Jun 45?	Enroute to 20 RS at end of war		Abandoned at Biak?
Unknown	Unknown	B-24M-25/30?	97078-R?			Jun 45?	Enroute to 20 RS at end of war		Abandoned at Biak?
Unknown	44-51802	B-24M-30-FO	DOM 131-B, DOM 124C		Cheyenne – 31 May 45	N/A	March Field – 26 Jul 45		Turned in to RFC, 21 May 46
Unknown	44-51356	B-24M-25-FO	DOM 126-B, DOM 124C		Cheyenne – 31 Mar 45	N/A	March Field – 20 Jul 45		Turned in to RFC, 1 Jun 46
Unknown	44-51282	B-24M-25-FO	DOM 126-B, DOM 124C		Cheyenne – 22 Mar 45	N/A	March Field – 3 Jun 45		Turned in to RFC, 18 May 46
Unknown	44-51784	B-24M-30-FO	97047S		Cheyenne – 31 May 45	Oct 45	404 BS, 17 Oct 45		Crashed at Shemya, AK 16 Jun 46
Unknown	Unknown	B-24M-30-FO?	98271-S		Unknown if modification started prior to end of war		For 1 PRS?		
Unknown	Unknown	B-24M-30-FO?	98271-S				For 1 PRS?		
Unknown	Unknown	B-24M-30-FO?	98271-S				For 1 PRS?		
Unknown	Unknown	B-24M-30-FO?	98271-S				For 1 PRS?		

Note 1 – Based on entry from Individual Aircraft Data Card

Field Modified Ferrets

Theater	Tail No	Aircraft Model	Date Modified	Location Modified	Assignment	Nose Art	Fate
SWPA – 13 AF	44-41464	B-24L-5-CO	Feb 45	Noemfoor Island, Dutch New Guinea	13 AF – 868 BS	Lady June II	14 Oct 45 RFC Kingman
SWPA – 5 AF	41-30276	B-25D	Feb 45	Unknown	499 BS – 5 AF 'radar buster'	Dirty Dora II	
SWPA – 5 AF	Unknown	B-25	Feb 45	Unknown	499 BS – 5 AF 'radar buster'		
SWPA – 13 AF	43-27983	B-25J	Nov 44	Either Sansapor, New Guinea or Noemfoor Island, Dutch New Guinea	100 BS – 13 AF 'radar buster'		Beautiful Ohio Abandoned at Puerto Princessa, Palawan?
SWPA – 13 AF	(likely 43-27958)	B-25J	Jun 45	Puerto Princessa, Palawan	100 BS – 13 AF 'radar buster'		Abandoned at Puerto Princessa, Palawan?
SWPA – 13 AF	(likely 43-28126)	B-25J	Jun 45	Puerto Princessa, Palawan	100 BS – 13 AF 'radar buster'		Abandoned at Puerto Princessa, Palawan?
Mediterranean	42-3358	B-17F-65-BO	Oct 43	Foch Field, Tunisia	16 RS	Thunder Head	Turned in, Hunter Field, GA, 14 Nov 44
Mediterranean	42-30379	B-17F-100-BO	Oct 43	Foch Field, Tunisia	16 RS		Lost 25 Jan 44
Mediterranean	41-9016	B-17E	Oct 43	Foch Field, Tunisia	16 RS		Lost 6 Dec 43
Mediterranean	42-30437	B-17F	Oct 43	Unknown location, UK	16 RS		Turned in, Hunter Field, GA, 14 Nov 44
Europe – 8 AF	44-10507	B-24J-60-CF	Feb 45	1st SAD, Honington, UK	36 BS		
CBI – 14 AF	42-40635	B-24D-80-CO	Jun-Jul 44	Agra Airfield, British India	308 BG	Interim Ferret/ Tail Heavy	Salvaged overseas, 28 Nov 45

Known Ad-hoc Ferrets

Alaska – Eleventh Air Force	**404 BS**
	B-24D-CO s/n 41-11924 "Duchess" – modified Dec 44- Jan 45; only flew 2 missions in Jan 45
Europe – Eighth Air Force	**36 BS**
	B-17G-10-DL s/n 42-37743 – from 96 BG, came with search eqpt
	B-17F-75-DL s/n 42-3518 – search eqpt from s/n 42-37743
	B-24J-5-DT s/n 42-51308 – search eqpt in rear of bomb bay, Sep-Dec 44
	B-24J-1-FO s/n 42-50622 – search eqpt in rear of bomb bay, Dec 44- Apr 45; eqpt from s/n 42-51305
	B-24J-1-FO s/n 42-50671 – search eqpt in rear of bomb bay, Aug 44, possibly Dec 44-Apr 45
	P-38J-15-LO s/n 43-28479 – modified by 192 Squadron, 100 (SD) Group, RAF?
	P-38J-20-LO s/n 44-23156 – modified by 192 Squadron, 100 (SD) Group, RAF?
	P-38J-20-LO s/n 44-23501 – modified by 192 Squadron, 100 (SD) Group, RAF?
SWPA – 1943	**435 BS**
	B-17E s/n 41-9194
	403 BS/43 BG
	B-17F s/n 41-24543 "Pluto II"
	B-17F s/n 41-24548
	B-17F s/n 41-24554 "The Mustang"
	90 BG
	B-24D-1-CO s/n 41-23731 "Dirty Gertie"
	B-24D-5-CO s/n 41-23759
	380 BG
	B-24D-53-CO s/n 42-40369 "Shady Lady"
	B-24D-65-CO s/n 42-40496 "Juarez Whistle"
	B-24D-65-CO s/n 42-40500 "Care Less"
	B-24D-65-CO s/n 42-40512 "She 'Asta"
	B-24D-70-CO s/n 42-40532 "Little Joe"
	B-24D-105-CO s/n 42-40827 "Old Hickory"
	B-24D-120-CO s/n 42-40967 "Black Widow"
SWPA – 1944-5	**868 BS**
	B-24D-100-CO s/n 42-40822 "Bums Away"
	B-24J-85-CO s/n 42-100271 "Lady June"
	B-24J-185-CO s/n 44-40897
	B-24J-185-CO s/n 44-40899 "Lady Luck II"
	B-24J-185-CO s/n 44-40902
	B-24J-190-CO s/n 44-41025 "So Round, So Firm, So Fully Stacked"
	B-24J-195-CO s/n 44-41080
	22 BG
	B-24L-10-FO s/n 44-49644
	B-24M-1-CO s/n 44-41820
	90 BG
	B-24J-110-CO s/n 42-109857
	B-24J-130-CO s/n 42-110055 "8 Ball"
	B-24J-160-CO s/n 44-40426 "Ruby's Ricksha"
	B-24J-175-CO s/n 44-40728 "Boise Bronc"
	380 BG
	B-24D-130-CO s/n 42-41071 "Morbid Moe"
	B-24D-155-CO s/n 42-72790 "Sandra Kay"
	B-24J-1-CO s/n 42-72964 "Dottie's Double"
	B-24J-15-CO s/n 42-73133 "Sad Sack"
	B-24J-45-CO s/n 42-73464 "Angel in de Skies"
	B-24J-160-CO s/n 44-40398 "Patty's Pig"

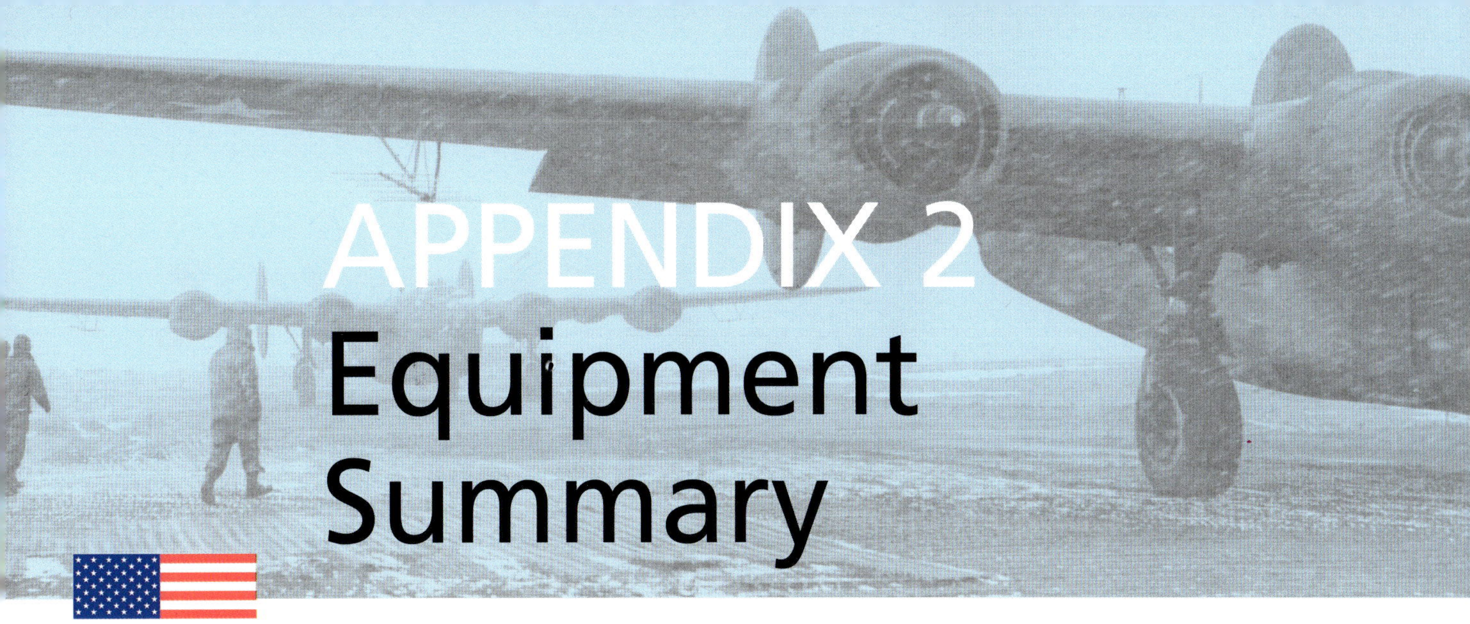

APPENDIX 2
Equipment Summary

Signal Analysis Equipment

AN/APA-6: Pulse analyzer; worked with AN/APA-6X, designed for use with the SCR-587
AN/APA-6X: Audio oscillator; military version of HP 200, worked in conjunction with AN/APA-6
AN/APA-10: Panoramic adapter – replaced BC-1032
AN/APA-11: Panoramic Indicator – replaced AN/APA-6 and AN/APA-6X with one unit

Receivers

ARC-1: USN receiver airborne and shipborne use used by Australians starting in September 1942; US Army designation SCR-587, then AN/APR-1
AN/APR-1: USN search receiver, known in US Army usage as SCR-587; coverage of 40-3000 MHz accomplished with separate Tuning Units; replaced by AN/APR-4
AN/APR-2: Search receiver that could be manually or motor-tuned; coverage of 85-1000 MHz; also known as RC-160.
AN/APR-4: Improved version of AN/APR-1; coverage of 38-3200 MHz accomplished with separate Tuning Units;
AN/APR-5: Wide range microwave receiver; coverage of 1000-3100 MHz
AN/APR-6: Wide range microwave receiver; coverage of 3000-6000 MHz
AN/APR-7: Coverage of 1000-3500 MHz
AN/ARQ-5: Panoramic receiver for use with countermeasures; coverage of 16-77 MHz
AN/ARR-5: Commercial Hallicrafters S-27 UHF receiver; coverage of 27-140 MHz; replaced S-36
AN/ARR-7: receiver; coverage of .55-42 MHz; replaced SX-28
RC-160: See AN/APR-2
RC-164: Warning receiver to note enemy radar station or night fighter is in proximity; coverage of 40-3000 MHz
S-27: see AN/ARR-5
S-36: Commercial Hallicrafters UHF receiver; coverage of 27.8-143 MHz
SCR-587: See AN/APR-1
SX-28: Commercial Hallicrafters HF receiver: coverage of .55-43 MHz
AN/APA-23: Thermal paper recorder; commonly used with AN/APR-4
AN/ANQ-1: Wire recorder

Direction Finding Antennas

C-2100 DF antenna
AN/APA-17: coverage 250-1000 MHz
AN/APA-24: coverage 100-750 MHz

Navigation Equipment

SCR-521: Search and navigation radar
SCR-717: Search and navigation radar
AN/APN-1: Radio altimeter
AN/APN-4: LORAN receiver

APPENDIX 3 Select Ferret Missions

Table One: 3rd PRS R Flight

Mission #	Date	Ferret	Location	Base
1	18-May-45	XIV/44-41981	Haha Jima	North Field, Guam
2	24-May-45	XVI/44-41994	Kito Iwo, Haha Jima, Chichi Jima	North Field, Guam
3	29-May-45	XVI/44-41994	Kito Iwo, Haha Jima, Chichi Jima	North Field, Guam
4	29-May-45	XIV/44-41981	Nanpo Shoto Island chain	North Field, Guam
5	31-May-45	XVIII/44-41996	Kito Iwo, Haha Jima, Chichi Jima	North Field, Guam
6	2-Jun-45	XIV/44-41981	Nanpo Shoto north to Tori Jima	North Field, Guam
7	7-Jun-45	VI/44-41124	Hachijo Jima	North Field, Guam
8	4-5 June 45	XVIII/44-41996	Tori Jima	North Field, Guam
9	4-Jun-45	XVI/44-41994	Aoga Shima and Bayonnaise Rocks	North Field, Guam
10	9-Jun-45	XIV/44-41981	Tori Shima, Aoga Shima and Bayonnaise Rocks	North Field, Guam
11	15-Jun-45	XVI/44-41994	Haha Jima	North Field, Guam
12	15-Jun-45	VI/44-41124	Hachijo Jima	North Field, Guam
13	22-Jun-45	VI/44-41124	Miyake, Mikura-jima and Inamba-jima	North Field, Guam
14	25-26 Jun 45	unk B-24M	Coast search from Shionomi Saki to Iho Saki, Honshu	North Field, Guam
15	26-Jun-45	XIV/44-41981	Miyake and Mikura Jima	North Field, Guam
16	28-Jun-45	XVIII/44-41996	Haha and Chichi Jima	North Field, Guam
17	2-3 July 45	VI/44-41124	Honshu, Shikoku	North Field, Guam
18	3-4 July 45	XIV/44-41981	KII Suido, coast of Shikoku and Honshu	North Field, Guam
19	6-7 July 45	XVI/44-41994	Honshu coast	North Field, Guam
20	6-7 July 45	XVIII/44-41996	Nanpo Shoto and Honshu coast	North Field, Guam
21	6-7 July 45	VI/44-41124	Off coast of Japan	North Field, Guam
22	9-10 July 45	XVIII/44-41996	Miyake, Mikura and O'Shima	North Field, Guam
23	16-17 July 45	VI/44-41124	Coastline to south of Tokyo	North Field, Guam
24	12-13 July 45	XIV/44-41981	Coastline to south of Tokyo	North Field, Guam
25	16-17 July 45	XVI/44-41994	Kyushu-Shikoku coasts	North Field, Guam
26	16-17 July 45	XVIII/44-41996	Southern coast of Shikoku	North Field, Guam
27	19-20 Jul 45	XVI/44-41994	Off coast of Shikoku-Honshu to a point south of Nagoya	North Field, Guam
28	19-20 Jul 45	XVIII/44-41996	Along coast of Japan, south of Hamamatsu	North Field, Guam
29	19-20 Jul 45	XIV/44-41981	South of Tokyo, eastern coast of Honshu from Chosi to Hitachi	North Field, Guam
30	23-24 Jul 45	VI/44-41124	Off coast of Shikoku-Honshu south of Osaka	North Field, Guam
31	23-24 Jul 45	XVI/44-41994	Off coast of Honshu, south of Nagoya	North Field, Guam
32	23-24 Jul 45	XVIII/44-41996	Off coast of Honshu near Hamamatsu to Island Chain	North Field, Guam
33	28-29 Jul 45	XVI/44-41994	Shikoku, Tokyo Bay	North Field, Guam
34	28-29 Jul 45	XIV/44-41981	Nagoya area off Hamamatsu	North Field, Guam
35	28-29 Jul 45	VI/44-41124	Nagoya area off Hamamatsu	North Field, Guam
36	31 Jul-1 Aug 45	VI/44-41124	Off coast of Honshu, around Nagoya, Tokyo Bay	North Field, Guam
37	5-6 Aug 45	XVI/44-41994	COMINT, 30 miles east and south coast of Kyushu	North Field, Guam
38	5-6 Aug 45	XIV/44-41981	30 miles off south coast of Honshu	North Field, Guam
39	7-8 Aug 45	XIV/44-41981	Kyushu	North Field, Guam
40	7-8 Aug 45	44-41124	50 miles off coast of Shikoku	North Field, Guam
41	13-14 Aug 45	XVI/44-41994	50 miles off coast of Shikoku	North Field, Guam
42	13-14 Aug 45	XVIII/44-41996	Nagoya, Osaka area, off coast of Honshu	North Field, Guam
43	14-15 Aug 45	VI/44-41124	Off Honshu	North Field, Guam

Table Two: 20th RS

Mission #	Date	Ferret	Mission	Base
1	3 Jul 45	XI/44-40943	Investigate enemy radars on Batan Island, Itbayat Island, and Koto-Sho	Clark Field, PI
2	4-5 Jul 45	XI /44-40943	General search on Canton-Hong Kong area and investigation on radar at Tankan Island attacked by 499 BS 'radar buster'	Clark Field, PI
3	9-10 Jul 45	XII/44-40815	General search on Canton-Hong Kong area and investigation on radar at Tankan Island attacked by 499 BS 'radar buster'	Clark Field, PI
4	10-11 Jul 45	X/44-41076	General search of Batan Island, Itbayat Island, and Koto-Sho	Clark Field, PI
5	13-14 Jul 45	XII/44-40815	General search of Formosa Island with focus on NW area	Clark Field, PI
6	15-16 Jul 45	X/44-41076	General search of East Formosa Coast	Clark Field, PI
7	23-24 Jul 45	XII/44-40815	General search of East Formosa Island with focus on NE area	Clark Field, PI
8	24-25 Jul 45	XII/44-40815	General search of the Sakishima Gunto area	Clark Field, PI
9	27-28 Jul 45	X/44-41076	General search of the Ryuku Rotto Islands	Clark Field, PI
10	29-30 Jul 45	X/44-41076	General search of the Ryuku Rotto Group of Islands	Clark Field, PI
11	2 Aug 45	XIII/44-40817	General search of the Sakishima Gunto group of islands	Clark Field, PI
12	5-6 Aug 45	XIII/44-40817	General search of the Sakishima Gunto group of islands	Clark Field, PI

Table Three: 404th BS, Eleventh Air Force

Mission #	Date	Ferret	Mission	Base
1	20 Jan 45	41-11924	Weather, general search of Kuriles	Shemya
2	23 Jan 45	41-11924	General search of Kuriles	Shemya
3	29 Mar 45	I/41-23886	Search Shimushu and Paramushiru Islands	Shemya
Non-ferret, RCM support	2 Apr 45	I/41-23886	Investigate whether Kresta Point radar was being jammed; weather reconnaissance	Shemya
Non-ferret, RCM support	4 or 5? Apr 45	I/41-23886	Investigate whether Kresta Point radar was being jammed; weather reconnaissance	Shemya
4?	7 Apr 45	I/41-23886	Paramushiru and Harumukotan	Shemya
5?	16 Apr 45	I/41-23886	Unknown, likely Shimushu and Paramushiru Islands	Shemya
6	25 Apr 45	I/41-23886	General search of Shimushu and Paramushiru Islands	Shemya
7?	27 Apr 45	I/41-23886	Shimushu and Paramushiru Islands	Shemya
8	5 May- 45	I/41-23886	Weather-general search-shipping recce of Paramushiru Strait	Shemya
9	9 May 45	I/41-23886	Search of Shimushu and Paramushiru Islands after bombing of Kataoka; trailing bombers	Shemya
10	15 May 45	I/41-23886	Shimushu and Paramushiru Islands	Shemya
11	18 May 45	I/41-23886	Shimushu and Paramushiru Islands	Shemya
12	23 May 45	I/41-23886	Weather, general search of Shimushu and Paramushiru Islands	Shemya
13	3 Jun 45	I/41-23886	Kataoka, followed by 8x strike/recce B-24	Shemya
14	18 Jun 45	I/41-23886	East coast of Paramushiru Island with 6x B-24s attacking Kataoka Straits and base	Shemya
15	10 Jul 45	I/41-23886	Shimushu and Paramushiru Islands	Shemya
16	26 Jul 45	I/41-23886	Shimushu and Paramushiru Islands	Shemya
17	12 Aug 45	I/41-23886	Unknown, likely Shimushu and Paramushiru Islands	Shemya

Table Four: Tenth Air Force

Mission #	Date	Ferret	Mission
1	Oct 44?	XII/44-40815	Unknown
2	10-11 Nov 44	XII/44-40815	Burma/Thailand area; aircraft operated singly
3	14-15 Nov 44	XII/44-40815	Unknown; aircraft operated singly
4	19-20 Nov 44	XII/44-40815	Burma/Thailand area; accompanied a B-24 strike
5	27-28 Nov 44	XII/44-40815	Search west coast of Burma up to and including St Matthews Island; aircraft operated singly
6	1 Dec 44	XII/44-40815	Accompany 7 BG B-24 strike to Morgui, Burma; emergency landing at Cox's Bazaar due to low fuel
	Unknown	XII/44-40815	Early December missions?
	20 Dec 44	XII/44-40815	test flight
	21 Dec 44	XII/44-40815	Taungup, Burma supply depot; accompanied a strike
	23 Dec 44	XII/44-40815	Taungup, Burma; accompanied a strike
	Unknown	XII/44-40815	Late December missions?
13	29-30 Dec 44	XII/44-40815	Burma/Thailand area
14	7 Jan 45	XII/44-40815	Gwa Bay Area, Burma; aircraft operated singly
15	9 Jan 45	XII/44-40815	Pagoda Pt, Rangoon; accompanied a strike
16	13 Jan 45	XII/44-40815	Mandalay, Meiktila; accompanied a strike
17	18 Jan 45	XII/44-40815	Meiktila; accompanied a strike
18	21 Jan 45	XII/44-40815	Ramree Island Area; accompanied a strike
19	23 Jan 45	XII/44-40815	Bassein, Moulmein, Pagoda Pt, Rangoon; accompanied a strike
20	27 Jan 45	XII/44-40815	Bassein, Tavoy, Pagoda Pt, Bangkok; accompanied a strike
21	31 Jan 45	XII/44-40815	Mandalay, Meiktila; accompanied a strike
22	3 Feb 45	XII/44-40815	Pagoda Pt, Victoria Pt; accompanied a strike
23	7 Feb 45	XII/44-40815	Moulmein, Pagoda Pt, Rangoon; accompanied a strike
24	9 Feb 45	XII/44-40815	Moulmein, Pagoda Pt; accompanied a strike
25	15 Mar 45	XII/44-40815	Bassein, Gwa, Pagoda Pt; aircraft operated singly
26	17 Mar 45	XII/44-40815	Bassein, Gwa, Pagoda Pt, Great Coco Island; aircraft operated singly
27	29 Mar 45	XII/44-40815	Bassein, Gwa, Rangoon; accompanied a strike
28	31 Mar 45	XII/44-40815	Bassein, Pagoda Pt, Great Coco Island, Andaman Island; aircraft operated singly
29	2-Apr 45	XII/44-40815	Bassein, Pagoda Pt, Great Coco Island, Andaman Island; aircraft operated singly
30	4-Apr 45	XII/44-40815	Bassein, Pagoda Pt, Mergui, Victoria Pt; aircraft operated singly
Unknown	9 Apr 45	XII/44-40815	Unknown
Unknown	13 Apr 45	XII/44-40815	Unknown
Unknown	17 Apr 45	XII/44-40815	Unknown
Unknown	21 Apr 45	XII/44-40815	Unknown
Unknown	24 Apr 45	XII/44-40815	Unknown; last ferret flight?

Table Five: Fourteenth Air Force

Mission #	Date	Ferret	Mission
1?	4 Sep 44	42-40635	Lunchow Peninsula and Canton?
2-4?	4-9 Sep 44	42-40635	Flew missions from Liuchow from 4-9 Sep; returned to Chengkung on 9 Sep 44
5	24-25 Sep 44	42-40635	Yochow-Hankow area
6	30 Sep – 1 Oct 44	42-40635	Accompany a bombing mission to Canton area
7	15-16 Oct 44	42-40635	Liuchow Peninsula and Hainan Island
8	17-18 Oct 44	42-40635	Liuchow Peninsula, Kiungsha, and Hanoi
9	27-28 Oct 44	42-40635	Changteh-Changsha-Shasi-Hankow area
10	30-31 Oct 44	42-40635	Accompany mine laying aircraft to Canton-Hong Kong area
11	5-6 Nov 44	42-40635	French Indo-China from Hanoi-Haiphong to Tourane
12	8-9 Nov 44	42-40635	Hainan Island
13	16-17 Nov 44	XIII/44-40817	Yochow-Shasi-Hankow-Changsha area
14	22-23 Nov 44	42-40635	Yochow-Hankow-Changsha area
15	24-25 Nov 44	42-40635	Changsha-Tuagting-lae Shahi area during 308 BG mission
16	26-27 Nov 44	XIII/44-40817	Hainan Island
	Unknown	Either ferret	December missions?
21	5-6 Jan 45	XIII/44-40817	Check on Japanese comms during local bombing raid
22	8 Jan 45	Either ferret	Kunming Area – "China Ferret Project" mission
23	11 Jan 45	Either ferret	Kunming Area – "China Ferret Project" mission
24	12 Jan 45	Either ferret	Kunming Area – "China Ferret Project" mission
25	14 Jan 45	Either ferret	Kunming Area – "China Ferret Project" mission
26	16-17 Jan 45	XIII/44-40817	Kunming Area – "China Ferret Project" mission; COMINT
27	28-29 Jan 45	XIII/44-40817	Shasi, Yochow, Hangkow, and Changsha Areas
28	30 Jan 45	42-40635	Hainan Island Island in conjunction with sea search
29	2-3 Feb 45	42-40635	China coast from St John's Island to Amoy – COMINT?
	6 Feb 45	42-40635	South China Sea?
	14 Feb 45	XIII/44-40817?	Plane 817 was part of a 373 BS three plane anti-shipping patrol along French Indo China coast; recovered at Chengkung
	16 Feb 45	XIII/44-40817?	Plane 817 was part of a 373 BS two plane anti-shipping patrol along French Indo China coast; recovered at Chengkung due to wx
	Unknown	Either ferret	Additional February missions?
35	8-9 Mar 45	XIII/44-40817	Hengyang and Poyang Lake area
36	2-3 Apr 45	42-40635	Hungtze Lake, Shanghai and Yangtze River areas

Table Six: 16th RS

Mission #	Date (Note 1)	Ferret	Mission
1	17 May 43	III/42-29644	By 9 July, when Operation HUSKY kicked off, Ferret III had completed nine missions covering the coasts of Sardinia and Sicily
	Unknown	III/42-29644	
8	26 Jun 43	III/42-29644	
	Unknown	III/42-29644	
	5 Aug – 20 Aug 43	Ferrets III – V	4 missions – coast of Sardinia and Corsica; west coast and heel/toe of Italy
	20 Aug – 5 Sep 43	Ferrets III – V	12 missions – thorough coverage of Sardinia and Corsica; west coast of Italy, Genoa/Naples areas along with jamming missions on 1, 5 Sep
23	1 Sep 43	V/42-3055, B-17F 42-30379	Cagliari area of southern coast of Sardinia; experiment to determine effectiveness of Mandrel jammer against German EW radars, 379 with jammer, 055 to observe; 379 attacked by flare-dropping night fighters and flak
24	3 Sep 43	IV/42-29881	Genoa area; quick check to verify info from previous flight
25	5 Sep 43	V/42-3055, B-17F 42-30379	Cape Spartivento and Cape Rizzuto; follow-on to 1 Sep mission on testing jamming; weather impacted
26	6 Sep 43	IV/42-29881	Italian coast from Tiber River north to Cape Palinuro; weather forced mission to south of Tiber River
27	8 Sep 43	V/42-3055	East coast of Sardinia, west coast of Italy; check Freya radar coverage
28	11 Sep 43	IV/42-29881	Italian coast from Monte Circeo to Genoa and east coast of Corsica to Sardinia
29	12 Sep 43	III/42-29644	Circle the islands of Sardinia and Corsica
30	13 Sep 43	III/42-29644	Italian coast from Ponte Circeo to La Roca Forte
31	16 Sep 43	V/42-3055	Italian coast from Ventotente Island to La Roca Forte, east coast of Sardinia
32	17 Sep 43	V/42-3055	Genoa, IT to Nice, FR and Corsica
33	18 Sep 43	III/42-29644	Eastern coast of Sardinia and Italian coast from Roca Forte to Guardia Point
34	19 Sep 43	V/42-3055	Islands of Sardinia and Corsica
35	20 Sep 43	IV/42-29881	West coast of Italy, east coasts of Sardinia and Corsica
36	23 Sep 43	IV/42-29881	Radar coverage from Ventotene Island to La Roca Forte
37	24 Sep 43	III/42-29644	Coast of France from Nice to Spanish border
38	25 Sep 43	III/42-29644	Italian coast from Ventotente north to Genoa
39	26 Sep 43	IV/42-29881	Western Adriatic as far south as Greece
40	27 Sep 43	III/42-29644	Italy – Monte Circio to La Rocca Forte
41	30 Sep 43	III/42-29644	Investigate radar coverage of the east coast of Italy and west coast of Yugoslavia and Albania
42	2 Oct 43	V/42-3055	South coast of France
43	3 Oct 43	IV/42-29881	La Spezia to St Tropez, FR; weather impacted mission
44	4 Oct 43	IV/42-29881	Night mission to observe Mandrel jamming of formation of 99, 301 BG bombers; flew behind formation
45	5 Oct 43	IV/42-29881	Italian coast from Elba to Monte Circeo/La Rocca Fort
46	6 Oct 43	IV/42-29881	Adriatic Sea radar survey – Ravenna to Trieste
47	1 Oct 43	V/42-3055	Italian coast from Elba to Monte Circeo/La Rocca Fort; mission cut short due to electrical storm
48	15 Oct 43	IV/42-29881	Italian coast from Monte Circeo, IT to Nice, FR
49	16 Oct 43	V/42-3055	Adriatic Sea; routine check of radar sites
50	18 Oct 43	IV/42-29881	Coast of Greece, from Corfu south and east
51	20 Oct 43	IV/42-29881	Italian coast from Monte Circeo, IT to Genoa; cut short at Spezia, IT due to wx
52	22 Oct 43	IV/42-29881	Accompany RAF mission to Ancona, IT
53	24 Oct 43	41-9016	Day mission with 97 BG to Wiener Neustadt, some of which were carrying 16 RS Carpet radar jammers. First daylight mission accompanied by a ferret; ferret carried a full bomb load; flew from Foggia, IT
	25 Oct 43	III/42-29644	Weather cancel
54	26 Oct 43	III/42-29644	Adriatic coastline to Corfu; flown from Grottaglia
55	27 Oct 43	III/42-29644	Greek coast, Albania; flown from Grottaglia; weather cut mission short
56	29 Oct 43	41-9016	Accompany RAF mission to Port Ferrato, IT, orbit near target area for duration of raid, 12k ft – over water near Grosseto, IT; then Italian coast from Elba Island to Nice, FR
57	30 Oct 43	III/42-29644	Accompany RAF night bombing mission to Perugia, IT; equipment failure (SCR-587) cut mission short
	31 Oct 43	V/42-3055	Maintenance cancel
58	1 Nov 43	42-3358	Leghorn-Spezia area; daylight 97 BG mission, wx divert
59	1 Nov 43	41-9016	Support RAF raid on Viareggio and patrol south coast of FR
60	2 Nov 43	42-30379	Wiener Neustadt, Austria; daylight 97 BG mission to Austria, dropped bombs
61	6 Nov 43	V/42-3055	Circle Adriatic, emphasis on Durrazo, Albania; flown from Grottaglia, IT
62	11 Nov 43	V/42-3055	Rome-Leghorn
63	12 Nov 43	V/42-3055	South of France – Nice to Spanish border
64	13 Nov 43	42-30437	South of France
65	15 Nov 43	41-9016	west coast of IT near Elba to e. of Toulon, FR
66	16 Nov 43	42-30437	Rome, IT to Nice, FR; three ferrets spaced at 15 min intervals to see German reaction
67	16 Nov 43	41-9016	

Mission #	Date (Note 1)	Ferret	Mission
68	16 Nov 43	V/42-3055	
69	18 Nov 43	V/42-3055	South of France – Nice to Spanish border; two ferrets spaced at 15 min intervals to see German reaction
70	18 Nov 43	42-30437	
71	19 Nov 43	42-30379	Rome-Nice; two ferrets spaced at 15 min intervals to see German reaction; weather cnx – turned back at Savona
72	19 Nov 43	41-9016	
73	21 Nov 43	42-30379	Monte Circeo – Spezia, IT
74	23 Nov 43	42-30379	Adriatic; flown from Brindisi
75	24 Nov 43	41-9016	Near Genoa, off west coast of IT; accompanied RAF night mission; ASV jamming, went over land – lost?
76	27 Nov 43	V/42-3055	Gulf of Lions – Med coast of France; weather cnx
77	29 Nov 43	42-30379	Monte Circeo – Elba, IT
78	30 Nov 43	42-30379	South of France – Nice to Spanish border
79	28 Nov 43	41-9016	Adriatic from Yugoslav border up east side and down west side
80	1 Dec 43	41-9016	Adriatic from Yugoslav border up east side and down west side
81	2 Dec 43	41-9016	Central Adriatic, focusing on islands off Yugoslav coast
82	3 Dec 43	41-9016	South east Adriatic coast along Greece to Crete then recover at Foch Field
83	3 Dec 43	V/42-3055	Italian coast from Monte Circeo to La Rocca Fort; weather cnx – turned back at Elba
84	4 Dec 43	41-9016	South of France – Toulon to Spanish border
86	5 Dec 43	41-9016	Toulon, FR to Leghorn, IT
86	6 Dec 43	41-9016	Mediterranean coast of France/Gulf of Lion – from Toulon to French/Spanish border; aircraft crashed
87	12 Dec 43	42-30379	Rome-Genoa; weather cnx – turned back at Elba
88	18 Dec 43	42-30379	Rome-Genoa
89	22 Dec 43	42-30379	Gulf of Lion as far east as Nice
90	27 Dec 43	42-30379	Nice to Marseille, FR; daylight J-Mission
91	27 Dec 43	42-30437	Nice to Marseille, FR; daylight J-Mission
92	3 Jan 44	42-30379	Forward deployed to Brindisi to fly missions over the Adriatic; only one msn flown due to weather
93	8 Jan 44	42-30379	Italian coast from Monte Circeo to La Rocca Fort; J-Mission
94	8 Jan 44	42-30437	Italian coast from Monte Circeo to La Rocca Fort; J-Mission
95	1 Jan 44	42-30437	From Bari area around the Adriatic to Valona area
96	12 Jan 44	42-30437	Adriatic – Cazza Island, Lagosta Island, Valona
97	13 Jan 44	42-30437	Ionian Sea – Corfu, Crete
98	13 Jan 44	42-30379	Gulf of Lions – Toulon to Spanish border
99	18 Jan 44	42-30379	Nice – Genoa – Mont Circeo
100	21 Jan 44	42-30379	Northern Adriatic; RAF raid on Klagenfurt, Austria; flown from Foggia; accompanied a RAF night raid; returned 23 Jan 44
101	22 Jan 44	42-30379	Northern Adriatic, west coast and north coast
102	25 Jan 44	42-30379	Rome area; aircraft crashed
102?	4 Feb 44	42-30437	Gulf of Lions – Nice to Spanish border; wx impacted msn
103	15 Feb 44	42-30437	Littoral Yugoslavia; short mission- cut short by wx? Flown from Grottaglia, Italy
104	16 Feb 44	42-30437	Littoral Yugoslavia; short mission- cut short by wx? Flown from Grottaglia, Italy
105	18 Feb 44	42-30437	Littoral Yugoslavia; short mission- cut short by wx? Flown from Grottaglia, Italy
106	4 Mar 44	42-30437	West coast of IT – Spezia, Genoa, Cape Martin; flown from Borgo, Corsica
107	7 Mar 44	42-3358	Southern Adriatic – Fano Island, Cape Arilla to Corfu; fFlown from Brindisi; first flight of C-2100 D/F antenna; short 3 hr mission
108	9 Mar 44	42-3358	Southern Adriatic – Fano Island, Cape Arilla; flown from Brindisi; very short mission
109	11 Mar 44	42-3358	Adriatic – up one coast, down the other; flown from Armondola/Foggia
110	18 Mar 44	42-30437	Up west coast of IT starting at La Rocca Fort, along coast to Marseille, then across the Med back to Tunis
111	19 Mar 44	42-30437	Up west coast of IT starting at La Rocca Fort, along coast to Marseille, then across the Med back to Tunis
112	25 Mar 44	42-30437	Cape Camarat, FR to Spanish border; recovered in Foggia
113	31 Mar 44	42-30437	Adriatic – Dubrovnik, YU to Corfu; first mission from new base at Foggia
114	4 Apr 44	42-30437	Northern Adriatic – east from Foggia, up the coast and back down the other
115	4 Apr 44	42-30437	RAF raid – Budapest
116	11 Apr 44	42-30437	RAF raid – shipbuilding yards north of Trieste; combined with survey of central and northern Adriatic
117	18 Apr 44	42-3358	Tyrrhenian Sea – west coast of Italy; flown from Pomigliano near Naples in search of U-Boat radars
118	20 Apr 44	42-3358	Tyrrhenian Sea – west coast of Italy; flown from Pomigliano near Naples in search of U-Boat radars
119	3 May 44	42-3358	West coast of Italy, La Rocca Fort to Spezia/Genoa; flown from Borga, worked with 1st Signals Service Platoon (SP)
120	3 May 44	42-3358	West coast of Italy, Elba Island to Toulon, FR; flown from Borga, worked with 1st Signals Service Platoon (SP)
121	6 May 44	42-3358	Corsica direct to Toulon, along coast to Marseille and return; flown from Borga, worked with 1st Signals Service Platoon (SP)
122	6 May 44	42-3358	West coast of Italy, La Rocca Fort to Spezia/Genoa; flown from Borga, worked with 1st Signals Service Platoon (SP)
123	11 May 44	42-3358	Calibrate CPN-3 beacon; involved flying over Adriatic
124	16 May 44	42-3358	Eastern Adriatic – Dubrovnic north to Zadar; investigate Freya radar near Split
125	21 May 44	42-30437	Eastern Adriatic – Dubrovnic north to Zadar

Mission #	Date (Note 1)	Ferret	Mission
126	23 May 44	42-30437	Ionian Sea – Crete
127	26 May 44	42-30437	Northern Adriatic; enemy shipping spotted on radar
128	27 May 44	42-30437	Adriatic – Corfu to Dubrovnik
129	27 May 44	42-3358	West coast of Italy, La Rocca Fort to Spezia/Genoa; short night msn, flown from Borga
130	28 May 44	42-3358	Corsica direct to Toulon, along coast to Spanish border and return; short night msn, flown from Borga
131	29 May 44	42-3358	West coast of Italy, Elba Island to Toulon, FR; short night msn, flown from Borga
132	5 Jun 44	42-30437	Adriatic north of Foggia
133	10 Jun 44	42-3358	Adriatic south of Foggia to Corfu
134	13 Jun 44	V/42-3055	RAF raid – Munich
135	9 Jun 44	42-30437	Toulon, FR to Valencia, SP then south of Mallorca Island; flown from Borga, looking for German radars on Balearic Island
136	12 Jun 44	42-30437	West coast of Italy, Elba Island to Toulon, FR; short night msn, flown from Borga
137	13 Jun 44	42-30437	Along FR coast to Marseille; short night msn, flown from Borga
138	16 Jun 44	42-3358	Adriatic north of Foggia
139	22 Jun 44	42-30437	Adriatic south of Foggia to Crete; tried to alert German radars through the use of chaff
140	23 Jun 44	42-30437	Adriatic east of Foggia south to Fano Island north of Corfu
141	23 Jun 44	42-3358	West of Corsica to Gulf of Lyon; out in the water, not near coast; flown from Borga, looking for German radars on Balearic Island
142	25 Jun 44	42-3358	Gulf of Genoa/Ligurian Sea; short night msn, flown from Borga
143	26 Jun 44	42-30437	Adriatic north of Foggia
144	28 Jun 44	42-3358	Adriatic – NE from Foggia to Mljet Island, then south to Corfu
145	29 Jun 44	42-30437	Leghorn, IT to St Tropez, FR; short night msn, flown from Borga
146	30 Jun 44	42-30437	Toulon, FR to Spanish border
147	1 Jul 44	42-3358	Adriatic north of Foggia
148	3 Jul 44	42-30437	East of Foggia into Adriatic, along Greek coast to Corfu
149	7 Jul 44	42-3358	Adriatic north of Foggia
150	6 Jul 44	42-30437	Leghorn, IT to west of Nice, FR; short night msn, flown from Borga
151	7 Jul 44	42-30437	Gulf of Lyons – Toulon to west of Marseille; short night msn, flown from Borga
152	10 Jul 44	42-3358	South of Foggia into Adriatic, along Greek coast to Cape Matapan
153	15 Jul 44	42-30437	East of Foggia into Adriatic, along Greek coast to Corfu
154	13 Jul 44	42-3358	Gulf of Lyons – Toulon to Spanish Border; short night msn, flown from Borga
155	15 Jul 44	42-3358	Leghorn, IT to Toulon, FR; short night msn, flown from Borga
156	24 Jul 44	42-3358	Northern Adriatic, then inland into northern Italy as far as Mote Venda and back over Adriatic north of Ravenna
157	25 Jul 44	42-30437	East of Foggia into Adriatic, along Greek coast to Corfu
158	26 Jul 45	42-3358	Gulf of Lyons – Toulon to west of Marseille; short night msn, flown from Borga
159	29 Jul 45	42-3358	Leghorn, IT to west of Nice, FR; short night msn, flown from Borga
160	4 Aug 44	42-3358	From Borgo out to a point off the coast of FR in Gulf of Lyon and return; pre-invasion reconnaissance
161	5 Aug 44	42-3358	From Borgo out to a point off the coast of Marseille and return; pre-invasion reconnaissance
162	7 Aug 44	42-30437	Flight inland of St Tropez; SCR-717B radar scope images to support Troop Carrier Command pathfinder aircraft
163	12 Aug 44	V/42-3055	Overland Yugoslavia – Banja Luka, Zagreb to investigate partisan report of a new German radar
164	11 Aug 44	42-30437	Marseille – Nice; check effectiveness of Allied fighter attacks on radar sites
165	12 Aug 44	42-30437	Nice to Spanish border; check effectiveness of Allied fighter attacks on radar sites
166	13 Aug 44	42-30437	Marseille – Nice; check effectiveness of Allied fighter attacks on radar sites
167	15 Aug 44	V/42-3055	Gulf of Lyon – away from invasion beaches; large triangular route to observe German reaction to the invasion
168	16 Aug 44	42-30437	Adriatic north of Foggia
169	21 Aug 44	42-3358	Corfu up coast to Dubrovnik
170	19 Aug 44	42-30437	Toulon to Montpelier, then back to Nice (but well off coast); post-invasion reconnaissance
171	22 Aug 44	42-3358	Adriatic south of Foggia from Corfu to Crete
172	24 Aug 44	42-3358	Nice to Spanish border; post-invasion reconnaissance
173	25 Aug 44	42-3358	Nice, FR to Leghorn, IT; post-invasion reconnaissance
174	26 Aug 44	V/42-3055	Adriatic from Corfu to Split
175	26 Aug 44	42-3358	Adriatic north of Foggia
176	3 Sep 44	42-3358	Nice, FR to Leghorn, IT; short mission, flown from Borga
177	4 Sep 44	42-3358	Nice, FR to Leghorn, IT
178	7 Sep 44	42-3358	Corfu up coast to Dubrovnik
179	11 Sep 44	42-3358	Corfu up coast to Dubrovnik
180	13 Sep 44	42-3358	Northern Adriatic – Ancona to Dubrovnik
181	14 Sep 44	42-3358	Nice, FR to Leghorn, IT
182	23 Sep 44	42-3358	Corfu up coast to Dubrovnik
183	24 Sep 44	42-3358	Central Adriatic, focusing on islands off Yugoslav coast
184	26 Sep 44	42-3358	Nice, FR to Leghorn, IT

Note 1: Many missions take off at 2300 ZBT – those are logged as missions occurring the next day

Table Seven: Section 22

Mission #	Date	Ferret	Mission	Base
1-21	Feb – Mar 44	VII/42-63991, VIII/42-64045	New Britain, New Ireland, and North Coast of New Guinea.	Dobadura, New Guinea
Unknown	10 Feb 44	VII/42-63991, VIII/42-64045	Unknown	Dobadura, New Guinea
22	10 Mar 44	VII/42-63991	Kavieng and Mussau Island	Dobadura, New Guinea
23	11 Mar 44	VIII/42-64045	Wewak and Admiralty Islands and Matthias Group; investigate signal at Wewak	Dobadura, New Guinea
24	11 Mar 44	VII/42-63991	Investigate signal at Wewak	Dobadura, New Guinea
25	13 Mar 44	VIII/42-64045	St Georges Channel, Kavieng and Wewak; confirm locations of radars at Borpop, East Cape and Talilis Plantation	Dobadura, New Guinea
26	16 Mar 44	VII/42-63991	Investigate signal at Wewak and patrol north coast of New Guinea	Dobadura, New Guinea
27	16 Mar 44	VIII/42-64045	Southern New Ireland; investigate signal heard on msn 25	Dobadura, New Guinea
29-32	Unknown	Unknown	Unknown	
33	7 Apr 44	VIII/42-64045	Circuit of Tanimbar, Aroe and Kai Islands	Fenton Field, Australia
34	10 Apr 44	VIII/42-64045	Circuit of Tanimbar, Aroe and Kai Islands	Fenton Field, Australia
35	13 Apr 44	VIII/42-64045	Past Utarom to Geelvink Bay	Fenton Field, Australia
36	16 Apr 44	VIII/42-64045		Fenton Field, Australia
37	19 Apr 44	VIII/42-64045	Ceram?	Fenton Field, Australia
38	22 Apr 44	VIII/42-64045	Island of Ceram – locate Ambon radar	Fenton Field, Australia
39	25 Apr 44	VIII/42-64045	General search of Timor Island	Fenton Field, Australia
40	28 Apr 44	VIII/42-64045	Timor Island; follow up on msn 39	Fenton Field, Australia
	19 May 44	VII/42-63991		Fenton Field, Australia
	26 May 44	VII/42-63991		Fenton Field, Australia
	31 May 44	VII/42-63991		Fenton Field, Australia
	2 Jun 1944	VII/42-63991		Fenton Field, Australia
	6 Jun 1944	VII/42-63991		Fenton Field, Australia
	9 Jun 1944	VII/42-63991		Fenton Field, Australia
	13 Jun 1944	VII/42-63991		Fenton Field, Australia
	15 Jun 1944	VII/42-63991		Fenton Field, Australia
	19 Jun 1944	VII/42-63991		Fenton Field, Australia
	21 Jun1944	VII/42-63991		Fenton Field, Australia
	26 Jun 1944	VII/42-63991		Fenton Field, Australia
	23 Jun 1944	VII/42-63991		Fenton Field, Australia
	30 Jun 1944	VII/42-63991		Fenton Field, Australia
	7 July 44	VII/42-63991		Fenton Field, Australia
	10 July 44	VII/42-63991		Fenton Field, Australia
	11 July 44	VII/42-63991		Fenton Field, Australia
57	16 July 44	VII/42-63991	Balikpapan via Makassar Strait	Fenton Field, Australia
	19 July 44	VII/42-63991		Fenton Field, Australia
	25 July 44	VII/42-63991		Fenton Field, Australia
	29 July 44	VII/42-63991		Fenton Field, Australia
	31 July 44	VII/42-63991		Fenton Field, Australia
	3 Aug 44	VII/42-63991		Fenton Field, Australia
63	6 Aug 44	VII/42-63991	General search of Tanimbar, Aroe, Kai Groups; recover at Owi Island	Fenton Field, Australia
64	7-8 Aug 44	VII/42-63991	General search of Palau Group	Owi Island
65	9-10 Aug 44	VII/42-63991	General search of Palau Group	Owi Island
	11 Aug 44	VII/42-63991		Fenton Field, Australia
	13 Aug 44	VII/42-63991		Fenton Field, Australia
	16 Aug 44	VII/42-63991		Fenton Field, Australia
	18 Aug 44	VIII/42-64045		Fenton Field, Australia
	21 Aug 44	VIII/42-64045		Fenton Field, Australia
	24 Aug 44	VIII/42-64045		Fenton Field, Australia
	26 Aug 44	VIII/42-64045		Fenton Field, Australia
	26 Aug 44	VII/42-63991		Fenton Field, Australia
	29 Aug 44	VIII/42-64045		Fenton Field, Australia
	31 Aug 44	VII/42-63991		Fenton Field, Australia
78?	6 Sep 44	Unknown	Morotai, Talaud, Davao Gulf (11 24N 126 25E), Palau and return	Owi Island
79?	10 Sep 44	Unknown	Sea search; RTB after reaching Noemfoor Island due to oil leak on engine #3	Owi Island
80?	11 Sep 44	Unknown	Owi to Halmahera Sea, Morotai Island, Talaud Island, North Celebes, Ceram Sea, MacCluer Gulf and return	Owi Island
81	13-14 Sep 44	Unknown	General search of Halmahera, Molucca Passage, Moro Gulf, North Celebes	Owi Island
82	15 Sep 44	Unknown	Accompany strike to Halmahera	Owi Island
83?	24 Sep 44	Unknown	Borneo – Owi to Waigeo, Halmahera, Celebes, Borneo and return	Owi Island
	24 Sep 44	Unknown	Philippines – incomplete, RTB – mechanical	Owi Island

Mission #	Date	Ferret	Mission	Base
84	26 Sep 44	Unknown	Mindanao – Owi to Celebes Sea, Moro Gulf, Mindanao Sea, Surigao Sea, return	Owi Island
85	27 Sep 44	Unknown	Mindanao – Owi to Talaud, Surigao Strait, Moro Gulf and return; 90% of route covered, RTB due to compass and radar	Owi Island
86	27 Sep 44	Unknown	Balikpapan via Gulf of Tomini, Waigeo to verify blind spots in Balikpapan radar coverage; RTB due to radio failure after 25% of route covered	Owi Island
87	29 Sep 44	Unknown	Owi to Mapia Islands, Talaud, Zamboanga, Negros, Panay, Leyte and return	Owi Island
	1 Oct 1944	Unknown	North Celebes Zamboango	
	2 Oct 1944	Unknown	Philippines; RTB due to radar malfunction	
	3 Oct 1944	Unknown	Philippines	
	5 Oct 1944	Unknown	Philippines	
	9 Oct 1944	Unknown	Central Philippines; Owi to Catanduanes Island, Middleburg and return	Owi Island
	10 Oct 1944	Unknown	Philippines – Owi to Mindanao, Samar and return	Owi Island
	12 Oct 1944	Unknown	Philippines – Owi to Mayo Bay, Leyte Gulf and return	Owi Island
	16 Oct 1944	Unknown	Philippines	
	19 Oct 1944	Unknown	Moro Gulf	
	21 Oct 1944	Unknown	Surigao, Mindanao Sea	
	23 Oct 1944	Unknown	Philippines	
	29 Oct 1944	Unknown	Philippines; RTB due to radar failure after flying 4 hours; no mission number assigned to mission	
	30 Oct 1944	Unknown	Philippines	
	2 Nov 1944	Unknown	Philippines	
	5 Nov 1944	Unknown	Northern Philippines – Morotai, Moro Gulf, Mindanao Sea, Visayan Sea, Sibuyan Sea, South China Sea, Lamon Bay	Owi Island
	7 Nov 1944	Unknown	Philippines – 90% of route covered, RTB at Mindoro due to weather	
	10 Nov 1944	Unknown	Manila	
	13 Nov 1944	Unknown	Philippines	
	16 Nov 1944	Unknown	Sulu Sea	
	22 Nov 1944	Unknown	Southern Luzon	
111	28 Nov 1944	Unknown	General search, Central, Eastern Philippines	Owi Island with RON at Morotai
112	30 Nov 1944	VII/42-63991	Catanduanes, "special DF" in Legaspi Area	Owi Island
114	12 Nov 1944		General search, Manila, Central, Southern Philippines	Owi Island with fuel stop at Morotai
	1 Dec 1944	VII/42-63991	Mindanao-Leyte-Samar-SE Luzon	
	8 Dec 1944	VII/42-63991	South Luzon	
	12 Dec 1944	Unknown	Cebu, Negros, Panay	
115	30-31 Dec 44	VII/42-63991	Central PI	Angaur Island, Palau
116	4 Jan 1945	VII/42-63991	Legaspi, Catanduanes	Angaur Island, Palau with RON Tacloban, Leyte, PI
117	7 Jan 1945	Unknown	Philippine Islands up to Lingayen Gulf	Owi Island with fuel stop at Tacloban, Leyte
118	15 Jan 1945	VII/42-63991	Halmahera, PI, Formosa	Owi Island to Tacloban, Leyte
119	18 Jan 1945	VII/42-63991	Northern Philippines and Formosa	Tacloban to San Jose
120	8 Feb 1945	VII/42-63991	PI, Borneo, Palawan Group, Panay	Tacloban, Leyte
121	15 Feb 1945	X/44-41076	Northern Luzon and around Formosa	Tacloban, Leyte
122	16 Feb 1945	X/44-41076	Northern Luzon and Formosa	Tacloban, Leyte
123	18 Feb 1945	X/44-41076	China	Tacloban, Leyte
124	25 Feb 1945	VII/42-63991	China coast and Formosa	Tacloban, Leyte
125	3 Mar 1945	X/44-41076	China coast from Indo China to Hong Kong	Tacloban, Leyte with RON San Jose, Mindoro, PI
126	5 Mar 1945	X/44-41076	Indo China from Saigon to Hainan Island	Tacloban, Leyte with RON San Jose, Mindoro, PI
127	8 Mar 1945	X/44-41076	China coast, from Hainan to Hong Kong	Tacloban, Leyte
128	22 Mar 1945	X/44-41076	China coast and west coast of Formosa	Clark Field, Luzon, PI
129	24 Mar 1945	X/44-41076	China coast, from Hong Kong to Saigon	Clark Field, Luzon, PI
130	26 Mar 1945	X/44-41076	Formosa and China coast	Clark Field, Luzon, PI
131	2 Apr 1945	X/44-41076	China Coast	Clark Field, Luzon, PI
132	5 Apr 1945	X/44-41076	Formosa-China Coast	Clark Field, Luzon, PI
133	8 Apr 1945	X/44-41076	South China coast	Clark Field, Luzon, PI
134	12 Apr 1945	X/44-41076	Southern coast of China	Clark Field, Luzon, PI
135	18 Apr 1945	X/44-41076	Southwestern Formosa	Clark Field, Luzon, PI
136	20 Apr 1945	XI/44-40943	China coast and Formosa	Clark Field, Luzon, PI
137	22 Apr 1945	XI/44-40943	South China coast	Clark Field, Luzon, PI
138	26 Apr 1945	XI/44-40943	Southern coast of Japan	Clark Field, Luzon, PI

Mission #	Date	Ferret	Mission	Base
139	29 Apr 1945	XI/44-40943	China coast and Formosa	Clark Field, Luzon, PI
140	2 May 1945	X/44-41076	South China coast	Clark Field, Luzon, PI
141	5 May 1945	XI/44-40943	China coast and Formosa	Clark Field, Luzon, PI
142	8-9 May 45	XI/44-40943	China coast and Formosa	Clark Field, Luzon, PI
143	11 May 1945	X/44-41076	Hainan and South China coast	Clark Field, Luzon, PI
144	15 May 1945	X/44-41076	Shanghai and China coast	Clark Field, Luzon, PI
145	18 May 1945	XI/44-40943	Taihoku, Formosa; search for AI frequencies	Clark Field, Luzon, PI
146	21 May 1945	XI/44-40943	Hainan and South China coast	Clark Field, Luzon, PI
147	22 May 1945	XI/44-40943	Taihoku, Formosa; search for AI frequencies	Clark Field, Luzon, PI
148	25 May 1945	XI/44-40943	Taihoku, Formosa; search for AI frequencies	Clark Field, Luzon, PI
	2 Jun 1945	X/44-41076	Nanking; radar failure, RTB to Clark, wx bad, so divert to Laong	
	4 Jun 1945	X/44-41076	Unk – Nanking? Radar failure, RTB to Clark	
	15 Jun 1945	X/44-41076	Nanking; RTB early due to low fuel	
	19 Jun 1945	X/44-41076	Nanking	
	22 Jun 1945	X/44-41076	Hong Kong, Canton, and down coast to Cam Ranh Bay	
	25 Jun 1945	XI/44-40943	China coast from Amoy to Hong Kong	
	27 Jun 1945	X/44-41076	Shanghai-Nanking area	Clark Field, Luzon, PI
	28 Jun 1945	XI/44-40943	Hong Kong/Canton area; intercepted by an U/I aircraft	Clark Field, Luzon, PI

Index

Personalities

Places

Q-Birds

The Impact of American Manned Aircraft as Drones

This is an account of a fascinating but largely unknown aspect of post World War 2 US military aviation history, the conversion and use of former frontline aircraft to serve as remotely piloted drones. This story begins as far back as the 1920s, gains momentum during World War 2 and peaks with the postwar glut of airframes during the Cold War era.

The list of manned aircraft converted to drones over the decades is long and includes at least the following: P-12, B-17, PB4Y-2, SB2C, F-80, T-33, F6F, F-86, B-29, B-47, F9F Panther and Cougar, F-100, F-102, F-104, F-106, F-4, F-16, P-39 and Boeing 720. These aircraft were used in a wide range of capacities; as test beds, flying bombs and targets for missiles and other aircraft to intercept and shoot down. One example of the sort of secret projects covered by this book, was a postwar scheme to use remotely controlled B-29s as one-way nuclear delivery devices under the code name Banshee.

Since the 1970s the author has visited a number of drone sites, including the plant that converted F-100s and F-102s as well as ranges where drones were used. His files include many photographs, mostly never previously published of the many and varied types of drone which were created including the last B-17G Boeing that rolled out the door in Seattle and was ultimately consumed as a QB-17 drone.

Aviation historians and enthusiasts will find so much of interest in this genuinely original, thoroughly researched, well-illustrated and utterly absorbing book which explores in detail a neglected but compelling aspect of recent US military aviation history.

ISBN: 9781800352797
Price: £34.95
Provisional publication date: June 2024
Pre-order at **crecy.co.uk**

American Secret Projects 2

Airlifters

This book charts the history of the US airlifter from its origins in World War II to today's transport giants. In doing so, it reveals and describes numerous designs which never saw the light of day, examining the thinking behind them and giving insights into why they did, or did not, succeed. In many ways, this untold story of aviation history reflects both the changing face of conflict and the exercise of geo-political power; it has also had a major bearing on the development of civil aviation.

The book has been made possible by the authors being given unprecedented access to major aerospace company archives, uncovering scores of design proposals which have never previously been revealed. It is profusely illustrated, much in full colour, with artwork and three-view drawings extracted from manufacturers' archives and with photographs of original project models. As well as describing how airlifters were progressively developed to meet ever-more demanding military transport requirements, the book looks at other roles for which they were adapted, from nuclear test-beds to Space-Shuttle carriers.

This previously untold story describes over 200 unknown, or little known, designs, and contains over 400 illustrations detailing some of the largest and most incredible aircraft ever conceived.

ISBN: 9781910809167

Price: £27.50

Order at **crecy.co.uk**

American Secret Projects 3

U.S. Airlifters since 1962

This brings the story of the US airlifter from the early 1960s to today's transport giants and tomorrow's stealth assault aircraft; revealing numerous designs which never saw the light of day, examining the thinking behind them and giving insights into why they did, or did not, succeed.

This untold story of aviation history also has a major bearing on the development of civil aviation. The book, and its companion volume, American Secret Projects 2, covers airlifter designs from WWII to the start of the 1960s, and has been made possible by the authors being given unprecedented access to major aerospace company archives, uncovering scores of design proposals which have never previously been revealed. As well as describing how airlifters were progressively developed to meet ever-more demanding military transport requirements, the book looks at their other roles, from nuclear test-beds to Space-Shuttle carriers.

Describing over 100 unknown, or little known, designs, including all the competitors to the C-5 and entries for the Tri-Service V/STOL transport competition, the book has over 400 illustrations, the majority of which have never previously been published, detailing some of the largest and most incredible aircraft ever conceived.

American Secret Projects 4

Bombers, Attack and Anti-Submarine Aircraft 1945-1974

Having completed the revision of his series of British Secret Projects titles, Tony Buttler has now begun the same treatment for his early volumes on American Secret Projects. This first revised book describes the design and development of American bomber and attack aircraft from the end of World War II to the mid-1970s, both for the Air Force and the Navy. Once again the emphasis is placed on designs that were never built, particularly within the context of competitions between the various manufacturers against official requirements.

The projects and programmes described range from the largest and most outrageous ideas for heavy strategic bombers down to much smaller anti-submarine and ground attack types. The majority of the work has been compiled from extensive research using primary source material and this second edition includes many additional and previously unseen three-view drawings, original artist's impressions and photographs of manufacturer's models. They are accompanied by a new selection of photos, many in colour, which makes this revised and expanded edition a great resource for modellers in particular. In addition to the comprehensive text, supplementary appendices list the projects by manufacturer and their specifications

ISBN: 9781910809907
Price: £27.50
Order at **crecy.co.uk**